SELECTED WRITINGS OF
James Fitzjames Stephen

James Fitzjames Stephen, 1857. Photographer unknown; from Harry Furniss, *Paradise in Piccadilly: The Story of Albany* (1925) (plate 8 in *Life*, OUP, 2017).

SELECTED WRITINGS OF
James Fitzjames Stephen

On the Novel and Journalism

EDITED BY
Christopher Ricks

OXFORD
UNIVERSITY PRESS

Great Clarendon Street, Oxford, OX2 6DP,
United Kingdom

Oxford University Press is a department of the University of Oxford.
It furthers the University's objective of excellence in research, scholarship,
and education by publishing worldwide. Oxford is a registered trade mark of
Oxford University Press in the UK and in certain other countries

Introduction and Editorial Matter © Christopher Ricks 2023

The moral rights of the author have been asserted

All rights reserved. No part of this publication may be reproduced, stored in
a retrieval system, or transmitted, in any form or by any means, without the
prior permission in writing of Oxford University Press, or as expressly permitted
by law, by licence or under terms agreed with the appropriate reprographics
rights organization. Enquiries concerning reproduction outside the scope of the
above should be sent to the Rights Department, Oxford University Press, at the
address above

You must not circulate this work in any other form
and you must impose this same condition on any acquirer

Published in the United States of America by Oxford University Press
198 Madison Avenue, New York, NY 10016, United States of America

British Library Cataloguing in Publication Data

Data available

Library of Congress Control Number: 2022939634

ISBN 978–0–19–288283–7

Printed and bound by
CPI Group (UK) Ltd, Croydon, CR0 4YY

Links to third party websites are provided by Oxford in good faith and
for information only. Oxford disclaims any responsibility for the materials
contained in any third party website referenced in this work.

Selected Writings of
James Fitzjames Stephen

A General View of the Criminal Law of England
Liberty, Equality, Fraternity
A History of the Criminal Law in England
The Story of Nuncomar and the Impeachment of Sir Elijah Impey

ALSO FOUR VOLUMES OF SELECTED ESSAYS:
On History and Empire
On Justice and Jurisprudence
On the Novel and Journalism
On Society, Religion, and Government

AND

The Life of Sir James Fitzjames Stephen
by Leslie Stephen

ACKNOWLEDGEMENTS

An award from the Mellon Foundation established the *Selected Writings of James Fitzjames Stephen*, and made it possible to bring to Boston University's Editorial Institute, as a General Editor, Frances Whistler from Oxford University Press. *On the Novel and Journalism* is indebted in particular to her and to those who edited or contributed to the five volumes already published (by the year 2022): Hermione Lee, Lisa Rodensky, Thomas E. Schneider, K. J. M. Smith, Julia Stapleton, and Christopher Tolley. Further help came from Archie Burnett, Jeff Gutierrez, R. A. Marriott, Jim McCue, Jan-Melissa Schramm, and from those who attended the Editorial Institute.

CHRISTOPHER RICKS

CONTENTS

Selected Writings of James Fitzjames Stephen (JFS)	xi
Note on Attribution	xiii
Introduction by Christopher Ricks	xv

'The Relation of Novels to Life' (excerpts) (*Cambridge Essays*, 1855)	1
'Woods *v.* Russell' (*Saturday Review*, 19 January 1856)	27
'Religious Journalism' (*Saturday Review*, 16 February 1856)	35
'The Sunday Papers' (*Saturday Review*, 19 April 1856)	43
'Our Civilization' (*Saturday Review*, 28 June 1856)	49
'Newspaper English' (*Saturday Review*, 9 August 1856)	54
'The Enigma' (excerpt) (*Saturday Review*, 30 August 1856)	59
'The Green Hand' (excerpts) (*Saturday Review*, 4 October 1856)	61
'Mrs. Caudle's Curtain Lectures' (excerpts) (*Saturday Review*, 1 November 1856)	63
'Groans of the Britons' (*Saturday Review*, 22 November 1856)	65
'Barry Lyndon' (*Saturday Review*, 27 December 1856)	71
'Mr. Dickens as a Politician' (*Saturday Review*, 3 January 1857)	77
CHARLES DICKENS, from the Preface to *The Pickwick Papers*	77
CHARLES DICKENS, from the Preface to *Bleak House*	78
JFS on Parliament: A Note	84
'Railroad Bookselling' (*Saturday Review*, 31 January 1857)	85
'Little Dorrit' (*Saturday Review*, 4 July 1857)	91
CHARLES DICKENS, Preface to *Little Dorrit*	92
'Light Literature and the *Saturday Review*' (excerpt) (*Saturday Review*, 11 July 1857)	98
'Madame Bovary' (*Saturday Review*, 11 July 1857)	99
'The License of Modern Novelists' (*Edinburgh Review*, July 1857)	104
'The *Edinburgh Review* and Modern Novelists' (*Saturday Review*, 18 July 1857)	133
CHARLES DICKENS, 'Curious Misprint in the *Edinburgh Review*' (*Household Words*, 1 August 1857)	138
'Light Literature in France' (*Saturday Review*, 5 September 1857)	142
'La Daniella' (*Saturday Review*, 12 September 1857)	146
'Balzac' (*Saturday Review*, 19 December 1857)	150
'Mr. Dickens' (*Saturday Review*, 8 May 1858)	156

SYDNEY SMITH, 'The Noodle's Oration', From 'Fallacies of
Anti-Reformers' (1824), Part III   161

'Gentlemen Authors' (*Saturday Review*, 17 July 1858)   163

'Manon Lescaut' (excerpts) (*Saturday Review*, 17 July 1858)   167

'The Spectator' (*Saturday Review*, 14 August 1858)   171

'Novels and Novelists' (excerpt) (*Saturday Review*, 18 September 1858)   177

'The *Revue des Deux Mondes* on English Romance' (excerpts)
(*Saturday Review*, 2 October 1858)   179

'Guy Livingstone' (excerpts) (*Edinburgh Review*, October 1858)   183

'The Romance of Vice' (*Saturday Review*, 13 November 1858)   185

'Sentimentalism' (excerpts) (*Saturday Review*, 25 December 1858)   188

'The History of British Journalism' (excerpt) (*Saturday Review*,
29 January 1859)   191

'The Minister's Wooing' (excerpts) (*Saturday Review*, 22 October 1859)   193

'A Tale of Two Cities' (*Saturday Review*, 17 December 1859)   198

'Journalism' (excerpt) (*Cornhill*, July 1862)   205

'Novelists' Common Forms' (*Saturday Review*, 13 June 1863)   207

'Mr. Thackeray' (excerpts) (*Fraser's*, April 1864)   211

'Senior's Essays on Fiction' (excerpt) (*Saturday Review*, 23 April 1864)   217

'Detectives in Fiction and in Real Life' (*Saturday Review*, 11 June 1864)   219

'Sentimentalism' (excerpts) (*Cornhill Magazine*, July 1864)   223

'Mr. Matthew Arnold and his Countrymen' (*Saturday Review*,
3 December 1864)   228

MATTHEW ARNOLD from the Preface to *Essays in Criticism* (1865)   235

and FROM 'THE FUNCTION OF CRITICISM AT THE PRESENT TIME'
Essays in Criticism (1865)   236

'The Mote and the Beam' (*Saturday Review*, 3 December 1864)   239

AN EDITORIAL IN *The Times* (26 Nov 1864)   239

'Mr. Matthew Arnold amongst the Philistines' (excerpts) (*Saturday Review*,
25 February 1865)   245

'Mr. Arnold on the Middle Classes' (excerpts) (*Saturday Review*,
10 February 1866)   247

'Mr. Matthew Arnold on Culture' (*Saturday Review*, 20 July 1867)   251

Index   255

SELECTED WRITINGS OF
JAMES FITZJAMES STEPHEN (JFS)

Essays by a Barrister (*Reprinted from the Saturday Review*). Anon, 1862. [*Essays*]

A General View of the Criminal Law of England. By James Fitzjames Stephen, M.A. Of the Inner Temple, Barrister-at-Law, Recorder of Newark-on-Trent (Macmillan and Co., 1863). Ed. K. J. M. Smith; *Selected Writings of James Fitzjames Stephen*, Oxford University Press, 2017. [*Gen. View 1863*]

Liberty, Equality, Fraternity (Smith, Elder, & Co., 1873; 2nd edn, 1874). Ed. Julia Stapleton; *Selected Writings of James Fitzjames Stephen*, Oxford University Press, 2017.

A History of the Criminal Law of England (3 vols, 1883) Forthcoming, *Selected Writings of James Fitzjames Stephen*, Oxford University Press. [*Hist. Crim. Law*]

The Story of Nuncomar and the Impeachment of Sir Elijah Impey (1885). Ed. Lisa Rodensky; *Selected Writings of James Fitzjames Stephen*, Oxford University Press, 2013.

A General View of the Criminal Law of England (revised edn, 1890). [*Gen. View 1890*]

Horae Sabbaticae: Reprint of Articles Contributed to The Saturday Review (3 vols., Macmillan and Co., 1892). [*Hor. Sab.*]

The Life of Sir James Fitzjames Stephen Bart., K.C.S.I. A Judge of the High Court of Justice. By His Brother Leslie Stephen (Smith, Elder, & Co., June 1895; 2nd edn, Aug. 1895). Ed. Christopher Tolley, with an Introductory Essay by Hermione Lee and a Bibliography of James Fitzjames Stephen's Articles and Reviews by Thomas E. Schneider; *Selected Writings of James Fitzjames Stephen*, Oxford University Press, 2017. [*Life*]

On Society, Religion, and Government. Ed. Thomas E. Schneider; *Selected Writings of James Fitzjames Stephen*, Oxford University Press, 2015.

On History and Empire. Forthcoming, *Selected Writings of James Fitzjames Stephen*, Oxford University Press.

On Justice and Jurisprudence. Forthcoming, *Selected Writings of James Fitzjames Stephen*, Oxford University Press.

NOTE ON ATTRIBUTION

There is an indispensable 'Note on Attributions', as also a 'Note on the Texts', in *On Society, Religion, and Government* (Oxford University Press, 2015), edited by Thomas E. Schneider, to whom all are indebted for the bibliography of Stephen's articles and reviews, identifying sources and witnesses, that is appended to *The Life of Sir James Fitzjames Stephen, by His Brother Leslie Stephen* (ed. Christopher Tolley, 2017; with an introductory essay by Hermione Lee). Of this present selection *On the Novel and Journalism*, almost all its writings were published anonymously, exceptions being duly noted.

INTRODUCTION

The essays and reviews that are selected here to constitute *On the Novel and Journalism* were written between 1855 and 1867, escorting Fitzjames Stephen from the age of twenty-six to thirty-eight. At the Bar from January 1854 when he was twenty-four, Stephen promptly prosecuted two callings: barrister and journalist. 'In nine cases out of ten, a writer in the position of which we have been speaking is called to the bar, and this is greatly to his advantage. He obtains a recognised social status, which, until journalism is more of an acknowledged profession than it is at present, is a gain not to be despised.'[1]

To be free to despise, for Stephen, was itself a gain, one of the many pleasures left in life, and there proved to be plenty of things that permitted of his despising. Making an example, he put in the stocks *The Life and Travels of Herodotus*, an 'imaginary biography' by J. Talboys Wheeler. The second number of the *Saturday Review* (10 Nov. 1855) boasted Fitzjames Stephen's swingeing review, the first of his three-hundred-or-so contributions to the polemical journal that Leslie Stephen, in his unimaginative unimaginary biography of his brother, was to characterize shrewdly: 'The writers were for the most part energetic young men, with the proper confidence in their own infallibility.'[2]

Of Edmund Burke's *Philosophical Enquiry into the Origin of Our Ideas of the Sublime and Beautiful* (anon., 1757), Stephen remarked at thirty-eight that 'It was written when Burke was under thirty, and it has that disproportion of logical scaffolding to ultimate result, which is common in early performances.'[3] In Stephen's own case, what was disproportionate was not scaffolding-to-ultimate-result, but the recidivism with which Stephen repeatedly staged the ultimate result as taking place on the scaffold. His two professions came together in all those early performances of his that have at centre-stage 'the Rugeley Poisoner', William Palmer, who is seen and heard in a dozen presentations by Stephen. Palmer had his case regularly affiliated not only to journalism's bad behaviour but to the world (in certain respects criminal, in Stephen's judgment) of novels.

'The Case of William Palmer' (Stephen attended the trial in 1856) was reproduced by him at thirty pages or so within not only *A General View of the Criminal Law of England* (1863) and its revision, *A History of the Criminal Law of England* (1883), but also within *The Indian Evidence Act* (1872). George Orwell was to keep Palmer's memory green: 'Our great period in murder, our Elizabethan period, so to speak, seems to have been between roughly 1850 and 1925, and the murderers whose reputation has stood the test of time are the following: Dr Palmer of Rugeley, Jack the Ripper...'[4] And on from Ripper to Crippen.

---

[1] JFS, 'Periodical Writing' (*Sat. Rev.*, 12 Feb. 1859).

[2] *The Life of Sir James Fitzjames Stephen, by His Brother Leslie Stephen* (1895); *Life* 104.

[3] 'The Works of Burke' (*Sat. Rev.*, 19 Oct. 1867; *Hor. Sab.* iii 102).

[4] Ellipses that are raised ··· indicate an omission editorially introduced. Note also the two-point ellipsis of the *Oxford English Dictionary*, where . . = an omitted part of a quotation. 'Decline of the English Murder' (*Tribune*, 15 Feb. 1946; *The Collected Essays, Journalism and Letters of George Orwell* IV, ed. Sonia Orwell and Ian Angus, 1968). Palmer's role goes marching on in Robert Graves, *They Hanged My Saintly Billy* (1957). Within literary studies: John Sutherland, 'Wilkie Collins and the Origins of the Sensation Novel', *Dickens Studies Annual* 20 (1991) 243–58; Ian Burney, *Poison, Detection, and the Victorian Imagination* (2012).

xvi ON THE NOVEL AND JOURNALISM

Fitzjames Stephen's brother Leslie was well able to stand the test of time as soon as he founded in 1885—and edited until 1891—the *Dictionary of National Biography* (63 volumes, 1885–1900). Loath to admit reputations that might stand the trial of time solely by virtue of having stood trial (and been found guilty of, for instance, murder), the *DNB*'s judgement originally turned down any such appeal to be nationally biographied. But in the fullness of time the *DNB* and then the *Oxford Dictionary of National Biography* in 2004 (60 volumes; *ODNB* hereafter), came to judge otherwise, and criminals—along with celebrities from sport or entertainment—at last found themselves accommodated, and the *ODNB* passed its sentences on William Palmer.

This introduction to *On the Novel and Journalism* makes its way to the crux: the responsibilities of the novel and of journalism. This, while seeking to identify the ways in which Stephen and those with whom he contended—in particular, Dickens—were at odds, although not in some premises and respects. The steps are these:

The relations of the journalist to the novelist, of periodical articles to substantiated criticism, and of Stephen to Dr. Johnson.

Stephen's having not only the eye of a journalist but that of a novelist—and then, panoptically, the gaze of the barrister-judge, in the conviction that a due judging is made possible once we compare the trials and tribulations that the novel imagines with those of the State Trials in all their reality.

His belief that the novel, in its nature and in what should therefore be its claims, should rest content to be no more than entertainment, a light slight thing (not *quite* the same as Stephen's slighting the novel, for there are successes open to the smaller special kinds; take the limerick, the clerihew, and most aptly—in its intercalation of fact and fiction—the photo-bubble cartoon).

Stephen's cast of mind and the point, compression, and clearness of his style.

The responsibilities and irresponsibilities of the novel and journalism, involving (as does everything) the nature of evidence, along with the use and abuse of caricature and exaggeration, and of fictions literary and legal.

Many questions cross-examine Stephen (and he them). Fortunately, we have wise counsel in two books by Lisa Rodensky: *The Crime in Mind: Criminal Responsibility and the Victorian Novel* (2003), which moves compellingly to the forty pages of its final chapter, 'James Fitzjames Stephen and the Responsibilities of Narrative', and ten years later (published within the *Selected Writings of James Fitzjames Stephen*), Rodensky's exemplary edition of Stephen's last major work, his deep study of an accusation—of judicial murder—that had forced late-nineteenth-century England and its history to grapple with India and its history: *The Story of Nuncomar and the Impeachment of Sir Elijah Impey* (1885). Rodensky's achievement is all the greater for her books' having independent life while being fulfillingly interdependent—no repeating, no repudiating, nothing less than, or other than, further knowing and noticing.

(i)

It is always a dangerous experiment to reprint newspaper articles. Even if they are of substantial and permanent importance, the fact of their having been already published is usually a great drawback to their success. If they have the characteristic and appropriate merits of newspaper articles, it is as difficult to read them a year after publication as to eat stale buns. It is the essence of an article to be fugitive and, if it were not read to-day and forgotten to-morrow it could hardly be said to fulfil its natural destiny.[5]

---

[5] 'M. Prévost-Paradol' (*Sat. Rev.*, 11 June 1864).

INTRODUCTION xvii

In re printing, Stephen appreciated that there were risks in bringing to book what had been an article, as he did in the case of *Essays by a Barrister* (anon., 1862) and *Horae Sabbaticae* (three volumes, 1892). But the other side of any matter must never go unacknowledged, and he granted, with an air of mild surprise, that there was—and long had been—journalism and, well, *journalism*. Take, to your surprise, Jeremy Taylor.

It may seem a paradox, but it is neverthless true, that there was a good deal of the journalist in Taylor, as in many of our other great ecclesiastical writers. The change which journalism has produced in the whole organisation of literature in modern times is very insufficiently understood. Look over the works of most of the great writers whose names are better known than their works, and you will find that a very large proportion of the many volumes which they fill consists of what, in the present day, would be articles in reviews, magazines, or newspapers.[6]

The republication of occasional essays, which has now become so common amongst men of real or imaginary eminence, is a practice which has many obvious advantages, the greatest of which is that where the author is a really considerable man, such a book usually gives the measure and picture of his mind far more completely than more elaborate publications. A man who forms, and keeps up, the habit of periodical writing is his own Boswell.[7]

The 'really considerable man', in Stephen's mind and at his heart, was he who had been realized by James Boswell, a singular case of the biographer's being second only to the biographee in powers of self-consideration. Leslie Stephen discerned in his brother Fitzjames a brotherhood with Johnson:

His friends not unfrequently compared him to Dr. Johnson, and, much as the two men differed in some ways, there was a real ground for the comparison. Fitzjames might be called pre-eminently a 'moralist', in the old-fashioned sense in which that term is applied to Johnson . . . If, like Johnson, he was a little too contemptuous of the sufferings of the over-sensitive, and put them down to mere affectation or feeblemindedness, he could sympathize most strongly with any of the serious sorrows and anxieties of those whom he loved.[8]

On his brother's behalf, Leslie Stephen called as a character witness the Rev. H. W. Watson, of Cambridge days, who remarked in Fitzjames 'his Johnsonian brusqueness of speech and manner, mingled with a corresponding Johnsonian warmth of sympathy with and loyalty to friends in trouble or anxiety.' Fitzjames Stephen's own well-judged tribute to Dr. Johnson culminates in a turn that is itself Johnsonian, augmenting 'gentility'—an abstraction from the social world—with a fullness of experience that is expressly a judgment: 'The greatest literary man of the last half of the eighteenth century came out of Grub-street and conquered the polite world by something that was better than gentility.'[9]

Within hailing distance of Johnson there will often pass a reflection by Stephen.

The mistake of novelists lies not so much in overrating the importance of marriage, as in the assumed universality of the passion of love, in their sense of the word. The notion which so many novels suggest—that if two people who have a violent passion for each other marry, they have necessarily acted wisely—is as unfounded as the converse, that if two people marry without such a passion, they act unwisely.[10]

---

[6] 'The Liberty of Prophesying' (*Sat. Rev.*, 30 Sept. 1865; *Hor. Sab.* i 209–10).
[7] 'Mr. Mill's Essays' (*Sat. Rev.*, 9 July and 16 July 1859).
[8] *Life* 91–2, 66.
[9] *Essays* 168.
[10] 'Relation of Novels to Life', p. 11.

xviii ON THE NOVEL AND JOURNALISM

At the head of *Cambridge Essays* (1855), p. 171, on 'The Relation of Novels to Life', a charge was made: *Undue prominence of Love*. Dr. Johnson had observed, in *his* novel, of 'a youth and maiden meeting by chance, or brought together by artifice', that 'they find themselves uneasy when they are apart, and therefore conclude that they shall be happy together.'[11] What Stephen was to deplore in most novels, Johnson had deplored in most plays, making Shakespeare the great exception:

> Upon every other stage the universal agent is love, by whose power all good and evil is distributed, and every action quickened or retarded...But love is only one of many passions, and as it has no great influence upon the sum of life, it has little operation in the dramas of a poet, who caught his ideas from the living world, and exhibited only what he saw before him. He knew, that any other passion, as it was regular or exorbitant, was a cause of happiness or calamity...This therefore is the praise of Shakespeare, that his drama is the mirrour of life; that he who has mazed his imagination, in following the phantoms which other writers raise up before him, may here be cured of his delirious ecstasies, by reading human sentiments in human language; by scenes from which a hermit may estimate the transactions of the world, and a confessor predict the progress of the passions.[12]

Praise of Johnson himself as to 'the transactions of the world' can rest upon his never forgetting his and our responsibility 'to distinguish nature from custom, or that which is established because it is right, from that which is right only because it is established' (*The Rambler* No. 156, 14 Sept. 1751). Our esteem for Stephen may be founded upon an allied wisdom: 'It is absurd and bigoted to resist change, to cling to what is old because it is old, to do what our ancestors did because they did it, or to refuse as opportunity offers to enlarge the circle of experience and to multiply relations with the world; but surely it is no less absurd and bigoted to look upon change as the one thing needful, as the one object of human wishes, and the one subject of human study.'[13] Of human wishes and of human bondage.

Leslie Stephen acknowledged that his brother had 'some singular defects'. 'He was absolutely contemptuous of things that he did not understand: scientific matters, for example, and literature and religion & so on.'[14] (& so on?) Of the articles collected as *Horae Sabbaticae*, Leslie Stephen says, levelly despite being *de haut en bas*, that 'It would be unfair to treat them as literary criticism, for which he cared as little as it deserves.'[15] When Fitzjames came to ponder in 1865 his 'Choice of one of the three Learned Professions' (Law, Physic, and Divinity), he made clear just where he was not in the caring vein: 'For art of any kind I have never cared, and do not care in the very least. For literature, as such, I care hardly at all'.[16]

As such: yet that journalism and criticism might, on occasion, mount to literature, this is implicit in his praise of Johnson as 'the greatest literary man of the last half of the eighteenth century.' For Stephen, journalism's responsibilities—and its concomitant

---

[11] *The Prince of Abissinia, A Tale* (1759), later *The History of Rasselas, Prince of Abissinia*; ch. xxix.

[12] Preface to the edition of Shakespeare (1765); *Johnson on Shakespeare*, ed. Arthur Sherbo (1968), ii 63–5.

[13] 'Buckle's *History of Civilization in England*' (*Edin. Rev.*, April 1858; not signed). 'of human wishes': see JFS, '"The Vanity of Human Wishes"', on Juvenal's satire and Johnson's 'Imitation' of it (*Sat. Rev.*, 29 Sept. 1860; *Essays* 183–90).

[14] Leslie Stephen to Charles Eliot Norton, 19 May 1894; Hermione Lee, Introductory Essay, *Life* xxviii.

[15] *Life* 149.

[16] *Life* 79.

INTRODUCTION   xix

irresponsibilities—made manifest the marked kinship of journalist and novelist. Stephen, by timing, by conviction, and by talent, served not only in the courts but at the court of a historic inauguration. 'Great is Journalism. Is not every Able Editor a Ruler of the World, being a persuader of it?': these trumpets were sounded in Carlyle's history of the toppling of some Rulers of the World, *The French Revolution* (1837). Carlyle was availing himself there of a recent word, its import as recent as 1833: '*Du Journalisme*'. *Oxford English Dictionary* (*OED* hereafter): The occupation or profession of a journalist, journalistic writing; the public journals collectively. *Westminster Review* (January 1833): '"Journalism" is a good name for the thing meant...A word was sadly wanted...The power of journalism is acknowledged...to be enormous in France.' For Stephen, the power of journalism is not only enormous but is one that lends itself, and often sells itself, to enormities. Novelists and journalists collude, not least when excoriating one another. Novels thrive on and in the public prints. 'The Thunderer' that had been *The Times* (London) was the ancestor of such scandal-sheets as *The Reverberator* (New York), to which in 1888 the Master, Henry James, devoted his impugning power. In a later day, with a nod to the organ in Evelyn Waugh's novel *Scoop,* there would issue forth *The Daily Beast* (2008–).

Stephen's observations on these matters are many and varied, and the tranche of his trenchancies does not limit itself here to selecting solely from articles that are included in *On the Novel and Journalism*. His powers of cohesive attention made time and space for the political world as well as the legal world, for cultural converse as well as for business dealings.

'Perhaps the sentimental novelist and the faithful journalist are not so far apart, after all.'[17] To be found among the unfaithful journalists was the recent phenomenon of the war-correspondent, and among the unfaithful novelists the Inimitable Boz. 'Mr. William Russell and Mr. Charles Dickens have respectively risen to the very top of two closely connected branches of the same occupation. The correspondence from the Crimea is constructed upon exactly the same model as *Pickwick* and *Martin Chuzzlewit*.'[18] Even so illustrious a name as that of Montaigne cannot be kept securely distinct.

Since his time we have been deluged with confessions and self-revelations. Novelists and journalists have vied with each other in beating out their own and their neighbours' experiences, feelings, and loose thoughts upon things in general into sheets of literary tinfoil; and Montaigne stands at the head of an immensely large and by no means respectable literary family.[19]

Stephen was the more wary of journalism's sibling, the novel, because of the overpowering and overbearing social pressure that it exerted—and still exerts, assisted or abetted now by film and 'social media'.[20]

---

[17] 'Light Literature and the *Saturday Review*' (*Sat. Rev.*, 11 July 1857).
[18] 'Mr. Dickens' (*Sat. Rev.*, 8 May 1858).
[19] 'Montaigne's Essays' (*Sat. Rev.*, 3 Nov. 1866; *Hor. Sab.* i 125).
[20] Rodensky attends to such social-question novels as Charles Reade's *It Is Never Too Late to Mend* (dissected by JFS): 'like television programs or films in our own time, these novels reached the largest audiences' (*The Crime in Mind* 186). JFS's unremitting concern with the *facts* of controversial representations has its combative counterpart today when the license of the modern film-maker is at issue, from D. W. Griffith's *The Birth of a Nation* (1915), through to Oliver Stone's *JFK* (1991), Spike Lee's *Malcolm X* (1992), and Steven Spielberg's *Lincoln* (2012).

xx ON THE NOVEL AND JOURNALISM

There are thousands upon thousands of young people, and a considerable number of people no longer young, whose principal experience of argument and discussion is derived from leading articles, and whose notions of the character and prospects of the world in which they live, of the nature of its institutions, and, in a word, of the general colour of life, are taken principally from novels.[21]

(ii)

He spoke as a dedicated journalist when he came to deplore journalistic irresponsibility. Although he could not speak as a novelist when he deplored the novelist's irresponsibility, he did often observe things with a novelist's eye—and with cognate experience of the courtroom. 'All the characters are on trial in any civilized narrative', wrote William Empson,[22] and there in the box was the God of *Paradise Lost*. Stephen as barrister and legal historian heard—and looked searchingly at—the language of the body and the glance of the eye.

All that any one person can, under any circumstances, positively know of any other is, that his body is of a certain shape, colour, &c., and that on particular occasions it moves in a certain way. The expression of the face, the tones of the voice, are all composed of or produced by subtle motions of different muscles and the flesh and skin which cover them. Every form of intellectual exertion, every impulse of passion, has to be translated into muscular or nervous motion of some sort before it can be signified to any one, perhaps even to the person who feels it. Much may be expressed by the glance of the eye or a motion of the nostril, but unless the eyeball or nostril does actually move the information will not be given.[23]

The Indian Evidence Act (1872) included not only 'an Introduction on the Principles of Judicial Evidence' but an evocation of what may be involved in *examining* a witness:

The most acute observer would never be able to catalogue the tones of voice, the passing shades of expression or the unconscious gestures which he had learnt to associate with falsehood; and if he did, his observations would probably be of little use to others. Everyone must learn matters of this sort for himself, and though no sort of knowledge is so important to a judge, no rules can be laid down for its acquisition.*

* I may give a few anecdotes which have no particular value in themselves, but which show what I mean. 'I always used to look at the witnesses' toes when I was cross-examining them', said a friend of mine who had practised at the bar in Ceylon. 'As soon as they began to lie they always fidgeted with them.'

As would a novelist, Stephen understands what footsteps and footprints can effect when it comes to following a story, a series of clues. 'Every step'—yes, every *step*—'by which the connection is made out must either be proved, or be so probable under the circumstances of the case that it may be presumed without proof. Footmarks are found near the scene of a crime...'. And so, (1)–(4), 'Here the steps are as follows:'. Or, thanks to a different sensing: 'she remarked that it smelt like bitter almonds.' Note by Stephen: '*I.e.*, of prussic acid. Lady Broughton perceived by smell the presence of the poison. Therefore she smelt a fact in issue.'[24] (And smelt a rat.)

[21] 'Mr. Thackeray' (*Fraser's*, April 1864; not signed).
[22] *Milton's God* (1961), 94.
[23] *Gen. View 1863* 109.
[24] *The Indian Evidence Act* 43, 54, 58.

INTRODUCTION   xxi

The mind creeps to the crime as a cat creeps towards a bird.[25]

Stephen's mind does not creep, it strides, marches even. The advance, his pursuit, is to maintain the claim that 'The State Trials' can take the place of the novel, can put the novel in its place. One place that he personally recalled was Paris.

Some years ago, a gentleman who passed some months in Paris, and was anxious to make himself familiar with the language and character of the people, was advised to obtain that object by frequenting the theatres. He preferred to devote his time to an assiduous attendance at the criminal courts; and whatever may be thought of his taste, we have little doubt of the correctness of his judgment. There is indeed no place in the world where so great and so interesting a variety of human transactions is described as in a court of criminal justice, and the descriptions given there have the advantage of being invested with all the authenticity that the most careful precautions can secure. The subject-matter of a criminal trial is always of a dramatic nature, but it has two enormous advantages over dramatic representations in point of interest. In the first place, there is no illusion or deception. Everything which is described at all is described as it really happened, and not as some imaginative person considers that it might have happened. And in the second place, the process itself is not a mere toy brought forward to amuse the spectators, but a most serious business, upon the issue of which liberty, and sometimes life, depends, and towards the transaction of which the presence of numerous spectators is a most important aid.

The great charm of the *State Trials* to common readers lies in the light which they throw upon a thousand apparently trivial but really characteristic incidents. Novels in the present day paint the daily life of all classes with the most elaborate minuteness, but a novelist can never be trusted. It is impossible to say how much allowance is to be made on the score of the necessities of the story, the temper of the individual writer, and a hundred other circumstances. In a trial, all the incidents are described on oath; and when there is perjury or inaccuracy, the matter stated is sure to be described as it probably would have happened, because no one knowingly tells an improbable lie or is deceived by a defect of memory into thinking that an improbable incident happened.

If anyone wants to know how poor people and vagrants passed their ordinary days just a hundred years ago, he cannot do better than read the trial (which made all England ring) of Elizabeth Canning for perjury...No novel could bring the common people and their average daily pursuits so vividly before the mind.[26]

True, there is in Stephen something of Johnson's thorough-going behaviour in argument ('when his pistol misses fire, he knocks you down with the butt end of it'[27]), and there is manifest injustice to the art of the novel and to drama, but Stephen's imagination is deeply engaged and there are ways in which it does its own justice and does justice to itself.

The horror of a story does not depend upon the dignity of the actors in it, and we do not think that Aeschylus himself ever imagined a more ghastly scene than must have been presented in that mean house in the midst of all the commonplaces of London life, whilst the mother was, for considerably more than a day, going about her ordinary domestic duties—cleaning the house, eating, drinking, and sleeping, in the presence of the bodies of her children, frightfully mangled by her own hands—and the father was attending to his ordinary employments, oppressed by the knowledge of the event.[28]

---

[25] 'Capital Punishments' (*Fraser's*, June 1864, signed F.S.).

[26] JFS, 'The State Trials' (*Sat. Rev.*, 8 Jan. 1859). Notably the edition by Thomas B. Howell and Thomas J. Howell (33 vols., 1809–26). On how law reports and novels meet and part, Ayelet Ben-Yishaim, *Common Precedents: The Presentness of the Past in Victorian Fiction* (2013). Elizabeth Canning (1734–1773; *ODNB*, convicted perjurer). Two women were found guilty of kidnapping her, but they were cleared when she was later convicted of perjury and was transported to Connecticut.

[27] Boswell's *Life of Johnson* (ed. George Birkbeck Hill, rev. L. F. Powell, 1934), ii 100.

[28] 'The Trial of the Bacons' (*Sat. Rev.*, 16 May 1857).

ON THE NOVEL AND JOURNALISM

There at this horrifying trial it is as if we might 'have seen in real life an exact repetition of the fearful story which forms the plot of Jane Eyre.'

The horror of a union with a person who, in successive fits of madness, murders her husband's mother, his and her own children, and sets fire to his house, is as great as that which hung over the family of Thyestes. On the other hand, if the wife's madness should be the instrument of discovering the past guilt of the husband by means of the death of his children, we shall witness one of those fearful instances of a retributive vengeance overtaking the evildoer, which may not be capable of being reduced to any very logical form, but which speaks in tones of thunder to the imaginations of mankind.

The imaginations of mankind, Stephen would insist, find themselves betrayed whenever facts are wrested to falsities. As with 'a report of the trial of a common thief, in the reign of Henry II', 'one of an immense number of stories of miracles, said to have been worked by his [Thomas Becket's] intervention after his murder. It probably has the same sort of relation to actual fact as an account of a trial by a modern novelist would have to what actually passes in courts of justice.'[29]

The license taken by the modern novelist and journalist was, if the culprit were a historian, all the more grave. Himself a historian, Stephen saw and often suspected the ways of such crafts and arts. The first and last thing first and last: *evidence*. Carlyle finds himself acquitted.

No attorney preparing a brief for counsel could have taken so much pains to get legal evidence of every fact which could possibly be relevant to the cause, as Mr. Carlyle has taken to elucidate everything which can in any way be brought to bear upon the history of his various heroes.[30]

It is only if there is confidence in the facts that there could be esteem for those character-studies of which Carlyle was master.

His object always is to construct in his own mind, from such materials as are accessible to him, a picture of the living man as he really was; and when he has got him, he invariably enlists our affections on the side of what was good in him, with as much vigour as the most powerful novelist, and, as it seems to us, with a truth and force of moral sentiment which hardly any writer of fiction, at least in our days, has ever attained to.[31]

In the same spirit, Stephen praised 'the descriptions of character on which the fame of Clarendon as a writer principally depends.'

Each of them shows how closely and with what searching curiosity he examined and revolved in his mind any fact which interested him. Every one, his dearest friend, his bitterest enemy, the objects of his deepest contempt and of his highest admiration, are all passed through the same crucible. He looks into them with all the curiosity of a modern novelist, and gives in a few phrases a summary which in the present day would, by the invention of characteristic illustrative instances, be made to fill the constitutional three volumes of a novel.[32]

For Stephen, contempt and admiration, in various ways and to different degrees, met not only in the *writings* of Edward Gibbon but in his person, as preserved in 'a portrait

---

[29] *Hist. Crim. Law*, i 78.
[30] 'Mr. Carlyle' (*Fraser's*, Dec. 1865).
[31] 'Mr. Carlyle' (*Fraser's*, Dec. 1865).
[32] 'Clarendon's History of the Rebellion' (*Sat. Rev.*, 29 Oct. 1864; *Hor. Sab.* i 314).

INTRODUCTION   xxiii

taken from a figure of him cut out from black paper, with a pair of scissors, in his
absence, by a Mrs. Brown':

It is the figure of a very short, fat man, as upright as if he had swallowed a poker, and surmounted
by a face a little like the late Mr. Buckle's. He wears a pigtail, and holds a snuff-box, which
balance each other in such a manner as to give the squat figure with its big head and its little bits
of legs, a strange look of formality, struggling with a desire to shine.[33]

This portrait of a Portrait of a Gentleman is not so much a matter of reservations about
Gibbon as a sense of the reserves that Gibbon commanded, there in 'a cross between
irony and pomposity which is admirably characteristic of the half-conscious grimace
which Gibbon never laid aside.'

The greatest challenge to Stephen, though, was not a matter of estimating the historian Clarendon and his diplomatic exactitude during our civil war, or Gibbon's distant ages of imperial rise and fall, or Carlyle's phantasmagoria of the ways we live now,
but the case of—even The Case of—Macaulay. A great historian in Stephen's eyes, a
great friend of British India, duly accompanied by great friendship with the Stephen
family (an immensely large and by all means respectable literary family): all this, to the
good. But had Macaulay hearkened to the evidence? Particularly when the evidence
came to—and from—British India?

Henry James asked, in the penultimate sentence of his review of *Middlemarch* in
1873, 'If we write novels so, how shall we write History?' *The Story of Nuncomar and
the Impeachment of Sir Elijah Impey* (1885) is the historical narrative by Stephen that
could not but invite its readers to ask what a novel is, in relation to what History—or a
history—is. Stephen On the Novel and Journalism has to admit Stephen on History,
and then Stephen and this history of his.

Lisa Rodensky opens her consummate edition with a succinct account of the complicated story that Stephen was moved to investigate.

The Story of Nuncomar and the Impeachment of Sir Elijah Impey (1885) announces its plot right
in the title: this book first tells (one version of) Nandakumar's 'story'—his trial and execution—
and next describes the attempt, 12 years later, to impeach the former Chief Justice of the court
that tried Nandakumar and ordered his punishment. That Chief Justice, Sir Elijah Impey, was
accused of engineering an unfair trial which issued in a legally sanctioned hanging: in short, a
judicial murder. But entangled with this complex plot is yet another, one Stephen outlines in his
first three entries for Thomas Babington Macaulay in his index. 'Macaulay, Lord, his attack on
Impey...; based on insufficient grounds and wholly unjust...; the author's admiration for
him...; splendour of the services he rendered to India...'
   The case provoked Macaulay to announce that 'it was then, and it still is, the opinion of
everybody, idiots and biographers excepted, that [Warren] Hastings was the real mover in the
business.' And, looking at the decision not to grant a reprieve, that 'no rational man can doubt
that [Impey] took this course in order to gratify the Governor-General.'

But Stephen was—no question—a rational man, as well as a man of pertinacity and
probity, and no amount of admiration for and gratitude to Macaulay would come
between Stephen and hearkening to the evidence. He had no choice but to apply to
Macaulay the very questioning that (twenty years earlier) he himself had brought to

---

[33] JFS quietly invites us to enjoy the coincidence of 'Buckle' and bodily strain. 'Gibbon's Memoirs' (*Sat.
Rev.*, 2 Feb. 1867; *Hor. Sab.* ii 403–4).

xxiv ON THE NOVEL AND JOURNALISM

bear down on Dickens and Charles Reade. For, as Rodensky shows, Macaulay's essay on Warren Hastings (*Edinburgh Review*, Oct. 1841) had claimed 'at once the authority of historiography and the license of fiction, the license to go directly into the interior lives of the figures it represents.'[34] Was not this, on Macaulay's part, an evasion of evidentiary responsibility? And was not *The Story of Nuncomar and the Impeachment of Sir Elijah Impey*) open to the same charge, even if, in the end, it were to be acquitted?

The case also had, as Stephen suggests in his letter to Lytton, a certain shape that readers would recognize as novelistic. Stephen moves with caution around the idea of this 'story' as a novel (it contains 'some of the characteristics of the legal novel', not all), but he registers the 'characteristics' nonetheless. What those characteristics are we must infer from the story Stephen tells, one that offers a complex plot, multiple accusations and suspects, and the thrill of both an execution and an attack on and later acquittal of the reputed executioners—executioners who happened to be the chief justice and the governor-general themselves. The story offered the attractions of conspiracy and dirty dealings. Central to this story is the unexpected twist that transforms Impey from judge to suspected murderer.[35]

To Lord Lytton,[36] Viceroy and versifier, Stephen wrote: 'Your poem to you is exactly what my Impey has been to me. I have no doubt it must be an absorbing thing to make poems and novels. I never at any time in my life had the least humour for either pursuit.'[37] Rodensky is moved to follow where Stephen proceeds: 'Yet in an April 29 [1885] letter to Lady Egerton, with whom he was also corresponding about his "Impey", he more readily imagines, at her suggestion, himself as a legal novelist'.

You suggest that I should write a novel. I should like some parts of it well enough, but the young women, and the love making, and the social scenes would completely beat me, and I am afraid that my criminal trial, and the murder, and the detectives, and the historical passages would be so much too much like the real things that nobody would read them. I have sometimes thought, in reading a novel, that it would be amusing to try to write a scene or two in one's own words. I am sure, for instance, I could make the conversations in Scott's novels, those, I mean which are not written in broad Scotch – infinitely more like real conversations than they are at present, but I do not think I should get further than that in the way of novel writing.

(iii)

When it came to such novels as were light literature, Stephen could be aptly light. 'It is an ordinary novel of the most commonplace kind. All the good people get into trouble first, and get out of it afterwards; and all the bad people do just the reverse.'[38] But we can judge that it was a loss to him as well as to us that he not only thought but liked the thought that there could not really exist any *un*-ordinary or extraordinary novels of a most *un*commonplace kind. He was happy with Thackeray's making out that when it came to novels one should not have great expectations. 'He knew perfectly well that a novel at its best estate ought to be regarded as nothing more than an elegant amusement,

---

[34] Rodensky, *The Crime in Mind* 34.
[35] *The Crime in Mind* 172.
[36] Robert Lytton Bulwer-Lytton, first earl of Lytton, *pseud*. Owen Meredith (1831–1891; *ODNB*, viceroy of India and poet).
[37] 23 Feb. 1885. Cambridge University Library. *The Crime in Mind* 173.
[38] 'The Enigma', by 'An Old Chronicler' (*Sat. Rev.*, 30 Aug. 1856).

INTRODUCTION   XXV

indirectly instructive.'[39] Anything *directly* instructive was held suspect, and Stephen, since he was very acute when he was on a case, often judged aright. Of the novel *Fair Oaks*:

> Such fictions tend to no higher end than that of furnishing their readers with the materials of a kind of hypocrisy rather more refined than the commoner varieties of that accomplishment. True self-denial must be learnt in a much rougher and less attractive school. We must, however, confess that our artistic objections to novels of this class are stronger than our moral objections. It is quite bad enough to have to make sacrifices in real life, without being called upon to admire them in fictions.

This, said with some justice, is followed immediately by summary injustice: 'A novel ought to be amusing, and to enable the reader to forget his duties and the other vexations of life.'[40] For not only was this particular novel without any 'higher end', all novels need to know their lowly origins.

On occasion (rare occasion), Stephen did find himself confronted by a novel that he sensed could not be reduced to 'nothing more than an elegant amusement'. His move, not dishonourable but insufficient, was to summon it in the company of a common-place novel that conveniently failed both as amusement and as anything more than amusement. The Italian setting of a novel by T. Adolphus Trollope moved Stephen to appraise Stendhal.

> A book which really did describe Italian life as it passed in the smaller Italian States might be a very great book, but it would require a considerable man to write it. Such a book as *Giulio Malatesta* is not to be mentioned in the same year with the *Chartreuse de Parme*...The *Chartreuse de Parme* is not a pretty story by any means, and it would require special acquaintance with Italy to say if it fairly represents the state of things which it claims to describe; but whether it does or not there cannot be a question that it does describe something, and something quite different from what we are accustomed to. It is, so to speak, good on the face of it. There is that sort of difference between the behaviour of the parties at the critical points in the story and the sort of behaviour which might be expected in the natives of other countries, which would naturally be produced by a long reign of superstition and despotism. Mr. Trollope cannot rise to this. He has not sufficient faith in himself or in his readers to introduce real defects into the characters that he likes.[41]

(iv)

Stephen wrote as he did—wrote as tellingly as he did—because of his cast of mind. Never plaster, usually cast in bronze for us (even if sometimes brazen), this earns him the praise that he bestowed upon the author of *The Light of Nature Pursued* (1768–77): 'He was one of that very small number of men who are incapable of making intellectual compromises, and who utterly refuse to be satisfied with anything short of an explicit understanding with themselves.'[42] Stephen's understanding of his contemporary Henry Thomas Buckle enjoyed esteeming him along the same lines, for courage as against compromise.

---

[39] 'Mr. Thackeray' (*Fraser's*, April 1864; not signed).
[40] 'Fair Oaks', by 'Max Lyle', Anna Maria Yule (*Sat. Rev.*, 21 Mar. 1857).
[41] 'Giulio Malatesta' (*Sat. Rev.*, 13 June 1863). *La Chartreuse de Parme* had been published in 1839.
[42] Abraham Tucker (writing as 'Edward Search'). 'Tucker's "Light of Nature" ' (*Sat. Rev.*, 12 Nov. 1864; *Hor. Sab.* iii 72).

XXvi ON THE NOVEL AND JOURNALISM

Intellectual cowardice is the only form of that vice which is at all common in this country, but it prevails to a lamentable degree. Most writers are so nervous about the tendencies of their books, and the social penalties of unorthodox opinion are so severe, and are exacted in so unsparing a manner, that philosophy, criticism and science itself too often speak amongst us in ambiguous whispers what ought to be proclaimed from the house tops. There are many of Mr. Buckle's speculations with which we do not agree, but we admire the courage with which he propounds them.[43]

Intrigued by Buckle, Stephen brings out the ways in which adversarial courage can prove to be co-operatively creative: 'It is by showing a man the foundation of the truth, which he holds already, that he is to be led into a wider view of it; for it is this which constitutes the ground common to himself and to his critic.'

In more than one way this should remind us of William Empson, who was to set out his reasons for thinking very highly of Buckle's *History of Civilization*,[44] and who (like Stephen) appreciated the valuable invitation that can be extended by a principled calling-in-question: 'An irony has no point unless it is true, in some degree, in both senses; for it is imagined as part of an argument; what is said is made absurd, but it is what the opponent might say.'[45] Buckle was the object of Stephen's irony, not sarcasm. 'In a note he admits that a small number of metaphysicians have pursued the course suggested in the text, but it is a habit of Mr. Buckle's to make admissions in notes which are not very reconcilable with the remarks to which they refer.' (This itself in a note by Stephen.) 'Our objection to Mr. Buckle is, not that he teaches an immoral doctrine, but that he seems to think that he does.' 'What we have called the working rules of life', Stephen insists, 'do nevertheless contain a very large proportion of truth; so large a proportion that, though to inquire into and revise them is perhaps the highest function to which the human mind can devote itself, they afford rules quite exact enough to be of the greatest possible importance in regulating the public and private affairs of life, and principles which may well serve as the foundation for institutions most necessary and beneficial to mankind.' The foundation for these beneficial institutions asked, or rather demanded, a style that is steely. 'To attempt to draw metaphysical or psychological conclusions from statistical data is no more than an elaborate way of inquiring into the distance between one o'clock and London Bridge.'

It certainly does not follow that, because a leading article or a review is dependent upon immediate success, it must be ill written. Some of the qualities which command immediate success are among the highest which can be displayed in literature. A periodical writer whose heart is in his work will try to command the success on which he depends by point, compression, clearness, and nervousness of style.[46]

Nervousness, *OED* Strength, vigour, force.[47] The very opposite of the next sense: Weakness of nerves. (Something from which Stephen suffered rather too little.) Point, compression, clearness, are marks of his thinking and wording, well turned, adept at squaring up and at rounding upon.

---

[43] 'Buckle's *History of Civilization in England*' (*Edin. Rev.*, Apr. 1858; not signed).
[44] *Milton's God* 252–4, Buckle having identified the historical growth of scepticism as the force that came to keep persecutory Christianity at bay.
[45] 'Double Plots', *Some Versions of Pastoral* (1935); ed. Seamus Perry (2020), 39.
[46] 'Life of Matthew Robinson' (*Sat. Rev.*, 18 Oct. 1856).
[47] Including 1839 HALLAM a spirit and nervousness of strength and sentiment. JFS wrote on Henry Hallam (*Sat. Rev.*, 29 Jan. 1859; *Essays* 16–30).

INTRODUCTION xxvii

The systematic vigour of his expressions must force his opponents, if they have any power of mind at all, into an attempt to invest their objections to them with something like equal clearness.[48]

People ought to say what they mean; and if what they mean to say is that something which is not a marriage is as good as if it were one, they ought to say so, without making the false assertion that God views it as being something which it is not. Correctness in phraseology is the first step towards correctness of thought, and the class of phrases in question keeps up in the minds of those who use them a delusion which has an extraordinary charm for people in general, and of which it is next to impossible to disabuse them.[49]

Stephen had the considerable intellectual and imaginative merit of being able to return to a crucial figure of speech in the awareness that he had not yet managed to get to the bottom of it, or to all sides of it.

His answer is simple and emphatic to the last degree – namely, that if you do right you will go to heaven, and if you do wrong to hell, which solution, he says 'goes to the bottom of the subject, as no further question can reasonably be asked.' No doubt the solution goes to the bottom of the question, but it does not go to all sides of it.[50]

As has been said, with extreme truth and wisdom, the uniform object of his arguments was not to find the bottom of a question, but to put a bottom into it.[51]

He believes things because he already believes something else more or less like them.

Everything else that can be said on the subject is only a more or less ingenious attempt to sit upon two stools. Mr. Rowland puts his two stools together with a considerable degree of ingenuity, and sits upon them perhaps with as much ease as people engaged in such a feat usually display.[52]

He has looked over, and in a sort of way studied, the most popular writers on morality, and he has also in a sort of way thought about their systems, but it is all in a sort of way.

The administration of justice rests on the principle that every one is acquainted with the law and fears its punishments. No one makes laws for cattle.[53]

We also think that it was very wrong to cut off his head; but, with considerable intellectual merits, he was utterly intolerable as a Prime Minister, and deserved almost anything short of what actually happened to him.[54]

Stephen's style has great and various strengths, including some that emanate perhaps from a co-operative subconscious (as in his letter to his sister-in-law as to his trials on the way towards a judgeship: 'I hope I have not been anxious to any unworthy or unmanly extent about the various trials which are now over').[55] But a weakness of his is the consequence of a truth that cries out 'Oh' within an imaginative masterpiece of legal acumen, *Measure for Measure*:[56]

---

[48] 'Lord Macaulay' (*Sat. Rev.*, 7 Jan. 1860; *Essays* 100).

[49] 'In the Sight of God' (*Sat. Rev.*, 31 Oct. 1863).

[50] 'Paley's Moral Philosophy' (*Sat. Rev.*, 9 Apr. 1859; *Essays* 303).

[51] 'Dr. Newman on Universities' (*Sat. Rev.*, 13 Dec. 1856).

[52] 'Rowland's Laws of Nature' (*Sat. Rev.*, 6 Feb. 1864).   [53] *Gen. View 1863* 117.

[54] 'Archbishop Laud' (*Sat. Rev.*, 9 Dec. 1865; *Hor. Sab.*, i 185).   [55] 4 Jan. 1879 (*Life* 256).

[56] A play profoundly attentive to the questions that arise from serious crimes attempted without success, questions that Stephen unsuccessfully attempted to settle (as have a great many thinkers). *Life* 280–1: 'Another man was convicted at Manchester of an attempt to murder his wife. He had stabbed her several times in the neck, but happened to miss a fatal spot... Fitzjames, in delivering sentence, told him that a man who had done the same thing, but with better aim, "stood at the last assizes where you now stand, before the judge who is now sentencing you. The sentence upon him was that he should be hung by the neck till he was dead, and he was hung by the neck till he was dead"... It was, he proceeded, by a mere accident that the result of the prisoner's crime was different, and that, therefore, the gravest sentence was the only proper sentence;

xxviii   ON THE NOVEL AND JOURNALISM

> Oh, it is excellent
> To have a Giants strength: but it is tyrannous
> To use it like a Giant. (II ii)

In the odd but usual way, every instance of Stephen's rhetorical coercion cannot but bear witness, in its very insistence, to a fissure in his arguing. Such an obduracy as 'surely' (at one with a kind of coaxing) is an uneasy covert acknowledgment of objections that are being denied admission. 'Our Civilization',[57] an essay of fewer than 3,000 words, enforces 'surely' twice in five lines and later in two successive paragraphs: 'surely most unjust…surely wrong…Surely it is much better…Surely all this can have nothing to do with "our civilization".' *I assure you*: this outstretched hand has nothing to do with genuine assurance or reassurance.

So that our pleasure in Stephen's words, like our due praise of them, needs to be wary of his propensity to be at once peremptory and collusive. The same goes for what might look like exactly the opposite of the forthrightness in him (his thinking largely in bold type): viz., the holding-operation that makes out that he will, of course, be attending further, somewhen, to these matters that he has been revolving. This air of the merely-interim report, although it may look like the opposite of *elbowing* us, serves a related turn in that it grants itself unspecified elbow-room for manoeuvre.[58] Stephen was not an '*almost*' man. This is among the reasons that he is real, and really valuable. He ought not to have affected otherwise, as he does whenever he calls upon his accomplice, *Almost*.

The history of English punishments is a history of a transition from almost barbarous severity to excessive lenity, both the lenity and the severity being tempered by a wide personal discretion reposed in the judge.[59]

Not authentically scrupulous, merely a gesture towards scruples, this recourse to 'almost barbarous', this rolling up and rolling away. For what was incumbent on Stephen (the judge of the matter here) was his thinking out, and his letting us in on, the precise ways in which 'barbarous' both *is* and *is not* the right word for the old 'severity'. The same goes for 'with almost excessive humanity'.[60] And again: 'Nothing is

---

and that is "that you be kept in penal servitude for the term of your natural life".' In 1842 JFS, a schoolboy, had 'left Brighton on the day, as he notes, upon which one Mister was hanged for attempting murder—being almost the last man in England hanged for anything short of actual murder' (*Life* 54–5 with n., JFS, 'Autobiog.' apparently misremembering, for Josiah Mister had been hanged a year earlier, on 3 Apr. 1841).

[57] *Sat. Rev.*, 28 June 1856.

[58] The author of *Liberty, Equality, Fraternity* did not live to read the words of 1910 that were prompted by Swinburne's poems: 'There is a lack of detail about Liberty, and she has indeed no positive quality at all. Liberty consists in the absence of obstructions; it is merely a preliminary to activities whose character it does not determine; and to write poems about Liberty is very much as if one should write an Ode to Elbow-room' (*A. E. Housman: Collected Poems and Selected Prose*, ed. Christopher Ricks, 1988, 279). AEH and JFS were (unsoulful) soul-mates. It is Leslie Stephen whom Housman quotes in his letter of condolence to his sister Katharine when her son was killed in action in 1915: 'I do not know that I can do better than send you some verses that I wrote many years ago [*Illic Jacet*, later *Last Poems* IV]; because the essential business of poetry, as it has been said, is to harmonise the sadness of the universe' (*The Letters of A.E.Housman*, ed. Archie Burnett, 2007, i 346–7).

[59] *Gen. View 1863* 108, from the final paragraph of ch. II.

[60] *Gen. View 1863* 124, the closing words of ch. III.

INTRODUCTION   xxix

more remarkable than the almost idolatrous admiration with which the leading writers of the sixteenth and seventeenth centuries regarded law.'[61]

(v)

'The dexterity of the novelist is proved by the fact, that he inclines his readers to dispense with evidence the study of which would supersede his unsupported assertions.'[62] Evidence is the battle-ground upon which Stephen attacks novelist and journalist alike for how they wage persuasion.

'The subject is one which reaches far beyond law. The law of evidence is nothing unless it is founded upon a rational conception of the manner in which truth as to all matters of fact whatever ought to be investigated.'[63] 'Your charge is to say whether he is guilty or not, *and hearken to the evidence*'.[64] For Stephen nothing had greater weight than evidence in every respect, and in 1885 he acknowledged a high hope:

I think, before I begin it [a history of British India], I must do another thing which has taken my fancy immensely and which will conclude my speculative works. This is a book on Evidence. It would be called 'The principles of Evidence Scientific Legal, and historical', and would embody the thoughts and experience of a great number of years. Its general object would be to show (what I am convinced is true) that there is one pretty simple principle which runs through all subjects of enquiry, whatever they may be whether Scientific, legal, or historical, according to which you may estimate the weight of evidence, which put shortly and imperfectly is that evidence is strong in proportion to the disposition of the witness to speak the truth, and also in proportion to his power of doing so, which again depends mainly on his means and opportunities for observing and recollecting the matter on which he testifies. This sounds so simple and commonplace as to be hardly worth stating, but if fully worked out and with proper illustrations it would be found to throw a new light on nearly every department of human knowledge and speculation. It shows for instance why scientific doctrines properly proved are more certain than any others, and it explains the reason why all religious belief is and must always be essentially doubtful. It shows the difference between ancient and modern history, and explains how far history deserves to be believed. It would I think show the view which ought to prevail about miracles ghosts odd stories etc., in a word it would be a book full of curiosity and in a sort of way of entertainment. It would for one thing try to draw the line between science and science, to show e.g. why Newton belongs to quite a different category from Herbert Spencer,[65] and how and why Darwin differs from his disciples. In short it is a book of which the idea fascinates me immensely, and which with writings about India would more than fill partem ultimam vitae which alas will not last so many years as I could wish.[66]

Such a book would have been the apotheosis of a great many memorable asseverations by Stephen. Of the works of Dr Thomas Arnold: 'they have all one marked

---

[61] 'Jeremy Taylor as a Moralist' (*Sat. Rev.*, 6 June 1868; *Hor. Sab.* i 250).

[62] 'Novels and Novelists' (*Sat. Rev.*, 18 Sept. 1858). *Gen. View 1863* 245, on 'the fact that juries ought to make conjectures in criminal trials': 'The phrase, "Circumstantial evidence", timidly and plausibly conceals this fact. It proposes a sham canon of proof, and leads jurymen to believe that they are deciding on a particular kind, and a highly scientific and ingenious kind, of evidence when, in fact, they are making a conjecture'. Further, see Alexander Welsh, *Strong Representations: Narrative and Circumstantial Evidence in England* (1992).

[63] *The Indian Evidence Act. With an Introduction on the Principles of Judicial Evidence* (1872), Preface.

[64] *Gen. View 1863* 68. ('The last clause was not in the old charge. It would have been needless, for the jurors themselves were the witnesses.')

[65] (1820–1903; *ODNB*, philosopher, social theorist, and sociologist).

[66] JFS to Julia Grant Duff, 25 June 1885. *Life* (Appendix 4: Letters), 347–8, with note to *partem*..., 'the last part of <my> life'.

XXX   ON THE NOVEL AND JOURNALISM

characteristic – they show that the author had a strong love for truth, but a weak love for evidence.'[67]

Nothing is more common than to assert the existence of an agreeable concealed quality, because, if it existed, it would present an effective contrast to a disagreeable apparent one. In novels this practice is so common that when a person is introduced who behaves with extreme brutality, it is morally certain that, a little further on, he will be found to act with romantic generosity. In real life people are not made on this plan. Manner, as far as it is any evidence of character, is evidence of a character corresponding with itself.[68]

We had better be atheists at once, if it must be so, than pretend to believe in a God and a future state on the sort of evidence which would be called to support a fraudulent *alibi*.[69]

The first answer is, that accounts of miracles, like all other historical statements, must be believed or not upon evidence. Destroy the weight of the evidence, and you destroy the belief. When, therefore, in answer to arguments destroying the weight of the evidence for the removal of the Holy House of Loretto,[70] it is said that the evidence of the Christian miracles is no better, this is an argument against the Christian miracles, and can be good only in the mouth of those who do not believe them, or (which is much the same) are determined to believe them whether true or not.[71]

The great majority of Liberals in the present day would admit that they are perfectly willing to believe any doctrines which can be proved to their satisfaction to have been revealed to men by God. All that they contend for is, that the question whether, in fact, alleged revelations are real is a question of evidence, to be decided by the common rules of evidence, and that the moral character of the alleged revelation is one item of the evidence to be considered.[72]

These stories give the keynote of Louis's mind. Faith, in his view, was the act of believing without evidence, or even against evidence.[73]

Leslie Stephen was aware, in Fitzjames's case, that 'It would be very easy to caricature him by dwelling on the rough side'. Aware, too, of 'Fitzjames's hatred of all exaggeration'[74]— and then of how such a hatred has a way of itself sharpening exaggeration to the point of caricature. Fitzjames was to write to his sister-in-law Emily Cunningham (8 Nov. 1872): 'My opinion is, and long has been, that the English people, though to blame, like all others, are considerably less to blame than they often appear, for their various social evils... In short I think exaggeration is the sin of the age.'[75] There, the deploring of the reform-ist breast-and-drum beating of such as Dickens is succeeded by some exaggerating of exaggeration. *The sin of the age*: were there not sins a-plenty? Stephen was unremit-tingly aware that there were *crimes* a-plenty. Of the flourishing word-sinners, though, the greatest had to be Charles Dickens. Rodensky pinpoints what is at work and in play:

Stephen could not recognize, as Ruskin—for instance—could, that there was truth in the caricatures that Dickens presented. Note this from Ruskin's commentary on *Hard Times*: 'The

---

[67] 'The *Edinburgh Review* on Doctor Arnold' (*Sat. Rev.*, 6 Feb. 1858).

[68] 'John Bull' (*Sat. Rev.*, 26 Nov. 1859; *Essays* 65).

[69] 'Superstition and Education' (*Sat. Rev.*, 14 May 1864).

[70] The basilica, a Marian shrine, that was believed to have been flown by angels from Nazareth to (in the end) Italy.

[71] 'The Miscellaneous Works of Conyers Middleton' (*Sat. Rev.*, 11 Feb. 1865; *Hor. Sab.* ii 359–60).

[72] 'Dr. Newman and Liberalism' (*Sat. Rev.*, 24 June 1865).

[73] 'Joinville and St. Louis' (*Sat. Rev.*, 10 Mar. 1866; *Hor. Sab.* i 11).

[74] *Life* 78.

[75] From a public letter by JFS, 'The Bishop of Carlisle upon Heathenism' (*PMG*, 9 Sept. 1872; *On Society, Religion, and Government* 217).

INTRODUCTION xxxi

essential value and truth of Dickens's writings have been unwisely lost sight of by many thoughtful persons merely because he presents his truth with some colour of caricature. Unwisely, because Dickens's caricature, though often gross, is never mistaken. Allowing for his manner of telling them, the things he tells us are always true.'[76]

The immense usefulness of this truth is not at all a matter of its relieving us of anything; rather, it should remind us of a good many unignorable questions that are usually (I would like to exaggerate this into *always, of course*) ignored. The responsibilities of caricature to truth, of this act of imagining to the unimaginary world (with 'the world' notoriously as 'everything that is the case'), are at once imperative and elusive. For a start, is all this a 'how much' question? How *much* is it alright to exaggerate? How much of *to-see-the-object-as-in-itself-it-really-is*, in proportion to how much of *to-see-the-object-as-in-itself-it-really-ISN'T* (but which we can *imagine* its being, while aware that imagining is what we are doing).

Ruskin is speaking all the more wisely because he acknowledges that any critical judgment, not cut for the chase but truly pursued, has to entail our patient attention to the ways in which the art of caricature, always a gamble, turns out to be worth the candle—not only socially but as art. Such are the central involvements of caricature in *likeness*, with there coming together, as a rewarding whole, the creative cooperation of several facets—expected likeness, surprising likeness, expected *un*likeness, and surprising *un*likeness. A cogent likeness has to be admitted within the art of caricature for it to come to anything. The nose of President Nixon needs to be—as Donald Davie once said of the words of a poem—at once surprising and just. (David Levine's caricature of Nixon's-nose-as-ski-slope seized its sporting chance.) And Davie is at one with Daumier, for no more than any other kind of achievement can caricature be relieved of responsibilities, its very own ones.

At which point, we stand in need of help with those moments in the Ruskin citation that are (we let ourselves hope and trust) not hedgings but pledgings. 'He presents his truth *with some colour of caricature* . . . Dickens's caricature, *though often gross, is never mistaken. Allowing for his manner of telling them,* the things he tells us are always true.' What exactly is the cash-value of this allowance that Ruskin makes and grants?[77]

For there is the aegis of another imaginative summing-up by Ruskin:

For it might be at first thought that the whole kingdom of imagination was one of deception also. Not so: the action of the imagination is a voluntary summoning of the conception of things absent or impossible; and the pleasure and nobility of the imagination partly consist in its knowledge and contemplation of them as such, *i.e.* in the knowledge of their actual absence or impossibility at the moment of their apparent presence or reality. When the imagination deceives, it becomes madness. It is a noble faculty so long as it confesses its own ideality; when it ceases to confess this, it is insanity. All the difference lies in the fact of the confession, in there being *no* deception. It is necessary to our rank as spiritual creatures, that we should be able to invent and to behold what is not; and to our rank as moral creatures, that we should know and confess at the same time that it is not.[78]

---

[76] *The Crime in Mind* 185–6.

[77] 'It is impossible to say how much allowance is to be made on the score of the necessities of the story . . .', xxi.

[78] 'The Lamp of Truth', *The Seven Lamps of Architecture* (1849), II iii.

xxxii ON THE NOVEL AND JOURNALISM

Stephen is always in danger of hardening his hostility towards caricature into a judging of it to be, by its very nature, irresponsible and of very little worth. Dickens, on the other foot, played fast and loose. Sometimes he implies a defence of caricature as quite happy to know its place, thank you, and knowing it. Sometimes he bridles at the suggestion that the picture he has painted is a caricature (or even fictitious) *at all*. These are markedly different positions to take, and often he is too impatient when it comes—or does not come—to differentiating them or attending to a particular case of one or the other. The Spontaneous Combustion that explodes Krook in *Bleak House* is not to be attenuated into a symbol, emblem, metaphor, or what-not. It is not a myth to be exploded. Like other bodily things, Spontaneous Combustion *happens*.[79]

But then Stephen has his own burly contradictions. There are contrarious impulses at work in his differing from his brother and sister as to the two busts of their father. Fitzjames 'owned and admired the Marochetti bust, which Leslie Stephen and his sister Caroline Emelia thought "a coarse caricature".'[80] Leslie judged that 'Fitzjames's preference of the Marochetti was to my mind characteristic'—oddly, given that Fitzjames distrusted the caricatural. But then Fitzjames also deprecated any hint of delicacy or weakness, features that caricature, after all, can likewise set its face against. Unlike the sculptor Munro, Marochetti 'made Sir James look like the statesman dictating a despatch to suppress a rebellion, but took all the delicacy out of his face. Fitzjames revered our father even more than I did, but could not help thinking that his sensitiveness was a weakness to be regretted.'[81]

Stephen's arguments lost ground because of his inordinate confidence that the world, or rather his England, no longer stood in any need of such dispositions and disputations as, in earlier times and other places, had served valuable functions, whatever their limitations and distortions. There was a generosity of acknowledgment whenever he granted such principled concessions, as, for instance, to 'the exercise of that tacit scepticism which is the great protector of mankind against spiritual tyranny.'[82] But no longer, it is intimated, do we need to protect ourselves against tyranny with the help of tacit scepticism, for what we need protection against is the full-throated scepticism that tyrannizes our days. Likewise with that 'levity of style' with which Montaigne resisted the tyrannies of his time.

He was not himself a penny-a-liner, though he was the father of the whole brood. He actually was what the modern gossip wishes to be, and he lived at a time when intelligent gossip was greatly required as a counterpoise to fierce, ignorant, and overbearing dogmatism...In Montaigne's

---

[79] MR. KROOK, *a marine–store dealer; an old and eccentric man*. Dickens in his Preface: 'There is only one other point on which I offer a word of remark' (in fact, about 300 words). 'The possibility of what is called Spontaneous Combustion has been denied since the death of Mr. Krook...I have no need to observe that I do not wilfully or negligently mislead my readers, and that before I wrote that description I took pains to investigate the subject...I do not think it necessary to add to these notable facts, and that general reference to the authorities which will be found at p. 534...' JFS, 'Authority is only another name for evidence' (what 'the Protestants might have replied' to Bossuet; *Sat. Rev.*, 17 Nov. 1866; *Hor. Sab.* ii 103).

[80] Hermione Lee, Introductory Essay in *Life* xxvii–xxviii. Also *Life* 47 n, and Plate 4: busts of Sir James Stephen by Carlo Marochetti (1805–1867; *ODNB*, sculptor), and Alexander Munro (1825–1871; *ODNB*, sculptor).

[81] Leslie Stephen, *Mausoleum Book* (ed. Alan Bell, 1977), 99–100.

[82] 'Vincenzo', by John Ruffini (*Sat. Rev.*, 30 Jan. 1864). The term 'tacit scepticism' is Buckle's.

INTRODUCTION xxxiii

time it was nearly the only available weapon of offence against a harsh tyranny which had so darkened counsel by words without knowledge, that the first and most pressing of all intellectual necessities was to get rid of the burdens which it had laid on the minds of men.[83]

Our civilization has, for Stephen, passed beyond requiring any such counterpoise; for Dickens, it was far from having done so.

'Novelists have everything their own way. As the prompter moves, the puppet squeaks, and the author of *The First Temptation* certainly succeeds in making the hero and all his friends talk as great nonsense as is to be found in Mr. Emerson's rhapsodies, and nonsense of much the same sort'.[84] The novelist, like the poetical rhapsodist, is judged by Stephen to be always open to The First Temptation, an Exculpation: 'He can always plead that he is writing a novel, and not a political treatise.'[85] (*Plead* is good.) 'Mr. Dickens, as we have remarked on former occasions, is always in a flutter of dissatisfied philanthropy; and, indeed, it would be hard to mention a writer whose literary aims are of the somewhat humble character in question, who does not frequently ignore the limits which divide the leading article from the novel.'[86]

All these are matters of particular responsibilities, and it should be regretted that although Stephen often turned his mind to the nature of legal fictions, he did not sustainedly do so in relation to literary fictions. It would have profited us if he had recognized that a legal fiction might be of great service to our thinking about literary fiction. For he had acknowledged 'the especial advantages and disadvantages of the literary temperament',[87] and it would have helped him to help us think (a further round of thought) if he had imaginatively considered the advantages as well as the disadvantages of both legal fictions and literary fictions.

Writing, with admiration, of 'the English nation' and its 'constitutional reforms', he admitted legal fictions.

There has never been at any period of our history a *tabula rasa*, like that which at the end of the last century existed for a time in France, on which homogeneous and consistent structures, either of law or government, could be raised. The consequence is, that our law is full of fictions, and our public offices full of intricacy. This is, no doubt, an evil to be remedied, but it is one which the present generation inherited, and which earlier generations considered a cheap price for the acquisition of political liberty.[88]

As often, 'no doubt' is an intimation of dubiety, and Stephen clearly has mixed feelings and mixed thinking as to legal fictions. For legal fictions cannot be simply an evil to be remedied; no inheritance can simply be repudiated; and any device that earlier generations considered a cheap price for the acquisition of political liberty is unlikely to have now become simply disavantageous—especially as, for Stephen, most judgements by 'the present generation' were not to be trusted.

---

[83] 'Montaigne's Essays' (*Sat. Rev.*, 3 Nov. 1866; *Hor. Sab.* i 126).

[84] 'The First Temptation' (*Sat. Rev.*, 9 May 1863).

[85] Pope, 'An Epistle to Dr. Arbuthnot' 317–18: 'Whether in florid Impotence he speaks, / And, as the Prompter breathes, the Puppet squeaks'. 'Novels and Novelists' (*Sat. Rev.*, 18 Sept. 1858).

[86] 'Harry Lorrequer' (*Sat. Rev.*, 7 Feb. 1857). *The Confessions of Harry Lorrequer* by Charles Lever.

[87] 'Mr. Carlyle' (*Sat. Rev.*, 19 June 1858; *Essays* 243). With relation to Matthew Arnold, p. 235.

[88] 'The License of Modern Novelists' (*Edin. Rev.*, July 1857), below.

xxxiv ON THE NOVEL AND JOURNALISM

Legal fictions lend themselves, or are leased for a fee, to language-gambits. A treatise on high treason maintained

'that, though such insurrections are not levelled at the person of the king, they are against his royal majesty, and, besides, they have a direct tendency to dissolve all the bonds of society, and to destroy all property, and all government too, by numbers and an armed force.' The words italicised were, obviously, the real reason which decided the judges to take this view; and they supply a conclusive reason why such insurrections should be severely punished, but no reason at all for holding that words intended to mean one thing should be taken to mean something entirely different.

The constructions put upon the words 'compassing the king's death' were of the same character; they enlarged themselves at about the same rate, and for analogous reasons... In other words, such conduct falls within what in my time would be a reasonable account of treason; therefore, the definition given three hundred years ago must be construed so as to include it.[89]

Must be, and should not be. (But easier said than done, the not-doing-this.)

The fictive uses of language had better be attentively listened to, but they have something to be said for them, as Stephen intimates when he speaks of them and their 'extensions' of earlier terminology as a 'device' which may effect some necessary things. 'The commonest and worst kind of homicide was where one man deliberately made up his mind to kill another'. To differentiate this from other homicides, *malice aforethought* was enlisted. It will not altogether do, but then doing without it might prove extortionate. Stephen is aware of the abuses to which such extensions will minister, but vigilance may be the best we can do.

The robber kills him not from any grudge, but to avoid detection, and in the heat of the struggle. To describe such cases as instances of 'malice aforethought' was impossible without violence to language; to treat them as anything else but crimes of the deepest atrocity would be an insult to common sense. In order to meet such cases, without sacrificing the established definition, the doctrine of implied malice was invented... Thus stated in plain words, the doctrine of implied malice amounted to a device, by which the judges were able from time to time to declare any case of homicide, in which they thought the criminal ought to be hung, a capital crime.[90]

Not quite cynical; dangerous, the upshot; but confronting a genuine difficulty of a kind that is not ever simply going to stop arising.

A legal fiction may mount to a 'constitutional fiction', such as Stephen silkily identifies within the case of King Charles v. Parliament. 'In a word, it was necessary to depose him, at least for a time. The Parliament wished to do this gently, and without disturbing the forms of the Constitution; and those forms, of course, implied that the King was still to be King'. Of course. Whereupon, acting on behalf of the royal actor, Clarendon became possessed of 'an inexhaustible supply of charges of hypocrisy and falsehood—charges which were well founded only on the supposition that there are to be no such things as constitutional fictions, and that a King of England ought to consider every phrase which the law uses about his office, as investing him individually

---

[89] Acute, again: 'The vehemence with which the author asserts that "the construction is in strict conformity with the statute, and to every principle of substantial political justice", betrays his consciousness that he ought to have said, "It would have been in strict conformity with the rest of the statute to have made this addition to it"' (*Gen. View 1863* 82–3).

[90] *Gen. View 1863* 86.

INTRODUCTION   XXXV

with the full amount of the power which the literal sense of the words professes to convey'.[91]

Perilous, the use of such fictions, but, whatever Stephen's misgivings, he does not sound like someone who is proposing that there are to be no such things &c. He may speak of 'legal fictions like those from which our own law has not yet worked itself clear',[92] but *not yet* does have a wistful or wishful air, with Stephen uncertain of his working wishes anyway. Except that he does wish us to understand not only the abuses but the uses of such fictions. 'The fact, that under the fiction of declaring the law the judges make it, has been recognized by everyone who has studied the subject with candour and intelligence, since the days of Bentham at least.'[93]

'Legal fictions are always matter of regret. Even if they are practically convenient, they have a strong tendency to make men indifferent to truth.'[94] Up to a point. And tendencies can be resisted. But anyway this would not mean that legal fictions, or (come to that) literary ones, are matter of regret only. Stephen's charges of hypocrisy and falsehood are well founded only on the supposition that there are to be no such things as fictions legal, constitutional, or literary. He had a strong tendency to make himself indifferent, not to the question *Is this true?*, but to the questions that novels, like all the arts, exist to ask: *What is truth?* and *What truth is there in this?*

CHRISTOPHER RICKS

[91] 'Clarendon's History of the Rebellion' (*Sat. Rev.*, 29 Oct. 1864; *Hor. Sab.* i 318).

[92] *Hist. Crim.* iii 84.

[93] *Gen. View 1863* 284, 288: 'The fiction that the judges declare, but do not make, the law, is still the recognized theory on the subject.' (A 'theory' that affects social practice in ways bad and good.)

[94] *Gen. View 1863* 269.

'The Relation of Novels to Life' (excerpts) (*Cambridge Essays*, 1855)

By Fitzjames Stephen, B.A. (subscribed, 'F.S.') in *Cambridge Essays*, contributed by Members of the University (1855; London: John W. Parker and Son). Of his 20,000 words, 13,000 are excerpted here. The selected running heads, intercalated here, are from *Cambridge Essays*. Several of the other essayists engaged with what were already interests of JFS's. For instance, the Crimean War, considered by Francis Galton,[1] 'Notes on Modern Geography', with maps of Crimea; by Robert Edgar Hughes, 'Future Prospects of the British Navy', with 'the present war' in Crimea; and by Charles Buxton, 'Limitations to Severity in War'. JFS's lifelong concern with the relations between public life, publicity, and the press, was shared with William George Clark, who summed up his essay on 'General Education and Classical Studies' (p. 289):

> Let us in fairness acknowledge that if we have less integrity among our shopkeepers, we have more among our statesmen, which may perhaps be owing to the growth of publicity, and the increased probability of being found out. If our great police-inspector, the press, would turn its dark lantern now and then from Downing-street, and flash it suddenly upon Cheapside, it would give a strong impulse to integrity there.

(Clark praises and quotes 'the distinguished Professor of Modern History', JFS's father.) Of the novels that provoked Stephen in 1855, many were recent, notably *Wuthering Heights* (1847), *Vanity Fair* (1848), *Dombey and Son* (1848), *The History of Pendennis* (1849–50), *David Copperfield* (1850), *Uncle Tom's Cabin* (1852), and *The Heir of Redclyffe* (1853). The wrapper titles of monthly parts, when so published, are given throughout JFS's essays, as pertinent to his sense of the presumptuous empire of the novel and its dealings; likewise with Dickens's identifications of his CHARACTERS.[2]

The Relation of Novels to Life (excerpts)

We have discarded many of the amusements of our forefathers. Out-of-door games are almost inaccessible to the inhabitants of cities; and if they were not, people are too much tired, both in nerve and muscle, to care for them. Theatres and spectacles are less frequented than they used to be; whilst the habit of reading has become universal. These causes increase the popularity and the influence of novels, and, measured by these standards, their importance must be considered very great.

The majority of those who read for amusement, read novels. The number of young people who take from them nearly all their notions of life is very considerable. They

---

[1] Sir Francis Galton (1822–1911; *ODNB*, biostatistician, human geneticist, and eugenicist). And the Stephen family, *Life* xxvi–xxvii.
[2] Charles Dickens (1812–1870; *ODNB*, novelist).

ON THE NOVEL AND JOURNALISM

are widely used for the diffusion of opinions. In one shape or another, they enter into the education of us all. They constitute very nearly the whole of the book-education of the unenergetic and listless.

* * *

[*They Contribute to Knowledge of the World*]

Novels, in the proper sense of the word, are used for a greater number of purposes than any other species of literature. Their influences on their readers may, however, be reduced within a very narrow compass. In early boyhood and in mature life they are read merely for amusement; and indulgence in them will be beneficial, or otherwise, according to the ordinary rules upon that subject. But at that time of life which intervenes between these two periods they exercise a far greater influence. They are then read as commentaries upon the life which is just opening before the reader, and as food for passions which are lately awakened but have not yet settled down to definite objects.

It may be questioned how far the habit of reading novels contributes to knowledge of the world. The undue prominence given to particular passions—such as love, the colouring used for artistic purposes, and a variety of other circumstances, are so much calculated to convey false impressions, that it may be plausibly doubted whether the impressions formed are, in fact, better than none at all.

Such a judgment appears to us too severe. If a young man were, according to Mr. Carlyle's suggestion,[3] to be shut up in a glass case from eighteen to twenty-five, and were, during that period, to be supplied with an unlimited number of novels, he would no doubt issue from his confinement with extremely false notions of the world to which he was returning; but if, during such an imprisonment, he had made it a point of conscience never to open a novel, he would, in the absence of extraordinary powers of observation and generalization, be strangely puzzled on re-entering life.

What we call knowledge of the world is acquired by the same means as other kinds of knowledge, and consists not in mere acquaintance with maxims about life, but in applying appropriate ideas to clear facts. This application can only be made by a proper arrangement and selection of the material parts of the facts observed; and this arrangement is effected, to a very great degree, by guesses and hypotheses. No one will be able to make any use of his experience of life, or to classify it in such a manner as to add to his real knowledge, unless he is provided in the first instance with some schemes or principles of classification, which he starts with, and which he enlarges, narrows, or otherwise modifies as he sees cause.

* * *

[*By Suggesting Interpretations of Conduct*]

It is, however, by the materials which it affords for self-examination that novel reading enlarges our experience most efficiently. It was, if we are not mistaken, Lord Chesterfield's

---

[3] Thomas Carlyle (1795–1881; *ODNB*, author, biographer, and historian). *Sartor Resartus* book 2, chapter 4: ' "I have heard affirmed (surely in jest)", observes he elsewhere, "by not unphilanthropic persons, that it were a real increase of human happiness, could all young men from the age of nineteen be covered under barrels, or rendered otherwise invisible; and there left to follow their lawful studies and callings, till they emerged, sadder and wiser, at the age of twenty-five...".'

THE RELATION OF NOVELS TO LIFE

advice to his son,[4] that if he wished to understand mankind he ought to be always saying to himself, 'If I were to act towards that man as he acts towards me, he would feel towards me as I feel towards him.' The thought that they often do act like characters represented in novels, and that people do in consequence feel towards them as they themselves regard such characters, must occur, we should think pretty frequently, to novel readers. It would be a great effort of self-denial[5] to many of us to read *Murad the Unlucky*, or *To-morrow*;[6] and we should think that few men could become acquainted with George Osborne[7] or Arthur Pendennis[8] without acquiring a consciousness of a multitude of small vanities and hypocrisies which would otherwise have escaped their attention. To produce or to stimulate self-consciousness by such means, may not be altogether a healthy process, but it is unquestionably one which has powerful effects.

In a large class of readers, novels operate most strongly by producing emotion. Strange as it seems, many people sympathize more intensely with fictitious than with historical characters. Persons who would read Carlyle's *History of the French Revolution*[9] unmoved, would not be proof against such books as *Uncle Tom's Cabin*,[10] or the *Heir of Redclyffe*;[11] and we suspect that Mr. Dickens has caused a great deal more emotion by some of his luscious death-bed scenes, than by what we have always considered one of the most fearful stories, both in matter and manner, which we ever read, the papers entitled *Transported for Life*,* in *Household Words*.[12] Habitual emotion, whatever may be the exciting cause, produces some moral effects. A man who had really seen a negro flogged to death, or had attended a young man on his wedding tour, in a fatal illness, would probably be in some respects altered for a longer or shorter time afterwards. Whatever would be the effect of habitually witnessing such scenes, the same effect would follow in a much slighter degree from habitually reading descriptions of them; but in order to make the parallel complete we must suppose the witnessing of the scenes to be as much a matter of choice as the reading of the novels; a person who went to see a man

---

[4] Philip Dormer Stanford, fourth earl of Chesterfield (1694–1773; *ODNB*, politician and diplomatist). JFS had in mind his advice: 'Observe carefully what pleases you in others, and probably the same things in you will please others' (16 Oct. 1847; *Letters Written by the Earl of Chesterfield to his Son, Philip* (1774). Noted in *Victorian Criticism of the Novel* (ed. Edwin M. Eigner and George J. Worth, 1985), p. 248.

[5] Apparently not in the *OED* sense, 'abnegation of oneself', 'sacrifice of one's personal desires', but as meaning that it would take a great effort by a reader to deny that she and he did themselves have such traits and frailties.

[6] 1818 and 1823, by Maria Edgeworth (1767–1849; *ODNB*, novelist and educationist).

[7] William Makepeace Thackeray (1811–1863; *ODNB*, novelist). *Vanity Fair: A Novel without a Hero* (1848).

[8] Thackeray, *The History of Pendennis. His Fortunes and Misfortunes, his Friends and his Greatest Enemy* (1849–50).

[9] *The French Revolution. A History* (1837).

[10] Harriet Beecher Stowe (1811–1896), American novelist, woman of letters. *Uncle Tom's Cabin; or, Life Among the Lowly* (1852). JFS was to review *The Minister's Wooing* (*Sat. Rev.*, 22 Oct. 1859; *Essays*), p. 193.

[11] Charlotte M. Yonge (1823–1901; *ODNB*, novelist), *The Heir of Redclyffe* (1853).

[12] Edited (1850–59) by Dickens. 'Transported for Life' (31 July 1852 and the following number), contributed by William Moy Thomas (1828–1910; *ODNB*, novelist, journalist, and translator). JFS, note: 'They are a simple relation of the experience (we believe) of Mr. Barber, transported twelve or thirteen years since for forgery, and pardoned on the discovery of his innocence. See *Household Words*, vol. v, p. 455, &c.' William Henry Barber, a solicitor convicted of fraud and forgery, was transported in 1844 to Australia and then Tasmania, but received a final unconditional pardon in 1848. *Household Words* has the first-person statement as having 'been taken down from the lips of the narrator, whose sufferings are described; with the object of shewing what Transportation, at the present time, really is.' Some of the regulations were no longer in force; *Household Words* (28 Aug. 1852) noted what had been reformed. (Note indebted to Dickens Journals Online.)

4 ON THE NOVEL AND JOURNALISM

die because he liked it would receive very different impressions from one who saw such a sight because he could not help it.

* * *

[*Suppressio Veri in Novels*]

One of the most obvious causes which makes novels unlike real life is the necessity under which they lie of being interesting, an object which can only be obtained by a great deal of *suppressio veri*, whence arises that *suggestio falsi*[13] of which it is our object to point out the principal varieties.

Who would infer from one of the trial scenes which occur in almost every one of the *Waverley Novels*,[14] what a real criminal trial was like? The mere *coup d'œil* presented by the judges, the barristers, the prisoner, the witnesses, and the crowd of spectators, might be pretty accurately represented to any sufficiently imaginative reader by the account of the trial of Fergus McIvor and Evan Dhu Maccombich. The *State Trials*[15] would give a juster notion of the interminable length of the indictments, the apparently irrelevant and unmeaning examinations and cross-examinations of witnesses, the skirmishing of the counsel on points of law, and the petitions of the prisoners, often painfully reasonable, for some relaxation of the rules of evidence, or procedure; but to any one who seeks mere amusement, such reading is intolerably tedious, and even when accomplished, it gives a very faint representation of the actual scene as it appeared to those who sat or stood, day after day, in all the heat, and dust, and foul air of the court-house at Carlisle or Southwark, half understanding, and—as the main points at issue got gradually drowned in their own details—half attending to the proceedings on which the lives and deaths of their friends depended. A man really present on such an occasion, and personally interested, would probably bring away impressions which a life-time would not destroy. In a novel, such a scene is at once more and less interesting than it is in fact. There are more points of interest, more dramatic situations; the circumstances are more clearly defined, and more sharply brought out than they ever would be in real life; but at the same time, that from which such circumstances derive their interest is wanting: the necessity of thought and attention, the consciousness that what is passing is most real and serious business, which it is not open to the spectators to hurry over, or to lay down and take up again at pleasure. In one word, the reality. It is in order to supply the absence of this source of interest that recourse is had to the other.

If we imagine a novel written for a reader seeking, not amusement, but information, it would be not only insupportably dull, but would be more laborious reading than any

---

[13] *OED* A misrepresentation of the truth whereby something incorrect is implied to be true; an indirect lie. Often in context with *suppressio veri*. 1815 (where the legal context happens to be Chancery); 1855 *Newspaper & Gen. Reader's Pocket Compan.* He was bound to say that the *suppressio veri* on that occasion approached very nearly to a positive *suggestio falsi*.

[14] The series by Sir Walter Scott (1771–1832; *ODNB*, poet and novelist) ran from *Waverley, or, 'tis Sixty Years Since* (1814) till 1831. The Edinburgh Edition of the Waverley Novels (1993–2012) is in 30 vols. The trial of the Jacobite rebels Fergus Mac-Ivor (a Highland chieftain) and Evan Dhu Maccombich (his lieutenant) figures in ch. 68 of *Waverley*.

[15] *Life* 99, 265: 'He often speaks of the strangely romantic interest of the incidents brought to light in the "State Trials"... and says in the "History" [*Hist. Crim. Law*], for example, that some of the State Trials are to him 'much more impressive than poetry or fiction'. JFS, 'The State Trials' (*Sat. Rev.*, 8 Jan. 1859).

THE RELATION OF NOVELS TO LIFE

other kind of literature. Suppose that in addition to the present novel of *Waverley*, we had the muster-roll of Captain Waverley's troop, with extracts from the *Army List*[16] of that time as to Gardiner's[17] dragoons; suppose we had full statements of the route of the Pretender's army, short-hand writers' notes of the proceedings of all his councils of war; suppose the MSS. of the Jacobite divinity of Waverley's tutor, or at any rate, the plan of the work, with copious extracts, were actually printed, and all the proceedings against Fergus McIvor, and respecting the pardon of Waverley and the Baron incorporated in the book; and suppose on the part of the reader sufficient interest and patience to go through all this mass of matter, no one can doubt that he would know much more about Waverley and his fortunes than ordinary readers do know. If, however, *Waverley* had been composed upon this principle, the conversations and descriptions, which give it all its charm, would have been greatly curtailed. A person who had toiled, notebook and atlas in hand, through all sorts of authorities, geographical, historical, antiquarian, and legal, about the Highland line, black-mail, and the heritable jurisdictions, would have little taste for the conversations between Waverley, Rose Bradwardine, Evan Dhu, and the Baron, upon the same subjects. They contemplate a frame of mind altogether different.

The *suppressio veri* which occurs in novels may therefore be considered as an essential feature of that kind of literature, but it involves a *suggestio falsi* which is not so obvious, and has more tendency to mislead readers.

It requires but very little experience of life to be aware that the circumstances stated in a novel form a very small part of what must have actually occurred to the persons represented; but it requires more experience to see in what respects the fact that all dull matter is suppressed, falsifies the representation of what is actually described.

* * *

[*Their Representations of Character: As Composed of Definite Qualities*]

Probably no one can look back upon his own history without recalling innumerable inconsistencies in his own conduct and in the conduct of those about him, with the principles which it has been their most earnest desire to recognize, and the habits which they have been forming for years. But though life is full of shortcomings and inconsistencies arising from this cause, novels are not. The difficulty of conceiving or representing differences which vary in every case would of course be very great, and the flow of the story would be interrupted by them. Character, in novels, therefore, is represented as far more homogeneous and consistent than it ever really is. Men are made cowards or brave, foolish or wise, affectionate or morose, just as they are represented as being tall or short, red-haired or black-haired, handsome or ugly.

It is to this origin that we are indebted for the mass of melodramatic or merely conventional characters, which form the staple of some novel writers, and which appear in greater or less numbers even in the most distinguished.

---

[16] The official list of commissioned officers. The earliest *OED* instance, *Waverley* (1814), ch. 61: 'This good lady had the whole army-list by heart.'

[17] Colonel James Gardiner (under whom Waverley served) commanded a regiment in Dundee.

6   ON THE NOVEL AND JOURNALISM

The heroes of the *Waverley Novels*, one and all, belong to this class. They have certain characters assigned to them, and act accordingly throughout the whole story, never
rising above or falling below a certain ill-defined, but well-understood, level of thought
and conduct which is appropriated to such persons. There is no effort, no incompleteness, about these characters. Any one of them could be described by a certain number of adjectives. All of them possess certain muscular and amatory qualifications for
their office of hero, all of them are brave, most of them generous, some determined,
and some irresolute, but none of them display the variety, the incompleteness, the
inconsistency, which almost all men show in real life.

* * *

[*Their Representations are Partial*]

The most remarkable instance of this is afforded by Mr. Thackeray. As there is no
writer who has shown greater genius in representing a particular view of life, so there
is none whose books contain greater omissions, or whose omissions are more likely to
mislead, on account of the wonderful impartiality and many-sidedness of his characters. The first impression received from reading almost any one of his books is, that it
exhausts the subject to which it refers; but a very little experience will show that the
perfection of the observation, so far as it goes, is only equalled by the narrowness of
its range. In the whole of Mr. Thackeray's books, there is hardly a hint of such a thing
as the serious business in life. All his characters are represented either in their leisure
moments, or as men whose whole life is leisure. Hardly any important transaction of
any kind whatever (except the usual number of marriages) enters into any one of his
books. Even when the course of his story brings him near an event in which the
stronger passions and energies are displayed, he instinctively avoids it, often with
consummate skill. The wonderful description of the scenes which passed at Brussels,
during the battle of Waterloo is, perhaps, the most striking instance of this.[18] *Scriberis
Vario*[19] is his constant motto; and we have the actors in one of the greatest scenes in
history set before us, as they flirted, and danced, and lounged—not as they planned,
and felt, and fought.

There is not in all Mr. Thackeray's novels a character who is described by his great
qualities; all are described by their small peculiarities. Yet a man of his genius cannot
have failed to observe that men differ from each other far more radically in the great
leading habits which they have acquired than in the small affectations or weaknesses by
which he generally specifies them. In *Pendennis*, for example, the principal characters
are literary barristers, but nothing turns upon their law or their literature, except that
it is stated as a matter of fact, that they earned an income by the last. Warrington[20] is
represented as being a man of great originality—full of powerful thought, scholarship,

---

[18] The scene at the ball (*Vanity Fair*, ch. 32), where George Osborne suggests to Becky Sharp that they
elope, is succeeded by the Battle of Waterloo, where he is killed.

[19] Horace, *Odes* i.6: 'Scriberis Vario fortis et hostium / victor, Maeonii carminis alite, / quam rem cumque
ferox navibus aut equis / miles te duce gesserit'. ('It takes a poet such as Varius, / Capable of Homeric flight
and range, / To praise your deeds of courage and the events / Of victory whether by ship or cavalry';
tr. David Ferry.)

[20] George Warrington, a journalist with whom Pendennis has lodgings.

THE RELATION OF NOVELS TO LIFE

and knowledge of various kinds; but we have none of the powerful thought, or scholarship, or knowledge, produced in the book; still less are any incidents introduced to give scope to them. We certainly get the impression that Warrington was a man of vigorous understanding; but we get it from learning that he behaved in the commonest affairs of life as such a man might be supposed to behave, not from any description of the remarkable things which he did. To prove that he really was what Mr. Thackeray calls him, we ought to have had an account of his social, political, and legal opinions, and the reasons why he adopted them. We ought to have had specimens of his reviews and leading articles.

* * *

[*Hero-Worship of Authors*]

The vexed question, as to the morality of representing bad characters in a novel, is possibly to be solved upon this principle. If it is universally true that the representation of wicked characters is objectionable, it would be hard to deny that all representation of human character is objectionable; inasmuch as there is no character which does not contain some admixture of wickedness. On the other hand, it is impossible to deny that there are some vices which can hardly be represented without mischief both to the writer and the reader. It would appear that the morality or immorality of such representations by no means depends upon the heinousness of the characters described. It would be difficult to imagine a more wicked character than Iago, or a less immoral play than *Othello*.[21] The Bible is full of descriptions of most atrocious crimes of all sorts, and it would be natural to suppose that the fact that they are related historically would make them more, and not less, injurious than they would be if related as fictions, because the interest is greater.

The moral effect of men upon each other depends upon their intimacy. No one is made wicked by knowing that bad people exist. Most people would become wicked if all their intimate friends were so. Characters in novels may be considered as being more or less intimate acquaintances.

* * *

It is to be observed, however, that the immoral writing which gives the greatest and most reasonable offence, is immoral specifically, and consists of detailed descriptions of subjects on which the mind cannot be suffered to rest without injury. This class of offences is mostly of a sufficiently obvious kind. It is nearly allied to what, in our own time and country, is a far more probable evil—a conscious delicacy, which suggests improper thoughts by carefully avoiding all mention of vices which must be referred to if life is to be depicted at all, and which would excite no improper feelings if referred to without unnecessary detail.

---

[21] *Hist. Crim.* iii 8: 'I am inclined to think that Iago would not have been convicted as an accessory before the fact to Desdemona's murder but for one single remark—"Do it not with poison, strangle her in her bed"' (IV i); with a footnote by JFS: 'As, however, Othello killed himself, Iago, in the then state of the law, could not even have been brought to trial in England.' On JFS and the legal arguments about accessories before the fact, see Rodensky, *The Crime in Mind*, 61–2.

8   ON THE NOVEL AND JOURNALISM

* * *

[*Secondary Characters Misrepresented*]

It is a great beauty in a novel to give glimpses of the life which the secondary characters lived when they were not within the field of the novelist's camera obscura. In *Pendennis* we get a most ingeniously contrived glimpse of the career of the gentleman who lent his chambers to the hero. How he was presented at court, and entangled himself in a lady's train, who turned out to be the daughter of 'that eminent Queen's Counsel, Mr. Kewsy',[22] who subsequently became his wife, and he a county-court judge. Many writers would have left on their readers no other impression about this person than that he had lent Mr. Pendennis his chambers, and was in the habit of making some pet speech, or indulging some whimsical caprice.

* * *

Even Miss Austen,[23] whose books convey an impression of reality altogether extraordinary, culls out and pieces together a succession of small incidents, so contrived as to develop, step by step, the characters of the persons represented. Each incident, taken by itself, is so exquisitely natural, and so carefully introduced, that it requires considerable attention to detect the improbability of the story. That improbability consists in the sequence of the incidents wanted. It is likely enough that incidents should sometimes happen which throw a light on character, but it is not probable that a series of incidents should occur, one after the other, all throwing light on different parts of the same character, as if they had been arranged for the express purpose of bringing out every feature of it in succession. Nor must it be forgotten that the importance and significance of an incident is much greater when it is one in a series, as in a novel, than where it stands by itself, as in real life.

* * *

[*Perspective in Novels*]

Few novels have been written with a plot more elaborately contrived, or dexterously brought out, than *Caleb Williams*;[24] but would the circumstances have impressed

---

[22] Mr. Serjeant Kewsy. *OED* A member of a superior order of barristers (abolished in 1880), from which, until 1873, the Common Law judges were always chosen. (Henry John Stephen, JFS's uncle, had become serjeant-at-law in 1828; *Life* 23 n.)

[23] Jane Austen (1775–1817; *ODNB*, novelist). Speaking at the Apostles in Cambridge, 'on his last appearance', the young JFS 'maintains the superiority of Miss Austen's "Emma" to Miss Brontë's "Jane Eyre" (*Life* 73). Leslie Stephen: ' "Jane Eyre" had then, I remember, some especially passionate admirers at Cambridge'. JFS on 'inequality between men and women': 'The proper reflection upon its approaching removal may be, The more's the pity. Mr. Woodhouse liked his gruel thin, but not too thin. At a certain point of wateriness he would probably have turned off the tap. If Emma had been a disciple of Mr. Mill's, she might have remarked, "Reflect, dear sir, that you are interrupting the stream of progress. Such remains of cohesiveness as are exhibited by the grits which form the substratum of your simple meal are relics of the past, and as such are probably defects in your gruel instead of merits".' *Liberty, Equality, Fraternity* (1873; second edition, 1874; ed. Julia Stapleton, *Selected Writings of James Fitzjames Stephen*, Oxford University Press, 2017), p. 132. *Emma. A Novel*. By the author of *Pride and Prejudice*, 1815, ch. iii: 'Such another small basin of thin gruel as his own was all that he could, with thorough self-approbation, recommend'.

[24] *Things as They Are; or, The Adventures of Caleb Williams* (1794). William Godwin (1756–1836; *ODNB*, philosopher and novelist), author of *An Enquiry Concerning Political Justice, and its Influence on General Virtue and Happiness* (1793).

THE RELATION OF NOVELS TO LIFE

themselves upon the mind of a person who witnessed their real occurrence in the connected pictorial manner in which they appear to the readers of the novel?

Caleb Williams is taken into the service of a rich gentleman, Mr. Falkland, whom he discovers to have murdered Mr. Tyrrel, some years before. Incautiously informing his master of his discovery, he tempts him to take advantage of an opportunity of accusing him, with every appearance of truth, of committing an aggravated robbery. His master, satisfied with destroying his character, offers no evidence against him at the trial, and he is acquitted. Wherever he goes he is followed by Falkland's agents, who expose his character and deprive him of one situation after another, until, at last, he resolves to turn upon his master in self-defence, reiterates accusations (which he had formerly made and retracted) of the murder of Tyrrel, and choosing his time for the accusation*[25] ingeniously, extorts from Mr. Falkland a confession, not only of his murder of Tyrrel, but of the falsehood of his accusations against himself.

Nothing can be more remarkable than the skill with which this story is developed step by step, each leading to, and each bearing upon the next. But if we suppose the events really to have occurred, would any ordinary person have remarked their connection? In the novel, Caleb Williams's introduction to Falkland's house, and the story he hears from the steward about his master's history, at once arrest the reader's attention, and introduce all that follows. In real life, the gossip of two servants about their master's affairs would attract no attention at all, or would only be noticed as one of the little vexations incidental to keeping a large establishment. When Falkland has been introduced in a manner calculated to awaken attention and curiosity, a variety of small characteristic conversations and allusions—immediately detected by the least experienced novel reader as being characteristic and important—are introduced in order to heighten the mystery and curiosity. In real life, such things would have passed unnoticed, or, if noticed, any one but a confirmed meddler and gossip would have set them down to the account of casual ill-temper or bad digestion, or to any other insignificant cause. The transaction about the robbery would have amounted to this—that

---

[25]* JFS, note: 'It is a curious instance of the almost universal inability of novelists to write about law without making mistakes, that Godwin, who had a considerable acquaintance with criminal law, forgets that Falkland could not be tried a second time for the murder of Tyrrel, although he seems quite aware that Williams could not be tried twice for the theft. ¶ In Miss Brontë's remarkable novel, *Wuthering Heights*, the legal relations of the different characters towards the close of the book are most perplexed. They involve a perfect wilderness of questions about disseisin, forcible entries, mortgages, and the wills and marriages of minors. Even Mr. Thackeray, generally so careful in such matters, falls, we conceive, into a legal mistake in *The Newcomes*. Mrs. Newcome leaves behind her a letter to her attorney written on the day of her death (before 1838) saying in effect, "I desire to bequeath" 5000*l.* to Clive Newcome. "Prepare a codicil to my will to that effect, and bring it on Saturday." This is written on Tuesday, on which day she dies. Mr. Pendennis, on the discovery of the letter, tells Miss Newcome that "it is not worth a penny", being only "a wish on the part of Mrs. Newcome", and Mr. Luce, the attorney, confirms this. ¶ Now, in *Passmore* v. *Passmore*, 1 *Phillim.* 218, Sir J. Nicholl expressly says, "That the instrument is in the form of a letter is no conclusive objection to it—nor has it been held necessary that they" (such instruments) "should be in direct and imperative terms, *wishes and requests have been deemed sufficient.*" ¶ In *Allen* v. *Manning*, 2 *Add.* 490, instructions to an attorney to prepare a will were admitted to probate on the ground that the testator died five days after giving them, and before he could execute the will. See, too, *Torre* v. *Castle*, 1 *Curt.* 303, and *Hattat* v. *Hattat*, 4 *Hagg.* 411. This would be somewhat minute criticism, if it were not for the fact, that Mr. Pendennis gives his opinion expressly as a lawyer.' *could not be tried a second time for*: compare *Gen. View 1863* 213 n.: 'See R. *v.* Newton, 13 Q. B. 716 (1849), for a case in which the prisoner was tried for the same murder three times. She was at last acquitted.' Emily Jane Brontë (1818–1848; *ODNB*, novelist and poet). *Wuthering Heights: a Novel by Ellis Bell* (1847).

ON THE NOVEL AND JOURNALISM

there was strong reason to suppose a clerk had robbed his master; that there was a kind of possibility that the master wanted to get rid of the clerk; and so the matter would have stood for many months, and in the meantime Falkland, and his relations, and servants, and acquaintance would have hardly given a thought to Caleb Williams and his affairs. They would have had business, and formed habits and connections far more interesting to themselves than any in which Williams had a part, and he and his trial would have subtended a very small angle indeed in their range of vision, instead of forming, as by the novelist's art they are made to do, the centre upon which all their fortunes depend.

* * *

[*Distortions of History*]

Perhaps the necessity of modifying the representation made by novels of the different events which occur in them, may be more fully illustrated by supposing that the story of *Caleb Williams* is only his way of accounting for, and connecting, certain admitted facts: such as the fact that Mr. Tyrrel was murdered; that Mr. Falkland was tried for the murder, and acquitted; that he led a retired life; that Caleb Williams was taken into his service, and left it under an accusation, true or false, of robbery; that Williams was committed to gaol; that he escaped, was retaken, tried, and, by the kindness of his prosecutor, acquitted; that he wandered about the country, and lost situations from a report of his conduct; that he went to Mr. Falkland's house during his last illness, accused him of murder, and caused him to make certain statements. Might it not be open to Mr. Falkland's friends to contend, and would they not contend with the greatest force, that the story was all false from beginning to end, and that it bore upon it every mark of being so; that all the tales about Falkland's conversations with Williams were mere fictions, artfully constructed on information obtained from a gossiping old man, in order to supply a means of explaining conduct which was in fact a treacherous robbery of a master by a confidential servant; that Williams's escape from prison was a confession of guilt; that his subsequent acquittal was simply owing to his master's reluctance to have him hanged; that his loss of his situations was the natural and necessary consequence of his crime; that his report of Falkland's last conversation was a garbled account of the weak, confused language of a dying man about matters in which he had at any rate suffered most cruelly; and that to suppose Falkland guilty of murder merely because a discharged servant, who had formerly made and retracted the same accusation, a probable robber, and a man who, according to his own confession, associated with a gang of highwaymen, said that his master had chosen him of all mankind as his confessor, would be to consider the solemn verdict of a jury as less cogent than the unsupported evidence of a single interested and untrustworthy witness.

This, however, is not the impression which the mere perusal of the novel leaves upon the mind. It is of the essence of a novel to assume not only the infallibility of the narrator as to the matters of fact which he relates, but also as to the bearing of the facts related upon each other; and it would lead to constant mistakes to suppose that the

THE RELATION OF NOVELS TO LIFE

circumstances which in a novel prove the guilt, or the love, or the wisdom, which the novelist attributes to his hero, would prove the same things in real life. A still more curious illustration of this is the alterations of facts which occur in historical novels. As novels cannot be taken to be histories without a good deal of management and allowance, so history cannot be readily woven into novels without corresponding distortions.

* * *

Far the most curious illustration of this predominance of the novel atmosphere over fact which we can remember, is to be found in Mr. Lockhart's novel of *Valerius*.[26] The curious Paleyan[27] process by which Valerius, on reading a MS. of one of the Gospels lent him by a Christian under persecution, becomes convinced of 'the candour and veracity of the author', would have astonished the contemporaries of Origen[28] about as much as the acquisition of an estate worth something like a million and a half sterling as the providential reward of a pagan's conversion to Christianity.

* * *

[*Undue Prominence of Love*]

Somewhat similar in its effects is the habit of supposing that the importance of events in real life is commensurate with their importance in novels. The well-known dogma of Aristotle, that the object of a tragedy is to excite terror and pity, might be paraphrased by saying that it is the object of a novel to describe love ending in marriage. Marriage in novels occupies almost always the position which death occupies in real life: it is the art of transition into a new state, with which novelists (with some very rare exceptions) have little or nothing to do. No doubt, a happy marriage is to a woman what success in any of the careers of life is to a man. It is almost the only profession which society, as at present constituted, opens to her. The mistake of novelists lies not so much in overrating the importance of marriage, as in the assumed universality of the passion of love, in their sense of the word. The notion which so many novels suggest—that if two people who have a violent passion for each other marry, they have necessarily acted wisely—is as unfounded as the converse, that if two people marry without such a passion, they act unwisely.

It would be impossible for any one to dispute altogether the existence of some such passion as is the foundation of most novels; but it may safely be affirmed that it is very

---

[26] John Gibson Lockhart (1794–1854; *ODNB*, writer and literary editor). *Valerius. A Roman Story* (1821).

[27] William Paley (1743–1805; *ODNB*, theologian and moralist). *A View of the Evidences of Christianity* (1794). *Liberty, Equality, Fraternity*, 184 n.: 'He was responsible for the analogy of God with a "watchmaker" that exponents of creationism still cite with approval: see his *Natural Theology, or Evidences of the Existence and Attributes of the Deity Collected from the Appearances of Nature* (1802)'. *Life* 86, 234: 'From the Benthamite point of view, the argument for Christianity must be simply the historical evidence. Paley, for whom Fitzjames had always a great respect, put the argument most skilfully in this shape . . . Fitzjames had given up the belief that the Gospel narrative could be proved after the Paley method, and that was the only method which, according to him, was legitimate. He had therefore ceased to believe in the historical truth of Christianity'. JFS, 'Paley's Evidences' (*Sat. Rev.*, 28 July 1866; *Hor. Sab.* iii 80): 'They obtained the questionable advantage of being made a University text-book, the result of which was that half of the imperfectly educated classes supposed that they understood the work.'

[28] Theologian (184–253) of Alexandria.

uncommon, that it is a very doubtful good when it exists, and that the love which the Prayer Book seems to consider as a condition subsequent to marriage,[29] is something much more common and very different. In novels it is considered as the cause, in the Prayer Book as what ought to be the effect of marriage; and we suspect that the divines have been shrewder observers of human nature than the men of the world. In the morality of almost all novelists, the promise ought to be, not 'I will love', but 'I declare that I do love.' The wisdom or otherwise of a step upon which so much of the happiness of life must turn, is made to depend, not on the mutual forbearance and kindly exertions of the two persons principally interested, but upon their feeling an exceptional and transitory passion at a particular moment.

To attempt to give an accurate definition, or even description of love, would be presumptuous, if not pedantic; but it may safely be affirmed that one of its most important constituent parts, if not its essence, is to be found in a willingness to discharge the duties implied in the relation of the persons loving, in order to please or benefit each other. Love between the sexes is not the only kind of love in the world. Its specific peculiarities arise, like the specific peculiarities of all other kinds of love, from the peculiar relations and duties implied in the relation of husband and wife, which, however, operate principally by giving colour to the common sentiments of friendship and confidence, and, above all, to those which spring from the habits of society. To use the language of a very great man*[30] (employed in maintaining a proposition which to some may seem questionable):

> It must be carefully remembered, that the general happiness of married life is secured by its indissolubility. When people understand that they must live together, except for a very few reasons known to the law, they learn to soften, by mutual accommodation, that yoke which they know they cannot shake off, and become good husbands and good wives from the necessity of remaining husbands and wives. For necessity is a powerful master in teaching the duties. If it were once understood that, upon mutual disgust, married persons might be legally separated, many a couple who now pass through the world with mutual comfort, with attention to their common offspring, and to the moral order of civil society, might have been at this moment living in a state of mutual unkindness, in a state of estrangement from their common offspring, in a state of the most licentious morality.

The habit of finishing a novel with the marriage of the hero and heroine, is quite in accordance with the view of love which we have been reprobating. It would seem ludicrous to conclude the history of a man's professional career with the act of his entering upon his profession; but it is an all but universal practice to conclude a representation of him, as a social and feeling being, with his marriage. Why? Because a person is supposed to enter on a profession in order to do something in it, and to marry only to gratify his passions.

---

[29] The Form of Solemnization of Matrimony: 'Wilt thou love her, comfort her, honour and keep her in sickness and in health?'

[30]* JFS, note: 'Judgment of Lord Stowell in *Evans* v. *Evans*. 1 *Hagg. Cons. Rep.* 36, 37.' William Scott, Baron Stowell (1745–1836; *ODNB*, judge and politician). JFS was to conscript him in 'Ecce Homo' (*Fraser's*, June 1866), to deplore J.R.Seeley, *A Survey of the Life and Work of Jesus Christ* (anon., 1865). Stowell and William Pitt—'English anti-revolutionary counterparts to the French revolutionary leaders' (*On Society, Religion, and Government* 204 n.)—are enlisted by JFS against the 'vanity verging on madness' of the 'world-betterer'.

THE RELATION OF NOVELS TO LIFE

*   *   *

[*Sentimentality*]

For our present purposes, therefore, 'sentimentality' may be described as being that way of writing which makes use of emotions of tenderness or the like, as accessories for the purpose of heightening an artistic effect, whether that effect is to be produced by the description of other feelings, or merely by the skilful handling of details. The state of human affairs is probably such that no one could conceive a consistent story without being naturally and unavoidably led to describe many painful things, and no one can be blamed for describing such subjects in a spirited manner, if he describes them gravely, and because they lie straight in his path; but we do not know of a habit more likely to injure the interests, both of art and of morals, than that of describing death and kindred subjects as accessories to matters of inferior importance, or for the sake of displaying skill in handling details.

There is one writer in our own day who entirely exemplifies our meaning: this is Mr. Dickens.

We will take only one instance of his sentimentality—his treatment of the subject of death. There are some aspects of death of which we wish to say nothing; but if we consider it simply as it affects the survivors, it cannot be regarded as connected exclusively with painful associations. The feelings excited by the death of a friend are, first, a feeling of solemn awe, which is not deepened, but weakened, by anything which diverts the attention from the naked fact. 'He is dead', is all that is to be said upon the subject; and any phrases whatever beyond that or its equivalents have a tendency to distract the mind, and so far to lessen the solemnity of the feelings excited. It would not be true to say that this sensation is entirely painful. To a sluggish imagination, the mere excitement is far from being altogether unpleasant. The dim view of a world of mysteries, in the midst of which we live and move, has something in it which relieves the tedium and ennobles the trivialities of common life; but when we weigh this against the utter separation, the end—for aught we know, the final end—of so many kindly sympathies and warm activities, there is something loathsome in the notion of a man's being willing to call up the one set of associations for the sake of playing with the other; and when we recollect the lighter associations which accompany death, the expressions of affection, the leave-takings, the little touching incidents to which the unconscious simplicity of the dying person may give rise, we cannot but feel that the mere recollection of such things involves an unutterable, an almost sacred sadness, and that there is an absence of feeling in displaying that which gives them all their sadness in order to set off their beauty, which reminds us of nothing so much as the mumbling satisfaction of the old Grandmother in the *Antiquary*,[31] at the wine and cakes handed round at her grandson's funeral. Now, Mr. Dickens, not once or twice, but continually, brings death upon the stage, apparently for no one reason but that of showing his skill in arranging affecting details so as to give them this horrible pungency. Paul Dombey, Eleanor Trent, Dora Copperfield, Richard Carstone (who dies partly to spite the Court of Chancery, and partly to give Miss Summerson an opportunity of showing how conscious she is of her

---

[31] *The Antiquary* (by the author of *Waverley* and *Guy Mannering*, 1816).

unconscious sweetness and piety), Oliver Twist's mother, and Smike,*[32] are a few of the instances[33] which occur to us of this toying with the disgrace of our nature.[34] We do not wish to write lightly on such a subject; but let us compare Mr. Dickens's treatment of death with some others.

Having to describe the death of a young woman who dies very unnecessarily, after rambling about the country with her grandfather, Mr. Dickens first introduces a little boy dying quietly enough, then he brings in an old sexton of seventy-nine, whose peculiarity is that he does *not* die, and does not expect to do so. Appended to the sexton are a church and out-houses, with carved wainscots, and windows looking out on the graves. Having arranged the scene, we have the time—a winter night and a snow-storm—and the chorus, in the shape of all sorts of anxious admirers; then comes the scene over which so many foolish tears have been shed, and which reminds us of nothing so much as the hackneyed quotation about the difficulty of driving a dog from a greasy hide. He gloats over the girl's death as if it delighted him; he looks at it from four or five points

---

[32]*   JFS, note: 'A list of the killed, wounded, and missing amongst Mr. Dickens's novels would read like an *Extraordinary Gazette*. An interesting child runs as much risk there as any of the troops who stormed the Redan.' (*Gazette*, as an official governmental publication; *Extraordinary*, as not the regular publication but an urgent particular notification.) John Ruskin (1819–1900; *ODNB*, art critic and social critic). 'Fiction, Fair and Foul' (*Nineteenth Century*, June 1880): 'the ultimate power of fiction to entertain is by varying to his fancy the modes, and defining for his dullness the horrors, of Death. In the single novel of *Bleak House* there are nine deaths (or left for deaths, in the drop scene) carefully wrought out or led up to, either by way of pleasing surprise, as the baby's at the brickmaker's, or finished in their threatenings and sufferings, with as much enjoyment as can be contrived in the anticipation, and as much pathology as can be concentrated in the description. Under the following varieties of method:

One by assassination	Mr Tulkinghorn
One by starvation, with phthisis	Joe
One by chagrin	Richard
One by spontaneous combustion	Mr Krook
One by sorrow	Lady Dedlock's lover
One by remorse	Lady Dedlock
One by insanity	Miss Flite
One by paralysis	Sir Leicester

Besides the baby, by fever, and a lively young French woman left to be hanged.' (Tim Peltason has pointed out an error by Ruskin: in *Bleak House*, Miss Flite stays alive, in her way.)

[33]   From *Dombey and Son* (1848), where the wrapper title of the monthly parts had been *Dealings with the Firm of Dombey and Son, Wholesale, Retail, and for Exportation*. PAUL DOMBEY, the young son and heir of Mr. Dombey. From *The Old Curiosity Shop* (1841), LITTLE NELL TRENT, a small and delicate child, of much sweetness of disposition, who lives alone with her grandfather. From *David Copperfield* (1850), where the wrapper title of the monthly parts had been *The Personal History, Adventures, Experience, and Observation of David Copperfield the Younger, of Blunderstone Rookery (Which He never meant to be Published on Any Account)*. Dora Copperfield, that is, MISS DORA SPENLOW, the only daughter of Mr. Spenlow; a timid, sensitive, artless little beauty, afterwards the 'child-wife' of David Copperfield. From *Bleak House* (1853), RICHARD CARSTONE, a ward of Mr. Jarndyce, and a suitor in Chancery. ESTHER SUMMERSON, the protégée of Mr. Jarndyce; a prudent and wise woman, and a self-denying friend. From *The Adventures of Oliver Twist* (1838), where the monthly parts had a sub-title: *or, The Parish Boy's Progress*. AGNES FLEMING, *mother of Oliver Twist*. From *The Life and Adventures of Nicholas Nickleby* (1839), where the wrapper title of the monthly parts had been *The Life and Adventures of Nicholas Nickleby, Containing a Faithful Account of the Fortunes, Misfortunes, Uprisings, Downfallings and Complete Career of the Nickleby Family*. SMIKE, a starved and half-witted inmate of Squeers's establishment.

[34]   Sir Thomas Browne (1605–1682; *ODNB*, physician and author): 'I am not so much afraid of death, as ashamed thereof; 'tis the very disgrace and ignominy of our natures' (*Religio Medici*, anon., 1642, pt. 1).

THE RELATION OF NOVELS TO LIFE   15

of view; touches, tastes, smells, and handles as if it was some savoury dainty which could not be too fully appreciated.

The description consists of six paragraphs (some in blank verse)[35] of which three begin with the words, 'She was dead.' The first is introductory; the second describes her as being asleep; the third relates to the bed; the fourth to a certain bird; the fifth to the subject's beautiful appearance; and the sixth to its face. The whole concludes with a questionable statement as to what the angels will look like,[36] which suggests that even upon artistic grounds it is as well not to intrude into things which we have not seen.

Perhaps the prophet Ezekiel thought of death as solemnly as Mr. Dickens, and loved his wife as much as Mr. Dickens cared for his little tragedy queen; but he tells us nothing of her bed, nor of what he put on it, nor about her face, nor her bird:

> Ezekiel xxiv. 15–18. 'Son of man, behold I take[37] from thee the desire of thine eyes with a stroke, yet neither shalt thou mourn nor weep, neither shall thy tears run down. Forbear to cry, make no mourning for the dead, bind the tire[38] of thy head upon thee, and put on thy shoes upon thy feet, and cover not thy lips, and eat not the bread of men. So I spake unto the people in the morning, and at even my wife died; and I did in the morning as I was commanded.'

Though Ezekiel was commanded not to mourn, it does not appear that he was forbidden to linger on the details of his wife's death, to describe her face, her bed, her ornaments, and to put little bits of pretty simplicity into her mouth. But he was not only an inspired prophet, but a brave man, who wrote with modesty and self-respect.

This is but one illustration out of ten thousand, of the spirit which leads people to indulge their timidity or their love of luxury, by disregarding the essential points of observation for the sake of accessories, and instead of looking death, and grief, and pain in the face, to trifle with the dramatic incidents by which they may be attended.

* * *

[*Machinery*]

Another consequence of the suppression of so large a proportion of the facts which in real life carry on the business of the world is to be found in the invention of masses of what the critics in the last century used to call 'machinery', and what is perhaps better

---

[35] ~Upon her little bed, she lay at rest~
   ~The solemn stillness was no marvel now~
   ~No sleep so beautiful and calm, so free~
   ~Dear, gentle, patient, noble Nell was dead~
   ~The pressure of a finger would have crushed~
   ~Where were the traces of her early cares~
   ~But peace and perfect happiness were born~
   ~Her tranquil beauty and profound repose~

Such cadences, remarked since the earliest publications by Dickens, are considered in Ricks, 'The Novelist as Critic', and 'Norman Mailer, Just Off the Rhythm' (both in *Along Heroic Lines*, 2021).

[36] ch. lxxi: 'the same mild lovely look. So shall we know the angels in their majesty, after death.'

[37] Read, 'take away'.

[38] *OED* Dress, apparel, raiment; *archaic* bonnet of tire, a cap of estate.

16 ON THE NOVEL AND JOURNALISM

known in the present day under its theatrical slang name of 'business'. Almost every author has his *Di minorum* or *majorum gentium*[39] in reserve for such knots as may occur in his story. Scott or Sir E. Lytton have generally some funny man—some Andrew Fairservice,[40] or Corporal Bung[41]—hanging about the story, ready to help matters on as a kind of prose comic chorus, or to disentangle any embarrassment which may arise, by throwing an air of absurdity over it.

If hardship, or poverty, or sickness is to be represented, almost all writers of novels bring in a Caleb Balderstone,[42] to invent shifts for filling his hero's larder, or a Mrs. Flanagan,[43] to steal his spirits under pretence of giving him medicine, that the reader's mind may not be unduly shocked.

Mr. Dickens seems to us the greatest master of this kind of artifice, but his method is most peculiar. It consists in giving an entirely factitious prominence to minute peculiarities. He constantly gives expression, almost personality, to inanimate objects. He invests the most ordinary affairs of life with a certain charm and poetry. It is abundantly clear that this is what none but a man of genius could do. Nor is it an illusion which would be likely to deceive any one. Nobody ever lived in the world without finding plenty of dulness in it, and no quantity of verbal artifice would make him forget it; but though artifices like these may not deceive, they are still deviations from reality, and are to be allowed for before a novel can be considered as a picture of life.

There are dwarfs in real life, and the circumstance of bodily deformity no doubt exercises a powerful influence over character, but a little imp, with some slight resemblance to a man and a vast preponderance of the devil, like Quilp,[44] or a 'recluse', like the Black Dwarf,[45] are what Addison calls 'machines' peculiar to novelists, and without representatives in real life.

Descriptions of scenery, especially in modern novels, often act as machines. We are tolerant of probability and of gaps in a story, such as 'Five years elapsed', &c. &c., when they are covered by pictures of still life, such as the charming descriptions of South America, which fill up about half a volume and three very uneventful years in the wanderings of Sir Amyas Leigh, knight.[46] Such, too, are some of Mr. Dickens's descriptions of nature, which contain extremely picturesque sentences, but generally offend our taste by their obvious effort and elaboration; such, for example, is the account of the great storm at Yarmouth or of the Swiss valley, in *David Copperfield*.[47] They would furnish very good drop-scenes to a theatre; but in the history of a man's life we can

---

[39] Of the first and second rank (senators, patricii); also of the gods, the superior being *dii maj.*, the inferior *min.*

[40] The servant of Frank Osbaldistone in *Rob Roy* (1818).

[41] Corporal Bunting in *Eugene Aram. A Tale* (by the author of *Pelham, Devereux*, etc., 1832).

[42] Steward to Edgar, Master of Ravenswood, in Scott's *The Bride of Lammermoor* (1819).

[43] Servant to Mrs. Clapp in *Vanity Fair*.

[44] From *The Old Curiosity Shop*. DANIEL QUILP, a dwarf; a sly, cunning, ferocious man.

[45] Scott, *The Black Dwarf* (1816).

[46] Charles Kingsley (1819–1875; *ODNB*, novelist, Church of England clergyman, and controversialist). *Westward Ho!; or, The Voyages and Adventures of Sir Amyas Leigh, Knight, of Burrough in the County of Devon, in the Reign of Her Most Glorious Majesty Queen Elizabeth* (3 vols., 1855).

[47] ch. lv, ch. lviii.

THE RELATION OF NOVELS TO LIFE

dispense with drop-scenes.*[48] The descriptions of nature in *Gil Blas*,[49] in Defoe, occasionally in Fielding,[50] and continually in Smollett, are never obtrusive or over elaborate. They are the simple vivid impression left by striking scenery upon men who had no inclination to go about the world in the spirit of landscape painters, but who could appreciate a fine view when it came in their way. Gil Blas' journey through the Asturias, the Cavaliers' wanderings in Yorkshire, the hill on which Tom Jones and Partridge lost their way, and the infinite variety of pictures hinted at rather than drawn, in Roderick Random's journey to London, are instances of our meaning.

It is a great beauty in a novel, when the story, as it were, tells itself, without the introduction of machines to help it out.

* * *

[False Morality]

Perhaps the most remarkable result of the arbitrary power which novel writers exercise in the selection of facts to be represented and facts to be suppressed, is to be found in the morality which they teach.

Nothing is more common than for novel writers to set out with the assumption of the truth of certain maxims of morality, and to arrange the facts of their story upon the hypothesis that every violation of those maxims entails all sorts of calamity; instead of looking at the world, and seeing for themselves whether, in point of fact, experience confirms them in the notions which they have formed as to the sanctions provided for the enforcement of such maxims. Those who act thus do not see that the honour which they intend to pay to morality is mere lip-service, and conceals a real doubt as to whether there is such a thing as a natural sanction of morality at all. If they believe that human nature and society are so constituted that the laws of morality are self-executing, they ought to recollect that the sanctions are adjusted by some fixed rule, and if so, the question, what those sanctions are, can be learnt only from experience.

Miss Edgeworth affords perhaps the most complete instance of this fault, and it is almost the only blemish which we can think of in her admirable works. Indeed, her morals are so good, so kindly, and so wise, that it seems unnatural to find fault with them. The number of capital punishments for small offences in her moral tales and tales of fashionable life is dreadful.[51] No one, we suppose, would doubt the evils of

---

[48] *OED* A term used loosely or incorrectly for *drop* [The painted curtain let down between the acts of a play] or act-drop; also for the final scene of a play or drama in real life, that on which the curtain drops. From 1815. * JFS, note at 'drop-scenes': 'It may be worth while to remark that Mr. Dickens often writes unintentional verse, like the "*Urbem Romam a principio reges habuere*", or the iambics, which occur sometimes in *Thucydides*. For example: "Yoho, beside the village green, / Where cricket players linger yet, / And every little indentation made / In the fresh grass / By bat or wicket, ball, or player's foot, / Sheds out its perfume on the night. Away, / With four fresh horses from the Bald-faced Stag." The last line is wonderfully Tennysonian. The following description of the shadow of a mail-coach might have well been written by Wordsworth: / "Yoho, yoho, through ditch and brake, / Upon the ploughed land and the smooth, / Along the steep hill-side and steeper wall, / As if it were a Phantom Hunter." (*urbem Romam*...: the hexameter, perhaps unintentional, that opens Tacitus, Germania.)

[49] Alain-René Lesage (1668–1747), *L'Histoire de Gil Blas de Santillane* (1715–35); Tobias George Smollett (1721–1771, *ODNB*, writer), translator of *The Adventures of Gil Blas of Santillane: A New Translation from the Best French Edition* (1748).

[50] Daniel Defoe (1660?–1731; *ODNB*, writer and businessman).   [51] *OED* Causing dread.

procrastination, but it is not a fair representation of life to call as a witness to its bad effects a man of great talents and many opportunities, who is five or six times on the point of making his fortune, and is as often baffled by putting something off which he might have done before. The character might, we apprehend, be objected to on artistic grounds. No one would be so inveterately and invariably procrastinating as the unhappy Mr. Lowe;[52] but independently of this, secondary[53] punishments would, we think, have answered Miss Edgeworth's purpose quite as well, and have been much more true to nature. She might have made him miss one or two openings in life, and succeed less well in others than a more punctual man; but in her anxiety to preach up punctuality, she seems to forget that there is no good in being punctual if a man cannot do his business when he has kept his appointment.

* * *

[*Hawkstone – Mystères de Paris – My Novel*]

There are, indeed, cases in which morals become absolute Juggernauts,[54] and the more questionable they are the bloodier are the sacrifices which they obtain. We do not recollect a more salient example of this than the fate of all the low-churchmen, freethinkers, and Jesuits introduced into *Hawkstone*.[55] The account stands thus:

Bentley. For being an evangelical clergyman, and for having belonged to a debating club at Cambridge—Subjected to extortion of money by threats of false accusations, unlawfully detained in custody, twice nearly murdered, and thrown at last into a quasi convent, by way of restitution.

Webster. For Atheism—Falls into melted lead, falling on his hands in the first instance, and sinking slowly on his face.

Pearce. For being a Jesuit—Eaten by rats in a secret passage of his own contrivance. From the position of what was left of him, it appeared that the vital parts had been attacked last.

The old French penal code was merciful compared to this. Webster, perhaps, might have met with treatment not materially milder at the hands of the judges who sentenced Damien and La Barre, but the fate of Jesuits in the time of Louis XV, or of Jansenists in that of Louis XIV, was far more tolerable than that of heretics convicted by the inexorable and infallible author of *Hawkstone*.

A parallel instance is that of Eugène Sue,[56] whom the author of *Hawkstone* so much resembles, and with whom, we suppose, he so fully sympathizes. Jesuits, hypocrites,

---

[52] In 'To-Morrow', *Popular Tales* (1804).

[53] *OED* Used to designate punishments other than capital. 1831 *Edin. Rev.* The difficulty of secondary punishments is much increased by observing that there is not a form of punishment which is not liable to some objections. JFS, *Gen. View 1863*, 141–2, on suicide: 'It would therefore be better to cease altogether to regard it as a crime, and to provide that any one who attempted to kill themselves, or who assisted any other person to do so, should be liable to secondary punishment.'

[54] *OED Hindu Myth* A title of Krishna; *specifically* the idol annually dragged in procession on an enormous car, under the wheels of which many devotees are said to have formerly thrown themselves to be crushed. Also *attributively*; *figurative* An institution, practice, or notion to which persons blindly devote themselves, or are ruthlessly sacrificed.

[55] William Sewell (1804–1874), *Hawkstone: A Tale of and for England* (anon., 1804).

[56] (1804–1857), *Les Mystères de Paris* (*Journal des débats*, 1842–43).

THE RELATION OF NOVELS TO LIFE

and immoral persons generally, get their poetical justice[57] served out, like the boiling pitch which Robinson Crusoe's cook distributed amongst the Chinese. Dying of recondite diseases, having holes burnt in their flesh with blow-pipes, being blinded, and kicked in tender parts—and in some of the less serious cases, drowning, hanging, guillotining, and other not very painful forms of death, are the punishments with which M. Sue visits the crimes which he takes so much pleasure in describing; and no doubt it is fair enough to hang all the characters, if the scene is always laid in Newgate.

Poetical justice is, however, not confined to such instances as these: it extends far higher, and is a taint from which few authors have escaped. Sir Edward Lytton generally puts on the black cap when his hero and heroine are, or are about to be, married. Surely the execution of Randal Leslie, in the last chapter of *My Novel*,[58] is very unnecessary. The character is certainly abundantly mean and base; but his very selfishness and insensibility of conscience would have prevented him from throwing up the game of life, which he had played so unscrupulously, merely because he was discovered in discreditable tricks by a set of people who must have kept their discoveries to themselves, for fear of compromising the character of their connections.[59] Leslie must have known very well that the wish to protect the character of the lady whom he had injured from public discussion, would have been quite motive enough to prevent his exposure by his former friends; and that many paths of life were open to him in which he might gratify his ambition. Instead of doing so, he utterly ruins himself, taking some trouble to do it, and takes to drinking, merely from a sense of duty to Sir E. Lytton; and because he feels that if a wicked man in a novel were to become rich, all the foundations of morality would be out of course. George Sand's[60] works abound in curious instances of an inverted poetical justice. We think it would be hard to prove that the arrangements of life, and the existing notions of morality, uniformly produce misery.

In this, as in almost every department of novel literature, Mr. Thackeray appears to us to have conferred immense benefits on novel readers. He is the only writer that we know who does not shrink from allowing all kinds of villainy to go unpunished, except by its own badness, and who makes his readers feel without preaching or effort how complete a punishment that is. The reason of this may perhaps be, that few authors feel so strongly as Mr. Thackeray that mere wealth and success in life are not all that we ought to live or to wish for; and that it is a beggarly reward, after all, for goodness, to make it heir to a large estate and a fine house. We think that Mr. Morgan[61] 'living to be one of the most respectable men in the parish of St. James's', and Becky Sharp[62] keeping one of the most well-conducted stalls in Vanity Fair, are really far more edifying representations than any number of saints, pampered, very strangely to all readers of the New Testament, with all sorts of luxury, and any number of sinners consigned to a fate to which they certainly were not accustomed, when they were not plagued like other

---

[57] *OED* The ideal justice in distribution of rewards and punishments supposed to befit a poem or other work of imagination.

[58] Edward George Earle Lytton Bulwer, first Baron Lytton (1803–1873; *ODNB*, writer and politician). '*My Novel'; or, Varieties in English Life* (by 'Pisistratus Caxton', 1803).

[59] *OED* Relationship by family ties, as marriage or consanguinity. With 1809 *Gil Blas* He is a youth of good connections.

[60] JFS, 'La Daniella' (*Sat. Rev.*, 12 Sept. 1857), p. 146.

[61] The dishonest valet to Major Pendennis.   [62] JFS has 'Sharpe', a frequent slip of his.

20 ON THE NOVEL AND JOURNALISM

men, nor afflicted like other men—when they had children at their desire, and left the rest of their substance to their babes.

* * *

[*Propagandist Novels*]

Another curious case of an extrinsic disturbing force acting upon novels is to be found in the habit, which of late years has become so common, of using novels to ventilate opinions.

It is a common, but not, we think, a very fair objection to such books, to complain that the author does not give his critics a fair shot—that he shelters himself behind his hero, and expresses, not his own, but his puppets' opinions... Opinions and states of mind may, no doubt, be as legitimately made the subjects of representation as adventures, but the dangers of partiality, of dishonesty, of false morality on the part of authors, and of hasty misconception on the part of readers, is obviously at a maximum in this class of books. *Pendennis* is, perhaps, the most notable and trustworthy specimen of the class which could be mentioned. The irresolute, half-ashamed, sceptical hero, conscious of his own weakness, conscious of his own ignorance, conscious, too, of his capacity for both power and knowledge—half envious of the vigorous delusions with which he sees one part of mankind possessed, half sympathizing with the vigorous pleasure-hunting of another class—governed by tastes and circumstances instead of principles, but clinging, firm to old habits, to traditional lessons of truth and honour— jotting down, sketch-book in hand, all the quaint irregularities or picturesque variations of the banks as he drifts, half-pleased, half-melancholy, down the river of life, not very bad, nor very good, nor very anything—looking, half-respectfully, half-derisively, at what the world venerates—despising, more or less, though on other grounds, what it hates—is one of the saddest, as it is one of the most masterly memorials of the times in which he lived which any writer ever drew for posterity.

* * *

[*Argumentative Novels*]

Novels are also made use of at the present day, as social or political *argumenta ad misericordiam*,[63] when they fall within the remarks which we have made upon novels written with a moral. Such, for example, are Mrs. Gaskell's novel of *Mary Barton*,[64]

---

[63] Appealing to, and exploiting, pity when making a case.

[64] Elizabeth Cleghorn Gaskell (1810–1865; *ODNB*, novelist and short story writer). *Mary Barton: A Tale of Manchester Life* (anon., 1848). JFS, 'The Morality of Advocacy' (*Cornhill*, April 1861): 'to attempt to mislead the court by garbling or misquoting cases; to insult or to attempt to confuse and bewilder a witness by a brutal manner or insolent questions; are practices which are looked upon by barristers in the light in which tradesmen look upon sanding sugar and wetting tobacco. To judge from the representations given by popular writers, it would appear to be the common opinion that such practices are regarded, both by the bench and by the bar, as triumphs of ingenuity. In *Mary Barton*, for example, a trial for murder is introduced, in which the counsel for the prosecution asks a witness for the prisoner a question which fills ten or twelve lines of print, which is so framed as to assert more than once that the prisoner is guilty, and that the witness is not only perjured, but bribed; and this question, it is asserted, was asked because the barrister saw, from the expression of the prosecutor's face, how anxious he was that the prisoner should be convicted. ¶ With a little more knowledge of the profession which she was attacking, the kindly and warm-hearted

THE RELATION OF NOVELS TO LIFE

written in order to bring forward certain observations of the author, and apparently to advocate a particular set of feelings respecting the condition of the poor in Manchester; and her novel of *Ruth*,[65] written, apparently, to show that the regulations of society, with respect to female virtue, sometimes produce hardship. We have already expressed our opinion upon the general question of the introduction of morality into novels; historically considered, all these novels will have to be read with large allowances, on the score of their having been, to a great extent, party pamphlets. It is curious to observe how the artistic bias of the writer's mind gets the better of her theories. *Mary Barton* remains an excellent novel after its utter uselessness, politically speaking, is fully recognized. That poor people out of work in Manchester were very discontented and very miserable, and that being so, they behaved much as the authoress of *Mary Barton* describes their behaviour, will continue to be a fact worth representing, however notorious it may always have been, long after everybody has recognized the truth, that that fact has little or nothing to do with either the cause or the remedy of their wretchedness.

Ruth has much in it that is beautiful, even in the eyes of those who cannot see that if it were literally true it would prove anything at all. All that it shows is, that it is possible to put a case of a person who, for violating the letter, and not the spirit of the law, gets more severely punished than she would have been if the law had been made to provide for her individual case. This must be the case with all human laws. What has to be proved is that the punishments of the social law, on the subject to which *Ruth* refers, are too severe, when not only the letter, but the spirit also, of the law is violated. You do not prove that imprisonment is too severe a punishment for theft by putting the case of a child being so punished, though it had hardly realized the notion of property: you must show that it is unjust to imprison a commonplace London pickpocket.

* * *

[*Robinson Crusoe*]

We do not know a better corrective for timidity and despondence than the tone of 'unabashed' Defoe. Most men would have described Robinson Crusoe's career as something between life in a mad-house and life in gaol. So, too, Lockhart's *Life of*

---

authoress of this scene would have known that if there were at the bar any man brutal enough to ask such a question, no judge who has sat on the bench in modern times could have permitted it to be asked... No doubt, if the scene were anything like a fair representation of the morals of advocates, they would deserve to be described as men willing to let themselves out to commit judicial murder for a few guineas; but,...'

[65] *Ruth: A Novel* (by the author of *Mary Barton*, 1853). JFS on *Sylvia's Lovers*: 'A really powerful writer might make a great deal of the torture which would be endured by a man with a conscience, who had obtained a woman's affections and admiration by false pretences. The most cutting sarcasm, the most wearing illtemper, would be more tolerable than fondness and confidence felt by the object of them to be given, not to him, but to his mask. To be incurably jealous of oneself would be the worst kind of jealousy, and the most horrible sustained torture that could well be inflicted on anyone. Imagine the feelings of a man who had to be constantly saying to himself, "This woman's love would be the most precious of all possessions to me, but if she had the faintest notion of the way in which I put myself into a position to gain it, it would not only be withdrawn, but be changed into horror and loathing." Any number of incidents might be contrived to set this sentiment in various lights, and to produce its gradual development. Something like this forms the main interest of Mrs. Gaskell's novel, *Sylvia's Lovers* [1863]' (*Sat. Rev.*, 29 Aug. 1863, reviewing a novel by 'Owen Meredith'—that is, Lytton).

ON THE NOVEL AND JOURNALISM

Scott[66] is a not uninstructive commentary on the *Waverley Novels*. There is another side to that prosperous, easy-going enjoyment of life, and fine scenery, and middle-age costume, which is to be taken into account before we can let the stalwart heroes—who are constantly 'accompanying their thanks with a kiss', and plausibly settling all the difficulties of the world—walk out of the canvas into real life. All those volumes of correspondence about plate, linen, and furniture—all the adding house to house, and field to field—the final bankruptcy—the tragical and fruitless efforts which followed it—and the gradual breaking up of a great genius and an iron frame, are melancholy proofs that the world has more in it after all than is to be solved by the sort of boisterous, noisy, straightforward sense—sense in more ways than one—which the *Waverley Novels* seem to suggest as that sum of the whole matter which the Wise Man expressed somewhat differently.

In conclusion, we will take as an illustration of the manner in which the disturbing forces of which we have spoken may be minimized, an instance of a novel which appears to us to be, these particulars, almost faultless; and which adds to the information and excites the feelings of its readers in a manner almost as natural and complete as if it were a real history of real facts. We allude to *Robinson Crusoe*.[67]

Whichever of the tests we have been discussing is applied to this book, we shall find it equally sound. Consider it with reference to the variations from real life introduced into it for artistic purposes. It is almost impossible to point out a single such variation. There is no factitious completeness in the incidents or scenery; characters come and go, and are mentioned and criticized as they happen to affect Crusoe's career, but they are never brought in for any other purpose, nor are their separate adventures followed farther than the occasion requires. Sir Walter Scott remarked, very justly, that the elder brother, who was colonel of the regiment of German infantry, and the boy Xury, both vanish from the book just as they would have vanished from the history of a real man's life, and are not brought in at the end, as they would have been in any ordinary novel, to rejoice in the hero's fortunate catastrophe. One of Mr. Dickens's critics praised *Bleak House* because it was so like life, in containing such an infinite variety of characters. Compare *Bleak House* with *Robinson Crusoe*. The old English gentleman—the eccentric bachelor, the surgeon, the heroine, Joe the sweeper, the law-writer, all the parties concerned in the Chancery suit, Mr. Jarndyce, the philanthropic lady, the attorney's clerk—who wants to make an offer of marriage 'without prejudice'[68]—and fifty

---

[66] J. G. Lockhart, *Memoirs of the Life of Sir Walter Scott, Bart.* (1837–38).

[67] *The Life and Strange Surprizing Adventures of Robinson Crusoe, of York, Mariner...Written by Himself* (anon., 1719). *Life* 105–6, summarizing JFS: 'A novel should be a serious attempt by a grave observer to draw a faithful portrait of the actual facts of life. A novelist, therefore, who uses the imaginary facts, like Sterne and Dickens, as mere pegs on which to hang specimens of his own sensibility and facetiousness, becomes disgusting...He, therefore, considers "Robinson Crusoe" to represent the ideal novel. It is the life of a brave man meeting danger and sorrow with unflinching courage, and never bringing his tears to market. Dickens somewhere says, characteristically, that "Robinson Crusoe" is the only very popular work which can be read without a tear from the first page to the last. That is precisely the quality which commends it to this stern reader, who thought that in fiction as in life a man should keep his feelings under lock and key.' *Life* 106 n.: 'Dickens thought Robinson Crusoe "the only instance of an universally popular book that could make no one laugh and could make no one cry"' (John Forster, *The Life of Charles Dickens* [revised 1854], iii 112).

[68] WILLIAM GUPPY, a lawyer's clerk, in the employ of Kenge and Carboy. '"It's one of our law terms, miss. You won't make any use of it to my detriment, at Kenge and Carboy's, or elsewhere. If our conversation shouldn't lead to anything, I am to be as I was, and am not to be prejudiced in my situation or worldly prospects. In short, it's in total confidence"' (ch. ix). *OED* without prejudice: in *Law*, without damage to one's

THE RELATION OF NOVELS TO LIFE

others, are all woven into one series of adventures, in which they are all interested, and from which, when they have performed their several tasks, they all depart in different dramatic positions, each with his appropriate piece of political justice. Can any one pretend that this is like life? Thousands of people affect us, and we affect thousands of others; but each of us works out the romance or history of our own life with but very occasional and fragmentary assistance from each other. Men are not, as Mr. Dickens seems to think, like characters in a play; they far more resemble a complicated set of forces, each acting in its own direction, and each influenced by, though independent of the others. In *Robinson Crusoe* this truth is far more fully apprehended. After the skipper of the Hull trader has been wrecked in Yarmouth Roads, and has given Crusoe some good advice, he goes on his way, and we see him no more. The old sailor who takes him a Guinea voyage dies when he returns. The Sallee rovers remain in the Mediterranean; the Portuguese captain and the Brazilian planters all stay at home; and when Crusoe wants them for a specific purpose, he has to go and look for them as any common person would. A modern novelist would have rolled them all into one mass; would have made the Portuguese captain marry the English captain's widow, who would have turned out to be connected with Friday, and to have a secret sorrow pressing on her on account of the bad behaviour of the colonel of Lockhart's foot,[69] and the book would have closed with eating and drinking, marrying and giving in marriage, according to the universal practice in that behalf.

* * *

[*Character of Crusoe*]

If we examine Crusoe's character, we shall see that it is a simple ordinary character, in no respect distorted for the purposes of art. What a picture of a stern, swarthy youth, scowling or smiling in horrible sympathy at the winds and the waves, and displaying the most heroic courage when the oldest sailors quailed, would many modern authors have painted if they had had to draw Crusoe on his first voyage. Defoe simply represents him as 'most inexpressibly sick both in mind and body'—as making all sorts of good resolutions only to break them—as cheering up and 'pumping as well as another', when there was something actually to be done.

Is there any modern novelist who, wishing to represent a very brave, adventurous, young man, would have sufficient confidence in himself to make him beat his breast, and sob and cry like a madman, trusting to his resources to prove that such conduct was a part of the bravest, hardiest, and most indomitable character that genius ever conceived? Defoe knew that courage is not a positive quality which some men have and others want; that it is that willingness to do disagreeable things which we have all acquired in some measure, but that there are acts of courage which the very bravest are only just able to do, and in which even they falter and tremble. How nobly is this brought out in Crusoe's behaviour on the island. At first he is in a passion of grief

own right, without detracting from one's own right or claims. *OED* breach of promise: *specifically* = breach of promise to marry. (breach: In colloq. use, short for breach of promise. 1840 DICKENS There's the chance of an action for breach.)

[69]   *OED* Foot-soldiers.

almost amounting to madness—'but I thought that would do little good, so I began to make a raft', &c. Little by little he calms down, often fairly giving way to the horrors of his situation, but always, after a time, setting to work manfully on whatever comes next to hand, until at last his mind grows into a state of settled content and cheerfulness, to which none but a man ribbed with triple steel would have attained. There is a fearless humility about the whole conception of Crusoe, of which we have almost lost even the tradition.

There is perhaps no novel which affords so little excuse for hasty generalization on the part of readers. The admirable fidelity to nature with which the book is executed would prevent anyone from supposing that it represented a larger section of society than it really does represent; and the plan of the work affords constant hints of states of society quite unconnected with each other or with the main purpose of the book.

No one passion is invested with an exaggerated importance. Even Crusoe's love for wandering is made to arise principally out of his unsettled circumstances. It is not a bad test of the propriety with which passions are represented in a novel, to look upon the novel as an autobiography of the hero, and to consider what would be the feelings with which we should look upon a man who so described the events of his own life. If we apply this test to *Robinson Crusoe*, we shall see with what self-respect and consistency the story is told. First in order comes the serious business of his life—his trade, his travels, his management of his affairs in his island. Then come the principles upon which he lived, his reflections upon Providence, and the Divine plans of which he conceived himself to be the subject. His purely personal matters, his marriage, his wife's death, and the like, are modestly kept in the background, as matters which he had no particular wish to publish to the world at large.

Contrast this with David Copperfield's memoirs, 'which he never meant to have been published on any account.'[70] If David Copperfield had been a real man, we think his intention would have been eminently judicious. What would be thought of a real autobiography disclosing all a man's most secret thoughts and most sacred affections. It would be considered a great breach of decency: and why is this less an offence in a novel than it would be in real life? It is seldom wholesome to dwell upon descriptions of those thoughts and feelings in others which we should instinctively veil if they were our own.

It is observable that Defoe never worships his hero. He does not in the least degree warp facts, or allow them to be coloured by his own peculiarities. It is impossible to read the book without feeling that it is, to use a much-abused word, eminently objective; that is, the circumstances are drawn from a real study of things as they are, and not in order to exemplify the workings of a particular habit of mind.

With respect to the manner in which Defoe's work acts upon the feelings, a few very simple instances will be sufficient to show his superiority over modern pathos. On gay subjects he is gay, on pathetic subjects pathetic, but he never goes out of his way to look for affecting incidents or details. When he returns to England, after nearly forty years' absence, he simply says, 'I went down to Yorkshire to look for my relatives.' We are not even told whether he went on horseback or by coach, whom he met on the road by a series of surprising coincidences, how many shops had been rebuilt, or young people grown old.

---

[70] *'Which He never meant to be Published on Any Account.'*

When he has occasion to speak of his wife's death he does it simply and quietly. We are not told whether there were any, and what, reflections of the sun upon the wall on the occasion, nor what his wife wore, nor who told him of her death, nor what the angels had to say upon the subject, nor, indeed, anything but the essential facts and the eternal feelings:

> But in the middle of all this felicity one blow from Divine Providence unhinged me at once. This blow was the loss of my wife. She was, in a few words, the stay of all my affairs, the centre of all my enterprises, the engine that, by her prudence, reduced me to that happy compass I was in, and from the most extravagant and ruinous project that fluttered in my head as above, and did more to guide my rambling genius than a mother's tears and a father's instructions, a friend's counsel, or all my own reasoning powers could do. I was happy in being moved by her tears and in listening to her entreaties, and to the last degree desolate and disconsolate in the world by the loss of her. When she was gone, the world looked awkwardly round me.

As for his descriptions of nature, we give but one instance in illustration of our remarks on that subject:

> Accordingly, we set out from Pampeluna, with our guide, on the 15th of November; and, indeed, I was surprised, when, instead of going forward, he came directly back with us on the same road that we came from Madrid, about twenty miles, when, having passed two rivers, and come into the plain country, we found ourselves in a warm climate again, where the country was pleasant, and no snow to be seen; but on a sudden turning to his left, he approached the mountains another way; and though it is true the hills and precipices looked dreadful, yet he made so many turns, such meanders, and led us by such winding ways, that we insensibly passed the height of the mountains without being much incumbered with the snow; and, all of a sudden, he showed us the pleasant fruitful provinces of Languedoc and Gascony, all green and flourishing, though, indeed, at a great distance, and we had some rough way to pass still.

* * *

[*Morality of Defoe*]

Perhaps the most extraordinary part of Defoe's book is its morality. The continual speculations upon the subject of Providence may seem, at first sight, to fall within the limits of that eagerness to justify existing notions which we have criticized. We apprehend, however, that this is not the case. All the incidents described are to the last degree simple, natural, and regular. The story is told so well, that the author can make the hero comment upon his own life as simply and quietly as if he were a real man commenting upon real occurrences. To invent facts in order to justify a theory is one thing—to apply facts fairly represented in a particular manner is quite another thing. That a sailor should be cast upon a desert island, escape from it, and travel over the world afterwards, is not in itself improbable. That he should have the piety and good sense to make such observations upon it as Crusoe makes, is much to be desired.

A somewhat similar justification may be offered for his constant introduction of omens and presentiments. It is well known, from other quarters, that Defoe had a strong belief in the existence of such warnings. Believing in them as matters of fact, it is natural that he should introduce them into a picture of life; but it is remarkable that the omens are not very specific. He arranges the details of the facts as is most suitable to the story; and introduces considerable variations between the facts and the presentiments. He dreams, for example, that a savage will run into his wood, but he says, 'I did not let my dream come true in this, for I took him another way', &c. A common writer would have made the details match exactly, in order to heighten the supernatural character of the warning, but Defoe gives the impression of not going beyond experience and reason, even where his opinions of what experience and reason teach are most peculiar to himself.

The historical and personal disturbing forces to be allowed for in reading *Robinson Crusoe* are few. There is hardly anything conventional in the structure of the story. The book is written to serve no turn—moral, political, or religious. It might probably be inferred, from the general character of the religious speculations contained in it, that it had been written by a man to whom the Act of Toleration[71] was the announcement of a new era, and who thought and felt upon those subjects as a contemporary of Locke would naturally think and feel.

We have already remarked that the charm of Crusoe's adventures is owing to the circumstance that they are described by a man who had, as he says, 'undergone as great risk as a grenadier on a counterscarp', through a great part of his life, and who was by nature pre-eminently qualified to run such risks; and that, described by a man more dependent on society—by Fielding, for example—they would have been a series of awful calamities and miseries.

Taken as a whole, there is probably no book in the range of novel literature which would form an addition to the experience of its readers so nearly equivalent to that which it would have formed if it had been literally true. In so far as a novel is a poem, or a satire, or a play, or a depository for beauties, *Robinson Crusoe* has been surpassed again and again; but if a novel is properly and primarily a fictitious biography, and if we have fairly stated its general objects and effects, it is not only unsurpassed, but we may almost say unsurpassable.

It may perhaps be regretted that novels should form so large a part of the reading of young men, though it is doubtful whether in any case they are an unmixed evil. Those who idle over novels would, in their absence, idle over something else; those who are unnaturally excited by them would find a vent for that habit of mind elsewhere. But be they good or bad, useless or necessary, they circulate over the land in every possible form, and enter more or less into the education of almost every one who can read. They hold in solution a great deal of experience. It would therefore surely be a most useful thing to provide rules by which the experience might be precipitated, and to ascertain the processes by means of which the precipitate might be made fit for use. We are not so vain as to suppose that we have done much towards the accomplishment of such a task. We have done our best to point out the limits and directions of the instructions which are wanted.

---

[71] 1688, allowing freedom of worship to nonconformist Protestants (such as Baptists, Congregationalists, or Presbyterians, though not to Roman Catholics, non-Trinitarians, or atheists).

'Woods *v.* Russell'
(*Saturday Review*, 19 January 1856)

On reports from the Crimean War, fought between the Imperial Russian Army and the allied armies of Britain, France, and the Ottoman Empire. Nicholas Augustus Woods (1813–1906) was the war correspondent of the *Morning Herald* (author of *The Past Campaign: A Sketch of the War in the East, from the Departure of Lord Raglan to the Capture of Sevastopol*, 1855), and William Howard Russell (1820–1907; *ODNB*, journalist), the correspondent of *The Times*. 'When war is declared, Truth is the first casualty': this was to be the epigraph to *Falsehood in Wartime* (1928) by Arthur Ponsonby, first Baron Ponsonby of Shulbrede (1871–1946; *ODNB*, politician and peace campaigner). For JFS at 26, the first casuistry is the rigging of evidence, and the question has to be 'What was the evidence…?' (His answer: 'miserably inconclusive'.) His cross-examination prosecutes 'the suggestion of the *Times* itself', being bent upon 'the differences between the two correspondents', 'our two authorities', their 'discrepancies'. Both of the authorities cannot be right although they could well both be wrong.

Woods *v.* Russell*

The popular view of the campaign in the Crimea is summed up in the apophthegm attributed to—perhaps invented for—the Russians, about the army of lions commanded by asses.[1] Two great historians—Messrs. Woods and Russell—have favoured the world with a republication of the correspondence which originally produced this impression. The work of the gentleman first named has been made the subject of a vehement panegyric by the *Times*, and his assertions have been triumphantly appealed to as confirming and bearing out the statements of the gentleman whose praise is in all the shop windows, and whom the Parthenon Club delights to honour.[2] As we happen to feel some regard for the reputation of our country—as we cannot quite acquiesce in the doctrine that the inferiority of England to France, the miserable imbecility of our Government and our soldiers, the stupid pride of our aristocracy, the slavish toadyism of our middle classes, and the brutal stupidity and inveterate sottishness of the poor, are proper subjects for noisy rejoicing, public festivities, and after-dinner exultation— we have gone through the task (not a very light one) of examining some of the authorities upon which the opinions in question rest; and we cannot say that the result has

---

* *History of the Late Campaign*, by N. A. Woods. London: Longmans, 1855. *History of the War*, by W. H. Russell. London: Routledge, 1855.

---

[1] 'Russians' perhaps, but circulated in French: 'L'armée anglaise est une armée de lions, commandée par des ânes'. (No secure source has been identified.)

[2] Charles Dickens, a member of the Parthenon Club.

28   ON THE NOVEL AND JOURNALISM

been to impress us with any great reverence for the abilities or truthfulness of our self-chosen censors.[3]

Of Mr. Russell we have spoken on former occasions. Our last new Thucydides[4] is Mr. N. A. Woods, late Special Correspondent of the *Morning Herald*. This candid gentleman disclaims in his Preface all 'pretensions to military criticism'. In fact, he seems to think it unnecessary, because 'opinion on military matters, though sometimes hasty, is seldom very wrong'—which opinion, from a gentleman who, by his own account, knows nothing about strategy, is of course entitled to great weight. Nevertheless Mr. Woods 'points to well known mistakes', and states 'less generally known deficiencies', and his readers, at any rate, 'cannot fail to see that' his 'narrative is true, and therefore impartial'. It is very characteristic of Mr. Woods to appeal to his readers for the truth of his narrative; and it is a blessing that the public are endowed with this unerring power of distinguishing truth from falsehood. If it were not so, they might be rather at a loss for an opinion upon the subject, for the question is entirely one of detail, and of very dry detail too. The questions to be decided are such as these— How many carts had the Commissariat at Varna? What was the evidence about the healthiness of the Camp there? How many surgeons were there at the Alma? What stores and other resources were at their disposal? What clothing was there at Balaklava? What was the morning state of the army on such a day? and so on. In fact, the questions upon which the whole inquiry hinges are as dry and as special as if they related to invoices, bills of exchange, dock warrants, and accounts current. It may, therefore, well be that Mr. Woods has drawn most lively pictures of the theatrical parts of the war, and yet that he is utterly untrustworthy when he comes to facts. Indeed, no artist's 'blood' is redder, no one's 'thunder' louder, no one's 'wounds' more frightful, no one deals so well with 'gangrene', 'maggots', 'filth unutterable', and 'festering masses of corruption'; but it does not follow that he is equally reliable when he says that such a regiment, on such a day, mustered only so many men, or that such a drug ran short in such an hospital. As upon these details everything depends, and as we have the advantage of being in a position to command the testimony of two such men as Messrs. Woods and Russell, we have compared some of their statements, acting upon the suggestion of the *Times* itself, which, whilst declining, with an engaging modesty, to execute the task on its own account, remarks that its readers will naturally make the comparison.

A striking instance of Mr. Woods's 'union' with Mr. Russell is, according to their common patron, to be found in their accounts of the mismanagement of the Government, and especially of the commissariat, at Varna.[5] Mr. Woods says:

> If ever the English were to have had good commissariat arrangements, they should have been at Varna; yet the very reverse was the case. Almost daily service letters went in to the heads of the commissariat departments from assistant commissaries in charge of divisions, stating that they were unable to provide the requisite amount of bread and meat for the support of the troops. (i. 86.)

---

[3] *OED* One who exercises official or officious supervision over morals and conduct. One who censures or blames; an adverse critic; one given to fault-finding. 1848 MACAULAY by eulogists or by censors. (Likewise, 'censorship', p. 34.)

[4] Athenian general (*c*.460 BC–*c*.404 BC), historian of the war between Sparta and Athens.

[5] Black Sea port, the main British and French naval base.

Mr. Russell says (June 9):

> Altogether the station seems excellent, and as the commissariat is not deficient in supplies of all the essentials of bread and beef, there is no cause for complaint. (83, 84.)

And again, June 26:

> The commissariat are doing their duty manfully. The quality of the meat is really very good.

On July 21, we are told:

> The meat furnished by the commissariat is excellent. Some of the surgeons think the ration is not large enough, as the meat is lean and deficient in nutritive quality, when compared with English beef and mutton; but it should be stated that, in order to compensate for that deficiency, the weight of the ration has been increased from three-quarters of a pound to one pound per day. (p. 103.)

Mr. Woods and Mr. Russell agree in thinking that it was on account of deficiency in the means of land transport that Silistria[6] was not relieved. Upon whom did the blame rest? Mr. Woods, writing of the middle of June, says:

> It was plain to every one at Varna that the French were not numerous enough to advance alone to its (Silistria's) help, and that, under any circumstances, the English were not able to advance at all. (i. 83.)

There was one person at Varna to whom this was not so obvious. A month later (July 21) Mr. Russell writes thus:

> They (the French) are not in a better condition to march into the interior than we are... They are obliged... to send on the general staff of the administration some sixteen days or a fortnight before they move... We, on the contrary, carry our stores with us, and are at this moment, as I have said, better able to march *en masse* than they are. (p. 124.)

Nor do Messrs. Woods and Russell agree upon the question of military luxuries. In a passage which the *Times* quotes with curious exultation, Mr. Woods says:

> Only 8000 lbs. of tea had been sent out by the Government, and this absurdly small stock was expended a few days after our landing. The men seldom got their full rations, that is to say, either the sugar, coffee, or meat were deficient, and *on very many occasions* they had only bread and water for breakfast. Even such a simple article as rice was not to be had on any terms. (i. 86, 87.)

Writing on the 14th of June, Mr. Russell says:

> Sorry am I to say that the men are dissatisfied, because the store of sugar is run out, and fellows who never were accustomed, before they enlisted, to anything better than a drink of buttermilk and a potato, declare they cannot take their tea or coffee without sugar. (p. 91.)

On the 20th of June, he writes:

> I regret very much to have to state that *for several days last week* there was neither rice, nor sugar, nor preserved potatoes, nor tea. The men had then to make their breakfast simply on ration brown bread and water... Within these last three or four days, a little rice has again been served out, and small quantities of tea. (p. 96.)

---

[6] Russian forces besieged the Ottoman fortress.

30 ON THE NOVEL AND JOURNALISM

And writing on the 21st July, he tells us that the quantity of food issued by the commissariat seems almost fabulous. In addition to 110,000 lbs. of corn, &c., issued for the horses, 27,000 lbs. of meat, 27,000 rations of bread, and '*the same quantity of rice, tea, coffee, sugar, &c.*', were issued daily. (p. 123.)

So that whilst Mr. Woods implies that the whole time spent at Varna was a time of hardship, Mr. Russell's only grievance is that between the 14th and 16th or 17th of June, the troops had no tea for breakfast; nor are the differences between the two correspondents at an end when they leave Varna. As our object at present is only to compare our two authorities, we will pass over various points which might require notice in narrating, and confine ourselves to a single point in which they are curiously at issue. Speaking of alleged irregularities in the disembarkation, Mr. Russell says:

> The greatest offender against the prescribed order of disembarkation was the Admiral himself, who, *instead of filling the place assigned to him* in the centre of his fleet, anchored four miles from the shore. (p. 160.)

And again:

> In our fleet, the whole labour and responsibility of the disembarkation rested with Sir E. Lyons. The Admiral remained, as I have said, aloof, and took no share in the proceedings of the day. (p. 161.)

Mr. Woods says:

> *Admiral Dundas was in his place* in the centre of the line-of-battle ships, which were moored about three miles off the shore, outside the transports, to protect them in case of the Russian fleet making any desperate attempt in the night.

Speaking of a village near the English position, Mr. Woods says:

> The outskirts were crowded with stacks of hay and barley, and large flocks of sheep and cattle. These, though we wanted fresh meat and forage, their owners declined to sell at any price. They had evidently been cautioned by the Russians against affording us any assistance. As strict orders had been issued that the property of the natives was to be respected, and as in nearly every instance, they refused to sell, the English did without their supplies as they best could. Such was not the case with our allies. They fixed a fair price on the articles they wanted, gave the money, and took the goods, and the people seemed very well content to have a market thus thrust upon them.

Mr. Russell, speaking apparently of the same place (though we cannot be quite sure of this), says that it 'was sacked by some French marauders, with every excess of brutal cruelty and ferocity. I need not repeat the details, indeed they are too shocking to humanity.' Not one word of this—wherever it happened—does Mr. Woods mention. Mr. Russell proceeds, 'They (the French razzias[7]) frighten them from our markets, and will soon deprive us of the vast supplies to be obtained from the natives' (p. 170.) Some more minute discrepancies are very instructive, because they show how little these gentlemen are to be depended upon in matters of detail. Mr. Woods says 'it will be scarcely credited that *nearly* 1200 sick' were placed on board the *Kangaroo* on a particular occasion. (i. 309.) Mr. Russell says, on the same occasion, that there were 'about 1500'. Where accuracy in number is the one thing needful, these gentlemen seem to

---

[7] *OED* A hostile incursion, foray, or raid, for purpose of conquest, plunder. From 1845.

make mere guesses. So, in speaking of the skirmish at Bouljanak, Mr. Woods says that 'we had only six-pounders', that our artillery could not effect much, that the Russians continued steady under fire, and then wheeled off and slowly retired. (i. 324.) Mr. Russell states that our cannon 'ploughed up the columns of the cavalry, who speedily dispersed into broken lines, wheeling round and round with great adroitness, to escape the six and *nine* pound balls' (p. 175).

Perhaps as curious a contradiction as any is one which relates to the battle of Balaklava. In a page of which the running title is 'Bravo, Highlanders! well done!' Mr. Russell tells a most picturesque story of how the Russian horse charged the 93rd, the ground flying under their feet, and the assailants gathering speed at every stride— how the Highlanders fired two volleys at them, one at 600 yards, which had no effect, and one at 150 yards, which 'carried death and terror into the Russians'—and how Sir Colin Campbell said, 'I did not think it worth while to form them even four deep.' According to Mr. Woods, this is a mere theatrical romance. His statement is that, at from 700 to 800 yards, a volley was fired at the Russians without effect—that then the Turks ran away—that the Russians advanced at a trot to within 400 or 500 yards—that the Highlanders then fired a second volley also without effect—and that the Russians slowly retired. (Mr. Russell says, 'they wheel about, open files right and left, and fly back faster than they came')—(Woods, ii. 70–1, Russell, 227.) As to Sir Colin Campbell's alleged speech, Mr. Woods declares that he never made any such 'absurd remark', adding that, if the Highlanders had been charged, Sir Colin would have ordered them to form square. Though both these gentlemen were eye-witnesses, both at Bouljanak and at Balaklava, they are in direct contradiction; and if Mr. Russell really made up this romantic story to flatter the public, what reliance can be placed on any statement he makes?

These are some of the discrepancies between these gentlemen's accounts which we have met with in a not very elaborate examination of their books. They bear a larger proportion to the total number of facts stated than our readers would suppose; for the mass of verbiage which is introduced into each book is not only surprising, but wearisome. We do not by any means wish it to be inferred from the above comparison that Mr. Russell is always in the wrong. He seems to us to be at times more reasonable than Mr. Woods, and indeed it must be allowed that Mr. Woods is about the lowest authority in matters of fact—perhaps we may except Mr. Russell—that we ever happened to meet with. We will not tire our readers with a criticism of the miserably inconclusive evidence on which he impugns the conduct of the war. 'I hear', 'It is said', 'I am told', is all he knows about it. He is, by his own confession, avowed nearly as often as he has occasion to make a statement, a mere retailer of gossip the correctness of which it is generally impossible to check. We will therefore confine ourselves to two or three flagrant instances of carelessness, which, upon such an occasion, is neither more nor less than dishonesty. Curiously enough, two of the statements to which we refer are clamorously and joyously adopted, and reiterated by the reviewer in the *Times* on the 9th inst. When the army arrived at Sebastopol, 'the English', says Mr. Woods, 'had no theodolites[8] with them'. A negative assertion like this is rather a wide one to receive, on the authority of a single person. It is curious that Mr. Woods should have said—carried

---

[8] *OED* A portable surveying instrument, originally for measuring horizontal angles.

away by love of picturesqueness and alliteration—that amongst the shops established at Varna were some in which you might buy anything 'from a *theodolite* to a toothpick' (i. 151.) Of course Mr. Woods was only looking out for something large which began with a *t*, but if we are to believe that theodolites were in such demand at Varna that private speculators brought them to the camp for sale, it is quite incredible that there should have been none at Sebastopol. This is a small matter, though characteristic, but what follows is of very different importance. We request our readers' attention to the following comparison:

WOODS, vol. ii. p. 253.—*On the 8th of January, of the 63rd Regiment, only seven remained fit for duty.* On the same day the 46th, which had landed on the 8th Nov., just two months before, mustered only *sixty* serviceable men. The 90th, a strong and healthy regiment, buried fifty men in eleven days; and one full company, during the same time, had only seventeen men out of hospital. The three battalions of Guards were mere names. *Out of 1562 men sent out to the Scots Fusiliers, from first to last, only 210 remained.*

RUSSELL, p. 303. Jan. 8.—*The 63rd Regiment had only seven men fit for duty yesterday.* The 46th had only *thirty* men fit for duty at the same date. A strong company of the 90th have been reduced, by the last week's severity, to fourteen file, in a few days; and that regiment, though considered very healthy, lost fifty men by death in a fortnight. *The Scots Fusilier Guards, who have had out, from beginning to end, 1562 men, now muster, including servants and corporals, 210 men on parade.*

Our readers see how exactly, almost verbally, these accounts tally. The sentences are sometimes clause for clause the same, and the regiments are referred to in the same order. Mr. Russell's statement purports to be a republication of his letter of the 8th January, and we suppose it is so; but Mr. Woods's statement does not purport to be taken from Mr. Russell, but from his own observation. In referring, however, to Mr. Woods's letters, in the *Morning Herald*, dated on the 8th, the 15th, the 20th, and the 27th of January, and on the 10th of February, and published on 29th of January and on the 3rd, 14th, and 27th of February—in which the sufferings of the army are dwelt upon at great length—we find that there is no reference whatever to the 90th Regiment or to the Scots Fusiliers, except in so far as the latter are comprehended under the general description of the losses of the Guards. The 46th Regiment are described as having, on the 8th of January, mustered seventy, not sixty, men; and the 63rd as having been reduced, not to seven on the 7th of January, but to ten on the 11th. The differences are unimportant in themselves; but the alteration in the case of the 63rd shows that Mr. Woods prefers Mr. Russell's authority to his own, and that which applies to the 46th shows that he will go as far to meet him as he can. The alteration must have been purposely made, for, on the 8th of January, Mr. Woods mentions the fact that the 46th had landed just two months,[9] which Mr. Russell omits, but which is mentioned in Mr. Woods's letter to the *Morning Herald* of that date. The statements about the Fusiliers and the 90th Regiment appear to be copied straight out of Mr. Russell's work, with slight alterations—we fear, to disguise the adoption. Yet this statement was paraded by the *Times* last Wednesday week as a confirmation of its own assertions, and Mr. Woods is complimented for his 'unalterable fidelity'. After this, it is, perhaps, superfluous to notice that, in his letter of the 8th of January Mr. Woods put the original

---

[9] That is, had been disembarked for just two months.

WOODS *V*. RUSSELL

force of the 40th at 850, whilst in his letter of the 20th he rates it at 1100. The *Times*, which mutilates its 'Own Correspondent's' despatches to suit its leading articles, must feel that Mr. Woods, who adapts his statements to Mr. Russell's, is a congenial spirit.

The most unblushing piece of impudence in Mr. Woods's book is to be found in a note in vol. ii. p. 206–7. In this passage Mr. Woods, after bitter complaints of the inefficiency of everything and everybody, gives for once an authority for his statements. 'All the facts I have mentioned in this chapter', he says, 'with others still more important which afterwards occurred, are detailed at length'—where does the reader suppose?—in an unpublished report in the possession of Government. Unless Mr. Woods has seen the report in question, his assertion is a simple guess, which, in such a case, is very like a simple untruth. What he says may be true or not, but he has no possible means of knowing whether it is so. He has the *naïveté* to add that the House of Commons' Report 'elicited nothing to criminate any one very deeply'. Surely the fact that such evidence as has been published exculpates the accused is a curious reason for saying that evidence given in a private inquiry criminates him.

Mr. Woods is, if his treatment of his own nest is any evidence, one of the least cleanly of all bipeds. Wherever he compares the English and French, it is to our disadvantage. A few phrases occur, no doubt, in which he says that it is painful and humiliating to do so, but Mr. Woods is a perfect ascetic in his passion for such humiliation. We will only notice two out of very many instances of this. In his account of the naval attack on Sebastopol, 'The French fleet', he says, 'was in long before the English. They came on in magnificent style, in two long lines.' The English, he says, came in an hour after, and Admiral Dundas anchored with several ships about 2000 yards from the forts, 'from which safe range' they kept up an incessant fire. He does not speak of the French as firing from 'a safe range'. Yet according to his own account, they were as far from the batteries as Admiral Dundas. Another most striking instance is the manner in which he hurries over the French expedition into the Dobrudscha. It is passed over in two or three pages, concluding with a notice of the 'most searching investigation' to which the general in command was subjected, and which terminated in his acquittal. If an English general had lost one-third of his men by sickness in twelve days, no language would have been strong enough to describe his wickedness, and any investigation which stopped short of shooting or breaking[10] all concerned would have been denounced as a delusion.

Of Mr. Woods's style we need not speak. It is familiar enough to all readers, showy, noisy, clever, and picturesque, but essentially vulgar and impudent. A dead dog is 'a decayed specimen of canine mortality'. He sees at sea '*a* phenomena'. 'Bosquet' and 'Canrobert', 'Lucan' and 'Cardigan', lose their several titles. Statements of the most vehement kind are made upon any or no authority. For example, Mr. Woods was on his way from Constantinople during the great storm of the 14th November; he arrived after it was over. Yet, in his letter to the *Morning Herald*, 'two or three days after the gale'—*i.e.*, immediately on his arrival, he says, 'I most decidedly charge the whole of the deplorable results of the late gale on the gross and culpable mismanagement of the naval authorities out here'—(II. 189). And he reprints this astonishing piece of impertinence, although he states (P. 171) that Admiral Lyons approved of the conduct of

---

[10] *OED to break an officer* to cashier, deprive him of his commission, degrade him from his rank.

34

those who kept the transports out of Balaklava Harbour, either because he thought the anchorage a safe one, or because he was aware of reasons which justified the measure. We should never have done if we pointed out all the follies and impudence which disgrace this book. After all, who are Messrs. Woods and Russell? They have assumed a censorship over our affairs, which, if it were a public trust, would not be granted to any one who had not some of the very highest mental qualifications which men can possess. The sternest impartiality, judicial habits of mind, the highest personal character, are some of the qualifications which, if united with profound knowledge, might give a man a right to pronounce *ex cathedrâ* upon the conduct of such an undertaking. Messrs. Woods and Russell may be the most sober, the most moral, the most upright of men, inaccessible to flattery, or to those delicate attentions which are a sort of indirect bribery; but the mere fact that they represent certain London papers in the Crimea proves nothing as to their respectability or their authority. There is a class of gentlemen of their profession whose business it is to describe processions, reviews, lord mayors' feasts, and executions; to tell how at an early hour the culprit partook of tea, and asked for broiled ham, which was supplied him; how the worthy sheriff and excellent chaplain arrived at seven; how, soon afterwards, Calcraft[11] was in attendance; and how the procession was formed, and as the bells of a neighbouring church tolled eight, the culprit was launched into eternity. We do not deny to these gentlemen plenty of fluency, picturesque eyes, and language to match; but when we come to look at their treatment of facts, and at the effect which their statements produce, we had rather have them confine themselves to the humbler vocation of the hangman's historians, than hold up our name and nation to the contempt of all Europe.

---

[11] William Calcraft (1800–1879; *ODNB*, hangman), 'the most famous hangman of the nineteenth century, a role he fulfilled for forty-five years' (*Liberty, Equality, Fraternity* 229 n.) See JFS, 'The Sunday Papers' (*Sat. Rev.*, 19 April 1856) p. 43. Also on the *Mémoires des Sanson* (*Sept Générations d'Exécuteurs*; *Sat. Rev.*, 7 Nov. 1863): 'The morals of one age are not those of another, but it is hard to acquit entirely the man who lived by breaking people on the wheel'; 'There is a point at which the fact that a system exists does not excuse those who work it.' On the other hand, 'The judge and the sheriff, after all, have no right to despise the hangman' (*Sat. Rev.*, 30 July 1864, 'Theodore Parker on Social Science'). 'Equality before the Law' (*Sat. Rev.*, 30 Jan. 1864), on capital punishment: 'Few minds do, in point of fact—as all reasonable minds ought—dwell on its expediency, and calmly approve its infliction on that ground. The mass of men view the gallows with a feeling compounded of superstitious awe and shuddering aversion, and look upon the execution of a murderer as something different in kind from a five-shilling fine. They do not quite know what to think of it, and therefore they do not think in a consistent, manly way, but drift about, catching at one sentiment or another as it happens'.

'Religious Journalism'
(*Saturday Review*, 16 February 1856)

JFS at 26 finds himself wishing a plague on both the newspaper houses. *Life* 105: 'The "Record" is lashed for its religious rancour, and the "Reasoner" for its vapid version of popular infidelity, though it is contemptuously preferred, in point of spirit, to the "Record".' 'Religious Journalism', as against—a couple of months later—'The Secular Press' (5 April 1856). The call is for evidence; one of the charges, prurience.

Religious Journalism

If we were to hear of any particular individual that he was eminently religious, what kind of person should we expect to see? As the word 'religion' is now generally used to denote the sum total of the relations between man and his Maker, and not merely, as was once the case, the external ceremonial of worship, we should have a right to expect that a very religious man would differ from his neighbours, not so much in the apparent objects or in the ordinary habits of life, as in being eminently wise and good—a man of truth, principle, honour, and charity—a judicious adviser, a man whose word could be trusted, one who feared nothing in the path of duty. In short, we should look for a man fearing and loving God, and acting upon these principles in all his dealings with men. If we were to hear of a newspaper as distinguished by the same peculiarity, we ought, by a parity of reasoning, to expect in it similar qualities. The function of a newspaper is to report and to comment upon passing events. A religious newspaper, one would suppose, ought to be distinguished from journals not so characterized by commenting more truthfully, and more generously, and more wisely than other newspapers upon the occurrences which might attract its notice. Words, however, are not readily divested of their appropriate meaning; and though the usage of the day may seem to sanction the notion that the word 'religious' is equivalent to 'righteous', it is sometimes used in its original sense of 'addicted', wisely or not, 'to ceremonial observances'. If the word be used in this sense, we have no difficulty in understanding what is meant by the 'religious' Press, and by the 'religious' world which it represents. The phrases, on this hypothesis, will denote that part of society and those particular newspapers which are distinguished by attaching—generally, sincerely enough—a peculiar importance to the maintenance of those outward and visible habits of conduct, of language, and of thought which are usually associated with devotion. Every one knows that in every theological denomination there are peculiarities which distinguish those who profess the strictest adherence to its principles. We do not wish to ridicule or to impute insincerity to those who adopt them. If we knew nothing whatever about two

36   ON THE NOVEL AND JOURNALISM

given individuals, except the fact that the one did and the other did not exhibit such peculiarities, we should think that there was some evidence that the first was a better man than the second. The aggregate of these bodies is what is generally called the 'religious world'; and the function of religious newspapers is to represent the opinions, feelings, and interests of the various classes into which it is divided. The universal profession of these papers is, that they wish to promote the interests of true piety. Their all but universal practice is founded upon some such argument as this: 'True piety is that which is believed and done by the truly pious. The truly pious are those who act upon certain principles in a certain manner. The principles, and the way of applying them, are such and such. The persons who hold and act upon them are that section of the religious world which we represent. Upon the whole, the body which we represent is truly pious, and by representing their feelings, wishes, opinions, and inter- ests, we are advocating the cause of true piety.'

Now, inasmuch as such bodies are distinguished, not only by their piety, but by the peculiarities which we have mentioned—and as it is much easier to recognise the out- ward and visible sign[1] than the inward and spiritual grace which gives it its value—the newspaper which represents it is pretty sure, for the sake of convenience and distinct- ness, to accept the sign which *can*, as conclusive evidence of the spiritual condition which *cannot* be ascertained. If all red-haired[2] men were eminently constitutional,[3] a newspaper established on constitutional principles would be very apt to distrust all whose heads were black, brown, or grey; and when a little heated in political contest, they would not scruple—of course, with every expression of tenderness for 'our black- haired brethren in all parts of world'—to attack all those who did not comply with the test, not on the ground of the blackness of their hair, but on the ground of their disloy- alty. Add to this circumstance the belief—very possibly quite sincere—of the infinite significance of the questions at issue, and there will no longer be any cause for surprise at the frightful vehemence and constant disregard of truth which are indissolubly asso- ciated in our minds with the words 'religious newspaper'. We have vulgar papers, we have unprincipled papers, we have disingenuous papers, and we have imbecile papers; but the full bitterness which the human heart is capable of feeling, the full ferocity which it is capable of expressing, is to be met with nowhere but in religious papers. We know of no spectacle more frightful than that of a 'religious' writer, raging with currish spite, and taxing his generally very narrow capacity to put into words the images famil- iar to a bad heart and a gloomy imagination. We know of no more awful responsibility than that of being a permanent scandal[4] and stumblingblock to those who wish to love and to serve their Maker, and a perpetual occasion to the enemies of religion to blas- pheme. Sometimes, in the midst of such displays, it is hardly possible to repress a smile

---

[1] The Book of Common Prayer: 'An outward and visible sign of an inward and spiritual grace.'

[2] JFS, contesting John Stuart Mill and offering a hypothetical rule: ' "All thieves except those who have red hair shall be imprisoned" ... In this sense equality is no doubt of the very essence of justice, but the ques- tion of whether the colour of a man's hair shall or shall not affect the punishment of his crimes depends on a different set of considerations. It is imaginable that the colour of the hair might be an unfailing mark of peculiarity of disposition which might require peculiar treatment' (*Liberty, Equality, Fraternity* 129); for JFS, Oscar Wilde, and A.E.Housman's 'Oh they're taking him to prison for the colour of his hair', Ricks, *Allusion to the Poets* [2002], 287–90.

[3] *OED* In harmony with, or authorized by, the political constitution. From 1765 BLACKSTONE.

[4] Etymologically cognate with the Latin and Greek, to stumble.

RELIGIOUS JOURNALISM

37

at a blundering ferocity which is at once amusing and disgusting. Take, for example, the following extracts (slightly compressed) from an article in last week's *Tablet*,[5] on *Crime in England*:

> The devil, according to St. Augustine, has certain moral attributes. He cannot get drunk. He is industrious. He is eminently intelligent, and would, with the most distinguished success, fill a professor's chair in any one of the godless colleges. Like the devil, the people of Protestant Britain are amazingly industrious, and like him, their industry had a Satanic origin. [Did the devil create himself?] We may see in Protestant England an industry which may be termed Satanic, a temperance which is Satanic, and an intelligence which is Satanic. This intelligence makes men at once chemists and atheists, alike godless and well informed. Lectures on chemistry which lead men to the use of strychnine have superseded sermons on Catholic dogma which lead men to the frequentation of the sacraments. Untiring efforts to assimilate the moral character of men to that of Satan are made by titled itinerant lecturers [poor Lord Stanley![6]]. Britain is fast becoming a hell upon earth. As men sow, so shall they reap.[7] Pernicious teachings are followed by more pernicious practices. Thus the world is horrified within one short month by the harvest of crime which mantles Great Britain with its disastrous and funereal shadow.

We suppose the murder of Miss Hinds[8] was only pretty Paddy's way,[9] and that the nine unfortunate victims hung last year in Ireland were Catholic martyrs. Our contemporary proceeds:

> We have first the fiendish felony [miserable misdemeanour would have been as good jingle and better law] of Sir John Paul,[10] who, with the same hand which opens a heretical Bible, despoils the widow of her mite and the orphan of his patrimony. After this grim and cowardly crawler follows the clumsy figure and coarse red face of William Palmer.[11]

It is some comfort to reflect that Palmer is not yet convicted. But it does not follow that England is a hell upon earth, because he has 'a clumsy figure and coarse red face'; nor were Sir John Paul's crimes discovered within a month of those imputed to Palmer, but nearly nine months before. Ebullitions of this kind are probably only the last efforts of the 'felon' press, sighing itself to rest; and we are not sorry that the heroes of the sword, the dock, and the cabbage-garden should carry their virulence into a sphere in which it only aggravates the symptoms of a chronic disease, instead of threatening to produce a civil war.

Certainly the conduct of many of the Irish Roman Catholics has not been such as to incline us either to respect or to admire them. There is, however, a body in England of which we wish to speak with the sincerest respect, and which has many undoubted claims to our admiration. It is caricatured by a paper as bitter as the *Tablet*, but less

---

[5] Founded 1840; owned and edited 1855–68 by John Edward Wallis, a Catholic barrister.

[6] Edward Lyulph Stanley, fourth Baron Stanley of Alderley (1839–1925; *ODNB*, educationist). [The square-bracketed words within the quoted lines are JFS's.]

[7] Galatians 6:7, For whatsoever a man soweth, that shall he also reap.

[8] Charlotte Hinds; the murder is discussed in William Edward Vaughan, *Murder Trials in Ireland, 1836–1914* (2009) 143ff.

[9] Thomas Parnell (1679–1718; *ODNB*, poet and essayist): 'And all that's madly wild, or oddly gay, / We call it only pretty Fanny's way' ('An Elegy, to an Old Beauty'). Parnell, born and educated in Ireland.

[10] Sir John Dean Paul, second baronet (1802–1868; *ODNB*, banker and fraudster).

[11] In the Palmer case, strychnine (mentioned here a few lines earlier) was the crux. See p. 16.

38   ON THE NOVEL AND JOURNALISM

able, and more totally unscrupulous. We allude to the Evangelical party and the *Record*[12] newspaper. No one who is a friend to the Church of England can doubt that the Evangelical party has rendered it inestimable service. The great religious revival of the last century—the foundation, the maintenance, and the government, conducted with extraordinary skill and vigour, of some of our most eminent charitable societies—the names of such men as Scott, Venn, Newton, and Simeon,[13] and of many living persons who not unworthily represent their spiritual ancestors, are most unquestionable titles to respect. In an evil hour, not only for themselves, but for the peace of English society, they have allowed themselves to be represented by a paper bitter, false, and malignant to an extent almost incredible. Of the theology of the *Record* we will say nothing, as we do not agree with our contemporary in thinking that such subjects can be profitably discussed in a newspaper. We will content ourselves with stating a general impression, which, we think, will be shared by all entitled to judge. Let any one compare books which the *Record* would greet with a Judas's kiss—H. Venn's *Complete Duty of Man*, J. Venn's *Sermons*, or Wilberforce's *Practical Christianity*[14]—with the theological art-icles in the *Record*, and he will feel the same kind of shock which would be occasioned by the substitution of the photograph of a corpse for the portrait of a face. In the one, he will find some peculiarities of expression and of opinion with which he would per-haps not be inclined to sympathize, but he would also find in every page the deepest marks of the love of God and the love of man. In the other, he would find the same expressions, and a caricature of the same opinions, petrified into a shape which would lead him to suppose that, whilst the object of the Master served by the one set of writers was to save the world, the characteristic of the Being worshipped by the other was to prepare and to rejoice in its destruction. No doubt the columns of the *Record* are full of lamentations over human wickedness and the consequences to which it tends, but it is impossible to read them without perceiving that they are crocodile's tears, and that in reality the writer rejoices over the corruptions which appear to prove his con-clusion. At the head of the column of correspondence in the *Record*, stands this notice—'We shall not insert anything opposed to the fundamental truths of the Gospel, without an immediate refutation.' On the 7th January, a letter, containing the following passage, was published in that column without note or comment, under the curious signature of 'P. O. P.' It calls the Editor's attention to 'A work called *Boyle v. Wiseman*, *which ought to be devoured* by every Englishman, whether Protestant, Dissenter, or Catholic.' Why? Because, 'never was a man so clearly convicted of lying, slander, and detraction as Cardinal Wiseman in this book. It would be wrong to say [but not to

---

[12] Founded 1828.

[13] Thomas Scott (1747–1821; *ODNB*, clergyman and biblical scholar). Henry Venn (1796–1873; *ODNB*, Church of England clergyman); his sister, Jane Catherine Venn, was JFS's mother. In 1841 'he was appointed honorary secretary to the Church Missionary Society, having been on the Committee since 1819' (*Life* 30). John Newton (1725–1807; *ODNB*, slave trader and Church of England clergyman, *Life* 29); see p. 40. Charles Simeon (1759–1836; *ODNB*, Church of England clergyman), Fellow of King's College, and vicar of Holy Trinity, Cambridge (*Life* 29).

[14] Henry Venn (1725–1797; *ODNB*, Church of England clergyman), *The Complete Duty of Man; or, A System of Doctrinal and Practical Christianity* (1763); *Life* 29. John Venn (1759–1813; *ODNB*, Church of England clergyman), a founder of the Church Missionary Society. William Wilberforce (1759–1833; *ODNB*, politician, philanthropist, and slavery abolitionist), author of *A Practical View of the Prevailing Religious System of Professed Christians, in the Higher and Middle Classes in this Country. Contrasted with real Christianity* (1797).

RELIGIOUS JOURNALISM

39

insinuate] that he is also convicted of perjury, but the statement of facts is such as to throw very strong suspicion on' his affidavits. We have no particular love for Cardinal Wiseman,[15] but we should be sorry to think him perjured. It is a 'fundamental truth of the Gospel', that there is joy in heaven over one sinner that repenteth;[16] but it would seem that there is joy in the pages of the *Record* over the detection of any one who needs repentance.

The *Record*'s estimate of itself is perhaps as surprising as its judgment of its neighbours. In a well-known essay, an eminent writer[17] had maintained the opinion that many persons who make little or no profession of religion are nevertheless distinguished by exemplary conduct, and that it is false and uncharitable to say that such actions are merely external, and have no spiritual value. On the 9th of last month, the *Record* published an article upon this subject, to the effect that there was a great difference between Mr. Jowett's theory and the fact. He asserted that the church and the world were separated from each other by very slight distinctions, and 'besought us not to keep up such a rigid line of demarcation'; whereas, says the *Record*, how wicked are all the Courts of Europe ('for obvious reasons, excepting our own and that of France'). How wicked the President of the United States would be, if he could—it is worth while to remark not only the charity of the assumption, but the ingenuity with which, by an after-thought, a foreseen objection is silenced. How wicked the respectable classes are—how wicked railway directors are—how wicked are the poor, as is shown by husbands beating their wives! In short, 'the present state of the human race, or at least of ninety-nine hundredths of it, is desperately wicked.' For these reasons the *Record* justifies itself in 'enforcing a rigid line of demarcation'. When the Pharisee in the parable arrived at the conclusion that he was not as other men, he had at least the grace to express his thankfulness. The *Record* does not even think it worth while to state the fact, but leaves it to be inferred. It rigidly marks itself off from the rest of the world— the ninety-nine hundredths are 'desperately wicked'.[18] What can we infer but that the other one hundredth is unimpeachably good? Perhaps, in some future edition, Mr. Jowett will draw the other side of the picture, and show that, as the world has many of the virtues of the church, the church is not exempt from the frailties of the world. Perhaps, amongst other things, he would say, 'How timid our spiritual reprovers are!' Is the Emperor of the French so spotless that he alone is admitted to share with the Queen, the Editor, and the admirers of the *Record*, the fold of the little flock? Or can it be that the 'obvious reasons' which exempt him from remark are mere cowardice and time-serving? Can we imagine Elijah saying to Israel, 'Hear, O Israel! the priests are

---

[15] Nicholas Wiseman (1802–1865; *ODNB*, cardinal and archbishop of Westminster).

[16] Luke 15:7, I say unto you, that likewise joy shall be in heaven over one sinner that repenteth, more than over ninety and nine just persons, which need no repentance.

[17] Benjamin Jowett (1817–1893; *ODNB*, master of Balliol College), elected in 1870. 'On the Interpretation of Scripture' in *The Interpretation of Scripture and Other Essays* (1860): 'Read Scripture like any other book.' In 1855, JFS 'is reading Jowett's "Commentary on the Epistle to the Romans", and calls it a "kind, gentle Christian book"—far more orthodox than he can himself pretend to be'. 'Certain clergyman of the Church of England had discovered—what had been known to other people for several generations—that there were mistakes in the Bible. They inferred that it was desirable to open their minds to free criticism, and that the Bible, as Jowett said, should be read "like any other book". The result was the publication in 1860 of "Essays and Reviews".' (*Life* 123–4). JFS was to act as counsel in 1861 for one of the contributors, publishing *Defence of the Rev. Rowland Williams, D.D., in the Arches Court of Canterbury* (1862).

[18] Jeremiah 17:9, The heart is deceitful above all things and desperately wicked: who can know it?

40   ON THE NOVEL AND JOURNALISM

very wicked, the people are very wicked, the tradesmen of Jezreel are very wicked. In short (though, for obvious reasons, what I say has no reference to Ahab and Jezebel) ninety-nine out of every hundred of you are desperately wicked?' Indeed, our contemporary's clumsiness puts his loyalty on a par with his charity and his courage; for he has placed in the same category, and for the same reasons, our own Sovereign, and a man whose friendship even worldly-minded people accept with some reservations.

One of the most curious circumstances in the conduct of the *Record* is the nature of its guardianship over that select number which it thus marks off. It is petty, spiteful, narrow, reminding one of a beadle who is so occupied in rapping the knuckles of little boys who look off their prayer-books in church, that he has no time to listen to the sermon, and little inclination to join in the prayers. On the 18th of last month, the *Record* published a favourable review of the Life of Captain Vicars,[19] a pious and gallant officer killed in the trenches at Sebastopol. Very rightly considering such a subject most useful at the present time, the *Record* devotes something more than two columns to it; but the authoress was so unfortunate as to insert in her book several quotations from Tennyson's poems, and to call the love of a son for his mother one of 'the holiest affections of man's heart', going on, moreover, to say, that through the instrumentality of that affection Captain Vicars was led to higher affections still. This would not seem very heretical, but the *Record* considers that it 'sounds far more like the language of the Maurician[20] school than the language of the *New Testament*', and proceeds to say, that such feelings 'after all, have in them', as the Article expresses it, 'the nature of sin'. It is, perhaps, fortunate for a sinful world that we have not all been so successful as our monitor in mortifying the carnal virtues of the unregenerate heart. A little further on, a reference, on the part of Captain Vicars to Newton's *Cardiphonia*,[21] suggests to his critic a late lecture of Mr. Alford's,[22] and he concludes thus: 'Hedley Vicars had not so learned Christ. He knew his Bible experimentally'—plainly suggesting that Mr. Alford, who is dragged into the question without having the slightest connexion with it, is destitute of 'experimental'[23] acquaintance with the Bible. Those who know what this ignorance is understood to imply,[24] will shudder at the malignity which makes it the subject of an ill-natured sneer. A little further on, the authoress is reproved for quoting, not only the poet laureate,[25] but 'even Willis and Longfellow', who 'all belong to

[19] 'Railroad Bookselling' (*Sat. Rev.*, 31 Jan. 1857), p. 85.

[20] Not in *OED*. Frederick Denison Maurice (1805–1872; *ODNB*, Church of England clergyman and theologian), professor of literature and history at King's College, London. 'His personal charm was remarkable, and if Fitzjames did not become exactly a disciple he was fully sensible of Maurice's kindness of nature and loftiness of purpose. He held, I imagine, in a vague kind of way, that here might perhaps be the prophet who was to guide him across the deserts of infidelity into the promised land where philosophy and religion will be finally reconciled' (*Life* 62).

[21] John Newton (p. 38), *Cardiphonia, or, The Utterance of the Heart. In the Course of a Real Correspondence. By the Author of Omicron's Letters* (1781).

[22] Henry Alford (1810–1871; *ODNB*, dean of Canterbury and biblical scholar).

[23] *OED* Based on or derived from experience as opposed to mere testimony or conjecture. 1869 GOULBURN To bring myself and others to an experimental knowledge of God. *experimental religion*: practical experience of the influence of religion on the powers and operations of the soul. The Experimental Knowledge of Christ was notably preached by Thomas Boston (1676–1732; *ODNB*, Church of Scotland minister and theologian) and John Elias (1774–1841; *ODNB*, Welsh Calvinist Methodist minister).

[24] That is, no salvation.

[25] Alfred Tennyson, first Baron Tennyson (1809–1892; *ODNB*, poet), Poet Laureate 1850–92.

RELIGIOUS JOURNALISM

the pantheistic school of Parker and Emerson.'[26] A criticism about as just and as intelligible as it would be to say that they all embrace the 'heresies' of Dr. Newman and his brother the Professor.[27] 'Charity thinketh no evil.'[28] The *Record* thinketh nothing but evil. One would have supposed that the most insane and inveterate enmity could have seen no harm in Mr. Macaulay's statement that the excellent General Mackay[29] said on a particular occasion, 'God's will be done.'[30] But the *Record* has the microscopic eye[31] and acute proboscis which are characteristic of some of the less savoury parts of the insect creation. In a note on the passage, it says that the expression really was, 'The will of the Lord be done', and remarks that many minds will recognize 'the existence of God which will shrink from naming the Lord Jehovah';—obviously imputing to Mr. Macaulay disbelief of the Old Testament, because he substitutes one equivalent for another.

The way in which the *Record* treats the public in general combines all those qualities which common honour and good feeling repudiate. If any one wishes to see a specimen of the malignity which imputes motives and suggests accusations which it has neither the courage to make good, nor the modesty to retract—if he wishes to see the kindest actions vilified, the best intentions misrepresented, and women dragged before the public and loaded with coarse abuse—let him read the articles on the Nightingale Fund[32] which appeared in the *Record* between the 14th and the 28th of January last. Indeed, this 'religious' periodical exercises over society a kind of surveillance not unlike that which was once wielded by the *Age* and the *Satirist*.[33] We do not, of course, suppose that the *Record* trades in hush-money;[34] but we do say that it trades upon scandal, and has the hypocrisy to profess to do so upon religious grounds. Suppose we were to publish an account of the pursuits of all the persons connected with it. Suppose we were to say, Mr. A. is in the habit of going to sleep in church, whilst Mr. B. preaches sermons bought of Mr. C. at 2*s.* 6*d.* a set; Mr. D. beats his wife; Mr. E. drinks too much port wine; and it is a fact that when Mr. F. dined at Mr. G.'s, they passed all their time in talking scandal about Mrs. H. and Mr. J. Would our contemporary's just indignation be qualified by the reflection that our slanders were published upon religious grounds,

[26] Nathaniel Willis (1806–1867), American man of letters, colleague of Henry Wadsworth Longfellow (1807–1882). Theodore Parker (1810–1860), Unitarian, American abolitionist. JFS engaged often with him; for 'Theodore Parker on Slavery' (*Sat. Rev.*, 14 Nov. 1863), p. 178. Ralph Waldo Emerson (1803–1882), man of letters.

[27] Francis Newman (1805–1897; *ODNB*, classical scholar and moral philosopher). Unlike his Cardinal brother, he did not enter the Church of Rome; rather, remained Anglican when not agnostic.

[28] 1 Corinthians 13.5.

[29] Hugh Mackay (*c.*1640–1692; *ODNB*, army officer), who led the Scots Brigade in the Glorious Revolution, suffering defeat at Killiecrankie.

[30] Macaulay, *History of England*, chapter 1: 'Mackay sent a pressing message...but all was vain. "God's will be done", said the brave veteran.' Thomas Babington Macaulay, Baron Macaulay (1800–1859; *ODNB*, historian, essayist, and poet). 'Lord Macaulay' (*Sat. Rev.*, 7 Jan. 1860; *Essays* 97–106). *Life* 116: Macaulay 'had been a model held up to him from infancy, and to the last retained a strong hold upon his affectionate remembrance.'

[31] Pope, 'Why has not Man a microscopic eye? / For this plain reason, Man is not a Fly' (*An Essay on Man* i 193–4). The fly enjoys, too, a proboscis.

[32] Inaugurated in Nov. 1855, inviting subscriptions to further the Crimean initiatives and other aspirations of Florence Nightingale.

[33] Weekly scandal-sheets, 1825–43 and 1831–49.

[34] *OED* Money paid to prevent disclosure or exposure, or to hush up a crime or discreditable transaction. From 1709 STEELE.

42 ON THE NOVEL AND JOURNALISM

to show people that they ought not to put confidence in their teachers, and that we plastered them over with quotations from the Bible? Yet this is what they do week by week continually. On the 4th of last month they had to retract false statements which they had made about the private affairs of the Duchess of Buccleuch, and had the impudence to make their retraction the occasion of insulting comments upon the amount of the confidence existing between that lady and her husband. We have not forgotten how, some years since, they had the baseness to employ spies to find out whether grace was said at the table of a party of gentlemen with whose affairs they had as much to do as with the balances at their bankers'. They condescended to hunt up the affairs of the Oxford Union and the King's College Debating Society.[35] In many instances, they have published to all the world the fact of the participation of clergymen in amusements, the propriety of which is surely a general and an open question; and whilst they have thus sedulously polished, according to their view of polishing, the outside of the cup and the platter, what has been their course with respect to the weightier matters of the law? Who would ever read the *Record* to learn whether a war was just, a law wise, a Ministry worthy of confidence? The reader will find there comments on 'nude' (it is so indecent to say naked) statuary, enough to fill half the parsonages of the kingdom with prurient curiosity. He will find column after column of indignant dulness—about the Band in the Parks and the opening of the Crystal Palace on Sunday; but he will find very little worth reading on the great questions which involve the honour and conscience of the nation. If we turn to the Prophets or to the Gospels, we shall find that the sins which call down God's judgments on a people are injustice, bloodguiltiness,[36] hypocrisy, falsehood, tyranny. If we turn to those who have the sacred volume in these days most frequently on their lips, we shall find that war, pestilence, and famine are poured out upon us for what, at the worst, are no more than a few insignificant external symptoms of sin, and what are, in many cases, mere matters of arrangement or accident—such as the superscription of a coin, the endowment of a college, or the proposed opening of the British Museum on a Sunday.[37]

Of all the phases of modern journalism, there is none more detestable than that which would lead an ignorant reader to suppose that either religion is principally concerned with trifles and ceremonial observances, or that it is the awkward mask of hypocrisy and the convenient tool of malice.

---

[35] JFS had entered King's College, London, in Oct. 1845. 'There was a debating society, in which he first learnt to hear his own voice, and indeed became a prominent orator' (*Life* 61). On the college and its 'General Course of Study' (largely preparing for Oxford and Cambridge), *Life* 61 n.

[36] *OED* blood-guilt (the guilt of unrighteous bloodshed). From 1535 COVERDALE Psalm 51: Deliver me from bloodguiltiness, O God.

[37] Hansard reported the debate in the House of Commons, 21 Feb. 1856: 'Sir Joshua Walmsley rose to propose the following Resolution—That, in the opinion of this House, it would promote the moral and intellectual improvement of the working classes of this Metropolis if the Collections of Natural History and Art in the British Museum and the National Gallery were open to the public inspection after Morning Service on Sundays.' In due course, the House divided: Ayes, 48; Noes, 376: Majority, 328. 'The Sunday Papers' (*Sat. Rev.*, 19 Apr. 1856) follows here.

'The Sunday Papers'
(*Saturday Review*, 19 April 1856)

The Lord's Day Observance Society, founded 1831, sabbatarianly opposed Sunday papers, postal deliveries, and travel by train.[1] JFS opposed the Society. (He was pleased to collect his *Saturday Review* pieces as *Horae Sabbaticae*, 1892.) In 'The License of Modern Novelists' (*Edin. Rev.*, July 1857) p. 108, he judged that it was not for a novelist—particularly if he were Dickens—to select 'one or two of the popular cries of the day', for instance the Poor Laws or the observance of Sunday. JFS selects cries popular with him, any 'inclination to infer the insanity of a criminal from the mere atrocity of the crime' and any supposition as to 'the undue severity of country justices'.

The Sunday Papers

If the circulation of a newspaper, and the proportion which it bears to the whole extent of the intellectual interests of its readers, afford the true test of its importance, the Sunday papers are almost, if not quite, our most important journals. To a man who labours habitually with his head, Sunday is especially grateful as a day of mental rest. To sit with his family, to take a walk out of London—in some way or other to relieve the strain which has been applied all through the week to his nerves and to his brain—is one, at any rate, of the principal enjoyments which Sunday affords to people engaged in public or professional life. To labouring men an entirely different kind of relaxation is equally indispensable. A man who has passed six days in the week in carting parcels from one railway station to another, in unloading ships, in watching the wheels of a machine, or in any other mechanical occupation, finds far more relief on the seventh day in some kind of occupation which engages organs almost dormant during the rest of his life, than in anything which adds still more to the fatigue of muscles and sinews already overwrought. Go to Kew Gardens, to Richmond Park, to Wimbledon Common on a Sunday, and you will hardly fail to meet a certain number of gentlemen enjoying the fresh turf and fresh air on horseback or on foot; but if you look for the labouring population, you will find them smoking, talking, or reading the newspapers in tea-gardens or public-houses. It is the object of the Sunday papers to afford occupation

---

[1] Samuel Butler (1835–1902; *ODNB*, writer and artist). *The Way of All Flesh* (written 1873–84, pub. 1903), ch. XXII: 'I was there on a Sunday, and observed the rigour with which the young people were taught to observe the Sabbath; they might not cut out things, nor use their paintbox on a Sunday, and this they thought rather hard, because their cousins the John Pontifexes might do these things. Their cousins might play with their toy train on Sunday, but though they had promised that they would run none but Sunday trains, all traffic had been prohibited. One treat only was allowed them—on Sunday evenings they might choose their own hymns.'

44   ON THE NOVEL AND JOURNALISM

and amusement on these occasions; and he must be a very rigorous and a very unsympathetic critic who would condemn such an object as wrong. The mind of an uneducated man cannot be a blank—it cannot occupy itself for a whole day with devotional or theological meditation. As a matter of fact, even in those who observe the Sunday most rigidly, this is not the case; and why it should be wrong to recal to the mind by the medium of printed paper what it would not be wrong to recal by the medium of spoken words, we cannot imagine. No human being would hesitate to tell another on a Sunday that he had been present at a trial for murder on Friday, and it is altogether impossible to give any reason why it should be wrong to read what it is not wrong to hear. It is a common objection to these papers that they cause a great amount of Sunday labour; but the fact is not so. They are uniformly, we believe, printed and published on Saturday, and are only read on Sunday. The objection, at any rate, comes with a bad grace from those who read in a Monday's *Morning Herald* denunciations of Sunday amusements, probably written, and certainly printed, on Sunday afternoon and evening. For these reasons we cannot look upon the Sunday papers as a *malum in se*.[2] We think their object a good one, and if the execution were as good as the design, we should feel great pleasure in their success.

It cannot be doubted that, for good or for evil, their influence is enormous. *Lloyd's Weekly Newspaper* (made familiar to most of our readers by the instrumentality of defaced penny-pieces[3]), according to its own account, has a circulation of no less than 170,000—nearly three times as great as that of the *Times*. The *Dispatch*, the *News of the World*, and the *Weekly Times* are also to be met with in every town in England. Constituting, as they do, a great proportion of the reading of those who read little else, on the only day in the week on which they read anything, it is most important to ascertain what is the nature of the influence of these journals. Whether from the circumstance of their publication on Sunday—or from reminiscences of offences charged against some of them in former times—or simply from the jealousy of those who consider themselves the only authorized directors and instructors of poor people—it is certain that there is a general impression abroad that they are unfailing sources of furious political incendiarism,[4] and panders to all kinds of prurient curiosity. Our knowledge of the subject is not extensive enough to warrant a very positive opinion; but if we look at the last week's numbers of the four journals which we have mentioned, nothing can be more unlike the impressions which we get from the papers themselves than the expectations which the general notion to which we have referred would excite. The quality of the news, and the decorum with which it is selected, both appear to us to be unexceptionable. There is, as might have been expected, an absence of that class of intelligence which is essential to the weight and to the circulation of a daily paper— that is to say, home and foreign news, unattainable except at a great expense, and by means of an extensive connexion with persons who are in a position to communicate it. But, after all, the difference between knowing a thing on Monday and knowing it on Thursday—between reading it in the paper in which it first appears, and reading it in

---

[2] *OED* Something intrinsically evil or wicked. From 1623. JFS, 'The Case of William Dove' (*Sat. Rev.*, 26 July 1856): 'any solecism which is a *malum in se*. The *malum prohibitum* is the contract'.

[3] That is, as tokens, not coins. *Lloyd's Weekly Newspaper* had sold for tuppence (as against sixpence for the *Illustrated London News*), but avoiding stamp duty did not last.

[4] *OED figurative*, from 1674.

THE SUNDAY PAPERS

some other paper into which it is copied—however important to that small class to whom politics are a profession, is nothing to the enormous class to whom a newspaper is only a luxury. The political information contained in these papers, though neither exclusive nor very new, is most abundant, and affords a convincing proof of the interest which, happily for the nation, every class takes in public affairs. The manner in which the information is conveyed is also well worthy of observation. It is for the most part so closely packed as to be by no means very light reading. It is clearly intended for a quiet, serious, reflective class of men. The *Dispatch*, for example, contains four columns of foreign news, abridged from the morning papers, and similar abridgments, containing six and three and a half columns, respectively, of Parliamentary debates, and of the proceedings of the Crimean Military Commission. To these *Lloyd* adds an account of the diplomatic relations of the Mosquito Territory,[5] and a series of extracts from the leading articles of the daily papers upon such subjects as the Income-tax, the Austrian occupation of the Danubian Provinces, the Drainage of London, Education, the Management of the National Gallery, and the American question. Among the lighter subjects is a report of a curious meeting of swell-mobsmen,[6] held by Mr. Mayhew,[7] in which the various calamities attending their profession, and the difficulty of emerging from it when once entered, are set forth in a very curious and anything but offensive manner; and we have also, as might have been expected, a very full report of criminal proceedings, both at the assizes and before the police courts. Here, if anywhere, we should have met with prurience, if it had been characteristic of this class of journals. We have accordingly examined the papers in question with some care. In the *Weekly Times* there is not a single line that a lady might not read. In the *News of the World* there is a report of breach of promise case at Gloucester (more fully reported in the daily papers), to which those who consider an absolute ignorance of the existence of vice a good preservative of virtue might possibly object—though, if they did, their objection would exclude from their houses every paper containing news. In *Lloyd's Weekly Newspaper*, and in the *Dispatch*, a police case is reported, in about eight lines, with the utmost conciseness and propriety, which in the first is headed, 'Indecency properly punished', and in the second, 'A Beast'. This is all that these four papers contain which a man would feel inclined to skip if he were reading aloud to his wife or daughter. Surely, when we consider that hardly a session of the criminal courts takes place without the most shocking revelations of the evil which is in the world—and that during the week in question, not only the Assizes but the sittings of the Central Criminal Court, and of the Middlesex Quarter Sessions, were going on—the fact which we have mentioned is extremely creditable to the readers and to the conductors of the journals in question. Another illustration of the same point may be found in the brevity with which all these papers tell a story which would, some years ago, have filled many columns of every paper on every breakfast-table in the West End—the murder which took

---

[5] The territory of the indigenous Miskito people, from Honduras to Nicaragua (the 'Mosquito Coast').

[6] *OED swell mob*, a class of pickpockets who assumed the dress and manners of respectable people in order to escape detection. Hence swell-mobsman. *slang*. Now *obsolete* or *historical*. From 1836 MARRYAT. With 1851 MAYHEW Swell mobsmen, and thieves, and housebreakers.

[7] Henry Mayhew (1812–1887; *ODNB*, author and social reformer). *London Labour and the London Poor. A Cyclopaedia of the Condition and Earnings of Those that Will Work, Those that Cannot Work, and Those that Will Not Work* (1851).

46   ON THE NOVEL AND JOURNALISM

place at Islington some weeks since, and for which a miserable woman was sentenced to be hanged at the last Old Bailey sessions.

Of the leading articles of the Sunday papers we cannot speak so highly as of the news. Those of the *Weekly Times* please us best. They are quiet, sensible, and manly; and one of them, upon the numerous murders which have taken place of late, is extremely kindly and humane, though we cannot agree with the writer's theory of the uselessness of capital punishments, or sympathize with his inclination to infer the insanity of a criminal from the mere atrocity of the crime. *Lloyd's Weekly Journal* enjoys, as its title announces to the world, the doubtful advantage of the editorship of Mr. Douglas Jerrold.[8] Every one of its leaders bears traces of the fact. They have a strong family likeness to those dreary serious articles which are familiar to readers of *Punch*—articles which read like sermons which were originally unctuous, but which have had gall substituted for the unction, without however, entirely, removing all traces of the original condiment. They are a constant series of growls—growls at the 'Immaculate' (satiric inverted commas)[9] Peace, growls about the Jews, about 'respectable criminals', about Kossuth and the Austrian Concordat,[10] and about 'our Naval sham at Spithead'.[11] One characteristic sentence will illustrate the sort of writing to which we allude—we all know where endless columns of the same material may be had: 'Austria's coat is for the present white, white as her liver—who knows how soon it may be red, red as her crimes?'

The *Dispatch* contains articles which are historically curious. They remind us of a time when journalism was quite a different thing, and journalists quite a different class of people, from what they are now. There is about them an effort to be clever, a jauntiness, an *obligato* satire, which were common in leading articles when the writers laboured under the consciousness that, unless they could attract notice by some such contrivances, they stood little chance of being read. Our meaning may be gathered from the following example:

> It was the 5th of the present month,
> > Wearied with business, labouring at the oar,
> > Which thousands once fast chain'd to leave no more,[12]
> we fairly rebelled against the slavery of town life and city work, and, playing truant from our daily carking cares, snapped our fingers in their face, and, in the true spirit of an eminent *pococurante*,[13] exclaimed inwardly, 'A fico for the world and worldlings base!'[14] Between the hawthorn hedgerows just viridating into leaf, we emerged to buffet the bluff West wind over the downs, and sauntered through the fields by the footways. The lark was

---

[8] Douglas Jerrold (1803–1857; *ODNB*, playwright and journalist). JFS on 'Mrs. Caudle's Curtain Lectures' (*Sat. Rev.*, 1 Nov. 1856; p. 63), and on 'The Life of Douglas Jerrold' (*Sat. Rev.*, 15 Jan. 1859).

[9] *OED* Free from fault or flaw. (Chiefly in negative or ironical use.) From 1832.

[10] Lajos Kossuth (1802–1894; in power, 1848–49) led Hungary's struggle for independence from Austria. The Concordat of 1855, an agreement between the Holy See in Rome and the Austrian Empire as to the powers of the Catholic Church.

[11] The site of the annual Naval Review.

[12] 'Hackney'd in business, wearied at the oar / Which thousands, once fast chain'd to, quit no more'. The opening couplet of William Cowper's 'Retirement' (1782).

[13] *OED* A careless or indifferent person; one who shows little interest or concern. From 1762 STERNE.

[14] Pistol: 'A foutre for the world and worldlings base! / I speak of Africa and golden joys", *2 Henry IV*, V ii (Folio, *footra*; Quarto, *footre*). In *The Antiquary*, ch. xli, Walter Scott adopted Henry Bowdler's emendation: 'A fico for the world, and worldlings base, / I speak of Africa and golden joys!' (fico = a fig).

THE SUNDAY PAPERS 47

at heaven's gate, serenading his mate in the furrow; there had been a warm shower, and you could almost *see* the wheat grow. Everything was clothed in the green of spring, and the bees were already busy among the daffodils. It was high noon, the sun was bright, the ploughmen and bird-boys were sitting in the hedges, with their dinner on their knees, while wife and mother waited beside them to return with the emptied prandial vessels. Their horses, unyoked but in their harness, were browsing in the furrows, or pursuing their inquiries into the nosebags.

A man who knows that he has got things to say which his readers will care to hear, does not introduce an article about the undue severity of country justices with this kind of flourish of trumpets. He does not speak of hawthorns as 'viridating', nor does he call pots and pans 'prandial vessels' or quote 'a fico for the world', &c., or 'the lark at heaven's gate sings',[15] *apropos de bottes*.[16] The rest of the article is just what might have been expected from the beginning. It is all about the severity and cruelty of society against petty offenders, and is composed of such matter as the following:

> Lo, where the hunger-bitten wretch in the winter wind gathers a few sticks among the hedges to muster a dismal fire for her shivering little ones against the return of their over-laboured father, wet and hungry, from the gravel-pit or the road. 'Off with her to jail', says our law; drag her between policemen; disgrace her among her neighbours; never heed her screaming little ones or her husband's heart rankling with contempt of society and execration of its authority. See! young Ralph, crossing the fields by the footway, steps aside and pulls up a turnip or gathers a pea or bean-pod; pounce comes Policeman X, hauls him off to 'the Bench', and 'lags' him for fourteen days if it happen to be Justice A, or a month if it be the sterner B. The law of God says, 'Forgive, not seven times, but seventy times seven'; to society it calls, 'Let him that is guiltless cast the first stone'; to the sinner it gently murmurs, 'Go in peace, and sin no more!'

Why is everybody who steals sticks 'a hunger-bitten wretch?' Why is a turnip-stealer 'young Ralph?' Would the *Dispatch* wish an Act of Parliament to provide that, if any hunger-bitten wretch steals wood, he shall be acquitted, but that, if such thief is not a wretch, or, being a wretch, is not hunger-bitten (for the meaning of which, see the interpretation clause), he shall undergo so much imprisonment? It is quite in keeping with this, that the article contains a profuse display of legal learning. Amongst other things, the writer has discovered that a child of nine cannot 'be held to plead to any charge'. If he will look at *Russell on Crimes*,[17] i. 7, he will find that a child was condemned to be hanged at nine, and that another actually was hanged at ten. It is fair to say that, though this article occupies the most prominent place in the paper in which it appears, it is, beyond all comparison, the worst.

One unfailing element of the *Dispatch* is its correspondence. 'Publicola'[18] and 'Caustic' are names known in many quarters where the paper itself is not read. Last week, Publicola occupied a column and a-half in discussing the question of women's property, and Caustic devoted the same space to advocating the necessity of preparing for war in the time of peace. Caustic's letter strikes us as sensible enough, though there is throughout

---

[15] Song, *Cymbeline*, III iii.   [16] *as to boots*...(that is, to change the subject, bootlessly).

[17] Sir William Oldnall Russell (1784–1833; *ODNB*, legal writer and judge in India). *A Treatise on Crimes and Misdemeanours* (1819).

[18] The correspondent who adopted the name of the Roman dissident and later consul Publius Valerius Poplicola or Publicola ('cherisher of the people') who died in 503 BC.

48   ON THE NOVEL AND JOURNALISM

an anxiety to justify the indignant signature, which leads to a curious combination of the quietest substance with a somewhat ferocious phraseology. Publicola's subject is a very difficult and delicate one. He seems to us hardly to appreciate its difficulty, and we think that he might avoid such strange errors as the assertion that the Roman law prevails in the South of France, and the Code Napoleon in other parts of that country.

A curious feature in these papers is the 'Answers to Correspondents'. They are most numerous in the *Dispatch*. Some are certainly sufficiently quaint. What, for example, would Dr. Cumming[19] think of the following?—'Ezekiel must apply to the Secretary of State for Foreign Affairs'. Had 'Ezekiel' been inquiring about the restoration of the Jews? For the most part, however, they contain really very sensible advice, sometimes on questions of some difficulty: For instance, A.B. wants to know how he can find out whether a brother in New Zealand is alive or not, and is advised to 'write a letter to be left till called for at the Post Office, and advertise the fact in some New Zealand paper.' He could hardly have got more judicious advice, and the answer is not one which would immediately present itself. 'Raphael' receives the following reply: 'As to the value of the old historical female portrait we can venture no opinion.' A man must be in a curious condition, one would suppose, who can find no one more willing to advise him in such a matter than the editor of a newspaper. Some of the answers are leading articles in italics—what they can possibly be answers to, we cannot conceive. For example, a gentleman, called 'The Last of the Gallows', gets half a column of small type, and extremely bad grammar, about the execution of Bousfield;[20] but whether he wrote it himself, or wanted to know something to which it was a reply—and, if so, what his question was—we cannot conceive. The great mass of the questions are about legal matters; and we should think that the attorneys must view the advice-gratis columns of the *Dispatch* with very considerable disgust. It is of course impossible, without seeing the questions, to form an estimate of the correctness of the answers; but some of them relate to subjects of considerable intricacy. There is one in particular, beginning, 'The Vicar is wrong', on which a great deal might be said. We very greatly doubt whether the Vicar was not right; and we would refer the gentleman who wrote the answer, to *Taylor on Evidence*, p. 1156, and to the cases there cited.[21]

On the whole, we think that there is a very unjust prejudice against the Sunday press. Its character appears to us to be very creditable to the readers and conductors, and far from discreditable to the writers, of the papers in question. We are sure, at any rate, that it is most unfair to speak of these journals as if their influence was altogether bad, and their very existence a nuisance.

---

[19] John Cumming (1807–1881; *ODNB*, Presbyterian minister). JFS, 'Dr. Cumming' (*Sat. Rev.*, 14 June, 21 June 1856): 'the craving for excitement which leads many who consider theatres wicked, and novels "dangerous", to work up all history into a romance more false and more extravagant than any that issue from the pen of Mr. G. W. M. Reynolds [1814–79]...Dr. Cumming preaches as weekly novelists write.' *Life* 105: Dr. Cummings 'was then proving from the Apocalypse that the world would come to an end in 1865'; denunciations of him in *Sat. Rev.* provoked 'some danger from the law of libel', and something of an apology from JFS (*Sat. Rev.*, 14 Feb. 1857).

[20] William Bousfield confessed to killing, on 3 Feb. 1856, his wife and three children; he was executed 31 March 1856 (Calcraft, the hangman, being gruesomely incompetent).

[21] John Pitt Taylor (1811–1888), *Treatise on the Law of Evidence as Administered in England and Ireland* (1848). On JFS and *The Indian Evidence Act* (1872): 'One gentleman [John Bruce Norton], who had himself written upon the subject, remarked that it had been apparently constructed by going through 'Taylor on Evidence', and arbitrarily selecting certain portions' (*Life* 179).

'Our Civilization'
(*Saturday Review*, 28 June 1856)

The column 'Our Civilization' in *The Leader* was a forerunner of a mid-twentieth-century feature in the *New Statesman*, where mockery of national complacency was often complacent. (A bookful of 'This England', 1934–68, bore this out.) 'Since the law of England is so stupidly bigoted as to consider a man a moral agent...': JFS was to move from this sarcasm, voiced at 27, towards a less rigid confidence in moral agency. In *A General View of the Criminal Law of England* (1863), Chapter III was to be constituted of 'Responsibility. Madness and Sanity. Why Madness may rebut Presumption of Malice. Madness Matter of Evidence only. Effects of different Sorts of Madness as Evidence of Irresponsibility[1]–Delusion. Insane Impulses. Moral Insanity. Defence of present Law.' *A History of the Criminal Law of England* (1883) would continue this principled reluctant conceding. *Life* 118 gives an account of a case in which the conscience of JFS, for the defence, had found itself in two more-than-minds. 'He was tormented by the conflict between his compassion and his sense of justice.' The conflict was later to be compounded by the madness, and confinement to an asylum, of his son Jem, J. K. Stephen. Leslie Stephen was duly reticent: 'it gradually became manifest that he was suffering from a terrible disease', 'there was something strangely pathetic in his whole behaviour' (*Life* 300 n.; also Hermione Lee, p. xxvi, Introductory Essay). 'Madness Matter of Evidence only', as was everything for JFS. In these few pages: 'is not conclusive evidence of goodness, but it is some evidence of it', 'in the absence of very strong evidence to the contrary', 'So long as the evidence is *bonâ fide*'.

Our Civilization

The comparative atrocity of the various cants which are canted in this canting world has been a favourite subject of speculation. Without pretending to decide the question of precedence, we may be allowed to doubt whether one of the most offensive is not that which is appropriated to the denunciation of conventionalism and respectability.[2] A weekly paper distinguished not only by its ability, but by its indignation against the unfortunate bugbears in question, has for some time past allotted a considerable portion of its space to a kind of artistic Newgate Calendar, under the heading prefixed to this article.[3] 'Our Civilization' is denounced, week by week, as the mother of several columns of criminal intelligence in small print—the suggestion being that the orderly

---

[1] *OED* Not answerable for conduct or actions; exempt from or incapable of legal responsibility.

[2] JFS, 'Anti-Respectability' (*Cornhill*, 1863; *On Society, Religion, and Government* 112–23).

[3] *The Newgate Calendar; Comprising Interesting Memoirs of the Most Notorious Characters who have been Convicted of Outrages on the Laws of England since the Commencement of the Eighteenth Century; with Anecdotes and Last Exclamations of Sufferers.* Published from 1773. Prisoners were held at Newgate prison before public execution at Tyburn.

ON THE NOVEL AND JOURNALISM

surface of society is but an external covering, and that it serves only as a cloak for bruises, wounds, and putrefying sores.

We cannot deny—on the contrary, we have taken every opportunity of urging—that external decorum frequently covers the most awful abysses of wickedness, and that the age in which we live peculiarly needs to be occasionally reminded of the fact; but to represent 'Our Civilization' as mere hypocrisy is surely most unjust. An age in which professions of goodness are common, is probably one in which true professions are common as well as false ones. It does not follow that because knaves find it convenient to go to church, and subscribe to 'missionary objects',[4] public worship and public charity are the causes of knavery; and it is surely wrong to publish the scandals of the day in a form which makes them look like the premises of such a conclusion. Outward decorum certainly is not conclusive evidence of goodness, but it is some evidence of it. If we knew nothing at all of A and B, except that A paid his bills, taught his children their catechism, went to church on a Sunday, and was decent in his language—whilst B was addicted to profane swearing, was separated from Mrs. B, and not separated from Mrs. C—we should certainly not rush to the conclusion that A was a saint, but, in the absence of very strong evidence to the contrary, we should greatly prefer him to B. When we see sobriety, outward decency, self-restraint in a thousand forms, spreading over the surface of society, including even, as a general rule, its most corrupt members, we do not expect a millennium—we do not expect that there will be no crimes at all, or none of a very deep dye—but we simply infer that in some classes of society, some vices will be less common, and some virtues more common, than in times of greater licence. To us, therefore, the co-existence in any community of much villany with much decorum is anything but surprising; and we deem it a libel on society to publish long accounts of the villany as something distinctive of, and peculiar to, the decorum. An inference of this kind is, however, to a great extent, matter of opinion. So long as the evidence is *bonâ fide* brought forward in support of the charge, and not for a sinister purpose, its publication can give rise to nothing more than a difference of opinion. But to publish long accounts of crime and of criminals, professedly with the object of denouncing the hypocrisy of society, and exposing the weak points of 'Our Civilization', but really for the sake of pandering to that prurient curiosity about wickedness which is one of the lowest appetites of human nature, is a very unpleasant compound of immorality and hypocrisy.

We make these remarks in reference to the articles which have recently appeared in the *Leader*,[5] on the Life and Death of William Palmer.[6] We are sorry to see a journal, with which we are far from agreeing, but which has always seemed to us to be conducted with honesty and ability, adopt such a line of conduct. In its last number, the

---

[4] *OED* The end to which effort is directed. (As with 'objectives'.)

[5] *The Leader* (1850–60), weekly journal of 'Christian liberal' convictions, founded by G. H. Lewes and Thornton Leigh Hunt.

[6] William Palmer (1824–1856; *ODNB*, poisoner and physician). 'The Rugeley Poisoner' (pron. *roo-j-lee*; Staffordshire). 'Hanged in 1856 for murdering his friend John Cook by poison, apparently with a view to concealing his thefts from Cook to cover gambling debts' (*On Society, Religion, and Government* 11 n.) 'The Trial of William Palmer' (*Sat. Rev.*, 31 May 1856), expanded by JFS as one of the Cases that conclude *Gen. View 1863* (Oxford 304–28; also 205–7), *Gen. View 1890*, and *Hist. Crim. Law*. 'Deus Ultionum' (*Sat. Rev.*, 17 Oct. 1857; *On Society, Religion, and Government* 11–15): 'If Palmer was a free agent, it was right to hang him. If he could not help poisoning Cook, neither could we help hanging him.'

OUR CIVILIZATION

51

Leader allots to the description of Palmer's execution no less than six columns 'from our Special Correspondent'. The suggestion, we suppose, is, 'See what a rogue a man may be who goes to church, takes the communion, and subscribes to missionary objects.' Admitting the importance of teaching the world such a lesson, we would ask any person reading that article to say whether it is credible that it was written for the purpose of enforcing it? Is it not obvious that it was written solely, or at any rate principally, for the purpose of gratifying the prurient feelings of which we have already spoken? That Palmer was a most atrocious villain, most deservedly hanged, and that the world since his death numbers one scoundrel the less, seem to us to be the only essential points in the matter. The peculiar incidents of his ignominious exit from life can prove nothing at all—they are all comprehended in the three words, 'he was hanged'. Surely it is much better to leave them there than to expand them into one of those detailed descriptions by which Dickens and Victor Hugo have debauched the public mind—frightening people by minute particularity of description from doing what it is essentially necessary to do. We suppress a great many of the disgusting minutiae which our contemporary thinks it is so edifying to publish, merely remarking that the description of what passed between Palmer's appearance on the scaffold and his death occupies just nineteen lines of small print. We subjoin a small specimen to justify our criticism:

> The bell tolls on, sad, but inexorable. The people bend forward with throbbing hearts and straining eyes, and deem each minute an hour. The pigeons on the chimney-top plume their feathers, or murmur soft amorous notes—too low in the scale of creation to practise fraud, forgery, seduction, murder, and the other pastimes incidental to beings endowed with reason.
>
> And now the hangman grasps the rope—Palmer bends his head—the noose is slipped over—his face grows yet more ghastly...the cap, or white bag, is pulled over his head—the peak blows out from his chin by the violent and rapid respiration—another second, the bolt is drawn.

However edifying Palmer's death may have been as a commentary on 'our civilization', what can be the moral value of such a description? Why enable every ill-regulated fancy to gloat over the details of a fearful scene like this, in the same spirit in which it would gloat over the nasty mysteries of Eugène Sue or Victor Hugo? Actually to witness the execution would, we have little doubt, have a far less injurious effect. Indeed, we can conceive that, to many minds, that rude decisive announcement of the moral indignation of society against a murderer might be salutary; but to transfer to paper a crowd of petty details, which ninety-nine spectators out of a hundred would overlook in the absorbing horror of such a spectacle, is to deprive the punishment of all its awful significance, and to degrade it into a sort of dirty luxury. This, however, offensive as it is, is not the most offensive part of the article in question. We have a long description of Palmer's person, of the appearance of his body after death, of the 'blue mark' left by the rope, and the different changes in the colour of the hands. Surely all this can have nothing to do with 'our civilization'. Such details might be in their place in a book of medical jurisprudence, but how do they illustrate the peculiar state of English society? They may gratify the propensities of a certain unfortunately large class of readers; but, revolting as they are, they are doubly revolting in a paper which puts them forward with a claim to be doing a sacred duty by society. Our contemporary will find it easier

ON THE NOVEL AND JOURNALISM

to dispute the especial authority than to deny the good sense of the injunction not to make a mock at sin[7]—that is, not to make it matter of amusement or enjoyment, and to avoid dwelling, or encouraging others to dwell, upon whatsoever things are unlovely, whatsoever things are impure, whatsoever things are of bad report.[8] We all know that there are very bad men in the world, and it may sometimes be well to remind us of the fact; but when we find many columns filled with all sorts of details like those which we have quoted, it is difficult not to suspect the motives which prompted the despatch of a 'special correspondent' to Rugeley, commissioned to collect and publish all the flying rumours of the neighbourhood about the number of women whom Palmer seduced, or the number of forgeries which he committed. Nor do we think that, because a man has been hanged for one murder and indicted for two others, a journalist has any right—for the sake of throwing imputations upon 'our civilization'—not only to assert that he was guilty of all the murders of which he was accused, but to insinuate that he was guilty of twelve others also—not to speak of forgery, adultery, robbery, and theft in all their forms. If the commission of crimes like these is to be made the ground of an accusation against society at large, it should at least be proved in the first place that they really were committed. 'Our civilization' ought not to be left at the mercy of every penny-a-liner[9] who can give a Dickenesque[10] description of an execution, and pick up the gossip of a country town.

The most curious proof of the bad moral effect of such publications is to be found in the writer himself. Speaking of Palmer's phrenological[11] development, he informs us that 'it was physically impossible for him ever to have been a good man.' 'He was organized to care for nothing but himself.' It is well for society that most men are so 'organized'[12] as to hang gentlemen whose peculiar organization leads to such results; but the 'organization' of the writer in the *Leader* is not of this mould. He thinks that Palmer ought not to have been hanged, but to have been punished on scientific principles. We can only do justice to the proposal by quoting it:

> Let us suppose that, instead of being strangled, Palmer had been placed at hard work in public, where he could have been frequently and freely seen; always under the eye of some intelligent and active-minded man, who could have learned from him his past life. Let us suppose that the circumstances attending his imprisonment should have been such as to induce him to confess; and that his labour might have been modified according to his conduct. Let us suppose also that the proceeds of his labour should be devoted, in some

---

[7] Proverbs 14:9, Fools make a mock at sin.

[8] Philippians 4:8, Whatsoever things are true, whatsoever things are honest, whatsoever things are just, whatsoever things are pure, whatsoever things are lovely, whatsoever things are of good report; if there be any virtue, and if there be any praise, think on these things.

[9] *OED* A writer for a newspaper or journal who is paid at a penny a line, or at a low rate (usually implying one who manufactures 'paragraphs', or writes in an inflated style so as to cover as much space as possible), a poor or inferior writer for hire; a hack-writer for the press (*contemptuous*). The earliest citation associates JFS's usual suspects: 1834 H.AINSWORTH Penny-a-liners and fashionable novelists. (With 1840 THACKERAY.)

[10] *OED* has this from JFS as its only instance, giving first place to 'Dickensesque'. ('Dickensian' from 1888.)

[11] *OED* The scientific study or theory of the mental faculties...the study of the external conformation of the cranium as an index. From 1815. 1846 POE The forehead, phrenologically, indicates causality and comparison, with deficient ideality. 1870 DICKENS the phrenological formation of the backs of their heads.

[12] JFS ignores the word's established medical sense, *OED pathology* conversion into living tissue (the 'organization' of a tumour, 1804, or of a thrombus, 1873).

OUR CIVILIZATION

indirect way, to compensate for the injuries that he had occasioned—paid, for example, towards a charitable fund in the neighbourhood distinguished by his crimes; those crimes being commemorated by the fact of the annual payment.

We wonder that our contemporary does not expatiate on the advantages of a Palmer scholarship in Toxicology at St. Bartholomew's Hospital, or a Palmer prize essay—the prize to be delivered by the founder, with an appropriate speech. Indeed, in the same article, some considerations of the kind are suggested:

> Homœopathists tell us that by a peculiar handling of drugs, their virtues can be brought out into much greater activity. The preparation of the human body by one drug will render another much more effective. This is well known in the ordinary practice of curative medicine, and Palmer, who was so earnest a student in anti-curative medicine, had probably tested the principle in that branch also. How much light could he have thrown upon the weapons by which the jealous wife, the wearied husband, the greedy heir, or the speculator in insurance, can work out his ends. Far more instructive would it have been for the world, if, instead of bringing his epic to a sudden conclusion before the gaol at Stafford, he had been made to work out another volume of autobiography in the presence of the public, while contributing from time to time materials for a retrospective volume.

It is all of a piece. Palmer's 'organization' is a curious one, and leads him to do odd things; and since the Government so far neglects its duty as to prefer ignominiously expelling him from human society to making him a curious study for the benefit of toxicological and psychological science—since the law of England is so stupidly bigoted as to consider a man a moral agent, and not a more or less cleverly constructed machine—since people have an obstinate prejudice against what they absurdly call flattering a criminal's vanity by making him a show and a study, and prefer getting rid of him in a summary manner—what can we do better than send a 'special correspondent' to cull all the delicacies of the gallows? Let us measure Palmer's stature, count his struggles, describe, in a picturesque manner, the crowd, the gallows, and the hangman; and let us frame the whole picture in a pastoral description of the streets and markets of Stafford, for the delight of our readers—for the extension of the circulation of our paper—and for the utter confusion of that transparent sham, 'Our Civilization!'

'Newspaper English'
(*Saturday Review*, 9 August 1856)

OED has as its earliest citation, late in the day, 1888 *Harper's Mag*. The phrase 'newspaper English' has come to have a significance which is not flattering to newspaper.

Newspaper English

Many of our readers must have observed the greatly increased taste for fine language which has become apparent of late years amongst uneducated or half-educated people. Of the many symptoms by which a gentleman may be recognised, none is more certain than his habitual plainness of speech. There is a large class of words which shopkeepers and bagmen[1] use without any particular affectation, but simply because they think it a proof of education and good manners—just as they say 'Sir' or 'Mr.' oftener than people of higher rank. A friend of ours once heard the following conversation in the commercial room of a country inn: 'Sir, have you visited the Exhibition of the Industry of all Nations?'[2]—'I have taken an opportunity of doing so, sir, and was deeply gratified by what I remarked.'—'May I ask, sir, what it was that principally attracted your attention?'—'The specimens of Manchester cottons and the statue of Godfrey of Bullion.'[3]—'Who, sir, was Godfrey of Bullion?'—'Godfrey of Bullion, sir, was the party who placed himself at the head of those parties who proceeded from France with a view to liberate the Holy Land from the other parties who held it—the—the—. It is a singular fact, that I am at present unable to recal the appellation which those parties selected.' After some more conversation in the course of which one of these Euphuists[4] asked the other whether *Jacob Faithful*[5] was 'a book of fiction or a narrative of fact', they parted, as they expressed it, 'to retire to the embraces of Morpheus.'

The harm done by this kind of folly is greater than might be supposed at first sight. It induces vagueness and inaccuracy of thought. The jury which recommended Dove[6]

---

[1] *OED* A commercial traveller, whose business it is to show samples and solicit orders on behalf of manufacturers, etc. (Dickens makes much of the 'Tale told by a Bagman' in *Sketches by "Boz"*, 1836.)

[2] The Great Exhibition of the Works of Industry…(1851), at the Crystal Palace. JFS, 'The Crystal Palace Frauds' (*Sat. Rev.*, 8 Nov. 1856).

[3] Godfrey of Bouillon, leader of the first Crusade.

[4] *OED* An imitator of the style of expression characteristic of Lyly's *Euphues*; one whose writing or speech is characterized by Euphuism. From 1820 SCOTT There he found the euphuist in the same elegant posture.

[5] 1834, by the author of *Peter Simple*. Frederick Marryat (1792–1848; *ODNB*, naval officer and novelist).

[6] 'The Case of William Dove' (*Sat. Rev.*, 26 July 1856). Further, *Gen. View 1863* (Oxford 328): 'On the 16th July, 1856, William Dove was indicted at York for the murder of his wife, Harriet Dove, and, after a trial before Baron Bramwell, which occupied four days, was convicted. His case is remarkable, as an illustration of the practical application of the principles of law relating to the criminal responsibility of madmen discussed

to mercy would never have stultified themselves as they did if they had not been able to shelter their folly under the unmeaning phrase, 'defective[7] intellect'—just as Westron's[8] jury talked nonsense about his 'hereditary predisposition to insanity.' A considerable curtailment of the nonsense which infests the world would be effected by the disuse of the 'great swelling words'[9] which enable so many people to talk about what they do not understand. The origin of this kind of language is easily detected. Our intelligent middle classes are not famous for extensive reading, and it is easy to observe in their dialect, whenever it becomes at all pronounced, traces of the fact that they form their style on the newspapers, and more especially on their penny-a-lining department.

We have frequently had occasion to speak of the style and character of 'Our Own Correspondent', but that great man's influence can never be fully understood until his peculiar position, as head of an extensive and influential profession, is properly recognised. We all know what the attorney-general or archbishop of correspondents can do, but we do not think that the influence of the junior members of the body which he represents is fully understood. The Israelites, when called upon to furnish a maximum of bricks, and supplied with only a minimum of straw,[10] are a type of the 'gentleman connected with the press' who has to fill his two or three newspaper columns with an account of the sayings and doings at some political meeting or other public ceremony. A man with a slight education, a fluent pen, and a certain amount of natural shrewdness, is sent off, on no notice at all, to make an amusing story out of an affair of the special purpose of which he has no more conception than he has of Hebrew. He describes a review at Spithead on Monday, a review at Aldershot[11] on Tuesday, a fête at the Crystal Palace on Wednesday, an agricultural meeting on Thursday, an Administrative Reform Association[12] dinner on Friday, and an execution on Saturday,

---

in a preceding chapter...The jury returned the following verdict: "Guilty, but we recommend him to mercy on the ground of his defective intellect." He was sentenced to death, and executed at York in pursuance of his sentence.' Note by K. J. M. Smith (*Gen. View 1863* 328): 'Comparing the *General View*'s and *History*'s [*Hist. Crim. Law*'s] analyses of *Dove* reveals a developed, more sophisticated understanding of the insanity defence in the later work. Whereas the *General View* (334–6) appears to assert the unconnected nature of cognitive and volitional impairment, the *History* (435) reflects Stephen's recognition of the possible interlinked quality of cognitive and volitional deficiencies and a widening of the scope of the M'Naughten rules.'

[7] *OED specifically* Mentally defective. (But the earliest citation is 1898.)

[8] Charles Westron, Feb. 1856, at the Old Bailey, the murder of George Waugh: 'GUILTY.—Recommended to mercy by the Jury on account of a strong predisposition to insanity. Aged 25.—DEATH recorded.' JFS's wording 'hereditary predisposition to insanity' is not to be found in the Proceedings. On this case among others, and contrasting with JFS's position, J. G. Davey, 'On the Plea of Insanity in Criminal Cases' (*Association Medical and Surgical Journal*, 1 Mar. 1856).

[9] 2 Peter 2:18–19, For when they speak great swelling words of vanity, they allure through the lusts of the flesh.

[10] Exodus 5:6–8: And Pharaoh commanded the same day the taskmasters of the people, and their officers, saying, Ye shall no more give the people straw to make brick, as heretofore: let them go and gather straw for themselves. And the tale [*OED* the number, all told], of the bricks, which they did make heretofore, ye shall lay upon them; ye shall not diminish ought thereof: for they be idle.

[11] Correcting *Sat. Rev.*, 'Aldershott'. In 1854, with the Crimean War, Aldershot Garrison in Hampshire was established as the first permanent training camp for the British Army, increasing Aldershot's population from 875 in 1851, to more than 16,000 by 1861 (about 9,000 from the military).

[12] From 1854 the Association (scrutinizing the Crimean War) dedicated itself to reforming army and government on principles different from those of the Circumlocution Office. JFS attacks the Association, and Dickens's association with it, in 'The *Edinburgh Review* and Modern Novelists' (18 July 1857), p. 133.

56   ON THE NOVEL AND JOURNALISM

in the profoundest ignorance of military or naval warfare, hydraulics, agriculture, politics, and mechanics; and yet he leaves on the minds of his readers a wonderful impression of his extraordinary vivacity and deep information. As an irreverent critic once said of a brilliant reviewer, his articles are worth reading twice 'to see the dodge of them'. They are all got up on the same principle, and sustained by the same artifices. On some future occasion we may perhaps direct our readers' attention to some of the more remarkable species of this genus of writers; but at present we confine ourselves to the manner in which, from the necessities of the case, they are obliged to corrupt the English language.

One of the indispensable requisites of this style of writing is a lax phraseology—something which commits the person who uses it to as few facts, and therefore lays him open to as few contradictions, as possible. It is a great art to be able to make a number of statements without committing oneself to a single fact; and the best way of doing this is to employ words which have no precise meaning, rather than those which have. We have already shown how useful this art is to juries in wording recommendations to mercy. We have little doubt that those who sit upon them learn it from penny-a-liners. A gentleman of the class in question not long since delighted the readers of the *Times* by an account of the meeting (of course he called it 'gathering', in inverted commas) at Mr. Mechi's farm at Tiptree, in Essex. His bulletin is full of such phrases as these—'practical agriculturists', 'liberal application of capital', 'national and adequate recognition'; and, amongst other things, it contains the following curious remark: 'A soil of this description precludes the operation of atmospheric changes, essential to a healthy and abundant vegetation.' To use such phrases as 'men actually employed in farming', or 'spending a great deal of money', would look tame by the side of the first two phrases which we have copied; whilst the third and fourth are not less remarkable for their want of definite meaning than for their extreme grandeur. We may take the following as another example of the same thing. Mr. Mechi, we are told, exhibited a machine for bringing rockets to 'the part of a beach most advantageous for effecting a communication' with wrecks. If the writer had said, 'from which the wreck might be reached most easily', he would have missed an opportunity of using words of Latin origin where plain English would have done equally well, and of employing fifteen syllables where seven would have been enough. It is a commonplace thing to speak of a 'dangerous habit'; but who can refuse to shudder at hearing that 'a practice obtains replete with danger to the public?' To mention the date of the building of the Hôtel de Ville at Brussels would require some knowledge, and might look pedantic; but it gives a delightful tone of taste to an article about the Belgian fêtes to allude to 'that renowned monument of mediaeval architecture'. A 'bloody battle' is coarse—an 'ensanguined battle' interesting. Anybody could have said that there were no beds to be had at Southampton the night before the naval review; but no one but a writer in the *Times* could have told us that on that night many persons were unable to take 'horizontal refreshment'.

We must not, however, suppose that the penny-a-lining principle affects only the words used. It has quite as strong an influence on the style. A certain jaunty affectation of ease, the constant introduction, *apropos de bottes*, of quotations or odd stories, a few withering sarcasms at the standing objects of the attacks of the newspaper in which the article appears, a ludicrous exaggeration of minute details, and a sort of affectation of

NEWSPAPER ENGLISH

omniscience are amongst its most characteristic features. On the 31st of last month, an article appeared in the *Times*, on a Review at Aldershot, which curiously exemplifies these peculiarities. The writer begins by saying that it was fine weather, and very hot, and he does it in the following elegant style: 'Nothing could exceed the beauty of the weather. The heat, no doubt, was occasionally oppressive, but the sky was *as blue as an amethyst*' (? red cornelian), 'and not one wandering cloud interposed between the sun and his nobility.' What is the sun's nobility, and how could you get between it and him? 'In fact, it was one of those glorious days when, to use the expressive phrase of an Oriental writer' (we should like to know who he is), "the green blood dances in the veins of the rose-trees", and you can almost fancy that you see the corn-fields growing.'[13] Nine lines and a half at 1½*d.*[14] are—the established newspaper phrase once dearly beloved by *Punch* would be, 'according to Cocker"[15]—1*s.* 1½*d.*, or just the price of a box of quack pills, including the stamp; and we think the information is dear at the price. After this ingenious and rather expensive exordium, comes the business of the day. We are introduced to certain stables, which, 'at first sight, remind the spectator of the ingenious little domicile improvised by Robinson Crusoe', and which supply the writer with an opportunity for displaying much virtuous indignation about Lord Lucan and Sir Richard Airey.[16] After a time, we come upon a criticism of the arrangements for spectators, which gives our friend an opportunity of mentioning the exclusion of 'the great body of the public—they of whom it has been proudly said that they are the true source of all legitimate power', and of remonstrating in a characteristic style about the rough manners of some 'fierce trooper who, flourishing his polished sabre in the air, threatens to cut them ["us" and others] off in the flower of their days unless they at once betake themselves to some remote region, from which the soldiers, like Shakspeare's famous samphire gatherer, look "no bigger than their heads".'[17] There is an amusing *naïveté* in the next sentence—'And the worst of it is, that you have no chance against such an antagonist.'

Of course we do not expect high literary excellence in reports which are necessarily written in haste; but we have a right to criticize elaborate and systematic offences against good taste and common sense. We seriously believe that the flashy, jaunty style of newspaper accounts of ordinary occurrences has a good deal to do with the preva- lence of similar faults in writings of much higher pretension. It is a great merit to be able to tell a plain story in a plain manner, and no one knows so well as those who see much of the current literature of the day how rare a merit it is. The style of newspaper

---

[13] 'Newspaper English', p. 54: 'you could almost *see* the wheat grow'.

[14] One shilling penny-ha'penny. 'Our Civilization' p. 47 for *penny-a-liner*; twelve pence (*d.*) to the shilling (*s.*).

[15] *OED* By or in accordance with strict rule or calculation. From 1818, with 1861 HUGHES *Tom Brown at Oxford*: 'So you ought to be, according to Cocker, spending all your time in sick rooms.' 'According to who?' 'According to Cocker.' 'Who is Cocker?' 'Oh, I don't know; some old fellow who wrote the rules of arith- metic, I believe; it's only a bit of slang.' JFS reviewed (*Edin. Rev.*, Jan. 1858, not signed) *Tom Brown's Schooldays* (By an old boy. 1857).

[16] George Charles Bingham, third earl of Lucan (1800–1888; *ODNB*, army officer), one of the senior officers responsible for the charge of the Light Brigade. Sir James Talbot Airey (1812–1898; *ODNB*, army officer), assistant quartermaster-general in the Crimean War. On which, 'Woods *v.* Russell' (*Sat. Rev.*, 19 Jan. 1856), p. 52.

[17] *King Lear*, IV v, Edgar imagining Dover Cliff: 'Half way down / Hangs one that gathers samphire: dreadful Trade: / Methinks he seems no bigger than his head.'

reporters is imitated by hundreds of persons who have not the same excuse for adopting it. A newspaper must be read. It must also be read on the day of publication, and in order to attain that object, great part of it is always written in a vulgar, garish style. Such artifices as these are mere bids for popularity; and although, in so far as they merely affect more or less the circulation of the paper in which they appear, they may be sufficiently unimportant, they become a serious evil when they infect our literature and enfeeble our every-day language.

'The Enigma' (excerpt)
(*Saturday Review*, 30 August 1856)

JFS's review of this novel (by 'An Old Chronicler') opened: 'We wish people would leave off writing novels about the origin of evil.' At the Apostles in Cambridge, JFS considered it 'impossible to frame a satisfactory hypothesis as to the origin of evil' (*Life* 73).

The Enigma (excerpt)

There is no particular harm in the *Enigma*. It is in no respect an offensive book, but we have hardly ever seen one in which the powers of the writer were so completely and ludicrously misconceived. We have noticed it principally because it affords a curious example of a very common mistake. There never was an age in which there was so much novel writing, and so much theological speculation, as there is in our own. As soon as any one has gone through any religious experience which leaves an impression on his mind, he—or more frequently she—makes it into a novel, on the principle that it cannot be uninteresting to others to read about anything which it was so deeply interesting to feel. The first requisite to a good novel is that the author should fully understand, and be master of, the matter on which he is going to write; and this can never be the case with religious experiences. The principles upon which they depend are so deep, so mysterious, so connected with considerations of all kinds, that very few persons indeed, however deeply they may feel them, can write about them without exposing themselves. 'He is in heaven, and thou art on earth, therefore let thy words be few'[1]—this is no less true as a canon of criticism than in its original application. This is more particularly true for female novelists. Quick, minute observation and representation of the ordinary affairs of life, is their *forte*—the inculcation of broad principles is apt to be their foible. So long as Miss Brontë, Mrs. Gaskell, Miss Yonge, or Miss Edgeworth confine themselves to describing what they have seen, they are amongst our very greatest writers; but when they come to draw or to insinuate conclusions as to broad general principles, we always regret that they should have left their proper sphere. *Ruth*, for example, and *Mary Barton*, are exquisite novels, but they prove nothing at all, though we think their authoress intended that they should. *Jane Eyre* and *Shirley* are works of genius, but we think that they suffer, both artistically and morally, from some of the discussions introduced into them. Miss Austen has always seemed to us far the greatest of female novel writers, precisely because there is nothing at all in the nature of a

---

[1] Ecclesiastes 5:2, Be not rash with thy mouth, and let not thine heart be hasty to utter any thing before God: for God is in heaven, and thou upon earth: therefore let thy words be few.

principle, or a speculation, or a moral, from one end of her books to the other. They are all pure representations of the life with which she was familiar—all the principles are assumed, and the reader is not annoyed by their elaboration or illustration. There is no indication, however, in the *Enigma* of powers which would place the authoress in the class of writers to which we have referred. The novel, as a novel, is poor—as a theological tract it is bad.

'The Green Hand' (excerpts)
(*Saturday Review*, 4 October 1856)

Captain Frederick Marryat (1792–1848) had set *Mr Midshipman Easy* (1836) during the Napoleonic wars. (In the twentieth century C. S. Forester and Patrick O'Brian were to set their novels in the same wars and waters.) George Cupples (1822–1891), Scottish journalist and novelist, has his hero 'go aboard a frigate to cruise round St. Helena to prevent Napoleon from escaping' (JFS). Dr. Johnson had been suspicious of literary recourse to sea-going terms, although 'Dryden was of opinion that a sea-fight ought to be described in the nautical language' (*The Lives of the Most Eminent English Poets*, ed. Roger Lonsdale, 2006, ii 133).

The Green Hand (excerpts)*

Philosophers have observed, as Sir Archibald Alison[1] would say, that men have a natural propensity to read novels. To this we may add the further observation, that landsmen have an especial propensity to read nautical novels. Such works possess not only the obvious charm of strange adventure, but the great advantage of a machinery by which the most unexpected results may be brought about without shocking the reader by any violent improbability. To a person who knows nothing about the sea, it is easy enough, by a proper use of technicalities, to make it seem the most natural thing in the world that a brig should take a line-of-battle ship, or go to the bottom and come up again, or sail straight upon a rocky coast and get no harm, or do anything else which might at first sight seem strange. When, for example, we read that 'she was topping the heavy seas as they rose with a long floating cleave, that carried her counter fairly free of the after-run, though nearly right before the wind', while 'the mainboom had been guyed over to the lee quarter', &c. &c., we feel as if we were listening to a magical incantation. For aught we know, it may be perfectly right that, after much other cunning of the same kind, the schooner in question should (as far as we can understand) turn over on one side—that the naval lieutenant should, 'as if by instinct', walk along the other, outside the bulwarks, to 'cut the lanyards of the shrouds and let the mainmast go', whilst the Byronic Jones 'eases the helm down to leeward'; and we participate, without much understanding it, in the delight of the whole party when 'the main staysail blows inway to leeward out of the bolt ropes', and everything comes right again as if by

---

* *The Green Hand: a Sea Story. Being the Adventures of a Naval Lieutenant.* By George Cupples. London: G. Routledge and Co., 1856.

---

[1] See p. 86.

62 ON THE NOVEL AND JOURNALISM

miracle. The occasional glimpses of a meaning sustain our interest, whilst the long intervals of obscurity afford an excuse for our easy acquiescence in improbabilities.

It is a long time since we have seen a more pleasantly prepared mess[2] of this kind than the *Green Hand*. It is, in our judgment, as good in its own way as almost any of Fenimore Cooper's novels, and not much inferior to the best of Captain Marryat's. We say 'in its own way', for a book of mere amusement is not, of course, to be tried by a very high standard.

* * *

To such a story there can, of course, be but one termination, which we may leave to our readers' experience. If they want to find out what was the mystery of the wonderful history—who Ugly Harry was—why Mr. Jones remarked, 'lying old Bluewater, you can't wash it out'—why Mr. Collins was called the Green Hand—or why, when you have a mad captain, lubberly officers, a semi-mutinous crew, and a barbarous coast to leeward, with the barometer suddenly fallen to 27°, an 'ox-eye' 'high over toward the ship's larboard bow', and a tornado obviously coming on, you are to take the helm, and tell a man in whom you have confidence to 'go and manage to get a pull taken on the starboard brace'—if they wish to learn the key to these and other pleasant riddles, we can only recommend them to expend eighteenpence on the *Green Hand* the next time they take a railway journey.[3] It is not a work of genius, but it is much the best sea story we have seen of late. The tale, as our readers will see, is not one which pretends to be anything more than a vehicle for an immense deal of adventure.

[2] *OED* A prepared dish (of a specified kind of food).
[3] 'Railroad Bookselling' (*Sat. Rev.*, 31 Jan. 1857), p. 85.

'Mrs. Caudle's Curtain Lectures' (excerpts) (*Saturday Review*, 1 November 1856)

Comic journalism by Douglas Jerrold (see p. 154). JFS, later reviewing *The Life and Remains of Douglas Jerrold*, by his Son, Blanchard Jerrold (*Sat. Rev.*, 15 Jan. 1859), was to make a concession of a sort (*reculer, pour mieux sauter*). 'In justice to Mr. Jerrold we ought to say that, though he was a man of most unbalanced mind, and entirely at the mercy of feeling and impulse, his feelings were at times very healthy, and were frequently expressed in a very forcible and even pathetic manner. In a letter to Mr. Dickens there occurs the following remark, which is not only very true, but tender and pathetic: "*Punch*, I believe, holds its course. Nevertheless I do not very cordially agree with its new spirit. I am convinced the world will get tired (at least I hope so) of this eternal guffaw about all things. After all life has something serious in it. It cannot be all a comic history of humanity. Some men would, I believe, write a comic Sermon on the Mount. Think of a comic history of England, the drollery of Alfred, the fun of Sir Thomas More, the farce of his daughter begging the dead head and clasping it in her coffin on her bosom. Surely the world will be sick of this blasphemy." Mr. Dickens's answer is equally honourable to him: "Anent the comic and similar comicalities, I feel exactly as you do. Their effect upon me is very disagreeable. Such joking is like the sorrow of an undertaker's mute reversed, and is applied to serious things with the like propriety and force." Unfortunately for both the correspondents, their notion of serious writing hardly went beyond sarcasm and sentimentality. They have done more in their respective lines to enervate their readers, and to throw discredit upon all the stronger faculties of the mind, than any other pair of English writers.'

Mrs. Caudle's Curtain Lectures (excerpts)*

Several of the more successful writers in *Punch* have been lately republishing their contributions in a collected form. It is a strange comment on the whole character of English wit at the present day that there should be comic newspapers at all; and it is perhaps a still stranger one that the writers in them should voluntarily submit their works to such an ordeal. It is not less unfavourable to wit to be pledged to joke about everything than it would be unfavourable to conjugal affection for a man to be under a solemn obligation to be always making love[1] to his wife; and the deliberate collection and republication of a series of jokes produced under such circumstances is in almost every case a mistake of the same kind, but of an infinitely higher degree. The caricatures in *Punch* are often, perhaps generally, excellent; but the letterpress is written

---

* *Mrs. Caudle's Curtain Lectures.* By Douglas Jerrold. London: Bradbury and Evans, 1856.

[1] *OED* to pay amorous attention; now more usually, to copulate. (JFS, then, the former.)

64 ON THE NOVEL AND JOURNALISM

under an inexorable necessity of making the British middle classes laugh—an undertaking generally neither easy nor graceful. Those classes have many admirable qualities, but they are certainly not elegant triflers.

* * *

The various collections of papers contributed to *Punch* which have been republished by their different authors, bear evident traces of the conditions under which they were originally produced. With hardly an exception, they are the smallest of small wit on the narrowest possible subjects. Even Mr. Thackeray is unable, under such conditions, to write like a man of genius. The *Snob Papers*[2] and *Jeames' Diary* are directed at such small follies, and are overlaid with such glaring ornament, that it is hardly possible to believe that their author should have been the most profound of modern satirists, and far the greatest of living novelists. If this is true of Mr. Thackeray, it is far more true of Mr. Douglas Jerrold.[3]

* * *

Passing from artistic to moral considerations, we cannot speak very highly of Mr. Jerrold's performance. The wit, such as it is, is of a very dismal and unpleasant kind. To read a long series of fretful, teasing lectures addressed by a wife to a husband, which have no other recommendation about them than their studied want of logic and common sense, can hardly be considered excellent fooling. Perhaps no greater calamity could befal a man than to marry a woman so bitter, so selfish, so monstrously absurd and cruel as the heroine of this singular monologue; and we confess that we do not exactly appreciate the joke of specifying to all the world the details of a misfortune which would make the most splendid position, and the most interesting occupation in life, a continual purgatory.

* * *

It would of course be absurd to charge Mr. Jerrold with any deliberate wish to bring marriage into discredit, but we think that exaggerated descriptions of the defects and irregularities, which are incidental to the working of all the relations of life, are very unwholesome reading. They give a false notion of the intensity of unavoidable troubles, and we can well imagine that they may often produce bad effects on melancholy and sensitive dispositions. Most men find it difficult enough to bear up cheerfully against the common trials of the world; and we do not think that they are likely to be aided in that undertaking by the floods of sentiment and ridicule with which, in the present day, a variety of birds, more or less unclean, are constantly fouling the common habitation of the human race.

---

[2] *The Book of Snobs* (1848), in *Punch* (1846–47) as 'The Snobs of England, by One of Themselves'. *Jeames's Diary* (1845).

[3] p. 50.

'Groans of the Britons'
(*Saturday Review*, 22 November 1856)

Groans of the Britons: *gemitus britannorum*, the final appeal by the Britons to the Roman army for help against the Picts and Scots. From Gildas' sixth-century *De Excidio et Conquestu Britanniae*, then Bede's History. Leslie Stephen seconded JFS's disapproval of Dickens (particularly 'the levity with which he treated serious political and social problems'): 'The attitude of mind represented is that of the ordinary newspaper correspondent, who imagines that a letter to the "Times" is the ultimate remedy for all the evils to which flesh is heir' (*Life* 107). JFS was to review Caroline Norton's novel, *Lost and Saved*: 'Such is the story. It was put before the world with a certain stern, uncompromising air. The authoress showed in the preface, in the occasional observances interwoven with the story itself, and in a subsequent letter to the morning papers, that she took a high moral view of what she had done' ('Anti-Respectability', *Cornhill*, Sept. 1863; *On Society, Religion, and Government* 114, ed. Thomas E. Schneider, 2015; *Selected Writings of James Fitzjames Stephen*, Oxford University Press, 114). Her letter had recently been published in *The Times* (18 June 1863): 'As to the general tenour and usefulness of purpose of *Lost and Saved*, it is objected that I have spoken out too plainly; and that, allowing that particular society calling itself "the world" to be what it is, no single voice can hope to amend the vicious injustice and general contempt of right and wrong which exist there...I think that, so far from individual protests being worthless, they are the small hinges on which the great doors of change for ever turn'. (Norton's letter was reprinted within subsequent issuing of the novel.) JFS was not above writing letters to *The Times*: seven in the 1860s, nine in the 1870s, seven in the 1880s, and two in 1891. 'Mr. Mozley on the Late Sir James Stephen' (6 July 1882) 'completely demolished' a scurrilous anecdote about the brothers' father (*Life* 38). For a characteristically outraged letter to *The Times*, by VERICUNDIA, p. 143, and for JFS's reservations about *The Times*, 'The Mote and the Beam', p. 239.

Groans of the Britons

To 'write to the *Times*' is the climax of an Englishman's threat, and one of the most powerful consolations of his disappointments. It has been wittily represented as an absolute necessity for an age which has ceased to believe in the invocation of saints; nor can there be any sort of doubt as to the sincerity or potency of the supplications, which are, in fact, the voice of public opinion.[1] The ballad of 'Jacob Omnium and his Horse',

---

[1] *OED* opinion. Qualified by *common, general, public, vulgar*, etc.: Such judgement or belief on the part of a number, or the majority, of persons; what is generally thought about something. The earliest citation (1735 BOLINGBROKE Let them stand, or fall in the publick opinion, by their merit) does not effect—since it attaches the article 'the'—what JFS's 'Public Opinion' was to do (p. 66), and the same is true of Burke's 'the public opinion'. So the earliest *OED* citation for the forceful abstraction is probably 1801 JEFFERSON The mighty wave of public opinion which has rolled over our great republic. Corroborated by 1841 D'ISRAELI

66   ON THE NOVEL AND JOURNALISM

and the 12 and 13 Vic. c. 75, jointly commemorate the victory of a groaning Briton over the Palace Court[2]—one of the last remnants of the glory of the Hereditary Grand Marshals of England. There is considerable reason to doubt whether there would have been any Minié rifles[3] at the battle of Inkermann if Sir Charles Shaw had not expounded their merits to the public through the columns of the morning newspapers. The Militia Bill of 1852 was owing almost entirely to what was known as the Invasion panic of that year;[4] and both Annette Meyers[5] and Kirwan[6]—the painter convicted of murdering his wife—were saved from execution principally by the efforts of those who discussed their cases in the daily papers.[7] It is curious to watch the issue of the various complaints which from time to time appear in this manner, for nothing can furnish a more remarkable comment on the nature and limits of the real influence of the press. At first sight, the operation would seem to be simplicity itself. It has become almost commonplace to say that newspapers are omnipotent. Mr. Carlyle speaks of the Fourth Estate, 'which let the other three hold if they can';[8] and there is a popular

---

How long has existed that numerous voice which we designate as 'Public Opinion'? (By 1892, the phrase is securely itself: *Pall Mall G.*, 'until then, parties must not attempt to influence public opinion.') JFS, 'On "Luxury"' (*Cornhill*, Sept. 1860, not signed): 'All the voices which have any real influence with an Englishman in easy circumstances, combine to stimulate a low form of energy, which stifles every high one. The newspapers extol his wisdom by assuming that the average intelligence which he represents is, under the name of public opinion, the ultimate and irresponsible ruler of the nation; the novels which he and his family devour with insatiable greediness have no tendency to rouse his imagination, to say nothing of his mind. They are pictures of the everyday life to which he has always been accustomed—sarcastic, sentimental, or ludicrous, as the case may be—but never rising to anything which ever suggests the existence of tragic dignity or ideal beauty.'

  [2] Matthew James Higgins, *pseud.* 'Jacob Omnium' (1810–1868; *ODNB*, journalist), celebrated in Thackeray's ballad, 'Jacob Omnium's Hoss: A New Pallice Court Chant'. (JFS quotes half a dozen stanzas in 'Mr. Thackeray', *Fraser's*, April 1864.) 'Who was this master good / Of whomb I makes these rhymes? / His name is Jacob Homnium, Exquire; / And if I'd committed crimes, / Good Lord! I wouldn't ave that mann / Attack me in the TIMES!' The ballad opens: 'One sees in Viteall Yard, / Vere pleacemen do resort / A wenerable hinstitute, / 'Tis called the Pallis Court / A gent as got his i on it, / I think will make some sport // The natur of this Court / My hindignation riles: / A few fat legal spiders / Here set & spin their viles; / To rob the town theyr privlege is, / In a hayrea of twelve miles.' *OED* Name of a court formerly held at the Marshalsea and having jurisdiction in personal actions arising within twelve miles of the palace of Whitehall, the city of London excepted. 1849 *Act 12 & 13 Vict.* From and after the thirty-first day of December 1849 all the power, authority, and jurisdiction of the said Court of the Marshalsea, and of the said Court of the Palace of the Queen at Westminster...shall cease and determine. (Thackeray was also to dedicate to him *The Adventures of Philip*, 1862.)

  [3] On the Caffre wars in the Cape Colony, a letter by Charles Shaw in *The Times* (3 Jan. 1852) argued that the army needed Minié rifles. The Battle of Inkerman in the Crimean War, 5 Nov. 1854.

  [4] The threat of invasion from France by Louis Napoleon, Napoleon III (on which Tennyson published half a dozen poems under pseudonyms).

  [5] Annette Myers murdered Henry Ducker in Feb. 1848. An editorial in *The Times* called for the commutation of her death sentence because of how he had treated her, and she was transported to Van Diemen's Land in 1850.

  [6] William Kirwan was found guilty of murdering his wife in 1852; tried in Dublin, he was sentenced to death but this was commuted after public insistence that her death was consistent with her having drowned, as Kirwan claimed.

  [7] *Hist. Crim. Law* iii 460, on a death sentence: 'The newspapers were filled with letters upon the subject...Some of the letters were of great importance; but the majority were nothing more than clamorous expressions of opinion, founded upon no real study of the case: for which, indeed, those who took their notions of it exclusively from newspaper reports had insufficient materials. A considerable number of the communications were simply imbecile.'

  [8] Thomas Carlyle, 'Diderot', *Foreign Quarterly Review* (1833): 'Lastly, the unutterable confusion worse confounded of our present Periodical existence; when, among other phenomena, a young Fourth Estate

impression that, in addition to the saintly attribute of being invoked, editors possess, in modern times, the apostolic power of binding and loosing.[9] But on looking more closely into the matter, we think that this impression will be very greatly modified. A newspaper is essentially and pre-eminently a mercantile speculation. Whatever else it may do, it must either pay or stop. The managers of a paper are therefore compelled to limit the patronage which they extend to gentlemen with grievances by the degree of interest which they suppose the public to take in the subject; and as the public at large care extremely little for any misdeeds unless they immediately affect the general comfort, and are capable of being dramatically presented to their notice and speedily and efficiently redressed, it is upon such subjects only that the power of writing to the papers is a really important privilege. To sweep away an obsolete court, to apply a new invention to the public service, to pardon a man unjustly condemned to death, are such obvious remedies for glaring abuses that the power of demanding is almost equivalent to a guarantee for obtaining them. On the other hand, when any question can be made to turn upon a disputed matter of fact or upon a set of obscure details, unless it is a matter of overwhelming public interest, the newspapers are nearly powerless.

This is, no doubt, the best side of the practice which we are examining; but it has other aspects, which may easily be confounded with this, though they are in reality fundamentally distinct from it. One large class of letters to the papers may be classified under the head of bores. There are persons who have *quasi* intellectual hobbies,[10] which an ungrateful public does not care to notice, but which, when intelligence is scanty and subjects are few, a despairing editor will thankfully admit to replenish his ill-furnished columns. The author of this class of contributions is generally well aware of the rights of his position. He fondly believes that his letters are a favour to the paper to which they are addressed, and will create a sensation, and he takes his line accordingly. We can never read such letters without a kind of pious awe, for we always feel that the writer's eye is upon us, and that if we skip a single sentence we are guilty of a wilful sin against light and knowledge. Yet, after all, what dreadful reading they are! Secondary punishments and reformatory schools[11] are usually the chosen themes. The writer begins by claiming some part of the editor's valuable space for a subject of deep—he might even say the deepest—social importance. He contends that we have gone too long upon the principle of punishing crimes which society has itself done much to produce, and that if we spent in prevention—and so on, through the history of the reformed boy who was taken up by a philanthropist at Bristol and exported to Canada, whence he wrote to say

---

(whom all the three elder may try if they can hold) is seen sprawling and staggering tumultuously through the world· · ·'. ('Burke said there were Three Estates [clergy, nobility, commoners] in Parliament; but, in the Reporters' Gallery yonder, there sat a *Fourth Estate* more important far than them all', 'The Hero as Man of Letters'.) In India in 1870, JFS was 'taunted with having been a member of the "fourth estate", and now desiring to fetter the liberty of the press. He therefore confessed . . . to the sin of having written for the newspapers' (*Life* 175).

[9] Matthew 16:19 (Christ to St. Peter), And whatsoever thou shalt bind on earth shall be bound in heaven: and whatsoever thou shalt loose on earth shall be loosed in heaven.

[10] *OED* A favourite occupation or topic, pursued merely for the amusement or interest that it affords, and which is compared to the riding of a toy horse (sense 3); an individual pursuit to which a person is devoted (in the speaker's opinion) out of proportion to its real importance. Formerly hobby-horse.

[11] *OED* 1851 (*title*) Reformatory Schools for the Children of the Perishing and Dangerous Classes, and for Juvenile Offenders. (*OED* 1859 In most of the European nations there are dangerous classes, dangerous, because uncared for and uneducated.)

68 ON THE NOVEL AND JOURNALISM

that he had saved 6s. 6d. in chimney-sweeping, and transmitted eighteen-pence for the Sunday schools of his native village. And this is followed by the counter story of the unreformed boy, who, when under sentence of transportation for life for a burglary with violence, told the chaplain that it was 'all along of the crushers[12] a-taking away his character when he looked out for work'—till at last we arrive at the long-expected conclusion, with a suppressed feeling that the world would be much more comfortable, and rather less dull, if some jovial tyrant would gag all the philanthropists and hang all the criminals. There is a regular round of subjects of this kind. Just before Parliament opens, we are pretty sure to have Mr. Locke King[13] and the Law Reformers. Immediately on the prorogation, we get some deadly-lively[14] writing from 'A Templar', or 'A Law Student', about the Inns of Court and Legal Education; and at the dead season of all, when a country paper would take to its gooseberries and frogs, Mr. Muntz[15] emerges like a nineteenth century Solomon Eagle,[16] with the awful cry—'Inconvertible[17] notes, inconvertible notes—yet ten years of a golden currency, and England shall be destroyed.'

The gentlemen with small, but real, grievances form another class of writers to the papers. If any one would take the pains to examine the files of the *Times* for some months or years, he would find the most striking confirmation of our view as to the limits of the influence of the kind of writing which we are considering. The occasional correspondents of the daily papers denounce a great number of very real grievances, but they go on protesting against them for years together without getting them removed, unless the grievance is glaring, and the remedy obvious and simple. We should like to know how long the great question of the passage of cabs through St. James's Park has been debated, or how often the wickedness of innkeepers and the dearness of travelling in England has been denounced. The schemes suggested by various correspondents of the papers for making a communication between the guard and the driver of a train, and the thrilling denunciations of the avarice of the directors who could not adopt them, would fill a small volume. Such topics as these are like the creaking hinge and the unpainted coach panel, which so grievously disturbed Uncle Toby and his father.[18] The reason why these small evils are not remedied by a machinery which possesses such enormous power in some directions, is curious. Of course, if

---

[12] *OED Slang* A policeman. From 1835. 1851 MAYHEW 'The blessed crushers is everywhere', shouted one.

[13] Peter John Locke King (1811–1885; *ODNB*, politician), whose Real Estate Charges Act (1854) brought protection for the bereaved against unscrupulous conduct as to mortgages.

[14] For 'dead-alive', 'The Romance of Vice' (*Sat. Rev.*, 13 Nov. 1858), p. 187.

[15] Philip Henry Muntz (1811–1888), business man and Liberal politician).

[16] Or Solomon Eccles (1618–1683). 'The famous Solomon Eagle, an enthusiast. He, though not infected at all but in his head, went about denouncing of judgment upon the city in a frightful manner, sometimes quite naked, and with a pan of burning charcoal on his head'. Defoe presents him several times in *A Journal of the Plague Year. Being observations or memorials, of the most remarkable occurrences, as well publick as private, which happened in London during the last great visitation in 1665. Written by a citizen who continued all the while in London. Never made publick before* (anon., 1722).

[17] *OED* Incapable of being exchanged for something else. *specifically* of paper money. 1833 MARTINEAU Inconvertible bank paper would have been everywhere refused. 1866 *Banking* This country had what it is to be hoped it will never see again—an inconvertible paper currency.

[18] Sometimes Tristram's father rose above such disturbance ('–My father thrust back his chair, –rose up, –put on his hat, –took four long strides to the door, – jerked it open, – thrust his head half way out, – shut the door again, – took no notice of the bad hinge, – returned to the table, –' (*Tristram Shandy*, vol. III, ch. xli).

the *Times* contained a column of castigation of the conduct of the directors of any one railway every day for months together, they would be brought to see the error of their ways; but as the public would soon be tired of the subject, the apparently boundless power of the paper is, in fact, confined to very occasional manifestations. It can only hit a blow now and then at considerable intervals. The attacks of a newspaper are like the fire of a cannon, the metal of which begins to run if the gun is discharged too often.

Sometimes the complaints which a bold Britain pours into the sympathizing bosom of his newspaper are the most curious illustrations of the intense and disinterested affection which an Englishman feels for himself. That he, the heir of all the ages in the foremost files of time,[19] should be uncomfortable, strikes him not so much in the light of a personal wrong as in that of a blot on the face of creation. His cultivation of his own comfort—as one of Eugène Sue's heroes remarks—*n'est pas une fonction, c'est un sacerdoce.*[20] His unexpressed, perhaps unconscious, but unalterable conviction—the universal postulate which lies at the root of all his beliefs—is that the world was made for him. This frame of mind breaks out at times in the most marvellous lamentations to the *Times*. Some time ago, a gentleman wrote to bewail the degeneracy of the age, because he had had to walk upwards of a mile in some remote part of London before he could find a cab at five o'clock in the morning. Another made similar remonstrances because there was no railing to the foot-path up Helvellyn; and two patriots debated for weeks about some disputed charge in an inn at Dover. Nor is it to English grievances alone that these utterances are confined. In the early part of the present autumn, there must have been some ten or fifteen complaints addressed to the English papers about the monstrous wickedness of the Swiss innkeepers and the prices which they charged for their horses. It is impossible not to feel a sort of admiration for the man who can nurse his wrath till it assumes this awful form. Most of us have taken the numbers of cabs, and have declared with indignant threats or impressive civility, according to our special idiosyncrasies, our unalterable determination to bring the offending driver before the judgment seat of a police-court; but who ever did it? '*Non sum qualis eram*',[21] is almost every man's feeling when he comes down to breakfast next morning. To be jostled about in a filthy court by greasy policemen, and to lose the morning in hearing people fined five shillings for being drunk and disorderly, is a penance too great for most men's public spirit. Let us, therefore, give due honour to those who make a note in their pocket-books of the sins of a Swiss guide, and keep their indignation warm enough for use all the way from Berne to Basle, from Basle to Strasburg, thence to Paris, and so home. Indeed, newspaper letters sometimes cast a wonderful light on a man's character. One would like to know the patriot who sent that awful instrument to the *Times*[22] the other day, which would so disfigure a robber, after 'caressing' his face for a single moment, 'that his own mother would not know him.' What did he think the editor would do with it? Or what special interest had he in protecting that gentleman against the friends who might embrace him somewhat too lovingly on his way home

[19] Tennyson, 'Locksley Hall' 178 ('I the heir...').
[20] Priestly office.   [21] Horace, *Odes* IV: i, I am not what I was.
[22] 10 Nov. 1856, AN ANTI-GAROTTER: 'manufactured the accompanying weapon...I send it for your inspection...if his face be but once caressed with it ever so gently, I think you will admit even his own mother would not recognize him afterwards.' JFS toys with 'instrument', *OED Law* A formal legal document whereby a right is created or confirmed, or a fact recorded; a formal writing of any kind, as an agreement, deed, charter, or record, drawn up and executed in technical form, so as to be of legal validity.'

70 ON THE NOVEL AND JOURNALISM

from Printing-house-square?[23] Even our old friend Paterfamilias gave us a new light as to his character yesterday, when he announced to all the garotters his habit of walking home with a loaded[24] cane and a set of 'knuckle dusters'[25]—whatever they may be. There is something touching in the freshness of the faith which such a veteran grumbler feels in his *Times*. Fancy a man *bonâ fide* loading himself with weapons of war, on account of an alarm excited solely by the indignation of a few noisy victims. It is as if the man who shows the whispering gallery at St. Paul's should be really frightened at hearing a nut cracked there.

The most wonderful man of all is the gentleman who sent his sons to Eton because he objected to flogging, in order, apparently, to have a chance of getting into a controversy with Dr. Goodford.[26] If he had lived in the days of Moloch,[27] he would probably have made his children pass through the fire for the sake of entitling himself to expose the system in the columns of the *Jerusalem Gazette* or the *Samaritan News*. What must be the patriotism of a man who exposes his sons to what he considers a filthy and degrading punishment, in order that he may, through the columns of a newspaper, incite the classic youth of Eton to follow the examples of Harmodius and Aristogeiton.[28] Perhaps his own heroic progeny will adopt the *rôle*, and sharpen their penknives.

After all, grumbling, which is the Briton's unwritten Magna Charta, has its secondary as well as its primary advantages. No age ever photographed[29] itself like our age. Whatever its faults may be, was there ever such a history of England as the broad sheet of the *Times*? What would we give for the files of some similar paper published in Greece or Rome! How it would make those dry bones live![30] How it would enable us to study not only the gravest transactions, but the minutest traits of an extinct character! Future Macaulays will put the nineteenth century on the stage in a manner which would drive Mr. Kean[31] to despair.

---

[23] First as the site of the King's Printer, then of *The Times*.

[24] *OED* Weighted, esp. with lead, as a *loaded stick, whip*.

[25] *OED* A formidable American instrument, made to cover the knuckles, so as to protect them from injury in striking, and at the same time to add force to a blow given with the fist thus covered. (From 1858 *The Times* and 1861 *All the Year Round*.)

[26] Charles Old Goodford (1812–1884; *ODNB*, headmaster), Eton in 1853 and then Provost in 1862. The letter in *The Times* (21 Nov. 1856) the day before JFS's remarks (which misrepresent it) was from M. Treherne.

[27] Leviticus 18:21, And thou shalt not let any of thy seed pass through the fire to Molech. 'Dr. Newman and Liberalism' (*Sat. Rev.*, 24 June 1865): 'It is possible to imagine a kind and degree of evidence which would induce the most sturdy Liberal to make his children pass through the fire to Moloch, but surely it is at least a respectable prejudice to think that the evidence ought to be carefully examined, and that nothing short of something approaching to demonstration ought to be sufficient for such a purpose. The vilest of all practices—murder, human sacrifices, sexual inquities of every sort—have been presented to mankind as divine revelations' (*On Society, Religion, and Government* 183).

[28] Tyrannicides in Athens, responsible for the assassination of Hipparchus and an attempt upon Hippias. (Thucydides is the principal historical source.)

[29] Antedating *OED figurative* To portray vividly in words; to fix or impress on the mind or memory. 1862 scenes. .are indelibly photographed on a memory; 1865 In the twenty-fifth chapter of Matthew [,] He photographs the transaction in a scene of judgment.

[30] Ezekiel 37:3, The valley which was full of bones…they were very dry. And he said unto me, Son of man, can these bones live?

[31] Edmund Kean (1787–1833; *ODNB*, actor).

'Barry Lyndon'
(*Saturday Review*, 27 December 1856)

JFS wrote often of Thackeray. Here, in high praise of *Barry Lyndon*; then in level rebuke of Thackeray for accommodating himself to the publicity world ('Gentlemen Authors', *Sat. Rev.*, 17 July 1858, p. 163); judiciously, of *The Virginians* (*Sat. Rev.*,19 Nov. 1859); and memorially, soon after Thackeray's death on 24 Dec. 1863 ('Mr. Thackeray', *Fraser's*, April 1864, not signed; p. 211). Thackeray's novels lent themselves (though they did not give themselves) to JFS's sense that a novel is an amusement that must not get above itself—as Dickens's novels presumed to do. *Barry Lyndon* 'has a moral, if the reader knows how to look for it; but it is kept in its proper place.' 'Hardly any one in these times ventures to moralize openly; but Mr. Thackeray infused into *Vanity Fair* and *Pendennis* as much of his reading of the book of Ecclesiastes as could conveniently be allied with the flirtations of Becky Sharp and the cigars of Mr. Pendennis' ('The Vanity of Human Wishes', *Sat. Rev.*, 29 Sept. 1860; *Essays* 185). JFS's relations with Thackeray were close, though sometimes as an atmosphere can be. Hermione Lee notes the clanship: 'Anny Thackeray Ritchie, Leslie Stephen's first wife's sister…wrote, in her old age, a kind of biographical pot-pourri, to her father William Makepeace Thackeray's complete works' (*Life* xxv). JFS reviewed her novel *The Village on the Cliff* (by the author of *Elizabeth*), in *Fraser's* (Oct. 1867; not signed).

Barry Lyndon*

Whatever we may think of the policy of republishing some parts of Mr. Thackeray's Miscellanies, there can be no doubt that English literature would have sustained a serious loss if *Barry Lyndon* had still been buried in the pages of a magazine.[1] In some respects, it appears to us the most characteristic and best executed of Mr. Thackeray's novels, though it is far less known, and is likely, we think, to be less popular than the rest. *Barry Lyndon* is the history of a scoundrel from his own point of view, and combines the habitual freshness of Fielding with a large measure of the grave irony of *Jonathan Wild*.[2] To be able, with perfect decency and propriety, to take up his abode in the very heart of a most unmitigated blackguard and scoundrel, and to show how, as a matter of course, and without any kind of denial or concealment, he *bonâ fide* considers himself one of the best and greatest of men, is surely one of the hardest tasks which could be imposed on an author; yet Mr. Thackeray has undertaken and executed it with perfect success.

---

* *Memoirs of Barry Lyndon, Esq.* By W. M. Thackeray. (London: Bradbury and Evans, 1856).

[1] Serialized in *Fraser's* (1844) as 'The Luck of Barry Lyndon'. *The Memoirs of Barry Lyndon, Esq., of the Kingdom of Ireland* (1856) differs from the *Fraser's* text.

[2] Henry Fielding (1707–1754; *ODNB*, author and magistrate). *The Life of Mr Jonathan Wild the Great* (1754).

Redmond Barry, who on his marriage takes the name of Lyndon, is the son of a man who runs through his property at gambling-tables and horse-races. He passes his boyhood in a sort of beggarly gentility, partly under the care of a handsome, proud, and vixenish mother, partly at a sort of Castle Rackrent[3] belonging to his uncle, Mick Brady. At sixteen, he falls madly in love with his eldest cousin, a silly and ugly girl of twenty-four, and in a mock duel, which he supposes to be real, shoots a rich and cowardly English rival with a tow bullet.[4] He leaves his home to avoid the consequences of his supposed murder—falls amongst sharpers at Dublin—is plundered by them— enlists as a common soldier—serves at the battles of Minden and Warburg[5]—robs a wounded lieutenant, after the latter action, of his money, clothes, and papers, and passes himself off as an officer. Whilst thus disguised, he is kidnapped by one of the man-stealers[6] who were so largely employed to recruit the armies of Frederick II,[7] and passes some years in the service of that sovereign. Impatient of the hardships to which he is exposed, he tries to mitigate them by assuming the occupation of a police spy, and in this character is set to watch the proceedings of his uncle, a professional gambler, who comes to Berlin in the exercise of his calling, and, as the police suppose, with some political object. The uncle finds means to enable his nephew to escape with him to Dresden, and Mr. Barry blazes out in the full glory of partner in, and bully to, a gambling establishment. After several strange adventures in this capacity, the uncle, a zealous Catholic, becomes anxious 'to make his *salut*', and goes into a convent for that purpose, whilst Mr. Barry, junior, returns to Ireland, after an absence of twelve years, in possession of some 5000*l*., and a dazzling reputation for resource and audacity. Here he falls in with a widow of enormous wealth, who being weak, clever, and romantic, had carried on a foolish literary flirtation with him in her husband's life-time. By fighting a duel with one of her admirers, and giving out with infinite vehemence his intention to do as much for any others who may appear, and by the fascination which courage, a strong will, and dashing vulgar display exercise over a frivolous mind, he bullies Lady Lyndon into marrying him, and becomes possessed in right of his wife of some six palaces and 40,000*l*. per annum. Having thus reached the pinnacle of his glory, Mr. Barry begins to descend. He cuts down his woods, raises money on his wife's life, quarrels vehemently with her son by her first husband, who is his heir, gets utterly drowned in debt, retires savagely to an obscure estate in Ireland, and there fights with the duns and bailiffs, eats his own mutton, and locks up his wife in her bed-room. By a stratagem she recovers her liberty, and her husband is sent abroad with a small pension from her relations, who stop it on her death, whereupon Mr. Barry Lyndon finishes his days in the Fleet Prison, where 'a small man, who is always jeering me and making game of me, asks me to fight, and I haven't the courage to touch him.'

Such is Mr. Barry's career—a riotous and miserable youth, a manhood of infamy, and an old age of ruin and beggary. Yet the genius of the novelist not only makes us feel that his hero would naturally look upon himself as a wronged and virtuous man—'the

---

[3] Maria Edgeworth, *Castle Rackrent: An Hibernian tale. Taken from facts, and from the manners of the Irish squires, before the year 1782* (anon., 1800).

[4] Of hemp or flax fibre; like a wax bullet (later, rubber), less lethal.

[5] During the Seven Years' War (1760 and 1759 respectively).

[6] *OED* from 1582, with 1769 BLACKSTONE *Comm.* IV Index, Manstealing.

[7] Frederick the Great (1712–1786), King of Prussia 1740–86.

victim', as he is made to say on his title-page, 'of many cruel persecutions, conspiracies, and slanders',[8]—but also that even in this wretched kind of existence all was not bad—that wheat as well as tares grow in the most unkindly and ill-cultivated soil. The ability with which this is managed is quite wonderful. The whole book is founded on the great principle, that if a man only lies hardily enough and long enough, nothing is easier for him than to impose upon himself. In nine cases out of ten, hypocrisy is nothing else than self-deception. Describe the transactions in which you are engaged, not as your neighbours would describe them, but as you yourself would wish them to be, and it is surprising how soon they will appear to be capable of no other construction. Barry Lyndon's fundamental and universal postulate is, that he is a good and gallant man, that he is a model of manly virtue, and that, therefore, though he may be occasionally subject to human infirmities, his actions must always be, on the whole, in accordance with his character. Take, as an example of the degree in which a man may bring himself to believe his own lies, the following wonderful account of Mr. Barry's family:

> As a man of the world, I have learned to despise heartily the claims of some pretenders to high birth who have no more genealogy than the lackey who cleans my boots; and though I laugh to utter scorn the boasting of many of my countrymen, who are all for descending from kings of Ireland, and talk of a domain no bigger than would feed a pig as if it were a principality, yet truth compels me to assert that my family was the noblest of the island, and perhaps of the universal world; while their possessions—now insignificant, and torn from us by war, by treachery, by the loss of time, by ancestral extravagance, by adhesion to the old faith and monarch—were formerly prodigious, and embraced many counties at a time when Ireland was vastly more prosperous than now.

Or take the following chastened reflections on the profession of gambling, as a specimen of the marvellous power which the mind possesses, or may acquire, of seeing things altogether upside-down. After describing some of the tricks by which he assisted his uncle in play, Mr. Barry proceeds:

> Some prudish persons may affect indignation at the frankness of these confessions, but Heaven pity them! Do you suppose that any man who has lost or won a hundred thousand pounds at play will not take the advantages which his neighbour enjoys? They are all the same. But it is only the clumsy fool who *cheats*, who resorts to the vulgar expedients of cogged dice and cut cards.[9] Such a man is sure to go wrong some time or other, and is not fit to play in the society of gallant gentlemen; and my advice to people who see such a vulgar person at his pranks is, of course, to back him while he plays, but never—never to have anything to do with him. Play grandly, honourably...When one considers the time and labour spent, the genius, the anxiety, the outlay of money required, the multiplicity of bad debts that one meets with (for dishonourable rascals are to be found at the play-table as everywhere else in the world), I say, for my part, the profession is a bad one; and indeed I have scarcely ever met a man who in the end profited by it.

The parenthesis which marks the point at which Mr. Barry has succeeded in convincing himself that his profession is, on the whole, highly honourable and noble, though

---

[8] On his title-page: 'and the many cruel persecutions, conspiracies, and slanders of which he has been a victim.'

[9] *OED to cog a die* or *the dice*, 1565: fraudulently to direct or control their fall. 1803 *Cut-cards*: having the good cards all cut shorter, and the bad ones cut something narrower.

74   ON THE NOVEL AND JOURNALISM

a few mean interlopers may disgrace it, is inconceivably ludicrous, and shows a depth of humour almost sublime. It is a sort of typical specimen of the spirit which makes a free negro talk with contempt of 'black fellows', or the vulgarest dandies who disgrace our name and nation on the Continent sneer at 'those English'. To show how Mr. Barry contrives to look upon himself as an ill-used man through the whole of his eventful life, would require little less than an abstract of the entire book. We may mention more particularly, however, his wonderful account of his relations to his wife, in which, after detailing with a high moral tone the measures which he thought necessary to bring her to a sense of her conjugal duties—consisting in a long series of the most brutal acts of tyranny and violence—he describes with a sort of contemptuous pity her low spirits, nervousness, bad health, and general dulness, and concludes by the quiet remark— 'My company from this fancied I was a tyrant over her; whereas I was only a severe and careful guardian over a silly, bad-tempered, and weak-minded lady.' We have not the slightest doubt that such a man would seriously and *bonâ fide* take exactly that view of such conduct. Indeed, why should he not? It is much pleasanter to consider oneself a man of sense and honour than a low-minded villain; and to one who wishes to do so, and knows how to set about it, it is quite as easy.

The conception of Barry Lyndon's character involves, however, some grains of good. Indeed, their absence in any man whatever would have been conclusive evidence that the book in which he was depicted was not written by Mr. Thackeray. His courage is genuine courage. He really is a very brave man; and although he knows it, and is inordinately vain of it, we think the picture is true to nature. Sydney Smith[10] long ago pointed out that where there is a great deal of vanity, there is generally some talent; and Mr. Thackeray seems to us to have shown his usual acuteness in exposing the fallacy of the common notion that a bully and a braggart is generally a coward. We should agree with him in thinking such faults some evidence of courage—though of a courage lower both in kind and degree than that which such a person would claim. There is great beauty also in the parental affection which Mr. Thackeray ventures to attribute to this utter scoundrel. He has a son by his second wife, and loves him tenderly, wildly, passionately, with a sort of fierce instinct such as any other brute might show. He is almost heartbroken at his death, and, in his lowest degradation, wears a lock of his hair round his neck. There is something not only touching, but deeply true, in such a representation. It recognises the fact that a strong, unbridled character, full of fierce appetites and ungoverned passions, is not utterly devilish—that it sometimes gives birth to virtues; rough and animal, if you please, but still genuine. The character of old Mrs. Barry, the hero's mother, is a further illustration of the same thing. She is a greedy, proud, unprincipled woman, capable by turns of meanness, haughtiness, fanaticism, and gross cruelty; yet she loves her son dearly through all. There is something wonderfully true in the unity with which the character is drawn. During her son's absence in Prussia, the fanatical side of her character comes out, and she falls under the dominion of a hypocritical scoundrel, called Jowls, who wants to marry her. Her son visits Ireland, fights a duel, and comes to his mother for refuge. Mr. Jowls is scandalized and frightened, and wants to turn out the fugitive, saying 'he would have had the gentleman avoid the drink, and the quarrel, and the wicked duel altogether.' Whereupon 'my

---

[10] (1771–1845; *ODNB*, clergyman, wit, and social reformer).

BARRY LYNDON

75

mother cut him short by saying "that such sort of conduct might be very well in a person of his cloth and his birth, but it neither became a Barry nor a Brady." In fact she was quite delighted with the thought that I had pinked an English marquis's son in a duel; and so, to console her, I told her of a score more in which I had been engaged.' The curtain ultimately falls upon the tough old lady, supporting her blackguard broken-down offspring in his captivity by the labour of her own hands, and on the wrecks of her property.

Artistically considered, we should almost be inclined to place *Barry Lyndon* at the head of the list of Mr. Thackeray's books. It has an immense advantage over his better known works in being far shorter—for which reason the plot is clearer, simpler, and more connected than it is in *Vanity Fair, Pendennis*, or the *Newcomes*.[11] Every page carries the story on, and with the exception of Barry's meeting with his uncle at Berlin, and of a rather melodramatic episode which takes place at a small German court, the story is as natural and easy as if it were true. We have attempted to show that the book has a moral, if the reader knows how to look for it; but it is kept in its proper place, and is suggested by the facts, instead of suggesting them. In most of Mr. Thackeray's more elaborate performances, his own views of the world appear to us to be insisted on too openly and too often; but there is nothing of this in *Barry Lyndon*. It is neither a melancholy nor a cheerful book, but a fair and wonderfully skilful portrait of a man whom we feel as if we had known personally. The accessories are described in as life-like and vigorous a manner as the main subject. We do not think that Mr. Thackeray's extraordinary power of description was ever more strongly illustrated than in the sketches which this volume contains of the wild, mad Irish life of Dublin and the provinces in the last century—of the horrible mechanism of man-stealing and espionage by which Frederick II maintained his power—of the strange career (half-highwayman, half-*grand seigneur*) of a professional gambler—or of the petty Courts in which, before the French Revolution, so many sham sovereigns played at kings and queens, with human beings for their counters. All these, and many other subjects of the same kind, are sketched off rapidly, easily, and with a life and distinctness altogether marvellous in a volume which will not last an active reader through a very long railway journey. We conclude our notice with a specimen of these strange pictures. The hero has been kidnapped, and is thrown, with several companions in misfortune, into a waggon, which is to carry him to the depôt of Frederick's recruits:

> The covered waggon, to which I was ordered to march, was standing, as I have said, in the courtyard of the farm, with another dismal vehicle of the same kind hard by. Each was pretty well filled with a crew of men whom the atrocious crimp who had seized me had enlisted under the banners of the glorious Frederick; and I could see by the lanterns of the sentinels, as they thrust me into the straw, a dozen dark figures huddled together in the horrible moving prison where I was now to be confined. A scream and a curse from my opposite neighbour showed me that he was most likely wounded, as I myself was; and during the whole of the wretched night the moans and sobs of the poor fellows in similar captivity kept up a continual painful chorus, which effectually prevented my getting any relief in sleep. At midnight (as far as I could judge) the horses were put to the waggons, and the creaking, lumbering machines were put in motion. A couple of soldiers, strongly armed, sat on the outer bench of the cart, and their grim faces peered in with their

---

[11] Thackeray (as 'Arthur Pendennis'), *The Newcomes: Memoirs of a Most Respectable Family* (1854).

lanterns every now and then through the canvas curtains, that they might count the number of their prisoners. The brutes were half-drunk, and were singing love and war songs, such as '*O Gretchen mein Täubchen, mein Herzenstrompet, mein Kanon, mein Heerpauk, und meine Musket*', '*Prinz Eugen der edle Ritter*',[12] and the like; their wild whoops and *jodels* making doleful discord with the groans of us captives within the waggons. Many a time afterwards have I heard those ditties sung on the march, or in the barrack-room, or round the fires, as we lay out at night.

[12] 'O Gretchen my dove, trumpet of my heart, my cannon, my army drum, and my musket.' 'Prince Eugen the noble knight', an Austrian-German folksong about the victory of Prince Eugene of Savoy in 1717 during the Austro-Turkish War.

'Mr. Dickens as a Politician'
(*Saturday Review*, 3 January 1857)

'Whatever philanthropists and public lecturers may say...', JFS's belief that philanthropy had become sentimentalized urges him to convict Dickens. 'Mr. Dickens, as we have remarked on former occasions, is always in a flutter of dissatisfied philanthropy; and, indeed, it would be hard to mention a writer whose literary aims are of the somewhat humble character in question, who does not frequently ignore the limits which divide the leading article from the novel.' (Not that Dickens was unaware of philanthropic falsities; he incarnated some of them in Mrs Jellyby, *Bleak House* ch. iv, 'Telescopic Philanthropy'.) JFS's 'Philanthropy' expresses its caveat as to all world-bettering institutions, assisted by an *and* ('and open to...') that really performs as a *but*: 'That such associations do produce a vast amount of good, there can be no doubt at all. They prevent a great deal of suffering, and open to an immense number of persons modes of escape from the consequences of their own guilt and folly...It would be wrong to say a word which could prevent a single kind action, but it is right to look upon the other side of the question' (*Sat. Rev.*, 20 Aug. 1859; *Essays* 41–2, 46). JFS was to write to his sister-in-law Emily Cunningham (8 Nov. 1872): 'My opinion is, and long has been, that the English people, though to blame, like all others, are considerably less to blame than they often appear, for their various social evils—pauperism and so on...In short I think exaggeration is the sin of the age, and I find it more in vogue in regard to philanthropy than in regard to almost anything else.' Noted by Thomas Schneider, 'The Bishop of Carlisle upon Heathenism' (*PMG*, 11 Sept. 1872, not signed; *On Society, Religion, and Government* 217). Here preceding JFS's 'Mr. Dickens as a politician' are excerpts from Dickens's Preface to *The Pickwick Papers* and from that to *Bleak House*.

CHARLES DICKENS
FROM THE PREFACE TO *THE PICKWICK PAPERS*

I have found it curious and interesting, looking over the sheets of this reprint, to mark what important social improvements have taken place about us, almost imperceptibly, since they were originally written. The licence of Counsel, and the degree to which Juries are ingeniously bewildered, are yet susceptible of moderation; while an improvement in the mode of conducting Parliamentary Elections (and even Parliaments too, perhaps) is still within the bounds of possibility. But legal reforms have pared the claws of Messrs. Dodson and Fogg; a spirit of self-respect, mutual forbearance, education, and co-operation for such good ends, has diffused itself among their clerks; places far apart are brought together,[1] to the present convenience and advantage of the Public, and to the certain destruction, in time, of a host of petty jealousies, blindnesses, and prejudices, by which the Public alone have always been the sufferers; the laws relating to imprisonment for debt are altered; and the Fleet Prison is pulled down!

Who knows, but by the time the series reaches its conclusion, it may be discovered that there are even magistrates in town and country, who should be taught to shake hands every day with Common-sense and Justice; that even Poor Laws may have mercy on the

---

[1] By railways, presumably.

ON THE NOVEL AND JOURNALISM

weak, the aged, and unfortunate; that Schools, on the broad principles of Christianity are the best adornment for the length and breadth of this civilised land; that Prison-doors should be barred on the outside, no less heavily and carefully than they are barred within; that the universal diffusion of common means of decency and health is as much the right of the poorest of the poor, as it is indispensable to the safety of the rich, and of the State; that a few petty boards and bodies—less than drops in the great ocean of humanity, which roars around them—are not for ever to let loose Fever and Consumption on God's creatures at their will, or always to keep their jobbing little fiddles going, for a Dance of Death.

CHARLES DICKENS
FROM THE PREFACE TO *BLEAK HOUSE*

A Chancery Judge once had the kindness to inform me, as one of a company of some hundred and fifty men and women not labouring under any suspicions of lunacy, that the Court of Chancery, though the shining subject of much popular prejudice (at which point I thought the Judge's eye had a cast in my direction), was almost immaculate. There had been, he admitted, a trivial blemish or so in its rate of progress, but this was exaggerated, and had been entirely owing to the 'parsimony of the public'; which guilty public, it appeared, had been until lately bent in the most determined manner on by no means enlarging the number of Chancery Judges appointed—I believe by Richard the Second, but any other king will do as well.

This seemed to me too profound a joke to be inserted in the body of this book, or I should have restored it to Conversation Kenge or to Mr. Vholes,[2] with one or other of whom I think it must have originated. In such mouths I might have coupled it with an apt quotation from one of SHAKSPEARE'S Sonnets:[3]

> My nature is subdued
> To what it works in, like the dyer's hand:
> Pity me then, and wish I were renew'd!

But as it is wholesome that the parsimonious public should know what has been doing, and still is doing, in this connexion, I mention here that everything set forth in these pages concerning the Court of Chancery is substantially true, and within the truth. The case of Gridley is in no essential altered from one of actual occurrence, made public by a disinterested person who was professionally acquainted with the whole of the monstrous wrong from beginning to end. At the present moment[4] there is a suit before the Court which was commenced nearly twenty years ago; in which from thirty to forty counsel have been known to appear at one time; in which costs have been incurred to the amount of seventy thousand pounds; which is *a friendly*[5] *suit*; and which is (I am assured) no nearer to its termination now than when it was begun. There is another well-known suit in Chancery, not yet decided, which was commenced before the close of the last century, and in which more than double the amount of seventy thousand pounds has been swallowed up in costs. If I wanted other authorities for JARNDYCE AND JARNDYCE, I could rain them on these pages to the shame of—a parsimonious public.

---

[2] MR. KENGE ('Conversation Kenge'), a portly important-looking person; senior member of Kenge and Carboy, solicitors. MR. VHOLES, Richard Carstone's Solicitor.

[3] Sonnet 111. [4] Note by Dickens: 'In August, 1853.'

[5] *OED* Of an action at Law: Brought between parties not really at variance, in order to obtain a decision on some point.

Mr. Dickens as a Politician

The age in which we live has produced, amongst other novelties, an entirely new school of politicians. In almost every department of public life, the task of obtaining results has been to a great extent superseded by that of inventing machinery. The world, we are all agreed, is out of joint, and it is touching to see how many doctors are anxious to reduce the dislocation. In politics, in law, and in twenty other walks of life, reforming has become a distinct branch of business. Almost every man who can in any way command the ear of the world has engaged himself in the hopeful task of 'doing good',[6] in preference to the ignoble selfishness of minding his own business, and, in one way or other, hoists the flag and wears the uniform of the noble army of world-betterers. As every system is said to culminate, and every idea to be embodied, it might have been expected *à priori* that an era of reform would find, sooner or later, its representative man. We do not know whether the restless, discontented, self-sufficient spirit which characterises so large a portion of modern speculation—especially on political and social subjects—could have had a more characteristic Avatar[7] than it has found in Mr. Dickens. The nature, the sphere, and the character of his influence, and the foundations upon which it rests, furnish a most curious commentary on a vast mass of phenomena which it is impossible for a serious person to view without profound disquiet. In his preface to a late edition of his earliest novel,[8] Mr. Dickens informed the world with satisfaction that, since its publication, a great part of the horrors of imprisonment for debt—the special evil which it denounced—have been removed by legislation; and he expressed a hope that, at the republication of each of his works, he might be able to say the same of the particular abuse against which it was levelled. Now, Mr. Dickens is the author of some twelve or fourteen books, each as long as three ordinary novels; and in each of them, in addition to the usual tasks which writers of fiction impose on themselves, he has discharged a self-imposed obligation of attacking some part or other of our rotten institutions. In *Pickwick*, he denounced imprisonment for debt[9]—in *Oliver Twist*, the Poor Laws—in *David Copperfield*, the inefficiency of Parliament—in *Bleak House*, the Court of Chancery[10]—and in *Little Dorrit*,[11] the system of administration. We say nothing at present of the satire which he has directed against the Americans, the aristocracy, the middle classes, charitable societies, and Calvinism. To do his best to persuade his neighbours that the institutions under which

---

[6] 'Doing Good' (*Sat. Rev.*, 17 Dec. 1859; *Essays* 78–88).

[7] *OED Hindu Myth*. The descent of a deity to the earth in an incarnate form. Manifestation or presentation to the world as a ruling power or object of worship (the first instance 1859 MASSON the avatar of Donne).

[8] *The Posthumous Papers of the Pickwick Club* (edited by 'Boz', 1837). The wrapper title of the monthly parts, 1836–37, added *Containing a Faithful Record of the Perambulations, Perils, Travels, Adventures and Sporting Transactions of the Corresponding Members*. The Cheap Edition of 1847 contained the new preface.

[9] The sub-sections in Chapter I of the *Life* on JFS's great-grandfather, grandfather, and father have a Dickensian look: JAMES STEPHEN, WRITER ON IMPRISONMENT FOR DEBT ('About 1769, James Stephen found himself confined for debt in the King's Bench prison', *Life* 9); JAMES STEPHEN, MASTER IN CHANCERY; JAMES STEPHEN, COLONIAL UNDER-SECRETARY. JFS on Dickens: 'He seems, as a general rule, to get his first notions of an abuse from the discussions which accompany its removal...This was his course with respect both to imprisonment for debt and to Chancery reform' ('The License of Modern Novelists', *Edin. Rev.*, July 1857, p. 114).

[10] A Master in Chancery was an important official though a low-level Chancery judge. The office had been abolished in English law in 1852 (*Life* 17 n.).

[11] 1857; in monthly parts 1855–57.

ON THE NOVEL AND JOURNALISM

they live encourage and permit the grossest cruelties towards debtors and paupers—that their Legislature is a stupid and inefficient debating club, their courts of justice foul haunts of chicanery, pedantry, and fraud, and their system of administration an odious compound of stupidity and corruption—is, perhaps, a sufficient responsibility for one man to assume; yet it is very characteristic that he should consider it so light a matter as to be anxious, in addition, to propagate similar views about almost every element of social life.

Such language may be considered too grave for such a subject. Who, it may be asked, takes Mr. Dickens seriously? Is it not as foolish to estimate his melodramatic and sentimental stock-in-trade gravely, as it would be to undertake a refutation of the jokes of the clown in a Christmas pantomime? No doubt this would be true enough if the world were composed entirely or principally of men of sense and cultivation. To such persons Mr. Dickens is nothing more than any other public performer—enjoying an extravagantly high reputation, and rewarded for his labours, both in purse and in credit, at an extravagantly high rate. But the vast majority of mankind, unfortunately, think little, and cultivate themselves still less. Whatever philanthropists and public lecturers may say, the mass of the poorer no less than of the richer classes are mentally idle, and are incapable of sustained and systematic thought or inquiry. Members of parliament, active professional men, merchants, manufacturers, shopkeepers in a large way of business, and enterprising farmers, form numerically an infinitesimally small proportion of the population. We have amongst us millions who are physically and intellectually weak, but whose collective sentiments go to form that moral atmosphere in the midst of which we all live and move. To these classes, such writers as Mr. Dickens are something more than an amusement. They are the most influential of all teachers—the teachers who make themselves friends and companions during those occasional intervals of rest and enjoyment which to many minds are far the pleasantest part of life. The production, among such readers, of false impressions of the system of which they form a part—especially if the falsehood tends to render them discontented with and disaffected to the institutions under which they live—cannot but be a serious evil, and must often involve great moral delinquency. Except the relations between men and their Maker, no subjects can be more grave than Legislation, Government, and the Administration of Justice; and we do not know that a man can misuse the trust imposed upon him by the possession of great talents and unbounded popularity more mischievously than by leading people to under-estimate the good, and over-estimate the evil, of the institutions of their country. Looking, therefore, at the sphere of Mr. Dickens's influence, we are compelled to think of him seriously. He is not entitled to the protection of insignificance. It may be admitted that he can scarcely attract the attention of the more intelligent classes of the community; but he may, and, as we believe, does exercise a very wide and a very pernicious political and social influence.

Our unfavourable opinion applies equally to the ends which he has in view, and to the means by which he seeks to accomplish them. He is the most prominent and popular of the innumerable preachers of that flattering doctrine, that, by some means or other, the world has been turned topsy-turvy—so that all the folly and stupidity are found in the highest places, and all the good sense, moderation, and ability in the lowest. As German students look upon themselves as the elect, and upon the members of

MR. DICKENS AS A POLITICIAN

the whole social hierarchy as 'philisters',[12] an opinion, or rather a sentiment, seems to be gaining ground amongst us—and it is carefully fanned by such writers as Mr. Dickens—that success in life is not only no evidence of a man's superiority, but is positive proof of his inferiority to his neighbours. For Parliament Mr. Dickens has an unlimited scorn. It is, he says, all talk, 'words, words, nothing but words'. The House of Commons, for him, is a stupid debating club, in which no business is transacted except the enunciation of innumerable platitudes. Nor does the law fare better. The Court of Chancery[13] is an abomination, to be cut down root and branch—a mere den of thieves, in which no man can long retain his honesty. But if our laws are made by fools and administered by rogues, what shall we say of those who manage our public affairs? They are all idiots and jobbers—they have neither the will nor the power to do right. Half-a-dozen families of Barnacles have contrived to attach themselves to the ship of the State, and have no other object than that of impeding its progress as far as possible, in order that their own parasitical existence may not be discovered and terminated. If a man makes a discovery, they treat him as a criminal—if he has a claim or a grievance, they baffle and cheat him—they have neither heart nor brain, but the widest of mouths and the most insatiable of stomachs. Such is the lesson which, month by month, Mr. Dickens reads to his fellow-citizens. He is, in the main, a kind-hearted man, and would perhaps be at a loss for opportunities of exercising his powers of vituperation, unless Providence had kindly created dignities on purpose to be evil spoken of; but as that arrangement has been made, he is enabled, with an easy conscience, to devote himself to the task of flattering his readers into the belief that, but for the intelligence of the middle classes and the unostentatious virtues of the poor, England would be a perfect paradise of fools and knaves.

Such is his end; and the means he employs are worthy of it. As there are reproaches which can be uttered by no one but a woman or a child, there are accusations which can only be conveyed through a novel. It would be impossible to make any more serious publication the vehicle of such calumnies—their grave and quiet statement would be their own refutation. But just as a foolish gossip in a country-town, who says what she pleases because all the world knows what her tongue is like, may babble away the purest character, a popular novelist may produce more disaffection and discontent than a whole army of pamphleteers and public orators, because he wears the cap and bells, and laughs in your face when you contradict him. A novelist has no responsibility. He can always discover his own meaning. To the world at large, *Jarndyce v. Jarndyce*[14]

---

[12] *OED* The German word for Philistine. A name applied by the students at German universities to the townsmen, or to all persons not students; an outsider; hence an unenlightened uncultured person. From 1828 CARLYLE He went to Mill (the British India Philister).

[13] JFS had made something of a concession the previous year: 'What with English, French, and Dutch jurisprudence, trover and conversion, embargoes and seizures by English frigates, the whole story, patiently elaborated as it is by M. de Loménie, leaves on the mind an impression like dreaming of a Chancery suit' ('Beaumarchais and His Times', *Sat. Rev.*, 23 Feb. 1856).

[14] *Bleak House*, ch. i: 'Jarndyce and Jarndyce drones on. This scarecrow of a suit has, in course of time, become so complicated, that no man alive knows what it means. The parties to it understand it least; but it has been observed that no two Chancery lawyers can talk about it for five minutes without coming to a total disagreement as to all the premises. Innumerable children have been born into the cause; innumerable young people have married into it; innumerable old people have died out of it. Scores of persons have deliriously found themselves made parties in Jarndyce and Jarndyce without knowing how or why; whole families have inherited legendary hatreds with the suit.'

82   ON THE NOVEL AND JOURNALISM

represents the Court of Chancery. To any one who taxes the writer with unfairness, it is merely, he is told, a playful exaggeration—pretty Fanny's way;[15] and who can have the heart to be angry with pretty Fanny? To the thousands of feverish artisans who read *Little Dorrit*, the Circumlocution Office is a *bonâ fide* representation of Downing-street. To any one who remonstrates, it is nothing but a fair representation of what exists, just exaggerated enough to make the subject entertaining. In this, no doubt, there is a certain amount of truth; and so there is in the plea of the old woman who destroys her neighbour's character over her tea, that she only adds colour enough to her story to make it piquant. No doubt Mr. Dickens does not really mean much harm. He only wants to sell his books; and by way of persuading himself that he is of some use in the world, he spices them with a certain amount of advocacy of social reforms, just as clergymen sometimes sugar their private letters with texts to make them improving. This is just what we complain of. He exercises considerable political influence with hardly any political convictions. He introduces the gravest subjects in a manner which makes it impossible that he should do them justice. He scatters fire, and says, Am I not in sport? The two fallacies which pervade all his writings are just those which nothing but care and education can guard against, and which are, therefore, particularly dangerous when addressed to uneducated people. One is the fallacy of artistic exaggeration. It was said of Swift[16] that he satirized mankind by describing men as vicious horses, and horses as virtuous men, and then asking which was the best. Something in the same way Mr. Dickens makes his intelligent tradesmen high-minded and highly-educated gentlemen, and his officials affected shop-boys, and then asks us whether the officials can bear a comparison with the tradesmen. If you are at liberty to allow some of the staring external marks of a class to stand unaltered, whilst its characteristic defects are exaggerated indefinitely, there can never be any difficulty in making out the world to be as absurd as you please. The other fallacy—that of minute description—is less obvious, but quite as effective. It consists in dwelling upon all the details of an incident till the mind invests it with as much dignity as such an introduction would demand. By the help of this device, nothing would be more easy than to make the operation of pulling out a tooth appear utterly intolerable. Describe the dentist's face, the arm-chair, the warm water, the basin with a hole in the bottom, the opening of the mouth, the insertion of the pincers, the cold feeling of the iron, and its tightening on the tooth, with sufficient minuteness—and the final wrench may be made to appear like the consummation of all things. In the same way, the inside of a workhouse may be made to look like an absolute torture-chamber; whereas, in fact, neither the pauper nor the dentist's patient feels half the agony which the novelist describes.

    The truth of the accusations which Mr. Dickens brings against society is on a par with the fairness of the manner in which they are urged. No one can deny that there are great abuses in the world in general, and in this country in particular. There is much that wants reform in Parliament, in the law, and in the administration; but no one can

---

[15] Thomas Parnell: 'And all that's madly wild, or oddly gay, / We call it only pretty Fanny's way' ('An Elegy, to an Old Beauty'); p. 37.

[16] 'Men and Brutes' (*Sat. Rev.*, 7 Nov. 1863): 'The history of the Houyhnhnms and Yahoos does not prove much, but it certainly does show that a good man in the shape of a horse is preferable to a vicious brute in the shape of a man' (*On Society, Religion, and Government* 125). *Travels into Several Remote Nations of the World ... By Lemuel Gulliver: Part IV. A Voyage to the Country of the Houyhnhnms* (1726).

reform wisely unless he knows what he is about; and that these institutions want reform is only half, or perhaps even less than half, of the truth. With all their faults, they have the very highest merits; and a man who represents to his fellow-countrymen only the faults, and none of the merits, fosters one of the worst of our national faults—the inveterate habit of self-depreciation. Whatever else our Parliament is, it is the only popular government in the world which has been able to maintain itself; and whatever Mr. Dickens may think, it really has done a very considerable amount of work since he began to denounce it, and will probably continue to do so. Our law has enormous faults, and we have always exposed them, and contended that they ought to be reformed; but to speak of the law with bitter contempt is to show the most profound ignorance of English history.[17] The great faults which every one now acknowledges must be viewed historically, as well as in their present condition; and though the historical fact that the defects of the law formed part of the price of our political freedom is no sort of reason for not reforming them, it is a very strong reason for speaking of the law, and of those who profess it, with some sort of respect and some approach to justice. Our administration, no doubt, had not the means of carrying on a gigantic war immediately after forty years of peace,[18] but, on the other hand, the deficiency was repaired with unexampled vigour; and with respect to other branches of Government, it should be remembered that a vast proportion of the national affairs are conducted fairly enough, and that there is no country in which the great ends of civil society—the security of person and property, and the absolute supremacy of law—are more fully attained, or in which the private character of public men stands higher. Human nature must be judged by an actual, and not by an ideal standard; and though it is true that we have a good deal of jobbing in England, it is quite as true that we have less downright bribery, less violation of confidence, less peculation, than most other countries. Our statesmen may sometimes provide for their cousins and nephews in the public service, but they do not sell their official secrets, or make fortunes on the Stock Exchange. That relations should be maintained with every nation in the world—that a revenue of some sixty millions should be collected and disbursed—that person and property should be secure in a very high degree—that espionage and individual oppression should be altogether unknown—are results which, as times go, we cannot despise, even if an inventor is sometimes snubbed, and an applicant occasionally kept waiting for his rights.

The most wonderful feature in Mr. Dickens's influence is the nature of the foundation on which it stands. Who is this man who is so much wiser than the rest of the world that he can pour contempt on all the institutions of his country? He is a man with a very active fancy, great powers of language, much perception of what is grotesque, and a most lachrymose and melodramatic turn of mind—and this is all. He is utterly destitute of any kind of solid acquirements. He has never played any part in any movement more significant than that of the fly—generally a gad-fly—on the wheel. Imprisonment for debt on *mesne* process[19] was doomed, if not abolished,

---

[17] 'Law Reform' (*Sat. Rev.*, 2 Feb. 1856): 'The popular notion, disseminated by writers like Dickens, is that the law is a mass of cruel absurdities invented by lawyers for their own profit, and that all that judicial decisions and statutory enactments have effected has been to perplex a very simple subject.'

[18] The Crimean War (1853–56), the Napoleonic Wars (1803–15).

[19] *OED mesne process*: that part of the proceedings in a suit which intervenes between the primary and the final process.

84 ON THE NOVEL AND JOURNALISM

before he wrote *Pickwick*. The Court of Chancery was reformed before he published *Bleak House*. In his attacks on Parliament he certainly relied on his own experience, and was utterly and hopelessly wrong. In his attacks on the administration he only followed the lead of Our Own Correspondent. And yet this man, who knows absolutely nothing of law or politics—who was so ignorant of the one subject that he grumbled at the length of an administration suit (which is like grumbling at the slowness of the lapse of time), and so ignorant of the other that he represented Parliament as a debating club—has elaborated a kind of theory of politics. He would have the pace of legislation quickened by the abolition of vain debates—he would have justice freed from the shackles of law—he would have public affairs conducted by officers of vast powers, unfettered by routine. He does not know his own meaning. He does not see the consequences of his own teaching; and yet he is unconsciously tending to a result logically connected with the whole of it. Freedom, law, established rules, have their difficulties. They are possible only to men who will be patient, quiet, moderate, and tolerant of difference in opinion; and therefore their results are intolerable to a feminine, irritable, noisy mind, which is always clamouring and shrieking for protection and guidance. Mr. Dickens's government looks pretty at a distance, but we can tell him how his ideal would look if it were realized. It would result in the purest despotism. There would be no debates to worry effeminate understandings—no laws to prevent judges going at once to the merits of the case according to their own inclination—no forms to prevent officials from dealing with their neighbours as so many parcels of ticketed goods. Whether a Mr. Dickens would then be able to point out the fact that arbitrary power is not uniformly wise, that arbitrary judges are sometimes corrupt, and that arbitrary officials are not always patriotic, is a very different question.

JFS ON PARLIAMENT: A NOTE

In 1873–74, JFS came to devote ten pages about Parliament to laying out the 'defects which grievously impair its efficiency', but he took care to introduce these in a way that distanced him from such as Dickens. 'Before attempting to prove this, I wish to disclaim any intention to undervalue the institutions under which we live. A person who spoke of them with disrespect would prove his own incompetence to discuss public affairs of importance, and his want of acquaintance with political institutions, and the conditions under which they must of necessity work. Whatever faults our institutions may have, they, or at least we who live under them, have solved the problems which are throwing the greater part of Continental Europe into convulsions.' 'Parliamentary Government' (*Contemp. Rev.*, Dec. 1873 and Jan. 1874, signed; *On Society, Religion, and Government* 226). When it came to Parliament's dealings with the law, JFS had sounded, ten years earlier, a note of well-grounded impatience, not so much grievous as aggrieved:

> Parliament appears to have thought—and, to judge from subsequent legislation, would appear still to be, to some extent, under the influence of the notion—that crimes exist independently of their definitions, and that it would be as wrong to attempt to correct an inconvenient definition by express enactment as to attempt to control natural agents by act of parliament. Parliament has never attempted to deal with the common law theory of theft, but has contented itself with making supplementary provisions for the cases to which it does not apply; until a matter, which in reality is simple, has become so complicated, that hardly any one understands it (*Gen. View 1863* 92).

'Railroad Bookselling'
(*Saturday Review*, 31 January 1857)

The booksellers, formed in 1792, became W. H. Smith & Son in 1846; their first book- and news-stand at railway stations had opened at Euston in 1848.

Railroad Bookselling

In these days of universal travelling, few of our readers can have failed to notice that, at almost all the larger railway[1] stations, book-stalls—which in some instances attain the proportions of shops—are established to enable passengers to relieve in some degree the dulness of their monotonous transit. Nearly all these establishments are branches of the single firm of Messrs. W. H. Smith and Son, who have for some years past supplied an enormous proportion of English railway travellers with their light reading. The courtesy of these gentlemen has enabled us to lay before our readers some account of a very curious matter. If it be true, as the proverb tells us, that no man is a hypocrite in his pleasures, nothing can throw more light on national character than trustworthy evidence as to the sort of intellectual amusement which a class so mixed as that of railway travellers prefers. The books in demand for railroad reading may be divided into the two great classes of dear and cheap. Taking two shillings or half-a-crown as the limit which divides the two, it may be said, roughly speaking, that nine-tenths in number and three-fourths in value of the books disposed of at the stations are cheap, and the remainder dear. The higher-priced works are on all kinds of subjects, and indeed the fact that some of them should find any sale at all at railway stations is a curious proof of the wealth of some classes of society. Messrs. Smith, of course, give no credit, and allow no discount; nor is it possible, from the nature of the case, that they should have regular customers. Those who buy of them buy upon the mere impulse of the moment, because it happens to strike them, between taking their tickets and their seats, that they should like to have something to read on their journey; yet such is the amount of spare cash which people have in their pockets, that there is a very large sale for publications at nine, ten, and twelve shillings, and even at higher prices. About 300 copies of the first two, and 100 of the last two volumes of Mr. Macaulay's *History*,[2] sold at the different railways. Indeed, the last two volumes were cried up and down the

---

[1] *OED specifically* railway. Cf. RAILROAD, at one time equally (or more) common in Great Britain and still usual in America. (JFS switches from one to the other.) *OED* adds that the great extension of railways from their original limited use [a way or road laid with rails] began with the opening of the Stockton–Darlington line in 1825, and Liverpool–Manchester in 1830.

[2] *The History of England from the Accession of James II*, vols. i–ii (1849), iii–iv (1855).

platform at York like a second edition of the *Times*. No human industry could ever read through more than one of the volumes during the longest journey; and yet people were so eager to know all about William III and Queen Mary, that, rather than wait a few hours for the knowledge, they were willing to encumber themselves on a journey with two heavy octavo volumes, and to pay 36s. for a book which was sold all over London on the day of publication for 27s. Interesting as it is, Mr. Layard's work on *Nineveh*[3] is a serious undertaking; yet it must have casually occurred to between 200 and 300 people, rich enough to gratify their whim, that they should like to have it, for about that number of copies were sold at different stations. Dr. Sandwith's book on Kars[4] reached a similar sale at the price of 12s. 6d.; and Miss Yonge's novels sell readily—especially on the South Western line—at 10s. 6d. and 12s. The most extraordinary instance of a combination of zeal for knowledge with the possession of wealth is to be found in the cases of three or four gentlemen who bought copies of Stephens's *Book of the Farm*[5]—the price being 3l. 3s., and the work consisting of two octavo volumes, each three or four inches thick. We should expect the person who made such a purchase to go into the refreshment-room at Swindon and ask for a barrel of salt pork and a puncheon of rum.

A good many books of a more moderate size and price, but of a very solid character, are sold on the railways. Dr. Smith's *History of Rome*, a translation of Guizot on the *English Revolution*, Mr. Prescott's historical works, Mr. Henry Taylor's *Notes from Life*, and Mr. A. Helps's *Companions of my Solitude* and *Friends in Council*, are in steady demand.[6] Mr. Helps is particularly popular at Manchester and Euston-square. The most singular proof of the voracity with which some people devour facts is to be found in the popularity of an epitome of Sir Archibald Alison's *History of Europe*,[7] which condenses into one small, but very thick and very closely-printed volume, most of the facts which are to be found in twenty crown octavo volumes. Between 200 and 300 copies of this book have been sold. We should like to know how an epitome of the author's reflections would sell! It is satisfactory to find that standard poets are in much favour. During the last six months, 100 copies of various editions of Shakspeare have been sold, at prices varying from 5s. to 10s. 6d.—a considerable number of a 5s. edition of Milton—about 100 of a two-volume edition of Pope—of Young and Thomson, not more than six—about 100 of a 5s. edition of Byron's poems—and the same number of a similar edition of Scott's. The sale of Rogers's poems has been about 40 copies; of Coleridge's, about 30; of Shelley's (at 7s.), 15; of Campbell's (at 9s.), six or eight.

---

[3] Austin Layard (1817–1894; *ODNB*, excavator, politician). *A Popular Account of Discoveries at Nineveh* (1851).

[4] Humphry Sandwith, *A Narrative of the Siege of Kars* (1856); the city fell to the Russians during the Crimean War, Nov. 1855. JFS, 'Comic Journalism' (*Sat. Rev.*, 1 Mar. 1856): 'A funny fellow, hearing of the fall of Kars, remarked that in Roman triumphs the Cars went up the hill of the Capitol, but that in modern wars our shame lay in the fall of Kars.'

[5] Henry Stephens, *The Book of the Farm: Detailing the Labors of the Farmer, Steward, Plowman, Hedger, Cattle-man, Shepherd, Field-worker, and Dairymaid* (many editions, including 2 vols., 1854).

[6] William Smith (1813–1893; *ODNB*, classical and biblical scholar). François Guizot (1787–1874), statesman, historian of *General History of Civilization in Europe* (1828).

[7] Sir Archibald Alison, first baronet (1792–1867; *ODNB*, historian and lawyer). One volume had been reviewed by JFS (*Sat. Rev.*, 22 Dec. 1855), and others were to be (2 May 1857, 27 Mar. 1858, and 18 June 1859). The *Epitome of Alison's History of Europe...for the Use of Schools and Young Persons* appeared in 1848 (many editions).

RAILROAD BOOKSELLING 87

Moore, Hood, and Longfellow, are decidedly the most popular of railway poets. About 200 copies of *Lalla Rookh*, the *Irish Melodies*, and the *Songs*, have been disposed of, and 20 copies of his complete works at 12s. 6d.;[8] also, 200 copies of Longfellow's poems, 100 copies of *Hiawatha*,[9] and from 200 to 300 of Hood's poems.[10] Mr. Tennyson is popular, but in a considerably less degree. The sale of religious books is not inconsiderable; but none are popular unless they are of the Low-church school. Barnes's *Notes*[11] and Hawker's *Portion*[12] are fair specimens of the kind of books of this class which sell upon railways—they are mostly bought in Wales. The most curious fact connected with this part of the subject is the wonderful popularity of a quasi-theological biography—*The Life of Captain Hedley Vicars*.[13] No less than 120,000 copies have been sold since its first publication. An edition of 20,000, lately published, went off in a single day; and Messrs. Smith could only obtain 365 as their share, though a larger number might easily have been disposed of. There is some sale for scientific books. Popular manuals on various sciences, especially on geology, sell well; and a cheap edition of Kirby and Spence's *Entomology*[14] has been extensively purchased. Lardner's *Museum of Science and Art*[15] is popular in the North—the engine-drivers and fitters are fond of buying books on mechanics. Cheap editions of *Oratorios*[16] are also sought after. Messrs. Smith and Son, to their great credit, exercise a vigilant censorship over the stalls under their care, and banish from them all works of an openly immoral character. People, we are informed, often ask for books in the *Index Expurgatorius*,[17] and look rather foolish on hearing that they are not kept. Charlatans, however, are successful on the railways, as elsewhere. Mr. Martin Tupper[18] is considerably more popular than Shakspeare—Dr. Cumming[19] goes down amazingly—and the exemplary Mr. S. W. Fullom[20] entraps a considerable audience by turning physical science into a cross between a raree-show and a meeting-house. It would be a real service to the nation if any one

[8] Thomas Moore (1779–1852; *ODNB*, poet), *Lalla Rookh: An Oriental Romance* (1817), *Irish Melodies* (1821), *Poetical Works* (1840).

[9] *The Song of Hiawatha* (1855).

[10] Thomas Hood (1779–1845; *ODNB*, poet and humorist). Most recently, *Poems* (1846).

[11] Albert Barnes (1798–1870), American theologian whose *Notes on the Old and the New Testaments* sold widely in the old world and the new world.

[12] Robert Stephen Hawker (1803–1875; *ODNB*, poet and Church of England clergyman), *The Poor Man's Morning and Evening Portions* (1819).

[13] Hedley Vicars (1826–1855; *ODNB*, army officer and evangelical), killed in the Crimean War. Catherine M. Marsh, *The Memorials of Captain Hedley Vicars* (1856): JFS, 'Religious Journalism' (*Sat. Rev.*, 16 Feb. 1856), p. 40.

[14] William Spence (1783–1860; *ODNB*, political economist and entomologist). With William Kirby (1759–1850; *ODNB*, entomologist and naturalist), he published *An Introduction to Entomology: or Elements of the Natural History of the Insects* (4 vols., 1815–26).

[15] 12 vols. (1854–56), ed. Dionysius Lardner (1793–1859; *ODNB*, writer on science and public lecturer).

[16] Perhaps *Oratorios unsuited to the House of Prayer, and inconsistent with a Christian profession: a sermon by the Rev. Richard Clayton* (1842).

[17] *OED* index. The list, published by authority, of books which Roman Catholics are forbidden to read, or may read only in expurgated editions. *Expurgatory Index*, an authoritative specification of the passages to be expunged or altered in works otherwise permitted. In English use, the name *Index Expurgatorius* has often been applied to the *Index Librorum Prohibitorum*.) 1845 THACKERAY Knowing well that *Fraser's Magazine* is eagerly read at Rome, and not. .excluded in the *Index Expurgatorius*. (JFS's application here.)

[18] Martin Tupper (1810–1889; *ODNB*, poet and writer), *Proverbial Philosophy* (1837–76).

[19] John Cumming (1807–1881; *ODNB*, minister of the Presbyterian Church of England).

[20] Stephen Watson Fullom (1818–1872), *The Marvels of Science, and their Testimony to Holy Writ* (1852; ten editions by 1856).

88 ON THE NOVEL AND JOURNALISM

could substitute for the works of these and some other gentlemen an equal number of copies of Soyer's *Cookery Book*,[21] of which we are glad to hear an ungastronomic generation has purchased no less than 20,000.

The shilling and eighteen-penny novels form the great bulk of the sales on railways. Cheap editions of the *Waverley Novels* are still very popular, as many as 200 a month of an eighteen-penny edition are disposed of. Sir E. Lytton, however, is at the head of the list. Next comes Captain Marryat; after him—*longo intervallo*[22]—Mr. James, Captain Grant, Miss Sinclair, Mr. Haliburton, Mrs. Trollope, Mr. Lever, Mrs. Gaskell, and Miss Austen.[23] The numbers sold range from 1200 to 25 monthly. People are willing to pay high for a good novel, and many works by popular writers sell almost if not quite as well at five or six shillings, as at two. Those who care to read them at all care enough about them to pay well for them. On the other hand, it requires an enormous sale to make a profit out of a shilling novel. The printing is so expensive that nothing but a sale of many thousands will prevent a loss. There are only two ways of producing this result. The first is the legitimate plan of being able to put a popular name on the title-page—the other consists in external decorations on the cover of the book. The quantity of absolutely worthless rubbish which is disposed of by the latter artifice is amazing. Our readers may have seen in shop windows copies of a song called 'The Language of the Eye',[24] on the outside of which is depicted a lady screening her mouth with a fan, and ogling the passers-by with intense pertinacity. This is copied from the cover of a tastefully-ornamented pamphlet bearing the same title, written by one Joseph Turnley, and dedicated to Lord Ellesmere.[25] It would be impossible to convey to our readers an adequate notion of the wretched absurdity of this book. It is so bad—so utterly and entirely bad—that to give reasons for disliking it would be like proving that toothache is unpleasant. Yet the scarlet-and-gold, the cream-coloured paper, and the ogling lady, have between them produced a sale of 4000 copies at Messrs. Smith's stalls alone; and we understand that between 20,000 and 30,000 have been sold altogether. That our readers may understand the force of our criticism, we subjoin an example of the author's style:

> The eye of some is all romance and feeling, and seems to portray varied pictures. In some you seem to see foreign lands, sweet wild scenery, and fancy walks by Ganges' side or Armenia's wilds. In some you may behold young love, as a pallid rose, in lighted halls of pleasure, where living stars of loveliness wear their silver and golden raiment. In some eyes you see genius pacing on some high tower, clad in the grandeur of contemplation, and wearing the damp and fervid heat of ambition: 'tis on such occasions you may see

---

[21] Alexis Soyer (1810–1858; *ODNB*, chef), many books, notably *A Shilling Cookery Book for the People* (1855).

[22] *OED* At some remove, though there is a gulf between them. From 1693.

[23] G. P. R. James (1799–1860), burlesqued by Thackeray. James Grant (1822–1887), his novels *The Romance of War* (1845), and *Adventures of an Aide-de-Camp: or, A Campaign in Calabria* (1848). Catherine Sinclair (1800–1864; *ODNB*, novelist and children's writer). Thomas Chandler Haliburton (1796–1865), Novia Scotian politician and novelist (Sam Slick, his best-known character). Charles Lever (1806–1872; *ODNB*, novelist).

[24] The song (words by J. Duff, music by Charles Hodgson) begins ''Tis sweet to hear a gentle voice'.

[25] Francis Egerton, first earl of Ellesmere (1800–1857; *ODNB*, politician and poet). Joseph Turnley, *The Language of the Eye: the Importance and Dignity of the Eye as Indicative of General Character, Female Beauty, and Manly Genius* (1856).

the spirit sitting on its throne of light eternal, and hear wild echoes from a voice with silver note,

'I dreamt I dwelt in marble halls.'[26]

The beauty and spirituality of some eyes exceeds the status of mere reason, and yields a path for the majestic step of imagination. Through the eye, joy oft beams and hovers, imparting a luxuriant animation which causes adoration.

A novel called *Verdant Green* has reached a sale, principally by the same means, of even greater extent. It consists of three parts, of which there have been sold no less than 50,000 copies.[27]

The sale of periodicals forms, of course, a very important branch of Messrs. Smith's business. A very large proportion of the newspaper circulation of the country passes through their hands, and there are probably some days on which they circulate as many as 100,000 copies of different journals, daily and weekly. Illustrated journals are much in request, and the experiment of publishing local penny papers would seem to have succeeded. The numbers disposed of are very great, but an enormous sale is necessary if any profit is to be made. On particular days, of course, the newspaper sale is immense. When the news of some of the battles in the late war arrived, the morning papers were soon out of print, and some of them sold on the next day for 1s., 1s. 6d., or even 2s. 6d. Palmer's trial created a 'war demand', and 25,000 copies of his life[28] were disposed of; but none of the other *causes célèbres* which have been so common within the last few years produced any perceptible effect on newspaper sale. Though, of course, there are many exceptions, the evening papers having suffered much of late years. The second editions of the morning journals have superseded them. The cheap novels have had a somewhat similar effect on the magazines. Periodical novels, of course, sell largely; but it is almost universally true of them that the demand is three or four times greater at the beginning than at the end of the story. A very small proportion of the amusement-hunters are in at the deaths and marriages.

Such are some of the results of the information with which Messrs. Smith have kindly supplied us. The most curious fact which it proves is the enormous demand which exists amongst us for books of mere amusement. No doubt, the great majority of publications sold on a railway must be at once cheap and light; for such travellers as want graver books would naturally choose them beforehand, and take them with them. But though the character of the sale is not matter of surprise, the extent of it is matter for serious consideration. The sales of Messrs. Smith are only a very small part indeed of the total traffic in books of this class. It is by no means difficult to dispose of 30,000 or 40,000 copies of a popular novel; and when we remember the number of such books that are annually published, it is probably no exaggeration to say that more than a

---

[26] 'The Gipsy Girl's Dream', Arline's aria from the opera *The Bohemian Girl* (1843) by Michael William Balfe, with lyrics by Alfred Bunn: 'I dreamt that I dwelt in marble halls, / With vassals and serfs at my side, / And of all those who assembled within those walls / That I was the hope and the pride.' Parodied by Lewis Carroll in *Lays of Mystery, Imagination, and Humour* (1855): 'I dreamt I dwelt in marble halls, / And each damp thing that creeps and crawls / Went wobble-wobble on the walls.'

[27] *The Adventures of Mr. Verdant Green, An Oxford Freshman* (1853).By Edward Bradley [*pseud*. Cuthbert Bede] (1827–1889; *ODNB*, author and Church of England clergyman). *The Further Adventures of Mr. Verdant Green* (1854); *Mr. Verdant Green, Married and Done For: Being the Third and Concluding Part of 'The Adventures of Mr. Verdant Green, An Oxford Freshman'* (1857).

[28] *The Trial of William Palmer for the Alleged Rugeley Poisonings* (London: James Gilbert, 1856).

million of them must be disposed of annually. Twenty years ago, a novel of any kind was an expensive luxury—at the present day, it costs only twice as much as a pot of beer. We have seen so many strange events that it is not easy to say what may be the effects of any revolution; but certainly such a deluge of *eau sucrée* must produce some results. It would seem as if, for the mass of mankind, thought had become almost impossible. We are all of us drowned in business on the one hand, and in amusement on the other. Indeed, if we consider the infinitely elaborate apparatus which we have constructed to satisfy our appetite for amusement, we shall be filled with a kind of awe. We take more trouble about idling than most nations do about working.

We would conclude by suggesting the possibility of adding to the present stock of railway libraries a certain number of second-hand copies of standard works, such as abound in every book-stall in London. Every one who cares for books knows the attractions of those establishments, and we should think that the better educated class of travellers would as often be tempted to lay out their loose shillings on 'something to read', by the sober leather coats of old copies of English or foreign classics, as by the most splendid combinations of gilding and scarlet that ever decorated the novels of writers otherwise unknown to fame.

'Little Dorrit'
(*Saturday Review*, 4 July 1857)

JFS opens this review of *Little Dorrit* with Mr. Merdle's cutting his throat, and duly closes with the name of John Sadleir who had killed himself with prussic acid in 1856. As well as Othello's suicide and Madame Bovary's, he considered Charles Reade's *It Is Never Too Late to Mend*; also *A Tale of Two Cities* where self-sacrifice is suicidal (Jan-Melissa Schramm, *Atonement and Self-Sacrifice in Nineteenth-Century Narrative*, 2012). JFS passes three judgments on suicide and the law:

from A GENERAL VIEW OF THE CRIMINAL LAW OF ENGLAND (1863) 141—2

One point in which the law of murder requires relaxation is the case of suicide. Suicide is by law murder and a person who is present aiding and abetting in the act is a principal in murder, and might be convicted and executed for the offence. Thus in the not very uncommon case of a joint attempt at suicide, if one person escapes and the other dies, the survivor is guilty of murder. That this is a hard case is apparent, from the fact that in practice, no one would be executed for such an offence. Suicide may be wicked, and is certainly injurious to society, but it is so in a much less degree than murder. The injury to the person killed can neither be estimated nor taken into account. The injury to survivors is generally small. It is a crime which produces no alarm, and which cannot be repeated. It would therefore be better to cease altogether to regard it as crime, and to provide that any one who attempted to kill themselves, or who assisted any other person to do so, should be liable to secondary punishment. In this way, substantial punishment would be inflicted for what may be a serious offence. Juries would be delivered from a conflict between duty and pity, and coroners' juries would be under no temptation to commit the amiable perjury of finding that the deceased killed himself in a fit of temporary insanity.

from A MODERN 'SYMPOSIUM' (1877)[1]
THE INFLUENCE UPON MORALITY OF A DECLINE IN RELIGIOUS BELIEF

Suicide is commonly regarded as wrong; and this moral doctrine is defended on theological grounds, which are summed up in the old saying that the soldier must not leave his post till he is relieved. I will not inquire whether any other argument can be produced forbidding suicide to a person labouring under a disease which converts his whole life into one long scene of excruciating agony, and which must kill him in the course of a few useless months, during which he is a source of misery, and perhaps danger, to his nearest and dearest friends. I confine myself to saying that, if it could be shown that there is no reason to suppose that God has in fact forbidden such an act, its morality might be discussed and

---

[1] *Nineteenth Century*, April–May 1877; *On Society, Religion, and Government* 255–6. Also 'The Sacredness of Human Life' (*Sat. Rev.*, 25 June 1864); *On Society, Religion, and Government* 169–72.

92   ON THE NOVEL AND JOURNALISM

decided upon on different grounds from those on which it must be considered and decided upon on the opposite hypothesis.

from A HISTORY OF THE CRIMINAL LAW OF ENGLAND (1883) III 104, 107

Suicide is by the law of England regarded as a murder committed by a man on himself, and the distinctions between murder and manslaughter apply to this (so far as they are applicable) as well as to the killing of others. There is, however, authority for saying that there is no such offence as self-manslaughter, and the true definition of murder of one's self seems to be where a man kills himself intentionally, to which Hale would add, 'or accidentally', by an act amounting to felony, as in the case where A., striking at B. with a knife, intending to kill B., misses B. and kills himself. Suicide is held to be murder so fully, that every one who aids or abets suicide is guilty of murder. If, for instance, two lovers try to drown themselves together, and one is drowned and the other escapes, the survivor is guilty of murder.

The Draft Penal Code proposed to make the abetment of suicide a special offence, subject to penal servitude for life as a maximum punishment. The attempt to commit suicide was to be punishable by two years' imprisonment and hard labour. The definition of homicide ('Homicide is the killing of a human being by another') excluded suicide.

The abetment of suicide may, under circumstances, be as great a moral offence as the abetment of murder. Suppose, for instance, the heir to a large property were to persuade the owner of it to kill himself by making him believe that a dog by which he had been bitten was mad, and that his choice was between suicide and a death of torture; or suppose the seducer of a girl on her becoming pregnant goaded her into suicide in order to rid himself of an incumbrance—such a person ought, I think, to be subjected to punishment of extreme severity. The difference between such offenders and accessories before the fact to murder is that their conduct involves much less public danger, though it may involve equal moral guilt. Suicide is the only offence which under no circumstances can produce alarm. It would, I think, be a pity if parliament were to enact any measure tending to alter the feeling with which it is and ought to be regarded. As an instance of popular feeling on the subject, I may mention a case I once tried at Norwich, in which a man—I think drunk at the time—tried to poison himself in a public house. When called on for his defence, he burst out with all the appearance of indignant innocence: 'I try to kill myself! I cannot answer for what I might do when drunk, but I was all through Central India with Sir Hugh Rose in 1857, I was in so many general actions, and so many times under fire, and can any one believe that if I knew what I was about I could go and do a dirty, cowardly act like that?' He was acquitted.

CHARLES DICKENS
PREFACE TO *LITTLE DORRIT*

I was occupied with this story, during many working hours of two years. I must have been very ill employed, if I could not leave its merits and demerits as whole, to express themselves on its being read as a whole.

If I might offer any apology for so exaggerated a fiction as the Barnacles and the Circumlocution Office, I would seek it in the common experience of an Englishman, without presuming to mention the unimportant fact of my having done that violence to good manners, in the days of a Russian war, and of a Court of Inquiry at Chelsea. If I might make so bold as to defend that extravagant conception, Mr. Merdle, I would hint that it originated after the Railroad-share epoch, in the times of a certain Irish bank, and of one or two other equally laudable enterprises. If I were to plead anything in mitigation

LITTLE DORRIT

of the preposterous fancy that a bad design will sometimes claim to be a good and an expressly religious[2] design, it would be the curious coincidence that such fancy was brought to its climax in these pages, in the days of the public examination of late Directors of a Royal British Bank. But, I submit myself to suffer judgment to go by default on all these counts, if need be, and to accept the assurance (on good authority) that nothing like them was ever known in this land.

Some of my readers may have an interest in being informed whether or no any portions of the Marshalsea Prison are yet standing. I myself did not know, until I was approaching the end of this story, when I went to look. I found the outer front courtyard, often mentioned here, metamorphosed into a butter shop; and then I almost gave up every brick of the jail for lost. Wandering, however, down a certain adjacent 'Angel Court, leading to Bermondsey', I came to 'Marshalsea Place': the houses in which I recognised, not only as the great block of the former prison, but as preserving the rooms that arose in my mind's-eye when I became Little Dorrit's biographer. The smallest boy I ever conversed with, carrying the largest baby I ever saw, offered a supernaturally intelligent explanation of the locality in its old uses, and was very nearly correct. How this young Newton (for such I judge him to be) came by his information, I don't know; he was a quarter of a century too young to know anything about it of himself. I pointed to the window of the room where Little Dorrit was born, and where her father lived so long, and asked him what was the name of the lodger who tenanted that apartment at present? He said, 'Tom Pythick'. I asked him who was Tom Pythick? And he said, 'Joe Pythicks's uncle.'

A little further on, I found the older and smaller wall, which used to enclose the pent-up inner prison where nobody was put, except for ceremony. Whoever goes into Marshalsea Place, turning out of Angel Court, leading to Bermondsey, will find his feet on the very paving-stones of the extinct Marshalsea jail; will see its narrow yard to the right and to the left, very little altered if at all, except that the walls were lowered when the place got free; will look upon the rooms in which the debtors lived; will stand among the crowding ghosts of many miserable years.

Little Dorrit*

Mr. Dickens has established a right to a careful examination of what he writes. He boasts—and it is at least a pardonable piece of exultation—of the number of his readers, the implied inference being that he was never so successful before. Apart from the question of taste, which in this quarter was scarcely to be looked for, the very prominent announcement of a large sale looks a little like a latent suspicion that it was not

* By Charles Dickens. London: Bradbury & Evans, 1857.

---

[2] JFS, next year, was to relate 'trading on imaginary capital' to 'the crimes to which religious men are perhaps more prone than their neighbours': 'We can see how narrow and technical an offence the crime which righteously consigned him to penal servitude must have appeared. How could the mere form of writing one name or another make much difference, when his whole life-time was passed in dealing with other men's property, and trading on imaginary capital? He is a terrible illustration of the character of the crimes to which religious men are perhaps more prone than their neighbours—quiet, respectable, gradual sins, which excite no scandal and give no alarm, and which are quite compatible, and indeed, on the principle of paying Paul after you have robbed Peter, have a certain sort of affinity with a great deal of church-going and charity—gentlemanlike sins, which imply no connexion with publicans or sinners—and, above all, good, hardy, practical, vigorous-minded sins, which demand a *mens sana in corpore sano*, and are not part of the mischief which Satan finds for idle hands to do' ('The Winter Assizes', *Sat. Rev.*, 2 Jan. 1858).

94 ON THE NOVEL AND JOURNALISM

quite deserved. 'Oh, I am very well', replied Mr. Merdle, after deliberating about it; 'I am as well as I usually am!' and the man went and cut his throat forthwith.[3] This may serve to remind Mr. Dickens that uncalled-for asseverations of well-doing do not prove the heart to be quite at ease; and if we are right as to his secret misgivings, we can assure him that he has ground for them. Mr. Dickens remarks 'that he has never had so many readers'—of course he means purchasers, though the terms are not convertible. In our slight experience we can assure him that we have yet to meet the man or woman, boy or girl, who can honestly say that he or she has read *Little Dorrit* through. It is the *cultus*[4] of the middle classes to purchase Dickens; but an Act of Parliament would fail to enforce the serious reading of his last production.

The simple fact is, that Mr. Dickens has been spoiled by success—or rather, like many other very clever men, he has mistaken his powers. The late Mr. Liston[5] was an admirable buffoon, but his honest earnest conviction was that *Hamlet* was his strong point. We once knew a Bampton Lecturer[6] who fancied that his real strength lay in knowledge of horse-flesh,[7] and he actually got up the stud-book as he crammed Thucydides and Butler.[8] So it is with Mr. Dickens. He is a great master of humour— not of wit, for of this faculty he is quite innocent—but he thinks that his vocation is that of the social reformer, perhaps of the prophet. He is eminently gifted to be the Jan Steen[9] of letters—he affects the historical canvas of Michael Angelo. Hogarth tried his hand at scriptural subjects[10]—Mr. Dickens thinks that he is a satirist. In either case, the result is the same. We admit that Mr. Dickens has a mission, but it is to make the world grin, not to recreate and rehabilitate society. Sam Weller, Dick Swiveller, and Sairy Gamp[11] are his successes, and we thank him most heartily for them. But when nothing less will content him than to reform the British constitution, to sit in judgment upon the whole law of England—to pronounce the bar, the Church, and all the Courts and institutions of England, its mercantile community, its legal community, its public servants, her Majesty's Ministers, all our charities, and all our politicians, our men of the Exchange, and men of the pulpit, to be downright shams and selfish hypocrites— we are forced to inquire whether this is not one sham among the universal crowd of shams—whether the preacher is not as his flock?

---

[3] MR. MERDLE, a popular financier on an extensive scale. Book the Second, ch. xxiv–xxv. (The final exclamation mark is by JFS, not Dickens, but then Dickens had one at the start, after 'Oh'.)

[4] *OED* An organized system of religious worship or ceremonial; also *transferred sense* 1838 EMERSON and 1846 DE QUINCEY.

[5] John Liston (*c*.1776–1846) happened to make his stage debut in *The Heir at Law*, and later appeared in *The Village Lawyer*.

[6] The annual Bampton Lectures on Christian theology, at Oxford, since 1780.

[7] *OED* Living horses collectively, usually with reference to riding, driving, or racing. 1711 *Spectator* A Person profoundly learned in Horse-flesh. *Life* 68: 'In sport of the gambling variety he never took the slightest interest; and when he became a judge, he shocked a Liverpool audience by asking in all simplicity, "What is the 'Grand National'?"'

[8] Bishop Joseph Butler (1692–1752; *ODNB*, theologian, philosopher).

[9] (*c*.1626–1679), Dutch genre painter.

[10] William Hogarth (1697–1764; *ODNB*, painter, engraver). *The Pool of Bethesda* and *The Good Samaritan*, for St Bartholomew's Hospital; *Moses brought before Pharaoh's Daughter*, for the Foundling Hospital, *Paul before Felix* at Lincoln's Inn, and his altarpiece for St. Mary Redcliffe, Bristol.

[11] From *Pickwick Papers*, Sam Weller (no identifying by Dickens of CHARACTERS in this book). From *The Old Curiosity Shop*, RICHARD SWIVELLER, an easy, careless, somewhat dissipated young man; clerk to Sampson Brass. From *Martin Chuzzlewit*, MRS. SAIREY [not 'Sairy'] GAMP, a professional nurse.

LITTLE DORRIT

We have, however, more specific complaints against Mr. Dickens in the case of *Little Dorrit*. We have a right to ask of an artist so practised the observance of some of the rules of his art. Perhaps, however, as in the case of the Pythoness,[12] the inspiration and the moral purpose were thought sufficient apologies for stumbling prosody and obscure meaning. Mr. Dickens may consider his design quite grand and religious enough to cover defects in composition. We do not think so. Of a writer of stories we claim some observance of the proprieties of a story. The literary execution of *Little Dorrit* is even worse than its inflated and pretentious sermonizing object. Mr. Dickens was never successful in his plots—he never yet constructed an artistic story. But in the present instance he never seems to have a whole before him. As far as we can judge, he wrote *Little Dorrit*, month by month, at haphazard, without ever having sketched out a plan, and failed in executing his own conceptions. He invests his characters with mystery, which he quite fails in clearing up. He suggests complications which involve nothing, and secrets which all end in no meaning. He hints at difficulties which are never unravelled, and we flounder on to the six hundredth page expecting to find a discovery when there is nothing to discover. Either idleness or inability compels him to abandon his characters with the unsatisfactory conclusion that they had no story to tell. Mrs. Clennam's house is haunted by some ghostly mystery—the weird old woman has some impenetrable secret—horrid anticipations of coming doom are in the garrets above and in the cellars below. Will Mr. Dickens assure us that the fall of the house in Tottenham Court Road was not a happy solution of a difficulty which he had not the skill to disentangle? Does he ask us to believe that, when he first introduced us to the old house in the City at p. 23, he foresaw the very prosaic catastrophe of its fall at p. 600?[13] Are we to understand that all Affery's horrors were meant to be resolved into the everyday phenomena of dry-rot?

Then take Miss Wade. It is plain that the author intended to connect her former history with the other characters. He throws out hints and suggestions of some such relation between her and old Casby; but it all comes to nothing. And we are put off with an interpolation of Miss Wade's previous history[14] as *apropos* to the story as the *Memoirs of a Lady of Quality*, which Smollett was paid for inserting in *Peregrine Pickle*.[15] So again with Tattycoram. It is impossible to believe that the parentage of a foundling was not intended to be developed and woven into the plot. Only, somehow or other, Mr. Dickens could not get her to work into the story. Blandois, too, and Mr. and Mrs. Gowan[16]—was it not at first meant that the future of the latter and the antecedents of the first should be connected with the drama of the tale?

In other words, the artistic fault of *Little Dorrit* is that it is no tale. It neither begins nor ends—it has no central interest, no legitimate catastrophe, and no modelling of the

---

[12] Pythia, high priestess of the Temple of Apollo at Delphi, uttering gibberish or dactylic hexameters.

[13] Book the First, ch. iii, and Book the Second, ch. xxxi.

[14] Book the Second, ch. xxi: 'The History of a Self-Tormentor'.

[15] *The Adventures of Peregrine Pickle. In which are included, Memoirs of a Lady of Quality* (1751), the latter by Frances Anne Vane, Viscountess Vane.

[16] MRS. AFFERY FLINTWINCH, wife of Jeremiah Flintwinch, [he being] servant and afterwards partner of Mrs. Clennam. MISS WADE, a sensitive woman, of sullen and ungovernable temper. CHRISTOPHER CASBY, landlord of Bleeding Heart Yard; a selfish, crafty imposter, who grinds his tenants by proxy. HARRIET BEADLE ('Tattycoram'), a handsome, but headstrong and passionate girl; maid to Miss Minnie Meagles. RIGAUD, alias BLANDOIS, alias LAGNIER, a smooth, polished scoundrel. HENRY GOWAN, an artist. 'Mr. and Mrs. Gowan': that is, Henry and his mother MRS. GOWAN, a courtly old lady, of lofty manners.

96   ON THE NOVEL AND JOURNALISM

plot into a whole. This is the fault of Mr. Dickens as an artist. He breaks down under his own conceptions, not having the skill, or not choosing to expend the time, to subordinate them to a general scheme. His characters remind us of the cheap theatrical prints of our schoolboy days, and of the inartificial[17] way in which boys used to act a play in the nursery. Every character strikes an imposing attitude—to use one of Mr. Dickens's own expressions—and he goes through all the scenes grimacing and gesticulating, with outstretched arms and one fixed spasmodic intensity of exaggeration. His actors are never in repose, never relax the stony stare, never vary from the monotonous rigidity of matter or manner. What effect there is, is produced by the wearisome repetition of the same details and the unflagging iteration of the same phrases and the same thoughts. Not one of his *dramatis personae* ever subsides into the commonplace speech of real life. Mrs. Finching,[18] a really good specimen of the grotesque, with her unpunctuated brain and parenthetic gabble of sentiment and kindness of heart, becomes an intolerable bore after (say) the fifteenth specimen of her manner of speech. A rather original conception is Mr. Blandois' French done into English, but after twenty times of 'Holy Blue!' we begin to think that a jest may be worn threadbare. The hard mechanical effort to make out character by elaborately stippling a single feature or a single expression, gives only the unnatural life of a daguerreotype.[19]

Nor is the morality of Mr. Dickens's later works so unexceptionable as he thinks. He knows, at least we know, that it is a libel on human nature to represent every man of five hundred a-year as fit for nothing but to grind the poor, or insult every class of society below his own. It is not the rule of English public men to throw every obstacle in the way of rising genius, as Mr. Dickens would have us to believe; and it would be just as fair to draw all the middle-class men of public life by the lineaments of 'Wiscount Villiams',[20] as it is to represent all official persons under the convenient type of Barnacle.[21] And—we dare to hint it—it hardly reconciles us to virtue and philanthropy, and every excellence that can dignify humanity, to present them in the guise of such intolerable bores as Mr. Arthur Clennam,[22] the incarnation of prosing imbecility, and *Little Dorrit*,[23] that most provoking of all she-saints. In Mr. Dickens's hands, the amiable characters are, we regret to say it, the most tedious of respectabilities. God forgive us—but just as we are tempted to sympathize with every breach of every Commandment, and every assault upon everything that is good and proper, after one of Lord Campbell's[24] sermons to the jury-box, so we must own, with all confusion of

[17]   *OED* Not in accordance with the principles of art; constructed without art or skill.
[18]   MRS. FLORA FINCHING, daughter of Christopher Casby; a well-to-do widow, sentimental and affected, but good-hearted.
[19]   Invented by Louis-Jacques-Mandé Daguerren in 1839, in wide use only till the late 1850s.
[20]   A character in *Punch*.
[21]   CLARENCE BARNACLE ('Barnacle Junior'), son of Mr. Tite Barnacle; a young gentleman employed in the Circumlocution Office. LORD DECIMUS TITE BARNACLE, a peer, and highly placed in the Circumlocution Office. FERDINAND BARNACLE, private secretary to the preceding; a good-looking, well-dressed, agreeable young fellow. MR. TITE BARNACLE, a high official in the Circumlocution Office.
[22]   MR. ARTHUR CLENNAM, the adopted son of Mrs. Clennam.
[23]   AMY DORRIT *('Little Dorrit')*, daughter of Mr. William Dorrit; a shy, retiring, affectionate little woman.
[24]   John Campbell, first Baron Campbell (1779–1861; *ODNB*, lord chancellor). *Life* 96: 'In 1856 he has some intercourse with Lord Campbell, then Chief Justice'; 'He was "overpowered with admiration" at Campbell's appearance. Campbell was "thickset as a navvy, as hard as nails", still full of vigour at the age of seventy-six, about the best judge on the bench now, and looking fit for ten or twelve years' more of work'. (To Mary Stephen, 23 July 1856.) *Life* 279: 'It may be truly said', as he remarks, 'that to hear in their

LITTLE DORRIT

97

face, that 'Fanny, dear',[25] is all but justified in rebelling against the fatiguing goodness of Miss Amy. Our taste may be wicked and corrupt; but if we had to choose between the Misses Dorrit, we confess that Mrs. Sparkler[26] would stand first. By the way, does not Mr. Dickens know the difference between a step-son and a son-in-law?[27] because the former was Mr. Sparkler's relationship to Mr. Merdle, not the latter, which seems to be Mr. Dickens's interpretation of the table of consanguinity.

Not that we are so unjust to Mr. Dickens as to say that he has not retained the elements of his unquestionable powers. In his slighter characteristics, even in *Little Dorrit*, the old manner and the old cunning hand are still discernible. The barrister, with his 'jury droop' and 'eyeglass', is little short of perfection. The Hampton Court dowager[28] is ill-natured and unfair, but vigorously sketched. Casby is as dexterously, as Flora's aunt[29] is coarsely, outlined. But in the dreary waste of tediousness which characterizes the whole community of Bleeding Heart Yard, the stupidity of Pancks and Plornish, and the absurdity of Mrs. General[30]—the woman who was always primming her mouth to the words 'prism' and 'prunes'—we can only ask with dismay where is the cunning hand which drew Pickwick and the two Wellers?[31] Mr. Dickens can, we believe, recover himself—he has simply mistaken his calling[32] and his powers; and, as he promises to meet us again, we trust it will not be with the cold cabbage of Crimean inquiries and Royal British Banks' Administrative Reformers, Tottenham Court Road accidents, Messrs. Redpath, Cameron, and John Sadleir.[33]

happiest moments the summing up of such judges as Lord Campbell, Lord Chief Justice Erle, or Baron Parke, was like listening not only (to use Hobbes's famous expression) to law living and armed, but to justice itself.' (*Hist. Crim. Law* i 456.)

[25] FANNY DORRIT, elder sister of the preceding [AMY DORRIT], of proud and ambitious temper.

[26] Book the Second, ch. xvi, sees Fanny Dorrit become Mrs. Sparkler. MR. EDMUND SPARKLER, a chuckle-headed young man; the son of Mrs. Merdle by her first husband.

[27] 'A son-in-law, with these limited talents, might have been a clog upon another man; but Mr. Merdle did not want a son-in-law for himself; he wanted a son-in-law for Society' (ch. xxi). Still, there has occurred *OED* son-in-law. A stepson. *Obsolete*. But with 1731 FIELDING, and 1738 The step-mother cannot discern the good qualities of her son-in-law.

[28] Mrs Gowan: JFS, 'ill-natured and unfair' (perhaps of her and of Dickens's caricaturing of her).

[29] MR. F.'s AUNT, a severe, grim, taciturn old lady.

[30] MR. PANCKS, the agent who collects Mr Casby's rents. MR. PLORNISH, a plasterer; one of Mr. Casby's tenants. MRS. GENERAL, a widow lady, of imposing and dignified appearance.

[31] Sam Weller and his father.

[32] 'Mr. Thackeray' (*Fraser's*, April 1864; not signed): 'Mr. Dickens expressed his regret, in the *Cornhill Magazine*, that Mr. Thackeray did not sufficiently appreciate the dignity of his calling. He understood it far better than his critics, for he knew that it consisted principally in minding his own business, and writing about matters which he understood. His memory has not to bear the disgrace of such ignorant and mischievous libels as the description of the Circumlocution Office, or the attack on the Court of Chancery in *Bleak House*. If Mr. Thackeray had written a novel about Law Reform, he would have thought it his duty to be acquainted with the elements of the subject.'

[33] The Royal British Bank, established by Royal Charter in 1849, collapsed in 1856; the trial of the directors for conspiracy to defraud the bank's customers was soon to come before the Lord Chief Justice, Lord Campbell (Feb. 1858). For the Administrative Reform Association, p. 55. John Redpath (1796–1869), Scots-Canadian business man, active in the Annexation Movement (proposing that the Canadian Provinces join the United States). John Sadleir (1813–1856), Irish financier, politician, who poisoned himself after the crash of his financial speculations. George Robb, *White-Collar Crime in Modern England* (2009): 'On the very heels of Sadleir's demise, the Royal British Bank failed amid revelations that the bank manager, Hugh Cameron, and two directors, Humphrey Brown and Edward Esdaile, had wasted the bank's resources in unsecured loans to themselves and their friends. Sadleir had implicated the Royal British directors in a letter which was published after his suicide and which caused a run on the bank. It transpired that Cameron, Brown and Esdaile had kept a separate ledger into which they entered certain accounts.'

'Light Literature and the *Saturday Review*' (excerpt) (*Saturday Review*, 11 July 1857)

The term 'light literature' is no longer current, unlike light music, light verse, and light reading. *OED* Of literature, dramatic works, music, etc.: Requiring little mental effort; amusing, entertaining. JFS, referring to the seventeenth century: 'There would seem to have been hardly any light literature in those days, plays excepted' ('Lord Clarendon's "Life"', *Sat. Rev.*, 6 Jan. 1866; *Hor. Sab.* i 334). *Life* 142: 'In the "Cornhill" [from 1860] he had been bound to keep within the limits prescribed by the tastes of average readers of light literature. In the "Pall Mall Gazette" [from 1865] he was able to speak out with perfect freedom upon all the graver topics of the day.' JFS would turn, two months later, to 'Light Literature in France' (*Sat. Rev.*, 5 Sept. 1857), p. 142.

Light Literature and the *Saturday Review* (excerpt)

We do most earnestly believe that the one nation which has reconciled law, liberty, order, and power, cannot be exhaustively distributed into knaves, fools, and literary men. We feel that whatever defects may disfigure our Government and our law—whatever anomalies in Church and State may delight the hearts of writers who are to society what rats and worms are to a ship's bottom—whatever foul scandals may be raked together for the gratification of those who think that our civilization[1] is adequately represented by the sewage of the Old Bailey—there is not, and there probably never was, a nation in the world which more truly feared and served God, or more nobly ruled man, than that English nation of which Mr. Dickens and his admirers ridicule and revile all the most important members. Thinking so, we must of course be reserved and cautious. We do not break with the whole past history of England. We do not pique[2] ourselves on being the sons of fools, the grandsons of jobbers, and the great-grandsons of slaves. We believe that the wonderful structure of which the present generation forms a part, has been built up by no common wisdom, by no vulgar skill; and though we recognise in it many defects and many inconveniences which it is most necessary to supply or to remove, our wish to reform and our wish to preserve are functions of each other. That in holding such views, and in combating those who ignorantly oppose reform, or who ignorantly insult the existing state of things, we are in complete sympathy with the deepest popular feeling, we are most entirely persuaded.

---

[1] 'Our Civilization' (*Sat. Rev.*, 28 June 1856), p. 49.

[2] *OED* To take pride *in*, to plume oneself *upon*. From 1705 POPE. JFS is piqued in the opposite sense (*OED* pricked to resentment): *We* do not break with ... *We* do not plume ourselves upon (our superiority to our ancestors...).

'Madame Bovary'
(*Saturday Review*, 11 July 1857)

The first instalment of Gustave Flaubert's novel was published in Paris in Oct. 1856; the whole, April 1857. Flaubert had been prosecuted in Jan. 1857 for publishing an immoral book; in Feb. he had been acquitted. Of an earlier scandalous novel, JFS had remarked that there is more than one way for such a book to be bad. 'French novels have not the best of reputations as it is; but hitherto no one has felt it necessary to complain of their dulness, whatever may have been thought of their immorality. Mr. Veron has contrived to neutralize the one fault by the other' ('Twenty Thousand a Year', *Sat. Rev.*, 29 Dec. 1855). On an English novel, by Caroline Norton: 'Another observation which such stories as *Lost and Saved* suggest arises from the common criticism upon them. They are always attacked by the same thrust and defended by the same parry. What an immoral book this is, says the critic. I must paint the world as I find it, says the author. Yes, but you should not be prurient, says the critic. No more I am, replies the author. The last issue—prurient or not prurient—involves a different question in respect to every book concerning which it is raised, and need not be further noticed here.'[1] JFS on Balzac (p. 154): 'Balzac has been repeatedly denounced as an immoral writer; and there can be no doubt that in some degree the charge is well founded, though, as we think, in a degree very much lower than that in which it is usually put forward.' JFS's high-minded indecency-threshold was very low, as is clear from his judgment on Montaigne: 'He is undoubtedly an indecent author, and his indecency is much more than mere plainness of speech. He constantly goes out of his way, if he can be said to have any way to go out of, to bring in indecent stories.'[2] The personal perplexity of JFS is genuine and disconcerting: 'There is something—I hardly know what to call it; indecent is too strong a word, but I may say unpleasant in the direction of indecorum—in prolonged and minute discussions about the relations between men and woman, and the characteristics of women as such.'[3] The relations between the French and English languages accommodated for JFS some scepticism about the way in which we 'constantly hear of the extreme precision of the French language' (on Tocqueville, 'Principes', *Sat. Rev.*, 3 Oct. 1863). JFS, 'Carlier's Early History of the American States' (*Sat. Rev.*, 2 April 1864), has quotations from Tocqueville 'in JFS's own translation, apparently' (*On Society, Religion, and Government* 154 n). *Life* 76–7: 'He passed the winter of 1850–51 in Paris, where he learnt French, and attended sittings of the Legislative Assembly, and was especially interested in proceedings in the French law-courts'. JFS: 'Some years ago, a gentleman who passed some months in Paris, and was anxious to make himself familiar with the language and character of the people, was advised to obtain that object by frequenting the theatres. He preferred to devote his time to an assiduous attendance at the criminal courts' (*Sat. Rev.*, 8 Jan. 1859). 'The Case of the Monk Léotade' (1848), 'The Affair of St. Cyr' (1860), and 'The Case of François Lesnier' were reported by JFS in detail and contrasted with English rules of evidence, with JFS keenly attentive to the exact French words of witnesses;

---

[1] 'Anti-Respectability' (*Cornhill*, Sept. 1863; *On Society, Religion, and Government* 122).
[2] 'Montaigne's Essays' (*Sat. Rev.*, 3 Nov. 1866; *Hor. Sab.* i 142–3).
[3] *Liberty, Equality, Fraternity* (1873; 2nd edn, 1874; ed. Julia Stapleton; *Selected Writings of James Fitzjames Stephen*, Oxford University Press, 2017), p. 132.

100 ON THE NOVEL AND JOURNALISM

seven Cases, including those three, concluded *Gen. View 1863*, *Gen. View 1890*, and *Hist. Crim. Law*.

Madame Bovary*

It was not without considerable hesitation that we determined to review *Madame Bovary*. The book has, however, we are informed, excited great attention at Paris, and has been hailed with much applause, as a specimen of 'realism' in fiction, by very eminent French critics. Though it is not a work which we can recommend any man, far less any woman, to read, its success appears to us to be a fact worthy of the attention of all who take an interest in the condition of French society. The story is told in a very few words. M. Bovary, a country apothecary, marries the daughter of a farmer, who is too highly educated for her rank in life. She finds herself extremely dull, and by way of satisfying her love for excitement carries on two successive intrigues, in the course of which she involves herself and her husband in debt to a large amount. His goods are taken in execution.[4] She appeals to her lovers to pay off the execution creditor, and, on their refusal, she poisons herself.[5] Her husband, who loved her passionately, though very foolishly, is inconsolable for her loss, but has implicit confidence in her purity. At last, by an accident, he discovers the letters which had passed between her and her lovers, and dies of grief. Such is the story; and it is obvious enough that it cannot be otherwise than offensive according to our views. Indeed, the volume contains not a few passages which would of themselves justify very strong language if there were any danger that M. Flaubert's example would be followed in this country, or that his book would become popular amongst English readers. We do not, however, feel ourselves called upon to make use of any very indignant expressions. There is no fear that our novelists will outrage public decency. Their weaknesses forbid such dangerous eccentricity quite as much as their virtues.

Whether *Madame Bovary* is a true representation of French life or not, is a question which could only be answered by persons possessed of a special knowledge of the subject, to which we make no pretensions. Some facts about it are, however, sufficiently plain. The author obviously belongs to what, for want of a better name, we must call the realist school of novelists. His style conveys to us the impression that it has been formed upon that of Mr. Thackeray, of whose influence it shows the strongest traces. Thus the first half of the book is taken up with a description of the education and early career of an obscure apothecary, whose widest experience of life consists of a short course of study at Rouen, and who settles down to practice in an obscure hamlet in Normandy, with a fond but troublesome mother[6]—a wife twenty years older than himself, and falsely supposed to be rich, who dies at the end of two or three chapters[7]—no tastes, no amusements, and very little occupation. The dulness of such an existence, its irritating effects upon the spoilt girl who is introduced to it, and the contrast afforded by the splendours to which Madame Bovary and her husband are

---

* *Madame Bovary. Mœurs de Province*. Par Gustave Flaubert. Paris, 1857.

---

[4] *OED* The seizure of the goods or person of a debtor in default of payment.
[5] Part Three, ch. viii.   [6] Mère Bovary.   [7] Héloise dies at the end of Part One, ch. ii.

MADAME BOVARY

introduced for one night by the politic invitation of a neighbouring electioneering marquis, are described with great spirit, and bear the marks of a good deal of patient and careful observation. There are also several descriptions of local scenes—especially one of an agricultural show—which are drawn with great spirit, and much apparent fidelity.

We do not therefore feel ourselves at liberty to doubt that the main facts of the novel might well occur without producing any very strong surprise amongst M. Flaubert's countrymen. If this be so, we can only say that not merely the facts and the language, but the whole framework and tendency of the story, are symptoms of the most fatal kind. It is indeed lamentable that any considerable or prominent portion of society in any country should be willing to recognise in such a book as this anything like a portrait of themselves; and it is perhaps even more lamentable that a man of talent should consider such a book a moral one, which we are inclined to believe to be the case with the author of the work before us. The character of Madame Bovary herself is one of the most essentially disgusting that we ever happened to meet with. It is one which we should be extremely sorry to attribute to any woman, and if it could ever become to any extent common, it could not for any length of time be compatible with the existence of society. The notion of duty or responsibility never seems to cross her mind. Neither as a daughter, a wife, nor a mother, does it ever occur to her that she has any other object in life than that of gratifying her own tastes, and especially her love of excitement. Her father's farm is dull—her husband's house is dull—he is not a man of genius—and as she only married him in order to be excited and roused by the society of a person with some aims in life, and some capacity to sustain them, she feels herself personally wronged by his dulness, and takes a vindictive pleasure in betraying him. Her child is only a transient amusement, of which she soon tires. Even in her love, when at last it is aroused, there is nothing generous or noble. She wishes to sacrifice each of her lovers to her own inclinations, trying in vain to persuade one of them to rob his employer, and the other to ruin his reputation by eloping with her. It must, however, be owned that the men are as bad as the woman. The lovers are paltry, heartless cowards, the husband a weak fool, and the other characters wretched compounds of cognate vices. From the first page of the book to the last, not a person is introduced calculated to excite any other feelings than contempt or disgust. No skill in the mechanical part of a novelist's art can redeem a defect so capital as this. We should be sorry to call the book a disgusting performance; but disgust is certainly the most prominent feeling that it awakens.

Perhaps the worst feature of *Madame Bovary* is the obvious intention on the part of the author to write rather a moral book. It may be quite true that breaking the seventh commandment is the only mode of passing her time in which the heroine takes much pleasure; but the most rigorous moralist could not wish her to be more severely punished for it. If the work could be looked upon merely in the light of a precedent, no one can say that it would tell in favour of immorality. Nor is it altogether an answer to this to say that the bad effect of full-length descriptions of vice is not done away with by the good effect of executing poetical justice upon it. This is no doubt true; but in considering the intentions of an author we must remember how very conventional is the standard of what it is permissible to say and to write. No one would call Milton or Shakspeare immoral. Yet *Paradise Lost* and *Othello* contain passages which could not be read aloud to English ladies. Indeed, if it were not for the force of habit, the same difficulty would constantly occur in reading the Bible. The real immorality which is involved in such a tale as *Madame Bovary*, lies in the want which it presumes in its readers of any moral distinctions at all. It says emphatically—though, like all such books, rather clumsily—that adultery may very possibly end in the utter ruin and destruction of the sinning woman; but it does not seem to recognise the fact that in itself, and apart from the occasional and exceptional cases in which it may be so punished, it is vile, hateful, and treacherous. Cut off the last chapter or two of *Madame Bovary*, and the impression left on the reader is that the author rather sympathizes with his heroine. Leave them in, and they show far more dislike of the consequences than of the character of the offence. In fact, strange as such a comparison may seem, *Madame Bovary* has a strong family likeness to a certain class of tracts—those which turn upon what we hope we may call, without offence, a sort of providential *tour de force*. When we hear of a boy who is drowned for boating on Sunday, the logical conclusion is that it is foolish to do that for which you may be drowned, but not that it is wrong to boat on Sunday; and in precisely the same way, we infer from *Madame Bovary* that poisoning by arsenic is a very painful death, and that it is well to avoid what may lead to it, however pleasant.

M. Flaubert's book suggests some reflections more interesting to Englishmen than any which concern either the book or the author. There are probably half a dozen scenes in it which no English author of reputation would venture to insert in any of his publications; and indeed there is no subject on which we are so apt to plume ourselves as the modern purification of our light literature. But is this true? And if it is, how far does it prove that we are more moral than our neighbours? It is true in one sense, no doubt, that our light literature is pure enough. That is, it is written upon the principle that it is never to contain anything which a modest man might not, with satisfaction to himself, read aloud to a young lady. But surely it is very questionable whether it is desirable that no novels should be written except those which are fit for young ladies to read. It is not so with any other branch of literature. Theology, history, philosophy, morality, law, and physical science are all studied at the reader's peril; and it would be just as prudish to affect to be shocked at finding indecent passages in Herodotus, or in *Cook's Voyages*,[8] as to cry shame on Hale's *Pleas of the Crown*,[9] or Taylor's *Medical Jurisprudence*.[10] Are works of imagination, then, such mere toys that they ought always

[8] James Cook (1728–1779; *ODNB*, explorer), with three voyages to Australia and New Zealand, 1770–79.

[9] Sir Matthew Hale (1609–1676), *Historia Placitorum Coronae, The History of the Pleas of the Crown*, a three-volume work on criminal law of which only the first volume was completed (published 1736). *Life* 11 n: Sir Edward Coke (1552–1634; *ODNB*), expounder of the common law in his *Reports* (1600–15) and *Institutes of the Laws of England* (1628–44). *Gen. View 1863* 101–2: 'In the course of the seventeenth century two remarkable works... still regarded as books of the highest authority... Coke's Third Institute, and Lord Hale's *History of the Pleas of the Crown*... Hale discusses at length the theory of punishments in general, and in particular that of capital punishments, and enters with more learning and greater sympathy than Coke into the history of the laws which he deals with, and of the occasions upon which they were passed'

[10] Alfred Swaine Taylor (1806–1880; *ODNB*, medical jurist and toxicologist). *On poisoning by Strychnia, with Comments on the Medical Evidence at the Trial of William Palmer for the Murder of John Parsons Cook* (1856). Gen. View 1863 122 n.: 'Alfred Swaine Taylor's pioneering Medical Jurisprudence first appeared in 1836. Subsequent editions (including that of 1861, probably used by JFS) became the leading reference work on the subject well into the twentieth century.' Gen. View 1863 304–28, 'The Case of William Palmer', with Taylor's expert testimony. Strychine came curiously to JFS's mind; for instance, of Burke on the Sublime: 'He oddly observes, "No smells or tastes can produce a grand sensation, except excessive bitters and intolerable stenches." According to this, a man tasting strychine in a sewer would be in a sublime situation.' Edmund Burke's *Philosophical Enquiry into the Origin of Our Ideas of the Sublime and Beautiful* (1757), part 2, sect. 22: 'Smell and Taste, Bitters and Stenches.'

to be calculated for girlish ignorance? If Shakspeare had never written a line which women in the present day could not read, he would never have been the greatest of poets. If we had only expurgated copies of the classics, we should have a most inadequate conception of Greece and Rome. No doubt our most popular writers of fiction accept, and are proud of, the position which we are describing. Many of them seem to think that the highest function of a poet is the amusement of children; but we are by no means prepared to say that, in literature, emasculation produces purity. Our statistical returns, the nightly appearance of our streets, and those verbatim reports of trials which are so disgusting that the papers which publish them[11] advocate the repeal of the laws which, as they affect to think, necessitate their publication, surely teach us that we are not so very immaculate. Whether a light literature entirely based upon love, and absolutely and systematically silent as to one most important side of it, may not have some tendency to stimulate passions to which it is far too proper ever to allude, is a question which is too wide for our limits on the present occasion; but it is one which we should do well to take into serious consideration before we preach the doctrine that the contemporaries of Mr. Dickens have made a vast step in advance of the contemporaries of Fielding.

---

[11] 'The Mote and the Beam' (*Sat. Rev.*, 3 Dec. 1864), p. 239.

'The License of Modern Novelists'
(*Edinburgh Review*, July 1857)

Dickens was to reply: 'The License of Modern Novelists is a taking title. But it suggests another—the License of Modern Reviewers' (p. 138). Jan-Melissa Schramm investigated the relation of the titular form, 'The License of . . .', to a crucial legal controversy that brought warnings of the collusion of advocacy with deceit, exaggeration, and inventiveness (ch. 3, 'Criminal Advocacy and Victorian Realism', *Testimony and Advocacy in Victorian Law, Literature, and Theology*, 2000). The license of advocacy raised the question of 'The Morality of Advocacy' (defended by JFS, *Cornhill*, April 1861). Schramm establishes the pertinence of Dickens's support of the work of Charles Phillips at the Old Bailey which had led to the Prisoners' Counsel Act of 1836 and its allowing counsel to speak on behalf of prisoners charged with felony; previously they had had to speak for themselves. Dickens (as 'Manlius') published in the *Morning Chronicle* (21 and 23 June 1840) two letters on 'The License of Counsel', the title of an essay that followed in *The Examiner* (12 July 1840, probably by Albany Fonblanque). Lisa Rodensky, in *The Crime in Mind* 181–6, scrutinizes the arguments and the argumentation of this central essay of JFS in relation to facts and fictions. 'Stephen goes too far in suggesting that novelists skilled in producing literary effects are not also skilled in applying reasons to those effects; however, more important is the idea of a leap to a foregone conclusion, the confidence with which hard-to-prove matters can be asserted as a "striking tale" in a manner that leaves nothing but an assurance that something doubtful or probable has become a sure thing.' JFS: 'The most influential of all indirect moral teachers—we mean contemporary novelists'—are colluding with 'the newspapers' to exaggerate 'the failures, the prejudices, and the stupidity of the executive'. His responsibility, then and there, is 'examining the justice of Mr. Dickens's general charges, and the accuracy of Mr. Reade's specific accusations' ('how much injustice', 'injustice to the institutions of English society', 'so unjust'). But the license of modern novelists was matched by that of JFS when he protested against Dickens's having castigated officers of the Government (in the persons of the Circumlocution Office) for their obstructive procrastination. JFS twice proclaimed there to have been, rather, a governmental triumph:

What does Mr. Dickens think of the whole organisation of the Post Office, and of the system of cheap postage, which was invented in this country, and has been adopted by almost every State on the Continent? Every branch of this establishment shows the greatest power of arrangement and contrivance—even mechanical contrivance. Mr. Dickens can never tear a penny stamp from its fellows without having before his eyes an illustration of the watchful ingenuity of this branch of the Circumlocution Office.

Or, to take a single and well-known example, how does he account for the career of Mr. Rowland Hill?[1] A gentleman in a private and not very conspicuous position, writes a pamphlet recommending what amounted to a revolution in a most important department of the Government. Did the Circumlocution Office neglect him, traduce him, break his heart, and ruin his fortune? They adopted his scheme, and gave him the leading share

---

[1] Sir Rowland Hill (1795–1879; *ODNB*, postal reformer and civil servant).

THE LICENSE OF MODERN NOVELISTS 105

in carrying it out, and yet this is the Government which Mr. Dickens declares to be a sworn foe to talent, and a systematic enemy to ingenuity.

Aware that JFS had been altogether wrong about this, and Dickens altogether right, Leslie Stephen in due course grudgingly conceded that JFS had 'included an injudicious reference to the case of the Post Office and Rowland Hill' (*injudicious* is very judicious but might ask to have genuine weight when judging a judge)—whereupon there was a brotherly move to damage-control: '...the case of the Post Office and Rowland Hill, which was not, I believe, due to Fitzjames himself, and which enabled Dickens to reply with some effect in "Household Words." '[2] Given below (p. 138) is Dickens's retort, 'Curious Misprint in the *Edinburgh Review*' (1 Aug. 1857). JFS's father wrote to JFS, warning him against Dickens:

> About Rowland Hill he is not far wrong...He is evidently very angry as a man who has so long been buried in public applause must be at the first indication of failing popularity. I do not know that he has a right to be angry—but I should doubt the wisdom of exciting him any more. He is rather a formidable enemy to deal with, and you are best without enemies...e.g. If the Govt. should offer you employment under the Attorney Genl's project Dickens would want neither the will nor the power to annoy you...also if a man is to fight he ought not to be handicapped, and the ER [*Edinburgh Review*] has tied your hands so much as to prevent your planting some of the most effective blows which might have been struck.[3]

The blows that JFS had struck against Dickens were aligned with those against Reade for his novel (1856), with the final blows being against a novelist who, for JFS's present censures, was arraigned as a biographer: E. C. Gaskell, for her *Life of Charlotte Brontë*. Published on 25 March 1857, with a second edition in May,[4] it incurred a prompt legal action by Lady Scott, and another from the Rev. William Carus Wilson. Letters by lawyers in the Scott action, offering and accepting a retraction, were in *The Times*, 30 May 1857.[5]

The License of Modern Novelists*

To give the young any direct instruction in morals or politics, unhappily forms no part of the customary and established system of modern English education. A youth may pass through our public schools and universities hearing little of his duties to society and to his country. Of classical and theological culture he will, indeed, experience no want, but he can receive no positive moral instruction except what comes to him through theological channels, or from the domestic influences of the society in which

---

* *Little Dorrit*. By CHARLES DICKENS. London: 1857. 2. *It is Never Too Late to Mend. A Matter-of-Fact Romance*. By CHARLES READE. Fifth edition. London: 1857. 3. *The Life of Charlotte Brontë, Author of 'Jane Eyre', 'Shirley'*, and *'Villette'*. By E. C. GASKELL, Author of 'Mary Barton', and 'Ruth.' 2 vols. London: 1857.

---

[2] *Life* 108. *Life* 110: 'I believe that the "Edinburgh Review" still acted upon the precedent set by Jeffrey, according to which a contributor, especially, of course, a young contributor, was regarded as supplying raw material which might be rather arbitrarily altered by the editor.'

[3] K. J. M. Smith, *James Fitzjames Stephen: Portrait of a Victorian Rationalist* (1988), 20–1.

[4] The third edition, Nov. 1857, includes a revised ch. iv and xiii.

[5] 'Mrs. Gaskell's Recantation' (*Sat. Rev.*, 6 June 1857), though held by K. J. M. Smith to be 'probably of Fitzjames' authorship', was not in Leon Radzinowicz's Publications of JFS (1957), and was not admitted by Thomas E. Schneider, after careful scrutiny, to the Bibliography of JFS's Articles and Reviews that is appended to the *Life*.

he lives. This defect in our higher education is in a great measure peculiar to the present generation. In the last century, a certain set of opinions upon subjects of a political and moral character formed part of the creed of every person of education. That the British Constitution combined the advantages and the defects of monarchy, aristocracy, and democracy; that the alliance between Church and State secured the liberties of both; that English law was the perfection of reason, and the birthright of every Briton; that every man had by his representatives a share in the government of his country, and that it was his duty and his right to take a corresponding interest in its politics: these, and many other beliefs of a similar kind, were as much part of the training of a gentleman as the doctrine that *verbum personale concordat cum nominativo*.[6] It certainly is as far from our intention, as it would be out of our power, to attempt to restore the currency of the old coin of political dogmatism, so effectually decried in Bentham's Book of Fallacies.[7] But we think that negative and critical conclusions are not the only results at which we ought to arrive upon these subjects, and that they are worse suited than any others to be made the staple of popular education. It ought not to be our object to instil into the minds of the young a blind admiration, or a blind contempt, of the institutions under which they live. In this, as in all other branches of education, the rule of truth is the only safe rule; and truth is outraged if contempt and ridicule are the only feelings excited in the mind of an educated man by the contemplation of the political and social arrangements of his country.

This doctrine, however, is much in favour amongst one class of writers who are, perhaps, the most influential of all indirect moral teachers—we mean contemporary novelists. The popularity of a form of literature which is at once a stimulant and an anodyne, and which engrosses the imagination, whilst it does not absolutely exclude the exercise of the understanding, needs no explanation; but there is another source of the educational influence of novels which most of us have felt, though it has not, we think, been usually recognised so explicitly as their other attractions. Through novels young people are generally addressed for the first time as equals upon the most interesting affairs of life. There they see grown-up men and women described, and the occupations of mature life discussed, without any *arrière pensée*[8] as to the moral effects which the discussion may have upon their own minds. To an inquisitive youth, novels are a series of lectures upon life, in which the professor addresses his pupils as his equals and as men of the world. There, for the first time, the springs of human actions are laid bare, and the laws of human society discussed in language intelligible and attractive to young imaginations and young hearts. Such teachers can never be otherwise than influential, but in the present day their influence is enormously increased by the facilities which cheap publication affords to them. Upwards of a million of the cheap shilling volumes which ornament railway book-stalls[9] are disposed of annually, and the effect of these publications on the whole mind of the community can hardly be exaggerated. Even Mr. Reade's novel, 'It is never too late to mend', is advertised to

---

[6] A verb in its 'person' agrees with its noun.

[7] Jeremy Bentham (1748–1832; *ODNB*, political and philosophical thinker). *The Book of Fallacies* (1824).

[8] Misused by JFS as though it meant second thoughts, reconsideration. But 'behind-thought', not 'later thought': *OED* A concealed thought or intention. From 1824 LADY MORGAN such views of society... concealed an '*arrière pensée*'.

[9] 'Railroad Bookselling' (*Sat. Rev.*, 13 Jan. 1857), p. 85.

have reached the twelfth thousand of its circulation, and we believe Mr. Dickens's tales sell about 40,000 copies on publication.

These facts furnish an apology, which we feel to be necessary, for devoting some attention to two books which justify the opinion we have formed on the influence exercised by such novels over the moral and political opinions of the young, the ignorant, and the inexperienced. That opinion is, that they tend to beget hasty generalisations and false conclusions. They address themselves almost entirely to the imagination upon subjects which properly belong to the intellect. Their suggestions go so far beyond their assertions that the author's sense of responsibility is greatly weakened, and by suppressing all that is dull, all that does not contribute to dramatic effect, and all that falls beyond a certain conventional circle of feelings, they caricature instead of representing the world. This applies even to those ordinary domestic relations, which are the legitimate province of novels. Love, marriage, friendship, grief, and joy are very different things in a novel from what they are in real life, and the representations of novelists are not only false, but often in the highest degree mischievous when they apply, not to the feelings, but to the facts and business transactions of the world. We propose to notice the two works before us, as an illustration of these observations, and we shall show before we conclude that Mrs. Gaskell's 'Life of Miss Brontë' is in some respects obnoxious[10] to the same criticism, though it claims a place in another branch of literature.

We do not of course undervalue the part which fiction has often played in the inculcation of truth, and a thousand imaginary characters crowd upon the mind which reflect with signal brilliancy the noblest graces and the purest virtues of our race. Where are we to find greater refinement than in Sir Charles Grandison[11]—greater ingenuity and perseverance than in Robinson Crusoe—more pathetic simplicity and devotedness than in Jeanie Deans?[12] But there is a very wide distinction between creations wrought up to the true ideal, and attempts to copy life by throwing a false and distorted light on real incidents. The incidents may in themselves be things which have actually taken place, yet they sometimes give most erroneous and exaggerated impressions when they are pressed into the service of romance.

'Little Dorrit' is not one of the most pleasing or interesting of Mr. Dickens's novels. The plot is singularly cumbrous and confused—the characters rather uninteresting— and the style often strained to excess. We are not however tempted, by the comparative inferiority of this production of a great novelist, to forget the indisputable merits of Mr. Dickens. Even those who dislike a good deal of the society to which he introduces his readers, and who are not accustomed to the language of his personages, must readily acknowledge that he has described modern English low life with infinite humour and fidelity, but without coarseness. He has caught and reproduced that native wit which is heard to perfection in the repartees of an English crowd: and though his path has often lain through scenes of gloom, and poverty, and wretchedness, and guilt, he leaves behind him a spirit of tenderness and humanity which does honour to his heart. We wish he had dealt as fairly and kindly with the upper classes of society as he has

---

[10] *OED* With *to*: Liable, subject, exposed, open.

[11] *The History of Sir Charles Grandison. In a Series of Letters Published from the Originals.* By the editor of Pamela and Clarissa [Samuel Richardson] (1753).

[12] Scott, *The Heart of Midlothian* (1818).

108   ON THE NOVEL AND JOURNALISM

with the lower; and that he had more liberally portrayed those manly, disinterested, and energetic qualities which make up the character of an English gentleman. Acute observer as he is, it is to be regretted that he should have mistaken a Lord Decimus for the type of an English statesman, or Mr. Tite[13] for a fair specimen of a public servant. But in truth we cannot recall any single character in his novels, intended to belong to the higher ranks of English life, who is drawn with the slightest approach to truth or probability. His injustice to the institutions of English society is, however, even more flagrant than his animosity to particular classes in that society. The rich and the great are commonly held up to ridicule for their folly, or to hatred for their selfishness. But the institutions of the country, the laws, the administration, in a word the government under which we live, are regarded and described by Mr. Dickens as all that is most odious and absurd in despotism or in oligarchy. In every new novel he selects one or two of the popular cries of the day, to serve as seasoning to the dish which he sets before his readers. It may be the Poor Laws, or Imprisonment for Debt, or the Court of Chancery, or the harshness of Mill-owners, or the stupidity of Parliament,[14] or the inefficiency of the Government, or the insolence of District Visitors,[15] or the observance of Sunday, or Mammon-worship, or whatever else you please. He is equally familiar with all these subjects. If there was a popular cry against the management of a hospital, he would no doubt write a novel on a month's warning about the ignorance and temerity with which surgical operations are performed; and if his lot had been cast in the days when it was fashionable to call the English law the perfection of reason, he would probably have published monthly denunciations of Lord Mansfield's Judgment in *Perrin* v. *Blake*,*[16] in blue covers adorned with curious hieroglyphics, intended to represent springing uses, executory devises, and contingent remainders.[17] We recommend him to draw the materials of his next work from Dr. Hassall[18] on the Adulteration of Food, or the Report on Scotch Lunatics. Even the catastrophe in 'Little Dorrit' is evidently borrowed from the recent fall of houses in Tottenham Court Road, which happens to have appeared in the newspapers at a convenient moment.

---

[13] Tite Barnacle and the extended family: JFS, '*Little Dorrit*' footnote, p. 96.

[14] JFS on Parliament, p. 84.

[15] LOUISA GRADGRIND (the eldest child of Mr. and Mrs. Gradgrind, afterwards the wife of Mr. Josiah Bounderby). She 'visits' STEPHEN BLACKPOOL (an honest hard-working power-loom weaver). *Hard Times*, book 2, ch. vi.

[16]* JFS, note: Lord Mansfield's Judgment in Perrin v. Blake. William Mansfield, earl of Mansfield (1705–1793; *ODNB*, judge and politician), reaffirming the law on contributory negligence and recovery of damages. *Life* 9, on JFS's grandfather ('writer on imprisonment for debt'): 'Stephen argued his case before Lord Mansfield. The great lawyer was naturally less amenable to reason than the prisoners. He was, however, impressed, it is reported, by the manliness and energy of the applicant.'

[17] *OED* springing *Law* = CONTINGENT. BLACKSTONE, *Comm*. Herein these, which are contingent or springing, uses differ from an executory devise. (Also *Comm*. Contingent or executory remainders are where the estate in remainder is limited to take effect, either to a dubious and uncertain person, or upon a dubious and uncertain event.) JFS, 'Berkeley's Metaphysical Works': 'There is a certain sublimity about this way of viewing the subject, yet it has also its grotesque side. When I leave this room all the furniture in it would cease to be till somebody else came in and looked at it, if the fact that it is perceived by God did not keep it in *esse*. This might be exactly expressed by saying, in the language of English conveyancing, that Berkeley regarded his Maker as a universal trustee to preserve contingent remainders' (*Sat. Rev.*, 7 Sept. 1867; *Hor. Sab.* iii 11). *Life* 230 on JFS and Berkeley.

[18] Arthur Hill Hassall (1817–1894; *ODNB*, physician and microscopist). *Food: Its Adulterations, and the Methods for their Detection* (1855). *Adulterations Detected; or, Plain Instructions for the Discovery of Frauds in Food and Medicine* (1857).

THE LICENSE OF MODERN NOVELISTS

Mr. Reade is less well known as a writer, but after publishing two popular, though not very edifying stories,[19] he has at last composed a novel of much greater length, which affords a convincing proof of the temptation to falsify and misrepresent the facts upon which such stories are founded. This book has propagated through the length and breadth of the country imputations against the Government, the judges, and private individuals, so grave, so unjust, so cruel, that we think it is the duty of criticism to expose them.

By examining the justice of Mr. Dickens's general charges, and the accuracy of Mr. Reade's specific accusations, we shall endeavour to show how much injustice may be done, and how much unfounded discontent may be engendered, by these one-sided and superficial pictures of popular abuses.

It is not a little curious to consider what qualifications a man ought to possess before he could, with any kind of propriety, hold the language Mr. Dickens sometimes holds about the various departments of social life. Scott, we all know, was a lawyer and an antiquarian. Sir Edward Lytton has distinguished himself in political life, and his books contain unquestionable evidence of a considerable amount of classical and historical reading. Mr. Thackeray hardly ever steps beyond those regions of society and literature which he has carefully explored. But in Mr. Dickens's voluminous works, we do not remember to have found many traces of these solid acquirements; and we must be permitted to say, for it is no reflection on any man out of the legal profession, that his notions of law, which occupy so large a space in his books, are precisely those of an attorney's clerk. He knows what arrest for debt is, he knows how affidavits are sworn. He knows the physiognomy[20] of courts of justice, and he has heard that Chancery suits sometimes last forty years; though he seems not to have the remotest notion that there is any difference between suits for the administration of estates and suits for the settlement of disputed rights, and that the delay which is an abuse in the one case, is inevitable in the other. The greatest of our statesmen, lawyers, and philosophers would shrink from delivering any trenchant and unqualified opinion upon so complicated and obscure a subject as the merits of the whole administrative Government of the empire.[21] To Mr. Dickens the question presents no such difficulty. He stumbles upon the happy phrase of 'the Circumlocution Office'[22] as an impersonation[23] of the Government; strikes out the brilliant thought, repeated just ten times in twenty-three lines, that whereas ordinary people want to know how to do their business, the whole art of Government lies in discovering 'how not to do it'; and with these somewhat unmeaning phrases he proceeds to describe, in a light and playful tone, the government of his country.

Everybody has read the following chapter of 'Little Dorrit'; but we are not equally sure that everybody has asked himself what it really means. It means, if it means anything, that

---

[19] Charles Reade (1814–1884; *ODNB*, novelist and playwright). *Peg Woffington: A Novel* (1852); *Christie Johnstone: A Novel* (1853).

[20] *OED transferred sense* The general appearance or external features of anything material.

[21] Hermione Lee, of JFS's father: 'The Right Honourable James Stephen was one of the most influential colonial administrators of the nineteenth century, known, only half-admiringly, as "Mr Over-Secretary Stephen" or "Mr Mother-Country Stephen". His main life's task (like his father's) was to work for emancipation in the Colonies, as counsel to the Colonial Office and Board of Trade, and as Under-Secretary (and in reality the dominant administrator) to the Colonies' (Introductory Essay, *Life* xxiv).

[22] *Little Dorrit*, Book the First, ch. x.

[23] A word enjoyed by Dickens: 'the very impersonation of good-humour' (*Barnaby Rudge: A Tale of the Riots of 'eighty* (1841), ch. iv.

110   ON THE NOVEL AND JOURNALISM

the result of the British constitution, of our boasted freedom, of parliamentary representation, and of all we possess, is to give us the worst government on the face of the earth—the clatter of a mill grinding no corn, the stroke of an engine drawing no water.

CHAPTER X
CONTAINING THE WHOLE SCIENCE OF GOVERNMENT

The Circumlocution Office was (as everybody knows without being told) the most important Department under Government. No public business of any kind could possibly be done at any time, without the acquiescence of the Circumlocution Office.[24]

This glorious establishment had been early in the field, when the one sublime principle involving the difficult art of governing a country, was first distinctly revealed to statesmen. It had been foremost to study that bright revelation, and to carry its shining influence through the whole of the official proceedings. Whatever was required to be done, the Circumlocution Office was beforehand with all the public departments in the art of perceiving—HOW NOT TO DO IT.

Through this delicate perception, through the tact with which it invariably seized it, and through the genius with which it always acted on it, the Circumlocution Office had risen to overtop all the public departments; and the public condition had risen to be—what it was.

It is true that How not to do it was the great study and object of all public departments and professional politicians all round the Circumlocution Office. It is true that every new premier and every new government, coming in because they had upheld a certain thing as necessary to be done, were no sooner come in than they applied their utmost faculties to discovering, How not to do it. It is true that from the moment when a general election was over, every returned man who had been raving on hustings because it hadn't been done, and who had been asking the friends of the honourable gentleman in the opposite interest on pain of impeachment to tell him why it hadn't been done, and who had been asserting that it must be done, and who had been pledging himself that it should be done, began to devise, How it was not to be done. It is true that the debates of both Houses of Parliament the whole session through, uniformly tended to the protracted deliberation, How not to do it. It is true that the royal speech at the opening of such session virtually said, My lords and gentlemen, you have a considerable stroke of work to do, and you will please to retire to your respective chambers, and discuss, How not to do it. It is true that the royal speech, at the close of such session, virtually said, My lords and gentlemen, you have through several laborious months been considering with great loyalty and patriotism, How not to do it, and you have found out; and with the blessing of Providence upon the harvest (natural, not political), I now dismiss you. All this is true, but the Circumlocution Office went beyond it.

Because the Circumlocution Office went on mechanically, every day, keeping this wonderful, all-sufficient wheel of statesmanship, How not to do it, in motion. Because the Circumlocution Office was down upon any ill-advised public servant who was going to do it, or who appeared to be by any surprising accident in remote danger of doing it, with a minute, and a memorandum, and a letter of instructions, that extinguished him.[25]

---

[24] JFS silently omits a passage: 'If another Gunpowder Plot had been discovered half an hour before the lighting of the match, nobody would have been justified in saving the parliament until there had been half a score of boards, half a bushel of minutes, several sacks of official memoranda, and a family-vault full of ungrammatical correspondence, on the part of the Circumlocution Office.'

[25] JFS silently omits a further passage: 'It was this spirit of national efficiency in the Circumlocution Office that had gradually led to its having something to do with everything. Mechanicians, natural philosophers, soldiers, sailors, petitioners, memorialists, people with grievances, people who wanted to prevent grievances, people who wanted to redress grievances, jobbing people, jobbed people, people who couldn't get

THE LICENSE OF MODERN NOVELISTS

Numbers of people were lost in the Circumlocution Office. Unfortunates with wrongs, or with projects for the general welfare (and they had better have had wrongs at first, than have taken that bitter English recipe for certainly getting them), who in slow lapse of time and agony had passed safely through other public departments; who, according to rule, had been bullied in this, over-reached by that, and evaded by the other; got referred at last to the Circumlocution Office, and never reappeared in the light of day. Boards sat upon them, secretaries minuted upon them, commissioners gabbled about them, clerks registered, entered, checked, and ticked them off, and they melted away. In short, all the business of the country went through the Circumlocution Office, except the business that never came out of it; and *its* name was Legion.[26]

This is no isolated ebullition. The Circumlocution Office forms one of the standing decorations of the work in which it is depicted. The cover of the book is adorned by a picture, representing, amongst other things, Britannia in a Bath-chair, drawn by a set of effete[27] idiots, an old woman, a worn-out cripple in a military uniform, and a supercilious young dandy, who buries the head of his cane in his moustaches. The chair is pushed on behind by six men in foolscaps, who are followed by a crowd of all ages and both sexes, intended, we presume, to represent that universal system of jobbing[28] and favouritism, which was introduced into the public service by Sir Charles Trevelyan and Sir Stafford Northcote,[29] shortly before the time when Mr. Dickens began his novel.[30] The spirit of the whole book is the same. The Circumlocution Office is constantly introduced as a splendid example of all that is base and stupid. Messrs. Tite Barnacle and Stiltstalking[31] are uniformly put forward as the representatives of the twenty or thirty permanent under-secretaries and heads of departments, by whom so large a portion of the public affairs is conducted, and every species of meanness, folly, and vulgarity is laid to their charge.

rewarded for merit, and people who couldn't get punished for demerit, were all indiscriminately tucked up under the foolscap paper of the Circumlocution Office.'

[26] Mark 5:9, Come out of the man, thou unclean spirit. And he asked him, What is thy name? And he answered, saying, My name is Legion: for we are many.

[27] JFS often uses the word with a touch of the original sense (*OED* that has ceased to bring forth offspring; with 1840 CARLYLE Nature. .was as if effete now; could not any longer produce Great Men.) *OED figurative* that has exhausted its vigour and energy . . . of persons: weak, ineffectual; degenerate. More recently, effeminate.

[28] Dickens, 'jobbing people, jobbed people' (Book the First, ch. x). The verb is more stark than the noun 'job'. (*OED* The action of using a public office or service for private gain or party advantage; the perpetration of corrupt jobs; jobbery.) *Life* 27: 'In 1813 Lord Bathurst . . . appointed James Stephen Counsel to the Colonial Department', with note by Leslie Stephen: 'My grandfather takes some trouble to show—and, as I think, shows conclusively—that the appointment mentioned in the text was not a job'. 'Competitive Examinations' (*Cornhill*, Dec. 1861): 'No one can affect to deny that the appointments to the less conspicuous offices under Government . . . were and are generally made from personal reasons, and are to that extent jobbed, if that word is restricted to appointments made with a view to private and not to public advantage, without implying that they are positively corrupt or improper . . . a pledge on the part of the Government to act with uprightness and impartiality in the distribution of its patronage . . . would, no doubt, be a great advantage, not merely in a political but also in a moral point of view, over and above the positive advantages of the removal of jobbery itself . . . No one proposes to appoint any officer by competitive examination whose position is conspicuous or important enough to afford in itself a guarantee that the appointment will not be jobbed' (*On Society, Religion, and Government* 77–8). JFS, 'Foster on the Improvement of Time': 'His theory appears to have been, that the Day of Judgment is a fearfully hard competitive examination, which can be passed only by a lifetime system of cram' (*Sat. Rev.*, 27 June 1863).

[29] Sir Charles Trevelyan (1807–1886; *ODNB*, administrator in India). In 1853 he joined Sir Stafford Northcote (1818–1887; *ODNB*, politician) in advocating reform of the organisation of the permanent civil service.

[30] The first instalment had been published in Dec. 1855.

[31] Tite Barnacle: 'he had intermarried with a branch of the Stiltstalkings, who were also better endowed in a sanguineous point of view than with real or personal property' (ch. x).

ON THE NOVEL AND JOURNALISM

It is difficult to extract the specific accusations which Mr. Dickens means to bring against the Government; but we take the principal counts in his indictment to be, that the business of the country is done very slowly and very ill; that inventors and projectors of improvements are treated with insolent neglect; and that the Government is conducted by, and for the interest of, a few aristocratic families, whose whole public life is a constant career of personal jobs.[32] Most men will consider these rather serious charges.

But the burlesque manner and extravagant language in which they are made are at once Mr. Dickens's shield and his sword. 'How can you suppose', he might say, 'that I mean any harm by such representations as these? I am neither a lawyer nor a politician; but I take a fling at the subjects of the day, just in order to give my writings a little local colour, and a little temporary piquancy.' Probably enough this is the true account of the matter, and it forms the very gravamen of our complaint. Men of the world may laugh at books which represent all who govern as fools, knaves, hypocrites, and dawdling tyrants. They know very well that such language is meant to be understood subject to modifications; but the poor and uneducated take such words in their natural and undiluted strength, and draw from them practical conclusions of corresponding importance; whilst the young and inexperienced are led to think far too meanly of the various careers which the organisation of society places before them, and to waste in premature cynicism and self-satisfied indolence some of the most precious opportunities which life affords.

It is not necessary to discuss the justice of Mr. Dickens's charges, but it is so much the fashion of the day to speak with unmeasured contempt both of the honesty and ability of the executive government, that we will lay before our readers a few considerations upon the general character of the public service, and upon the principles which ought to govern discussions as to its merits.

The first question which presents itself is, What is the standard of comparison? It would require a knowledge of the details of the administrative system of other countries, which we do not pretend to possess, to institute a detailed comparison between their governments and our own. But without entering on so vast a subject, we think that any person of ordinary fairness and information may easily satisfy himself that the British Government need not shrink from a comparison, either with the transactions of mercantile men, or with those of great public companies. Mr. Dickens, and many other denouncers of the incapacity of the Government, have long indulged in the pleasant habit of looking only at one side of the subject. They read in the newspapers of the failures, the prejudices, and the stupidity of the executive; and it never occurs to them that they do not hear of the cases in which the official mechanism works well. We must have some notion of the magnitude of the operations which the Government has to conduct, before we can duly estimate the immense weight of the testimony in its favour, which is conveyed by the absence of complaint on so many subjects. But the testimony so conveyed is positive as well as negative. Here, as in the other affairs of life, we must look at broad general results; and from them we may readily gather abundant confirmation of our position, that whatever defects may exist in the administration of public affairs, their general condition proves that much capacity and honesty is employed upon them.

[32] *OED* A transaction in which duty or the public interest is sacrificed for the sake of private or party advantage.

THE LICENSE OF MODERN NOVELISTS

If we turn, for example, to the management of the Revenue, is Mr. Dickens aware of the complexity and extent of the operations which are involved in collecting, disbursing, and accounting for, something like 60,000,000*l.*, and of making such arrangements with respect to it, that there shall always be enough in hand to make every payment at its appointed period, whatever irregularities may occur in the receipt of the income? Has he any notion of the variety and intricacy of the system of accounts which such transactions render necessary? If any mercantile firm had establishments at every seaport and in every considerable inland town; if they employed several thousand servants of different grades, in order to collect an income of the amount which we have mentioned; if they had to adjust their receipts and expenditure with such scrupulous exactness as to be able to pay away about half of their gross income to an immense body of mortgagees by quarterly instalments; and if all the business which these operations implied were conducted with the regularity of clockwork, without gross fraud, with little, if any, peculation, and with such method that the shareholders were annually furnished with accounts embracing the very minutest details of so enormous an outlay, how Mr. Dickens would triumph in contrasting the business-like habits of the middle classes with the blundering stupidity of the Circumlocution Office. Yet this is a literal and most scanty account of the occupations of one single department of that Circumlocution Office which is the subject of Mr. Dickens's extreme contempt.

The administration of the British Empire has no doubt many shortcomings and imperfections, but are we seeking to perpetuate them or to remove them? If a man's house is not to his mind, he either builds a new one or repairs the old one; and whichever of the two operations may be the wisest, there can be no doubt that the English nation have in all constitutional reforms adopted the latter. There has never been at any period of our history a *tabula rasa*,[33] like that which at the end of the last century existed for a time in France, on which homogeneous and consistent structures, either of law or government, could be raised. The consequence is, that our law is full of fictions, and our public offices full of intricacy. This is, no doubt, an evil to be remedied, but it is one which the present generation inherited, and which earlier generations considered a cheap price for the acquisition of political liberty.

Inefficiency, however, is only one of Mr. Dickens's charges against the Government. Neglect of useful inventions and gross corruption are thrown in by way of makeweight. Thus in the following oracular conversation in 'Little Dorrit':

> 'What I mean to say is, that however this comes to be the regular way of our government; it is its regular way. Have you ever heard of any proprietor or inventor who failed to find it all but inaccessible, and whom it did not discourage and ill-treat?'
>
> 'I cannot say I ever have.'
>
> 'Have you ever known it to be beforehand in the adoption of any useful thing? Ever known it to set an example of any useful kind?'
>
> 'I am a good deal older than my friend here', said Mr. Meagles, 'and I'll answer that. *Never.*' (p. 88.)[34]

---

[33] *OED* A tablet from which the writing has been erased, and which is therefore ready to be written upon again: usually *figurative*.

[34] ch. x; read, 'What I mean to say is', and not 'any proprietor' but 'any projector'. *OED* One who forms a project, who plans or designs some enterprise or undertaking. (Differentiated from the 'invidious use' where *OED* instances 'a promoter of bubble companies'—like Mr. Merdle.) Read, 'that I ever'. The italicizing of the final word, '*Never*', is by JFS, not Dickens.

ON THE NOVEL AND JOURNALISM

With respect to the first of these charges, we may mention one or two specific instances of the application of inventive power to the regular objects of administration. What does Mr. Dickens think of the whole organisation of the Post Office, and of the system of cheap postage, which was invented in this country, and has been adopted by almost every State on the Continent? Every branch of this establishment shows the greatest power of arrangement and contrivance—even mechanical contrivance. Mr. Dickens can never tear a penny stamp from its fellows without having before his eyes an illustration of the watchful ingenuity of this branch of the Circumlocution Office. To take another special illustration: what does Mr. Dickens say to the London Police? What he has said on the subject, anyone may see, by referring to 'Household Words', in which he will find the organisation of the force praised in almost hyperbolical language. It is not a little characteristic that Mr. Dickens should praise one branch of the Circumlocution Office in one of his organs, and shortly afterwards denounce the whole institution as a mass of clumsy stupidity in another. There can hardly be a more delicate administrative problem than that of protecting the persons and property without endangering the liberties of the public; and we should feel some curiosity to see a statement by Mr. Dickens of the comparative value of the solutions arrived at by the French, the Russian, and the English Governments.

As to the personal corruption, and the neglect of talent, which Mr. Dickens charges against the Government of the country, we can only say that any careful observer of his method might have predicted with confidence that he would begin a novel on that subject within a very few months after the establishment of a system of competitive examinations for admission into the Civil Service. He seems, as a general rule, to get his first notions of an abuse from the discussions which accompany its removal, and begins to open his trenches and mount his batteries as soon as the place to be attacked has surrendered. This was his course with respect both to imprisonment for debt and to Chancery reform; but in the present instance, he has attacked an abuse which never existed to anything like the extent which he describes. A large proportion of the higher permanent offices of state have always been filled by men of great talent, whose promotion was owing to their talent. Did Mr. Dickens ever hear that Mr. Hallam, Mr. William Hamilton, Mr. Phillips, Sir George Barrow, Sir A. Spearman, Sir James Stephen, Sir C. Trevelyan, Mr. Merivale, Mr. Henry Taylor, or Mr. Greg are, or have been, members of the permanent Civil Service?[35] Will he assert that these gentlemen were promoted simply from family motives, or that they are fairly represented by such a lump of folly and conceit as the Mr. Stiltstalking of his story? Or, to take a single and well-known example, how does he account for the career of Mr. Rowland Hill? A gentleman in a private and not very conspicuous position, writes a pamphlet recommending what amounted to a revolution in a most important department of the Government. Did the Circumlocution Office neglect him, traduce him, break his heart, and ruin his fortune? They adopted his scheme, and gave him the leading share in carrying it out, and yet this is the Government which Mr. Dickens declares to be a sworn foe to talent, and a systematic enemy to ingenuity.

[35] All in *ODNB*. Henry Hallam (1777–1859; historian); JFS, 'Mr. Hallam' (*Sat. Rev.*, 29 Jan. 1859, *Essays* 16–30). William Hamilton (1788–1856; philosopher). John Phillips (1800–1874; geologist). George Barrow (1806–1876; civil servant). Alexander Spearman (1793–1874; civil servant). Charles Merivale (1808–1893; historian). Henry Taylor (1800–1886; poet and public servant). William Rathbone Greg (1809–1881; industrialist and writer).

THE LICENSE OF MODERN NOVELISTS

We cannot, however, entirely confine ourselves to looking at the positive side of the question. We must for a moment direct Mr. Dickens's attention to its negative aspects; and we think that it would be a just, though an inadequate, punishment for the language which he has used, if he were obliged to learn from painful experience what other governments are like. If he had to do, for a very little time, with a system in which a set of ill-paid and needy underlings had it in their power to levy black mail[36] upon him, by a hundred petty interferences with the privacy of his house and the freedom of his movements, he might find that King Stork has his faults as well as King Log. It is not agreeable to feel doubts as to the prudence of making a handsome new year's gift to the judge who is to try your cause; nor can it be a pleasant thought for a patriotic mind, that there is not a despatch in any department of the Government of which copies may not be bought from highly efficient clerks at a very moderate premium. We individually should feel uneasy at the reflection, that several hundred thousand persons, in all classes of society, were absolutely dependent on the *sic volo sic jubeo*[37] of the Central Government for their daily bread; nor would it conciliate our confidence in public men, if rumours were extensively circulated that Ministers were in the habit of making fortunes on the Stock Exchange; and if all these, and many similar features, were extremely common in a great part of the world, and were utterly and absolutely unknown in our own country, we should doubt whether we were much worse governed than our neighbours.

It is one of Mr. Dickens's favourite themes, to compare the modesty, the patience, and the solid business-like sense of his intelligent mechanic, Mr. Doyce,[38] with the blundering inefficiency of the Circumlocution Office. We do not deny the justice of the praise which Mr. Dickens lavishes on Mr. Doyce and his class. It is no doubt well deserved, but we wish to call attention to the fact, that our faith in their good qualities is based entirely upon broad general results, precisely similar to those which, as we say, prove the general ability and honesty of the Government, although the mercantile and mechanical classes have also to account for a vast number of failures of an infinitely more serious kind than those which called into existence Mr. Dickens's extravagant fictions. Look, for example, at any of our great railways.[39] No one who observes the traffic, the organisation, the discipline, and all the various members of those immense establishments, can doubt that a vast deal of skill and energy has been employed in their construction; but if we were disposed to denounce them as utterly corrupt and effete, how superabundant the materials of denunciation would be. Imagine Mr. Dickens idealising Redpath,[40] and filling in the intervals of his story with racy descriptions of the opposition between the North-Western, the Great Northern, and the Great Western; sketches of trucks laid across the line for engines to run into; speculations as to the reasons which induce directors always to send on a coal train ten minutes before

---

[36] *OED* Any payment extorted by intimidation or pressure, or levied by unprincipled officials, critics, journalists etc., upon those whom they have it in their power to help or injure. Now usu. a payment extorted by threats or pressure, esp. by threatening to reveal a discreditable secret. From 1826.

[37] Juvenal, *Hoc volo, sic iubeo, sit pro ratione voluntas* (*Satires* 6:223). So do I will, so do I command. (Trans. Dryden: 'And give no other reason but my will'.)

[38] DANIEL DOYCE, an engineer and inventor.

[39] Thomas Edward Dicey (1789–1858), chairman of the Midland Railway, was related to JFS, as was Oscar Leslie Stephen (1819–1898), railway director. *Life* 7 n., 18–19, presents the Stephen / Venn family tree.

[40] John Redpath (1796–1869), business-man of Montreal.

ON THE NOVEL AND JOURNALISM

they despatch an express; tyrannical invasions of private property, and authentic comparisons of the sums spent in law expenses, with the returns from the branches for which those expenses obtained Acts of Parliament! Let the background of the picture be filled in with broken-hearted lovers mourning over a fall in the price of shares, by which their union is prevented for ever, and angelic widows reading with agonized hearts accounts of the 'smash'[41] which had deprived them for ever of the society of that virtuous bagman, whose faithful purity and earnestness had for hundreds of pages moved our contempt for the heartless aristocrats with whom he was contrasted. Such a description of English railways would be, neither in kind nor in degree, one whit more unjust, and would not be in its results one-hundredth part as injurious, as the description given in 'Little Dorrit' of the Executive Government of this country.

It is as hard to refute a generality as to answer a sneer, and we therefore feel that in combating such statements as those of Mr. Dickens, we expose ourselves to the retort that we are fighting with shadows of our own raising. With respect to Mr. Charles Reade, our task is far simpler. We have in his case an example of the inevitable necessity which this style of composition imposes upon novelists of distorting facts, which may be brought to a very simple issue indeed. Our objection to such novels is, that, inasmuch as facts are seldom or never so romantic as the exigencies of fiction require, the novelist is tempted to exaggerate, and thereby misrepresent, them, for the purposes of his book. This abuse is very strongly exemplified in the production entitled 'It is never too late to mend.'[42]

Some of our readers are probably aware that about four years ago great complaints were made of the manner in which prisoners were treated in Birmingham Gaol. From disclosures which took place on an inquest held on a boy named Andrews, who hanged himself in that prison, the attention of Government was directed to its management. A commission of inquiry sat upon it in the autumn of the same year, and published a Report, speaking in very strong terms of the conduct of the governor, together with a mass of evidence showing that illegal and cruel punishments had been inflicted on the prisoners during his tenure of office. From the offences thus brought to light, Lieutenant Austin, the governor, was tried and convicted on two indictments at the Warwick assizes in July, 1855, and in the following Michaelmas term was called up for judgment, and sentenced to three months' imprisonment in the Queen's Prison. Some seven or eight months ago Mr. Reade published a novel based on these facts; in which he has not only charged the governor with cruelties far exceeding any that were proved against him, but made them the ground of accusations against the government and the judges, expressed in language as intemperate as the charges themselves are false.

In order to show that there can be no doubt that—Gaol, in 'It is never too late to mend', is identical with Birmingham Prison, we need only say that every single incident in the novel is founded upon corresponding incidents related in the evidence taken before the Royal Commissioners; the main features of the story are identical with

---

[41] *OED* Commercial failure. From 1839.

[42] *Life* 107 n.: 'That novel was briefly a travesty of a recent case in which a prisoner had committed suicide in consequence, as was suggested, of ill-treatment by the authorities of the gaol. Fitzjames gives the actual facts to show how Reade had allowed himself, as a writer of fiction, to exaggerate and distort them, and had at the same time taken the airs of an historian of facts and bragged of his resolution to brand all judges who should dare to follow the precedent which he denounced.' JFS later praised Reade's *Hard Cash* (1863) for its fair treatment of the law (to Mary Stephen, 4 Mar. 1864).

THE LICENSE OF MODERN NOVELISTS

those which we have stated, and the names of the characters introduced are concealed under transparent disguises. Thus, the governor of the prison, Lieut. *Aus*-tin, is represented by Mr. Hawes. Freer, one of the warders, is called Fry; Captain Maconochie, the governor who preceded Lieutenant Austin, is O'Connor; Mr. Luckcock, a magistrate, is described as Mr. Woodcock; Taylor, a prisoner, as Naylor; and the boy, Andrews, who hung himself, is (probably with a reminiscence of Fielding)[43] named Josephs.

We do not propose to undertake the defence either of Lieutenant Austin or of the magistrates of Birmingham. Both, we have no doubt, were very greatly to blame. Lieutenant Austin for a severity of discipline, which, in the words of the Report, showed 'lamentable indifference to human suffering'; and the magistrates for reposing in him such undue confidence, that they allowed the supervision of the prison to pass almost entirely out of their own hands, and the duty of inspection to degenerate into little more than a formal routine.

Whatever practical defects the law of libel may contain, and they are no doubt many, one main feature of its theory has, by very recent legislation,[44] been brought into complete harmony with common sense. To publish any statement tending to injure another is *primâ facie* criminal, and in order to justify any such publication it is necessary to prove not only the truth of the matters charged, but that for some specific reason it was for the public benefit that they should be published. If it be true that the Government and a variety of public officers of various kinds, conspired to defeat the course of justice, and to protect the criminal, there can be no doubt that it is for the public benefit that the fact should be known; and Mr. Reade might say fairly enough that he was justified in bringing Lieutenant Austin again before the public, if by so doing he could prove that the Government had been guilty of great offences hitherto undetected. But Mr. Austin has already suffered severely, though deservedly, for his offences, both in person, in reputation, and in money; and surely, unless some public purpose is to be subserved by holding him up to execration, an author has neither the moral nor legal right to make him, or any man, the villain of a widely-circulated novel.

Blameable, however, as Mr. Austin's conduct undoubtedly was, it was far from being as bad as Mr. Reade represents it to have been. We have taken the trouble of comparing this novel minutely with the Report and Evidence of the Royal Commission and with the evidence on the trial. The result is highly unfavourable to this romantic mode of following in the track of criminal justice.[45] Most of the cruelties ascribed by Mr. Reade

---

[43] *Joseph Andrews* (1742).

[44] *OED* libel *Law*. Any published statement damaging to the reputation of a person. In wider sense, any writing of a treasonable, seditious, or immoral kind. *Gen. View 1863* 100, on the earlier law of libel: 'it enabled the courts of law, as the authorized exponents of morality and duty to the Government, to declare any writing to be criminal. The popular sentiment was undoubtedly right in denouncing the existence of this power as fatal to liberty, and the Libel Act [1792] was unquestionably a salutary measure ... The consequence of the Libel Act has been to define the liberty of the press as the unrestricted power of publishing anything whatever, subject to the chance that a jury may think that the author deserves, under all the circumstances, to be punished for having published it.' JFS, 'The Liberty of Prophesying' (Jeremy Taylor): 'To restrict the limits of heresy by definition was the way to bring people gently and by easy degrees to indifference to it, just as the gradual restriction of the law of libel to narrow limits by forensic discussion, gradually introduced practically unlimited freedom of political and religious discussion' (*Sat. Rev.*, 30 Sept. 1865; *Hor. Sab.* i 222–3).

[45] JFS, 'Are Madmen Irresponsible?': 'Still the reader may ask, Why did not the Court call Mr. Gibson? The answer is to be found in the theory which reconciles all the apparent contradictions of English criminal justice—namely, that it is the prosecutor's business to convict if he can; the prisoner's business to escape if

118 ON THE NOVEL AND JOURNALISM

to Lieutenant Austin have some foundation in fact. We have even been able to discover some which have been stated pretty fairly; but he has almost always added just as many incidents as were required in order to make the difference between unjustifiable severity and the required melodramatic devilishness of character. One or two specimens of this style of popular composition will suffice. We select a general description of what Mr. Reade leads his readers to consider the characteristics of prison discipline in English Penitentiaries, for which (if true) the Government, the Parliament, the Magistrates, and the Courts of Law are responsible.

> A thick dark pall of silence and woe hung over its huge walls. If a voice was heard above a whisper it was sure to be either a cry of anguish or a fierce command to inflict anguish. Two or three were crucified every day; the rest expected crucifixion from morning till night. No man felt safe an hour; no man had the means of averting punishment; all were at the mercy of a tyrant. Threats, frightful, fierce, and mysterious, hung like weights over every soul and body. Whenever a prisoner met an officer, he cowered and hurried crouching by like a dog passing a man with a whip in his hand; and as he passed he trembled at the thunder of his own footsteps, and wished to heaven they would not draw so much attention to him by ringing so clear through that huge silent tomb. When an officer met the governor he tried to slip by with a hurried salute lest he should be stopped, abused, and sworn at.
>
> The earnest man fell hardest upon the young; boys and children were favourite victims; but his favourites of all were poor Robinson and little Josephs. These were at the head of the long list he crucified, he parched, he famished, he robbed of prayer, of light, of rest, and hope. He disciplined the sick; he closed the infirmary again. That large room, furnished with comforts, nurses, and air, was an inconsistency.
>
> 'A new prison is a collection of cells', said Hawes. The infirmary was a spot in the sun. The exercise-yard in this prison was a twelve-box stable for creatures concluded to be wild beasts. The labour-yard was a fifteen-stall stable for ditto. The house of God an eighty-stall stable, into which the wild beasts were dispersed for public worship made private. Here in early days, before Hawes was ripe, they assembled apart and repeated prayers; and sang hymns on Sunday. But Hawes found out that though the men were stabled apart their voices were refractory and mingled in the air, and with their voices their hearts might, who knows? He pointed this out to the justices, who shook their skulls and stopped the men's responses and hymns. The animals cut the choruses out of the English liturgy with as little ceremony and as good effect as they would have cut the choruses out of Handel's 'Messiah', if the theory they were working had been a musical instead of a moral one.
>
> So far so good; but the infirmary had escaped Justice Shallow and Justice Woodcock.[46] Hawes abolished that.
>
> Discipline before all. Not because a fellow is sick is he to break discipline. So the sick lay in their narrow cells gasping in vain for fresh air, gasping in vain for some cooling drink, or some little simple delicacy to incite their enfeebled appetite.

he can; the judge's business to see fair play; and nobody's business to arrive at the truth. We do not see how this evil is to be remedied, so long as witnesses of this description are brought into court at the expense of the parties, not in order to tell the truth and the whole truth, but to tell such parts of it as make for the party calling them' (*Sat. Rev.*, 16 Feb. 1856).

[46] Justices of the Peace, *Henry IV, Part 2* (and *The Merry Wives of Windsor*), and Isaac Bickerstaffe, *Love in a Village: A Comic Opera* (anon., 1763).

THE LICENSE OF MODERN NOVELISTS

The dying were locked up at the fixed hour for locking up, and found dead at the fixed hour for opening. How they had died—no one knew. At what hour they had died—no one knew. Whether in some choking struggle a human hand might have saved them by changing a suffocating position or the like—no one knew.

But this all knew—that these our sinful brethren had died, not like men, but like vultures in the great desert. They were separated from their kith and kin, who, however brutal, would have said a kind word and done a tender thing or two for them at that awful hour; and nothing allowed them in exchange, not even the routine attentions of a prison nurse; they were in darkness and alone when the king of terrors came to them and wrestled with them; all men had turned their backs on them, no creature near to wipe the dews of death, to put a cool hand to the brow, or soften the intensity of the last sad sigh that carried their souls from earth. Thus they passed away, punished lawlessly by the law till they succumbed, and then since they were no longer food for torture, ignored by the law and abandoned by the human race.

They locked up one dying man at eight o'clock. At midnight the thirst of death came on him. He prayed for a drop of water, but there was none to hear him. Parched and gasping the miserable man got out of bed and groped and groped for his tin mug, but before he could drink the death agony seized him. When they unlocked him in the morning they found him a corpse on the floor with the mug in his hand and the water spilled on the floor. They wrenched the prison property out of its dead hand, and flung the carcase itself upon the bed as if it had been the clay cast of a dog, not the remains of a man.

All was of a piece. The living tortured; the dying abandoned; the dead kicked out of the way. (pp. 169–70.)

We might draw out illustrations of this kind to any length; but as our object is not to discuss the character of Lieutenant Austin, but to illustrate the character of novels founded on fact, we will content ourselves with the most specific misstatements.

The first, refers to the case of the boy Andrews, who hung himself. The punishments inflicted upon him consisted, partly in reducing his diet to bread and water, partly in depriving him of his bed and gas, and partly and principally in the application of an instrument called the punishment-jacket, by which the person punished was attached to the wall by a strap round his arms, which were also confined in a strait waistcoat, whilst a stiff leather collar was fastened round his neck. Mr. Reade's case is, that by excessive application of these punishments, the boy was driven to suicide, and that an excuse for punishing him was found, by setting him tasks of hard labour greater than he could perform, and which in fact he did not perform.

In this story we have detected the following exaggerations:

1. At p. 173, Mr. Reade calls the leather collar surrounding the boy's neck 'a high circular-saw'; and in another passage he describes it as left unbound at the edges, so as to be jagged. Of this there is no evidence whatever in the Report. The collar was unbound, but not jagged.
2. At p. 84, Mr. Reade says, 'that the governor gave the lad 8000 turns (of the crank) to do in four and a half hours.' At p. 170, he says, 'Between breakfast and dinner' (which would be four and a half hours) 'he was set 5000 turns of a heavy crank.' Both these numbers are exaggerations. The real number was 4000.
3. At the same pages, Mr. Reade says, that 'Josephs never succeeded in performing these preposterous tasks'; and that he (Hawes) knew the boy *could not do it*. It was only a formula he had for punishing the lad.' At p. xi of the Report, we find these

120 ON THE NOVEL AND JOURNALISM

words: 'We examined the amount of crank-labour[47] which Edward Andrews had performed, and found a record of his labour at the crank on every weekday, from March 30 to April 23. He was deficient on the 30th and 31st of March, and on the 16th and 19th of April. On all the other days he completed his assigned amount of labour, and on several (seven) days *exceeded it.*'

4. At p. 171, Mr. Reade describes Josephs as presenting the appearance of 'a small but aged man, shambling stiffly, with joints stiffened by perpetual crucifixion and by rheumatism, that had been caused by being perpetually wetted through.' This is incorrect. Andrews gained two pounds in weight during his confinement, and there were no marks of violence on the body.* As to the perpetual wetting, he was wetted once.

5. At pp. 172–3, Mr. Reade describes Josephs as having been confined in the punishment-jacket on the afternoon before his suicide. He was not so confined for three days before his suicide. This is important, because the proximate[48] cause of his hanging himself was not any punishment inflicted by Lieutenant Austin, but a threat to report him to the magistrates.

6. The governor is represented at p. 172 as abusing him. No such abuse took place, and the habitual use of profane language on the part of the governor was disproved on oath.

7. At p. 176, it is said that Josephs was deprived of his bed for the whole night. He was deprived of it only from eight to ten P.M., which left him eight hours' sleep. This is a most material exaggeration, as will appear immediately.

8. It is asserted in the same page, and at p. 174, that water was thrown over him when in the punishment-jacket, and that he was left all night in his wet clothes. It is true that the water was thrown over him, but not that he was kept in wet clothes.

9. It is asserted that when the boy was put into the jacket, the governor ordered the straps to be drawn tighter. This is quite imaginary.

10. It is asserted (p. 177) that Josephs hung himself at one A.M., watching till the prison officers were out of the way. He hung himself at ten P.M., when the warder would come round to bring in his bed. He was not quite dead when he was cut down**; and—though it was no part of the prison discipline—he had cleaned the can in which he would have received his breakfast next morning. We gather these facts from the subsequent proceedings at the trial, and in London, and not from the Report; so that Mr. Reade is perhaps not to blame for having omitted them, though he is greatly to blame for altering the time of the suicide so as to put beyond all doubt an intention which, on the evidence before the Commissioners, was only matter of conjecture.

* JFS, note: Evidence of Mr. Blount, p. 154, supported by affidavit of Mr. Lakin.
** JFS, note: Report of proceedings in London in R. v. Austin. Birmingham Journal, 28 Nov. 1855. (Lieutenant William Austin.)

[47] *OED* A machine for the punishment of criminals sentenced to hard labour, consisting of a revolving disc to which a regulated pressure can be applied, and which the prisoner is required to turn a certain number of times each day. 1847 Means should exist of rendering the discipline...more stringent...by placing crank machinery in the cells.
[48] *OED* Coming next (before or after) in a chain of causation, agency.

THE LICENSE OF MODERN NOVELISTS

After this illustration—and it is only an illustration of Mr. Reade's method—we may notice a few other points in a more concise manner. Mr. Reade, for example, makes a great deal of Mr. Austin's conduct towards a man named Hunt (called in the novel Carter), into whose mouth some salt was put by the surgeon. The exaggerations in this case resemble those which we have already noticed in the case of Andrews so much, that we will only say that Mr. Reade not only exaggerates the story, but omits all mention of the fact that it formed the subject of one of the indictments on which Lieutenant Austin was tried at Warwick, and that he was *acquitted* on the very same evidence, with an unimportant exception, which was laid before the Commissioners, and acquitted by the same jury which had convicted him of the assaults upon Andrews.

Such is a specimen of the misrepresentations into which a writer of fictions founded upon fact may be led.

The extent of Mr. Austin's criminality, which we have no wish to deny or to palliate, is only to be ascertained by a conscientious and dispassionate inquiry into facts; and it will be apparent from two extracts—the one from Mr. Reade's novel, the other from Mr. Justice Coleridge's address in passing sentence—that the way in which that investigation is conducted must make a most serious difference to the person principally concerned.

> 'This unhappy dolt', says Mr. Reade of the Governor, 'must still, like his prisoners and the rest of us, have some excitement to keep him from going dead. What more natural than that such a nature should find its excitement in tormenting; and that by degrees this excitement should become, first a habit, then a need? Torture had grown upon stupid, earnest Hawes; it seasoned that white of egg, a mindless existence.'

Considering that this is mere matter of inference, it is rather strong language, even for a novelist. Mr. Reade may not attach much importance to the opinion of the judge who passed sentence on Lieutenant Austin, inasmuch as he considers him a 'dolt', a 'fool', an 'idiot', 'vermin', and 'not a lawyer'. The rest of the world, however, have not yet learnt to apply this language to Mr. Justice Coleridge,[49] and will therefore perhaps be glad to hear that, after a careful judicial inquiry into these astounding and revolting charges, that Judge said to Lieutenant Austin, 'The Court are satisfied, from the character you have borne for a number of years, and from statements in your affidavits, that *deliberate cruelty and inhumanity were never conceived by you.*'

In quitting this part of the subject, we feel bound to warn our readers that the general conclusion which we have drawn from a careful examination of Mr. Reade's book, with the authorities on which it professes to be founded, is, that it hardly contains a single statement of a matter of fact which can be entirely depended upon, though every statement respecting—Gaol, which it contains, is founded upon something mentioned in the Report of the Commissioners who inquired into Birmingham Prison. We will now proceed to show that it has a most important bearing on a subject of far greater public interest.

Besides his attacks upon the governor of the prison, Mr. Reade speaks with the most extreme violence of the conduct of the visiting magistrates, of the supineness of the 'unconscientious flunkeys, humbugs, hirelings, whom God confound on earth', usually known as the Home Office; of the inspector of prisons for the district; and of a

---

[49] John Duke Coleridge (1820–1894; *ODNB*, judge).

corrupt conspiracy between a great variety of persons in order to pervert the course of justice: and inasmuch as the description of Lieutenant Austin's misdeeds affords the principal foundation for these attacks, it is obvious that by exaggerating the facts, additional weight is given to these inferences. The attack upon the magistrates, though exaggerated in one or two very material points, has nevertheless so strong a basis of truth that we shall only refer to it incidentally. There can be no doubt that they grievously neglected their duty in the careless manner in which the gaol was superintended, though several facts which make in their favour are omitted by Mr. Reade, whilst others which make against them are exaggerated, from his usual habit of looking upon the production of melodramatic effect as superior to every other human consideration. We will compare the facts attending the discovery of the mismanagement of the prison, as given by Mr. Reade, with the same facts as they appear in the Report.

Andrews hung himself on the 27th of April, 1853. The inquest on his body followed immediately. On the 3rd of May Mr. Wills, the Chairman of the Board of Visiting Justices, applied to the coroner for his notes of the evidence. He did not get them till the 4th, but from verbal information which the coroner gave him on the 3rd, he immediately went to the prison in company with another magistrate, conversed upon the matter with Lieutenant Austin, gave orders for the discontinuance of the illegal punishments then ascertained to exist, took possession of the leather collars which formed the worst part of the punishment-jacket, and ordered that the strait waist-coat and straps should only be used for purposes of restraint in cases of great personal violence, and not for purposes of punishment; and he made a report to the Committee of Visiting Justices on the very next day (Ev. p. 475–6).[50] Mr. Wills at this time had only been a visiting justice for ten days, though he had previously held that office for some months in the time of Captain Maconochie.

Now how does Mr. Reade represent these facts? The most prominent member (though he is not explicitly called the Chairman) of the visiting justices in the novel is called Mr. Williams, and he is represented as the unscrupulous partisan and advocate of Lieutenant Austin, whose credit he upholds notwithstanding the discoveries of the inspector; so that Mr. Wills is made in the novel to defend the very acts to which he in reality put a stop.*** But Mr. Reade withheld from Mr. Wills the credit of the exposure because he is an unpaid magistrate, a class for which Mr. Reade cannot express his contempt in sufficiently forcible language. As, however, it was necessary for the purposes of the novel, that the cruelties of the governor should be brought to light somehow, a totally imaginary chaplain is introduced, who unites all sorts of virtues, physical and moral, and who drags the culprits to punishment.

*** JFS, note: It is fair to Mr. Reade to add, that he may have been misled by a mistake in the Report as to the length of time during which Mr. Wills had held office. The Report, p. xxxvii, states that he had been a visiting justice for several months. It appears from the evidence that this was not the case. We should also remark, that Mr. Wills joined in a report from the visiting magistrates to the Home Office, which would certainly seem to have taken too lenient a view of Lieutenant Austin's conduct. But, in making that report, the whole of the evidence (partly, no doubt, in consequence of what would seem to have been a mistake in judgment on their part) was not before them; and the Commissioners say, 'We are satisfied that they (the magistrates) heard the details of the occurrences in the gaol, as they were disclosed before us, with much pain and regret.' (p. xxxvii.)

---

[50] Ev. (Evidence), the transcript of the proceedings as the testimony was taken on direct examination. Below, Rep. (Report), the panel's final opinion as issued.

THE LICENSE OF MODERN NOVELISTS

Mr. Reade always delights to contrast 'holy Church' and 'unholy State' to the disadvantage of the latter; and we shall point out immediately the manner in which the 'man of God' is said to have done what Mr. Wills actually did. In the meantime we will only remark that Mr. Reade's virtuous zeal would go a long way to leave us without any government at all, for he is quite as hard as Mr. Dickens upon the Circumlocution Office, as he is upon the unpaid magistracy. He is extremely indignant about the clerks in public offices, 'the eighty pounders,[51] who execute England'; and there could not be a more curious illustration of his views on that point than his abuse of Mr. Perry, the inspector of prisons. Not only does he make no complaint against that gentleman, but his representative in the novel, Mr. Lacy, is the *Deus ex machinâ* who turns Mr. Hawes out of the gaol, and sets up Mr. Eden in his stead. Still Mr. Lacy is guilty of the crime of being a public servant, a 'hireling', and Mr. Reade feels bound to express his sense of the offence in the following manner:

> Then in that gloomy abode of blood and tears Heaven wrought a miracle. One who for twenty years past had been an official, became a man for full five minutes. Light burst on him. Nature rushed back upon her truant son, and seized her long-forgotten empire. The frost and reserve of office melted like snow in summer before the sun of religion and humanity. How unreal and idle appeared now the twenty years gone in tape[52] and circumlocution! Away went his life of shadows—his career of watery polysyllables meandering through the great desert into the Dead Sea. He awoke from his desk, and saw the corpse of an Englishman murdered by routine, and the tears of a man of God dripping upon it.
>
> Then his soul burst its desk, and his heart broke its polysyllables and its tapen[53] bonds, and the man of office came quickly to the man of God, and seized his hand with both his, which shook very much, and pressed it again and again and again, and his eyes glistened, and his voice faltered. (p. 221)

The best reward that Mr. Reade can bestow upon an efficient public servant is the hope that he may have grace to repent of being one. Mr. Reade brings no charge whatever against Mr. Perry except that of being a public servant who performed his duty. But his antipathies grow like circles in water. After libelling Mr. Wills and abusing Mr. Perry, he goes a step further and attacks the Home Office. Mr. Eden (the imaginary chaplain) is represented as writing a letter to that department, in which he denounces the abuses of the prison. He is told, after some delay, that the inspector is on his circuit, and that in about six weeks time he will arrive in—Gaol. Hereupon Mr. Eden goes up into the seventh heaven of fury, and 'flesh and blood addresses gutta-percha'[54] in a series of dithyrambs conceived in a sort of madhouse style, in which, amongst other things, he states his intention of applying to the Queen in person, if he is not attended to. Hereupon he receives what he acknowledges to be a gentlemanlike letter, to the effect that 'a person connected with the Home Department would soon arrive'; and the much reviled Mr. Lacy comes accordingly. This is the novel. Now for the fact.

The first intimation which the Government, or Mr. Perry, received to the effect that there was anything wrong in the management of the prison, appears to have

---

[51] *OED* A person possessing, having an income of, or paying (e.g. as rent) a specified number of pounds sterling. *OED* execute, To follow out, carry into effect (an intention, purpose, plan, instruction, or command).

[52] See *OED* red-tape, red tape.

[53] *OED rare* Composed of tape. In quot. *figurative*. (This from Reade as the only citation.)

[54] *OED* The inspissated juice of various trees found chiefly in the Malayan archipelago, now extensively used in the arts. From 1845.

been derived from the newspaper reports of the inquest on Andrews. As soon as Mr. Perry read this report he wrote to the chaplain, to know whether his evidence was correctly reported, and on hearing that it was, he went down to investigate the subject. The inquest was concluded on May 3rd. Mr. Perry's inquiry began on May 16th, and ended on the 23rd (Ev. p. 492). These proceedings appear to have been known to, and were probably concerted with, the Home Office. (Rep. p. v.) So far therefore from its being true that the Home Office was warned of the misconduct of Lieutenant Austin many weeks before the suicide of Andrews, and that they neglected the warning till it was repeatedly urged upon them, it would seem that without any official intimation of the fact whatever, they directed an inquiry within a few days after it came to light.

Even this is not all. The climax of Mr. Reade's frenzy, as we have already observed, is reserved for the Courts of Law. No language except that of simple quotation can do justice to the indescribable mixture of folly, ignorance, and presumption which is contained in the following passages:

A Royal Commission sat on—Gaol, and elicited all the butchery I have related, and a good deal more. The journals gave an able sketch of the horrors of that hell, and a name or two out of the long list of the victims done to death by solitude, starvation, violence, and accumulated tortures of soul and body.

The nation cried 'shame', and then all good citizens waited in honest confidence, that next month the sword of justice would fall on the manslayer.

Well, months and months rolled away, and still, somehow, no justice came to poor little murdered Josephs and his fellow-martyrs. Their sufferings, and the manner of their destruction, had made all the flesh and blood in the nation thrill with pity and anger; but one little clique remained gutta-percha—the clerks that executed England.

Then 'The Times' raised its lash, and threatened that band of heartless hirelings. 'You shall not leave us stained with all this blood shed lawlessly', said 'The Times'. Then these hirelings began to do, for fear of the New Bailey in Printing-House Yard, what they had not done for fear of God, or pity of the deceased, or love of justice, or respect for law and public morals, or for the honour of the nation and the credit of the human race.

They brought an indictment against Messrs. Hawes and Sawyer. But the mannikin who marches towards his duty, because a man's toe is applied to his sense of honour, may show fight, but he seldom fights. Our hirelings of Xerxes illustrated this trait of nature at every step. They indicted Messrs. Hawes and Sawyer for what, do you suppose? He had starved men to death, which the law has, ere this, pronounced to be murder. A gaoler was hanged in Paris for a single murder thus effected. Did they indict this man for murder? No! He had driven men to suicide by illegal bodily tortures, and illegal mental tortures and felonious practices, without number, which is manslaughter. Did they indict him for manslaughter? No! They only indicted him for prisoner-slaughter; and they estimated this act at what? At a misdemeanour!

The misdemeanour of manslaughter in a prison was tried at last in open court at the country assize. The friendly prosecutor brought as few witnesses to Mr. Hawes's misdemeanours—or shall we say breaches of etiquette—as possible. I cannot find that any of the sufferers by his little misconduct were brought into court; yet they might have been; they were not all dead. Like soldiers in battle, there were nine wounded for every one killed. The prosecution seems to have been rested on the evidence of the prisoner's servants and confederates. Whether this arrangement was taken at the express request of the prisoner, or originated with his friendly antagonists, I don't know.

THE LICENSE OF MODERN NOVELISTS 125

Then came another phenomenon of this strange business. The judge, instead of completing the case, and taking his share in the day's business (as the counsel and the jury had theirs), by passing sentence on the evidence and on the spot, deferred his judgment.

Now this was an act opposed to the custom of English Courts in criminal cases. A judge is a slave of precedents.

Why, then, did the slave of precedent defy precedent?

We shall see.

Three mortal months after the trial, the promised judgment was pronounced. Where? In London, a hundred miles from the jury and the public that had heard the evidence. The judgment was not only deferred, it was transferred. Thus two objects were gained; the honest heart of the public had time to cool; fresh events, in an eventful age, had displaced the memory of murdered Josephs and his fellow-martyrs; and so the prisoner-slayer was to be shuffled away safe, unnoticed, and the absence secured of the English public from a judgment which the judge knew would insult their hearts and consciences.

The judgment thus smuggled into law, delivered on the sly before a handful of people who could not judge the judgment, because they were not the people that had heard the evidence. This judgment—what was it when it came?

It was the sort of thing this trickery had led discerning men to expect.

It was three months' imprisonment! (p. 462–4.)

Every single imputation contained in this passage is utterly baseless. Its style would, no doubt, protect it from criticism, if it did not deal with facts; but the relation between the facts and the novel is so instructive, that we will answer it at length. There was, says Mr. Reade, a plot to stifle justice, and this is proved by the delay in the prosecution. The report of the Commissioners is dated Jan. 25 1854, and it was shortly afterwards laid before the two houses of Parliament. Lieutenant Austin was not indicted till the spring assizes of 1855, when the indictment was removed by *certiorari*[55] in order to obtain a special jury. It was held at the following summer assizes. Thus two opportunities of proceeding against him, afforded by the Lent and Summer Circuits of 1854, were lost. If it be said that owing to the pressure of legal and parliamentary business, the prosecution of Lieutenant Austin was for some months postponed, we should be inclined to found upon this fact the obvious but prosaic conclusion, that we stand greatly in need of a more efficient system of public prosecutors, and of a redistribution of the legal year, arrangements by which the transaction of the criminal business of the country would be much facilitated. This is our conjecture. It is far too tame a solution to suggest itself to Mr. Reade. Nothing will satisfy him but the view that the delay was the result of a wicked conspiracy. Let us compare the probabilities of the two suggestions. The objection to that which we propose is simply that it is not amusing; but in order to arrive at Mr. Reade's, we must suppose that one of the most honourable judges on the bench, the attorney-general, three barristers quite unconnected with party, and occupying a distinguished position in their profession, the solicitor to the Treasury, and one of the largest firms at Birmingham, conspired to pervert the course of justice and to screen from punishment a delinquent in whom they had no conceivable interest; all which appears to Mr. Reade so perfectly natural, as to excite no surprise, and call for no other proof than the fact that the proceedings were tardy. If he were cool enough to

---

[55] *OED* A writ, issuing from a superior court, upon the complaint of a party that he has not received justice in an inferior court, or cannot have an impartial trial, by which the records of the cause are called up for trial in the superior court.

reason at all, it ought surely to occur to him to ask, what possible motive could incline so many persons to do an act so disgraceful. Who are the mysterious 'clerks' who could dictate to an English judge, and to members of the English bar, if they had ever so strong a desire to do so? And what clerks were there in any public office in the country who could have the smallest possible motive for shielding Lieutenant Austin? He was not the servant of the Government in any sense whatever. He held his appointment not from the Queen, but from the borough of Birmingham; and it is childish to suppose that the fate of a person, of whom the most that could be said was that he was a half-pay lieutenant, and that two years before he had been governor of a gaol, could be a matter of sufficient importance to induce five persons, one of them a judge, and the other four members of the 'Godlike public', which, according to Mr. Reade, delights to be governed by the greatest fools in the country, to join in a conspiracy against common humanity and the law of the land.

But Mr. Reade favours us with a little more law. He tells us that the proper witnesses were not called. Lieutenant Austin was indicted on seven indictments, charging him respectively with acts of cruelty to Andrews, to Hunt, to Brown, to Wilks, to Maiden, and to Plant, and with making false entries in the prison books. That in the choice of the cases to be prosecuted, Government showed no lenity to Mr. Austin is conclusively proved, as against Mr. Reade, by the fact that they are identical with those which he has selected for the basis of his exaggerations. Mr. Austin was tried upon two of these indictments, one relating to Andrews, on which he was convicted; and the other to Hunt, on which he was acquitted; and he pleaded guilty to the one which charged him with omitting to make entries in the prison books, stating, at the same time, that those omissions were not made from an intention to deceive the magistrates. The counsel for the Crown thereupon (we quote Mr. Whateley's affidavit in aggravation of punishment) 'consented and agreed to enter a *nolle prosequi*[56] upon the five remaining indictments...the same being, as was then stated by the said counsel, assaults and punishments of a like nature and character with those which had been proved upon the trial of the indictment relating to the case of the said Edward Andrews; and it was then also expressly stated, by said learned counsel, as a condition of not proceeding with the remaining indictments, that the case of said Edward Andrews should not be afterwards presented to this Honourable Court as a single and isolated case.' Who, then, were the witnesses called for the Crown in Andrews's case? They were Mr. Hillyard, William Browne, Thomas Freer, the Rev. Ambrose Sherwin, Thomas Brooks, John Wood, and William Taylor, who were officers of the prison, and Mr. Underhay, an engineer. In Hunt's case the witnesses were Daniel Hartwell and Alfred Wood. A third man, Pearce, also a warder, was present at the assault, and was before the commissioners: but at the time of the trial he was in the Crimea. The witnesses in both cases, with the exception of Pearce and Mr. Hillyard (whose evidence was of little importance), and that of Messrs. Austin and Blunt, who by law could not be called against themselves, were identical with those who were examined before the Commissioners. Andrews could not be examined, because he was dead. Hunt was mad, and was not examined before the Commissioners. Who else could have been called? This, however conclusive, is not all.

---

[56] *OED* An entry made upon the record of a court, when the plaintiff or prosecutor abandons part, or all, of his suit or prosecution against a defendant or defendants.

THE LICENSE OF MODERN NOVELISTS

The case was surrounded with difficulty. All the principal witnesses against Mr. Austin were technically, though not morally, involved in his guilt, and might have completely defeated the prosecution by refusing to answer questions criminating themselves. Here was a loophole for a friendly prosecutor. If the counsel for the prosecution had entered into the vile compact charged against them, how easy it would have been to have hinted to the counsel for the prisoner the propriety of taking this objection.[57] Did they do so? We call Mr. Reade's particular attention to the following fact, now made public for the first time, which we hope will teach him the value of such random accusations. In order to meet this possible objection a pardon under the Great Seal was procured for all the witnesses in the case, and was in court during the trial, to be used if the occasion should arise.

'But why was not sentence passed at the trial?' says Mr. Reade. 'An English judge is the slave of precedent; why did he break through it on this occasion?' Mr. Justice Coleridge not only did not break through precedent, but acted in the strictest conformity with it. When indictments are removed (in order to be tried by a Special Jury), to the Nisi Prius[58] side of the Court, the judges could not, in former times, pass sentence at once; they were only enabled to do so by the 11 Geo. 4., and 1 W. 4. c. 70. § 9.; and they only exercise that discretion when the offence is of a sufficiently simple and common nature to enable the judge to decide at once upon the punishment which it requires. The reason why judgment was deferred in Lieutenant Austin's case was, that it was a case of an important and complicated nature, in which punishment could not be fairly apportioned, without reference to the whole of the prisoner's character and conduct; and for this purpose, time was given to the prisoner to produce affidavits in mitigation, and to the Crown to produce affidavits in aggravation, of punishment. This was accordingly done; and we can only say, that if Lieutenant Austin had not felt that his case was one in which further investigation was likely to be beneficial to him, he would hardly have given an opportunity to Sir A. Cockburn[59] of addressing to the Court of Queen's Bench a speech in aggravation of punishment, strongly marked by his extraordinary ability and healthy indignation against wrong doing. It is mere folly and childishness to say, that a judgment given in full term, in the Court of Queen's Bench, after addresses from Sir F. Thesiger[60] and Sir A. Cockburn, was more private than a judgment given at the very fag end of the Warwick Assizes.

Having thus shown that Mr. Reade is wrong in his facts, wrong in his law, and wrong in his logic; we need not insist very much on the probability that he would be wrong in his conclusion upon the justice of the sentence of the Court. We shall therefore conclude our remarks by contrasting the view which Lord Campbell, Mr. Justice Coleridge, and Mr. Justice Erle took of Lieutenant Austin's case, with the grand concluding burst of the petulant *littérateur*, who has arraigned *them* at his bar. Mr. Justice Coleridge in passing sentence told the prisoner, that the Court were of opinion, that the omissions

---

[57] A witness declining to answer a question in fear of self-incrimination.

[58] *OED* unless previously. The significance of the phrase is thus explained by Blackstone, *Comm.* (1768): All causes commenced in the courts of Westminster-hall are by the course of the courts appointed to be there tried, on a day fixed in some Easter or Michaelmas term, by a jury returned from the county, wherein the cause of action arises; but with this proviso, *nisi prius justitiarii ad assisas capiendas venerint, unless before* the day prefixed the judges of assize come into the county in question.

[59] Sir Alexander Cockburn (1802–1880; *ODNB*, judge).

[60] Frederic Thesiger, first Baron Chelmsford (1794–1878; *ODNB*, lord chancellor).

128 ON THE NOVEL AND JOURNALISM

in the prison books arose from inadvertency; that if they had been of a contrary opinion, they should have punished him very severely. That they thought his system of punishment was 'capable of inflicting great pain', and that it might be feared that it had led to fatal results. That the position of the governor of a gaol was one of great difficulty; that it appeared to the Court that he was not guilty of deliberate cruelty; and that they felt that he ought to be punished for the assaults which he had committed, and not for the consequences which they might have produced. In consideration of these circumstances, they sentenced him to three months' imprisonment in the Queen's Prison. The sentence was no doubt lenient, but we think that our readers will agree with us in feeling that it was anything but illusory, and that it was one which the Court had a perfect right to pronounce.

Now for Mr. Reade's view of the case (p. 465):

> The vermin thought they were in the dark, and could do anything now with impunity. Nobody will track our steps any further than the want-of-judgment-seat, thought they, and I confess that I for one was weak enough to track them no further. Fools! they had heard of God's eye to which the darkness is no darkness, but did not believe it; but he saw and revealed it to me by one of those things that men call strange accidents.
>
> It now remains for me, who am a public functionary though not a hireling, to do the rest of my duty.
>
> I revoke that sentence with all the blunders on which it was founded. Instead of becoming, as other judicial decisions do, a precedent for future judges, it shall be a beacon they shall avoid. It shall lie among the decisions of lawyers, but it shall never mix with them. It shall stand alone in all its oblique pity, its straightforward cruelty and absurdity; and no judge shall dare copy it while I am alive; for if he does, I swear to him by the God that made me, that all I have yet said is to what I will print of *him* as a lady's whip to a thresher's flail. I promise him on my honour as a writer and no hireling, I will buy a sheet of paper as big as a barn door, and nail him to it by his name as we nail a polecat by the throat. I will take him by one ear to Calcutta, and from Calcutta to Sydney; and by the other from London via Liverpool to New York and Boston. The sun shall never set upon his gibbet, and when his bones are rotten his shame shall live—Ay! though he was thirty years upon the bench posterity shall know little about his name, and *feel* nothing about it but this—that it is the name of a muddlehead, who gained and merited my loathing, my horror, my scorn!
>
> The civilised races, and I their temporary representative, revoke that sentence from the rising to the setting sun in every land where the English tongue is spoken.

In quieter language, if any judge presumes to differ from Mr. Reade he will swear at him so frightfully that he shall never be remembered for anything else. We feel that no language of ours can add to the effect of this hysterical effusion. That a man should write such nonsense in a momentary fit of excitement is credible, though strange; but that he should print it, correct the proofs, and send out five editions of it to the world, and that the book in which it appears should achieve very considerable, and even remarkable success, are curious social phenomena.

We have quoted these passages, as we might quote fifty more, not in order to show the quality of the individual intellect of Mr. Reade, but as a sample of the structure of a mind which has so hearty a contempt for the constituted frame-work of society. Mr. Reade caricatures the views of the world, so often professed by men of his class; he goes, for example, a long way beyond Mr. Dickens, but whether the contempt expressed

THE LICENSE OF MODERN NOVELISTS 129

for society as it stands, is greater or less, it constantly appears in the class of books to which we are referring, and wherever it exists, it is an infallible indication of an irritable fibre and feeble understanding. We need not go far to see what consequences follow from the propagation of this fretful temperament. The French 'literature of desperation',[61] which was so popular under Louis-Philippe,[62] is a rather more violent form of the same disease; and we all know what were its consequences. A *muliebris impotentia*[63] of thought and speech paves the way to profligate morals, religious scepticism, and political tyranny, just as surely as drinking produces *delirium tremens*. We have not gone far in this miserable path; English life is too active, English spheres of action too wide, English freedom too deeply rooted to be endangered by a set of bacchanals, drunk with green tea, and not protected by petticoats. Still, in the midst of boundless luxury and insatiable thirst for amusement, we have raised a class of writers who show strong sympathies for all that is most opposite to the very foundations of English life. Mr. Reade is so illogical that it is impossible to prove that he would dislike any one form of government less than any other; but his sympathies, like Mr. Dickens's express doctrines, set toward despotism. In 'Little Dorrit' Russia is set up as the pattern for England. Our motto is, 'how not to do it'; theirs 'how to do it'. Mr. Reade always invokes some kind of moral 'big brother'[64] to come and settle his difficulties. An heroic clergyman, armed with all gifts, physical, moral, and intellectual; who can repeat by heart 'thousands of pages' of Greek and Latin; who is 'a pupil of Bendigo';[65] sets Birmingham Gaol to rights by a sort of *tour de force*. Unpaid magistrates are an abomination; judges who act by precedent are 'hirelings'. A good theatrical government, interfering in domestic affairs, like the virtuous British farmers, at the Adelphi,[66] to give the repentant lovers their blessing and a fortune, and destroy the villain of the piece, without judge or jury, would fulfil the ideal of the authors of 'Little Dorrit', and 'It is never too late to mend.' That the ignorant and the young should amuse themselves with such things, is to be expected, but it is utterly unpardonable in grown-up men, to draw such wretched conclusions as these, from the spectacle afforded to them by England as it is, and England as it has been. That they are ignorant of politics and of history is their only excuse. To a mind which has any sympathy with all that is most noble in real, not ideal, human nature, there is something so grand and so touching in that great drama of which the present generation forms a part, that it is hard to speak with patience of those who fail to recognise its existence. The infinite labour which has been expended upon various parts of the social edifice of this country; the vehement discussion which has attended every change in it; the conflicting influences, which lines of thought and feeling the most radically opposed have exercised over its various members; the calm forbearance which is daily shown in maintaining our innumerable social compromises; the freedom secured to all just criticism; the good

[61] Gustave Masson (p. 142), *Thirty Years of French Literature* 12: 'Then arose what has been aptly called "the literature of despair"; and we saw vanity, incredulity, moral cowardice, and the most extraordinary looseness of principle, conspiring together to produce an intellectual phasis, such as had never been witnessed since the last days of the Roman Empire'.

[62] (1773–1850), King of France 1830–48.

[63] Lack of control over one's passions, held to be womanish (Tacitus, *Annals*).

[64] *OED* big = elder. From 1851, of a sister; from 1863, of a brother. (Given that 'despotism' happens to occur two lines earlier in JFS, it is all the more imperative to exclude *OED* Big Brother 1949 ORWELL.)

[65] William [*known as* Bendigo] Thompson (1811–1880; *ODNB*, pugilist).

[66] The Adelphi Theatre (refounded 1819), notable for staging a great many adaptations of Dickens.

130 ON THE NOVEL AND JOURNALISM

temper and good sense which refuse to push principles partially adopted to inconvenient conclusions—unite to invest English society with an historical dignity; and we
regret that there are men living in it for no better purpose than to exaggerate and deride
its defects.

These observations are more particularly addressed to the misrepresentations and
exaggerations resorted to by modern novelists in their descriptions of public institutions and public abuses; but we are compelled to add that they have not always respected
the domain of private charity and the recesses of private life. It is impossible to speak
without the deepest interest and sympathy of the genius, the trials, and the fate of
Charlotte Brontë. Her novels hold, and deserve to hold, a place in English literature
from their intrinsic power, from their nervous style,[67] from their daring vigour and
subtle analysis, which few books of the same class have ever obtained. But when we
learn, from the records of her life, within how dark and narrow a boundary that fiery
spirit dwelt and toiled—when we see how that frail body, that suffering constitution,
that half-distracted family, that cheerless home, that scanty household, that still more
scanty experience of the pleasures and sympathies of life, crushed the vehement aspirations of a child of genius for love, and happiness, and freedom—we recur to her works
with amazement, and we grudge no portion of the fame which rests upon her melancholy story and her early grave. Yet it must be said that in drawing from her own experiences the materials of her novels—for Miss Brontë's writings partake more of reality
than of imagination—she greatly abused the license of her art. The description of the
Lowood school in 'Jane Eyre', is evidently the result of a morbid impression on the
mind of a highly sensitive child of nine years old, wrought by painful associations and
great imaginative fervour into a scene of torment; but it is due to the estimable persons
who have been connected with that institution, to state that the frightful charges
brought against it by Miss Brontë are denied, and that the charitable designs of its
founders have not been perverted in the manner she has led her readers to suppose. On
this point we are content to take Mrs. Gaskell's own account of her heroine's mode of
proceeding.

> Miss Brontë more than once said to me that she should not have written what she did of
> Lowood in 'Jane Eyre', if she thought the place would have been so immediately identi-
> fied with Cowan's Bridge, although there was not a word in her account of the institution
> but what was true at the time when she knew it; she also said that *she had not considered it
> necessary, in a work of fiction, to state every particular with the impartiality* that might be
> required in a court of justice, nor to seek out motives and make allowance for human feel-
> ings, as she might have done, if dispassionately analyzing the conduct of those who had
> the superintendence of the institution. I believe she herself would have been glad of an
> opportunity to correct the overstrong impression which was made upon the public mind
> by her vivid picture; though even she, suffering her whole life long, both in heart and
> body, from the consequences of what happened there, might have been apt to the last to
> take her deep belief in facts for the facts themselves—her conception of truth for the
> absolute truth. (*Life of C. Brontë*, vol. i. p. 64.)

Again, we are assured by persons who received their education (and a very good education Miss Brontë herself proves it to have been) at the school to which she was attached

[67] See Introduction, p. 9.

THE LICENSE OF MODERN NOVELISTS

in Brussels, that nothing can be more unjust than the aspersions she has thrown in 'Villette' on that establishment, and on the excellent persons who managed it. The three curates who figure in 'Shirley', conspicuous for different degrees of folly, vulgarity, and impertinence, are, we are told by Miss Brontë's biographer, three gentlemen well known at the time in the neighbourhood of Howarth, who have had the good taste to accept this caricature as a joke. But if the habits of social intercourse, if personal peculiarities, and even the arrangements of charitable institutions, are to be exhibited to the world in the colours of an *auto-de-fé*[68]—bedaubed with gamboge[69] and emblazoned with devils—the novelists will become a pest to literature, and they will degrade, as some of them have already degraded, their talents to the service of malignant passions, calumny, and falsehood.

Nor can we, with a due regard to literary justice, pass over in silence the grave offence of a similar character of which Mrs. Gaskell, the biographer of Miss Brontë, has herself been guilty. The life of this remarkable woman has been read with an avidity which does not surprise us, for both the subject and the manner of the book are well calculated to excite the deepest interest. But Mrs. Gaskell appears to have learnt the art of the novel-writer so well that she cannot discharge from her palette the colours she has used in the pages of 'Mary Barton' and 'Ruth'. This biography opens precisely like a novel, and the skilful arrangement of lights and shades and colours—the prominence of some objects and the evident suppression of others—leave on the mind the excitement of a highly-wrought drama, rather than the simplicity of daylight and of nature. To heighten the interest of this strange representation, and also to assert her own imperious sense of moral obligations, the biographer has thought it proper and necessary to introduce the episode of Branwell Brontë, a worthless brother of the three mysterious *Bells*,[70] whose misconduct added a pang to their dreary existence; and in giving the history of this scapegrace Mrs. Gaskell has allowed herself to enter into details affecting the character and conduct of living persons, on whom she proceeds to pass sentence in a tone for which she now feels, or ought to feel, great shame and regret. It turns out that these details were borrowed from imperfect or incorrect evidence; no effort seems to have been made to verify the facts on which Mrs. Gaskell proceeded to consign another woman to infamy and to brand her with maledictions. The name and station of the lady thus assailed were easily identified, and it became known that she is a member of a highly honourable family; legal proceedings were threatened, and we believe commenced, to vindicate her reputation; and on the 30th May a letter appeared in the 'Times' newspaper from Mrs. Gaskell's solicitor, stating that he was instructed '*to retract every statement* contained in that work which imputes to a widowed lady, referred to, but not named therein, any breach of her conjugal, of her maternal, and of her social duties, &c. All those statements were made upon information which at the time Mrs. Gaskell believed to be well founded, but which, upon investigation, with the additional evidence furnished to me by you, *I have ascertained not to be trustworthy*. I am, therefore, authorised not only to retract the statements in question, but to express the deep regret of Mrs. Gaskell that she should have been led

---

[68] *OED auto-da-fé, -de-fé* The execution of a sentence of the Inquisition; *esp.* the public burning of a heretic.

[69] *OED* A gum resin . . . used as a pigment, giving a bright yellow colouring.

[70] Acton Bell (Anne Brontë), Currer Bell (Charlotte Brontë), and Ellis Bell (Emily Jane Brontë).

132 ON THE NOVEL AND JOURNALISM

to make them.' This apology has been accepted; though the disavowal of the false statements would have been more becoming to both parties, if it had not been conveyed in the studied phraseology of an attorney.

We record these painful details in justice to the injured party, rather than to increase the punishment of this exposure of the biographer. Mrs. Gaskell erred, no doubt, from mistaken information and from mistaken motives; for she appears to have entirely misconceived the duties and the rights of her position as an authoress. She acted on the assumption that she was justified in dragging hidden offences to the bar of public opinion—in arraigning and condemning without trial or notice persons of whose real sentiments and conduct she was ignorant—and in applying the language of an avenging Deity to a being who is perhaps not more frail or liable to error than herself. Nay, she seems even to have thought, as Mr. Reade does, that it is a part of the high commission of literature to try offences which elude the repression of the law, and to denounce with hyperbolical violence actions which may not have been committed at all, or which have been committed from very different motives. Whether such allegations be true or false, it is perfectly certain that the laws of civilised nations and the usages of society prohibit and punish the publication of them. A man's honour, a woman's virtue, are not to be blown to the winds merely because it suits the humour of a romancer to rake up some imaginary or forgotten transgression—to dress it in the colours of fiction, heightened by the mischievous attraction of personal slander—and to set up a pillory in Paternoster Row.[71] The dignified administration of justice, the assiduous activity of those who are called by the nation to the management of its affairs, and the institutions which give method and order to free government, are not to be traduced, vilified, and outraged merely because they do not obey the hasty impulses of novelists or pamphleteers. The law, which might punish such attacks, is seldom put in force against them, and we entirely concur in the wisdom of this forbearance; but, as they are made in the name of literature, it becomes the duty of literary criticism to expose and to disown them; and for this reason we have commented on them more fully than the works before us can themselves be said to deserve.

[71] The home of London publishers.

'The *Edinburgh Review* and Modern Novelists' (*Saturday Review*, 18 July 1857)

JFS agreeably finds himself all-but-entirely agreeing with himself, this anonymous piece of his in the *Saturday Review* echoing his anonymous piece in the *Edinburgh Review*, 'The License of Modern Novelists' (July 1857, p. 104). 'Double reviewing' was a frequent duplicity but it seldom took the specious form of JFS here ('in a powerful and very curious article...', 'this instructive paper', 'well described by the *Edinburgh Review*...').[1] One week later (*Sat. Rev.*, 25 July 1857): 'Mr. Charles Reade and the *Edinburgh Review*':

> We have received the subjoined communication from Mr. Reade. In this case, contrary to our usual rule, we publish our correspondent's letter:
>
> SATURDAY REVIEW, You have brains of your own, and good ones. Do not you echo the bray of such a very small ass as the *Edinburgh Review*. Be more just to yourself and to me. Reflect! I must be six times a greater writer than ever lived, ere I could exaggerate suicide, despair, and the horrors that drive young and old to them; or (to vary your own phrase) write 'a libel upon Hell'.
>
> Yours sincerely,
>
> Garrick Club, July 21   CHARLES READE

The *Edinburgh Review* and Modern Novelists

The *Edinburgh Review*, in a powerful and very curious article, has directed attention to the serious mischiefs arising from the growing influence of novels with the half-educated classes, and the growing tendency of novelists to assume the functions of political censors.[2] The topics discussed in this instructive paper have been frequently handled in our own columns, but the space at the command of the *Edinburgh Review* enables it to give them a fulness of illustration which is scarcely possible with ourselves. The instances selected by the Reviewer are the caricature of the Government offices in Mr. Dickens's *Little Dorrit*—the libel on Birmingham Gaol, in the novel of Mr. Charles Reade called *It is Never too Late to Mend*—and that miserable story in *The Life of Charlotte Brontë* of which Mrs. Gaskell has recently admitted the untruth. The last example evidently stands on a rather different footing from the others. It no doubt shows the completeness with which the literary mind is apt to give itself up to its own foregone conclusions, and illustrates the distinction—a distinction implied in the difference between imagination and reason—which exists between skill in the

---

[1] Christopher C. Dahl, 'Fitzjames Stephen, Charles Dickens, and Double Reviewing' (*Victorian Periodicals Review*, summer 1981).

[2] See *OED* note, p. 104.

134   ON THE NOVEL AND JOURNALISM

production of literary effects, and skill in the verification and employment of alleged evidence. But Mr. Dickens and Mr. Reade are, as the Reviewer abundantly proves, deliberate perverters and falsifiers of facts. Mrs. Gaskell is open to no such accusation; and the worst that can be said of her is, that she allowed herself to assume that the resources of her own art included a faculty which is sometimes only imperfectly acquired by the special training of half a life.

The Reviewer deals rather more harshly, on the whole, with Mr. Reade than with Mr. Dickens. We think there is a little injustice in this, though the bias of the critic is amply explained by the habits of thought to which we have gradually accustomed ourselves. A class of writers—of which Mr. Dickens and the religious novelists[3] are samples at once curiously like and curiously unlike—have almost completely debauched our sympathies and understandings on the subject of the relation which opinions should bear to facts. We have got to think it quite natural and pardonable in a Puseyite romancer to make the exponent of Evangelicalism put the wrong name to a promissory note, or in an Evangelical novelist to send the Puseyite clergyman over to Rome in company with his neighbour's wife. The forgery of facts takes rank[4] with the fine arts, and we have Ruskins[5] who lay down canons to enable us to judge between the comparative values of imaginative flimsy.[6] Few of us have sufficient integrity of mind to perceive that Mr. Dickens was guilty of a moral offence in constructing a set of facts to support his condemnation of the Public Offices. Even the *Edinburgh Review* speaks in a tone which seems to imply that the writer who invents a falsehood is less guilty than the writer who exaggerates a truth. We cannot admit this. Mr. Dickens's facts are entirely imaginary. The evidence on which his conclusion was really based, consisting, as it did, of ignorant popular rumours and vague newspaper statements, was so worthless as to be absolutely null. But Mr. Reade had really some evidence to his second opinion. Either from sterility of invention, or (as we would hope) from a juster view of the conditions which should govern practical judgments, he took the Report and Evidence of the Royal Commission on the Birmingham Gaol, and formed them into the basis of the elaborate descriptions which fill the greater part of his first and second volumes. The authority was good, as far as it went; but Mr. Reade's offence lay in straining and tampering with every single datum which his authority gave him. This,

---

[3] JFS, 'Fair Oaks' (*Sat. Rev.*, 21 Mar. 1857). By 'Max Lyle' (Anna Maria Yule); it 'belongs to a class of novels which is very characteristic of, and almost peculiar to, the present day. It is not exactly what would be generally called a religious novel, and it is certainly not one of the commoner type. Perhaps—to put an additional burden on a much-abused word—we may call it an earnest novel...A sort of calm, resigned melancholy has seized upon a large and really very estimable class of clever young men and women in the present day. It is to the Byronic form of the disease what chicken-pox is to small-pox, but it belongs to the same family. The victims of this malady are too manly and too pious to complain. They are too good for this wicked world, and they know it; but as their lot is cast here—as they have duties to do and "brothers" to help—they will be cheerful, and even, as a point of honour, enthusiastic and interested about pursuits in which they feel that they never can succeed for want of wickedness, and which would bring them no happiness if by any strange accident they did. It is the peculiar characteristic of heroes of this description that they are always kept back by their own virtues. Arnold Osborne (the very name denotes the man) is such an admirable doctor, so devoted to his profession, such a thorough gentleman, so handsome, well-born, and well-bred, that of course he fails. What can such a man do but fail, and go to heaven for it?'

[4] *OED* a grade of station or dignity.

[5] *OED* 1851 RUSKIN To place in its true rank the general Gothic of the thirteenth century.

[6] *OED* A flimsy or thin kind of paper: esp. that used by reporters for the purpose of multiplying copies; hence, reporters' 'copy'. From 1857.

THE *EDINBURGH REVIEW* AND MODERN NOVELISTS 135

in our opinion, was extremely culpable; but we cannot agree with the view taken by the Reviewer—rather impliedly, it is true, than expressly—of the ratio which the delinquency bears to those habitually practised by Mr. Dickens. We hold that it is worse to tell a whole lie than half a one. The homage to truth involved in a partial adherence to it ought to be admitted in extenuation.

We are, however, indebted for much instruction to the prominence given to Mr. Reade in this article. Nothing can be more curious than the comparison which the Reviewer has instituted between the facts of the Birmingham Gaol case and the representations of them in the popular novel. In *Little Dorrit* we have only the result—the concrete phenomenon. Nobody can trace the mental operation by which the Barnacles and the other Circumlocutionists were conceived. It is Mr. Dickens's secret exclusively. But in *It is Never too Late to Mend* we have the chemistry of modern romance. The salts crystallize, the gases diffuse themselves, the metals agglomerate before our very eyes. The process consists in twisting, perverting, misrepresenting, adding to or taking away from, every single truth which enters into the material basis. Here are specimens of the manipulation which facts must undergo before they become fitted for the novelist's art. The cruel ill-treatment of a youth imprisoned in one of our gaols has to be described for the purpose of assisting prison reform. He had a stiff leathern collar placed round his neck—it has to be changed into a 'high circular saw'. He had 4000 turns of the crank—4000 is altered to 8000. He was once wetted with a bucket of water—the novel states that he was wetted perpetually. He was hard worked, but managed nearly always to do his allotted task, and sometimes exceed it—Mr. Reade states that it was physically impossible for him to complete it. He was certainly ill-used, but he gained in flesh during his imprisonment—in the novel he is transformed into 'a small but aged man, shambling in the joints, stiffened by perpetual crucifixion and rheumatism.' Many more misrepresentations than these, and much more important, are established by the Reviewer in regard to the conduct of Lieutenant Austin, the Birmingham magistrates, and the Home Office. We have merely selected a few which seem to us instructive in their very absurdity. In fact, most of Mr. Reade's exaggerations can be measured arithmetically. He seems to have reversed the policy of the Unjust Steward in the parable. Wherever he found the number 5, he took his paper, sat down quickly, and wrote 50.[7]

Whoever has fairly correct notions of the uses which facts are collected to subserve—whoever has an inkling of the truth that general propositions are valuable in so far as they cover actual facts, and worthless when they go a hair's-breadth beyond them—may be left to make up his mind as to the propriety of Mr. Reade's method. Unfortunately, long indulgence in a literature which is well described by the *Edinburgh Review* as 'at once a stimulant and an anodyne', has so depraved some of the most necessary faculties of the reading public as to render it almost incapable of applying the laws of inference to the generalizations of novelists. We well know the answer which will be made to the *Edinburgh Review*. It is one which, in effect, claims for novel-writers an immunity from sobriety of statement and caution in drawing conclusions. The Reviewer has anticipated it, when he suggests this plea for Mr. Dickens: 'How can

---

[7] Luke 16:5–6, How much owest thou unto my lord? And he said, An hundred measures of oil. And he said unto him, Take thy bill, and sit down quickly, and write fifty.

you suppose that I mean any harm by such representations as these? I am neither a lawyer nor a politician; but I take a fling at the subjects of the day, just in order to give my writings a little local colour and a little temporary piquancy.' We are told, in fact, that the paper which the novelist puts off on us is only a note of the Bank of Elegance, and that it is our own fault if we are taken in. We reply, however, that whatever be the nature of the counterfeit which the authors of *Little Dorrit* and *It is Never too Late to Mend* attempted to pass, they intended to pocket the change. These gentlemen seriously mean to be listened to as practical teachers; and it is the boast of those who admire their method of instruction, that their romances are more influential than fifty Blue-books.[8] Mr. Dickens's caricature of the Circumlocution Office was originally part of a more comprehensive attack on the administrative system of the country; nor would it have seemed to be isolated if the other part of the campaign had not miscarried so miserably. Just before these chapters of *Little Dorrit* appeared, its author marched down to Drury Lane,[9] with sackbut, psaltery, and all kinds of puffatory[10] music, to pull down the golden image which a series of kings had set up.[11] We hold that he was perfectly justified in doing so. If he subjects himself to the ordinary checks which wait upon political discussion, Mr. Dickens has as clear a right to be heard upon politics as anybody else. But when the Association to which he tried to lend assistance went out like a candle-snuff, Mr. Dickens was not entitled to invent in his novel the *data* which his associates had failed to establish on the platform; nor are his friends justified in asking for the romance-writer that immunity from deference to truth which it would have been impudence to demand for the spokesman of the Administrative Reformers. As for Mr. Reade, his assertions of the practical effects which are to follow from his novel are vehement and repeated. He prophesies against the Judges and the Home Office, like a sort of milk-and-water Ezekiel. Here is his reversal of the sentence of the Queen's Bench on Lieutenant Austin: 'It now remains for me, *who am a public functionary*, but not a hireling, to do the rest of my duty. I revoke that sentence...Instead of becoming a precedent for future Judges, it shall be a beacon they shall avoid...No Judge shall dare copy it while I am alive; for if he does...I will buy a sheet of paper as big as a barn-door, and nail him to it by his name, as we nail a polecat by the throat...The civilized races, and I, their temporary representative, revoke that sentence, from the rising to the setting sun, in every land where the English tongue is spoken.'

The disdain of their country which the novels of Mr. Dickens and Mr. Reade reveal, is attributable no doubt to the 'scavengering'[12] mission of the present age. We have cleared away so many abuses that some of us regard statesmen as created exclusively to cart off muck, and journalists to ferret it out in neglected corners. The holy and beautiful house in which this purification is but a menial office, has been almost forgotten by

---

[8] *OED specifically* one of the official reports of Parliament and the Privy Council, which are issued in a dark blue paper cover. (1715 citation, 'bound in blue Velvet'.)

[9] At the Theatre Royal, Drury Lane, on 27 June 1855, Dickens addressed the Administrative Reform Association, of which he was a founding member.

[10] *OED* [from 'puff', after such words as laudatory]. From 1823. 1854 Authors are better off seeing all reviews, unless the helplessly puffatory or malignantly abusive.

[11] Daniel 3:5, O people, nations, and languages, that at what time ye hear the sound of the cornet, flute, harp, sackbut, psaltery, dulcimer, and all kinds of musick, ye fall down and worship the golden image that Nebuchadnezzar the king hath set up.

[12] Carlyle, 'the long-expected *Scavenger Age*'; p. 156.

THE *EDINBURGH REVIEW* AND MODERN NOVELISTS 137

those whose hands are deep in dirt, and Mr. Dickens bids us pull it down rather than labour at it any longer. Happily, in the eloquent language of the Reviewer, 'we have not gone far in this miserable path; English life is too active, English spheres of action too wide; English freedom too deeply rooted to be endangered by a set of Bacchanals, drunk with green tea, and not protected by petticoats. In the midst of boundless luxury and insatiable thirst for amusement, we have raised a class of writers who show strong sympathies for all that is most opposite to the very foundations of English life...That they are ignorant of politics and of history is their only excuse. To a mind which has any sympathy with all that is most noble in real, not ideal, human nature, there is something so grand and so touching in that great drama of which the present generation forms a part, that it is hard to speak with patience of those who fail to recognise its existence. The infinite labour which has been expended upon various parts of the social edifice of this country; the vehement discussion which has attended every change in it; the conflicting influences which lives of thought and feeling the most radically opposed have exercised over its various members; the calm forbearance which is daily shown in maintaining our innumerable social compromises; the freedom secured to all just criticism; the good temper and good sense which refuse to push principles partially adopted to inconvenient conclusions—unite to invest English society with an historical dignity.' We regret, with the *Edinburgh Review*, that there are men living in it for no better purpose than to exaggerate and deride its defects.

Charles Dickens, 'Curious Misprint in the *Edinburgh Review*' (*Household Words*, 1 August 1857)

The Edinburgh Review, in an article in its last number, on 'The License of Modern Novelists', is angry with MR. DICKENS and other modern novelists, for not confining themselves to the mere amusement of their readers, and for testifying in their works that they seriously feel the interest of true Englishmen in the welfare and honour of their country. To them should be left the making of easy occasional books for idle young gentlemen and ladies to take up and lay down on sofas, drawing-room tables, and window-seats; to the Edinburgh Review should be reserved the settlement of all social and political questions, and the strangulation of all complainers. MR. THACKERAY may write upon Snobs, but there must be none in the superior government departments. There is no positive objection to MR. READE having to do, in a Platonic way, with a Scottish fishwoman or so; but he must by no means connect himself with Prison Discipline. That is the inalienable property of official personages; and, until Mr. Reade can show that he has so much a-year, paid quarterly, for understanding (or not understanding) the subject, it is none of his, and it is impossible that he can be allowed to deal with it.

The name of Mr. Dickens is at the head of this page, and the hand of Mr. Dickens writes this paper. He will shelter himself under no affectation of being any one else, in having a few words of earnest but temperate remonstrance with the Edinburgh Review, before pointing out its curious misprint. Temperate, for the honour of Literature; temperate, because of the great services which the Edinburgh Review has rendered in its time to good literature, and good government; temperate, in remembrance of the loving affection of JEFFREY, the friendship of SYDNEY SMITH, and the faithful sympathy of both.

The License of Modern Novelists is a taking title. But it suggests another—the License of Modern Reviewers. Mr. Dickens's libel on the wonderfully exact and vigorous English government, which is always ready for any emergency, and which, as everybody knows, has never shown itself to be at all feeble at a pinch within the memory of men, is License in a novelist. Will the Edinburgh Review forgive Mr. Dickens for taking the liberty to point out what is License in a Reviewer?

'Even the catastrophe in "Little Dorrit" is evidently borrowed from the recent fall of houses in Tottenham Court Road, which happens to have appeared in the newspapers at a convenient period.'

Thus, the Reviewer. The Novelist begs to ask him whether there is no License in his writing those words and stating that assumption as a truth, when any man accustomed to the critical examination of a book cannot fail, attentively turning over the pages of Little Dorrit, to observe that that catastrophe is carefully prepared for from the very first presentation of the old house in the story; that when Rigaud, the man who is crushed by the fall of the house, first enters it (hundreds of pages before the end), he is beset by a mysterious fear and shuddering; that the rotten and crazy state of the house is laboriously kept before the reader, whenever the house is shown; that the way to the demolition of the man and the house together, is paved all through the book

CURIOUS MISPRINT IN THE *EDINBURGH REVIEW* 139

with a painful minuteness and reiterated care of preparation, the necessity of which (in order that the thread may be kept in the reader's mind through nearly two years), is one of the adverse incidents of that social form of publication? It may be nothing to the question that Mr. Dickens now publicly declares, on his word and honor, that that catastrophe was written, was engraven on steel, was printed, had passed through the hands of compositors, readers for the press, and pressmen, and was in type and in proof in the Printing House of MESSRS. BRADBURY AND EVANS, before the accident in Tottenham Court Road occurred. But, it is much to the question that an honorable reviewer might have easily traced this out in the internal evidence of the book itself, before he stated, for a fact, what is utterly and entirely, in every particular and respect, untrue. More; if the Editor of the Edinburgh Review (unbending from the severe official duties of a blameless branch of the Circumlocution Office) had happened to condescend to cast his eye on the passage, and had referred even its mechanical probabilities and improbabilities to his publishers, those experienced gentlemen must have warned him that he was getting into danger; must have told him that on a comparison of dates, and with a reference to the number printed of Little Dorrit, with that very incident illustrated, and to the date of the publication of the completed book in a volume, they hardly perceived how Mr. Dickens *could* have waited, with such a desperate Micawberism, for a fall of houses in Tottenham Court Road, to get him out of his difficulties, and yet could have come up to time with the needful punctuality. Does the Edinburgh Review make no charges at random? Does it live in a blue and yellow glass house, and yet throw such big stones over the roof? Will the licensed Reviewer apologize to the licensed Novelist, for *his* little Circumlocution Office? Will he 'examine the justice' of his own 'general charges', as well as Mr. Dickens's? Will he apply his own words to himself, and come to the conclusion that it really is, 'a little curious to consider what qualifications a man ought to possess, before he could with any kind of propriety hold this language'?

The Novelist now proceeds to the Reviewer's curious misprint. The Reviewer, in his laudation of the great official departments, and in his indignant denial of there being any trace of a Circumlocution Office to be detected among them all, begs to know, 'what does Mr. Dickens think of the whole organisation of the Post Office, and of the system of cheap Postage?' Taking St. Martins-le-grand in tow, the wrathful Circumlocution steamer, puffing at Mr. Dickens to crush him with all the weight of that first-rate vessel, demands, 'to take a single and well-known example, how does he account for the career of MR. ROWLAND HILL? A gentleman in a private and not very conspicuous position, writes a pamphlet recommending what amounted to a revolution in a most important department of the Government. Did the Circumlocution Office neglect him, traduce him, break his heart, and ruin his fortune? They adopted his scheme, and gave him the leading share in carrying it out, and yet this is the government which Mr. Dickens declares to be a sworn foe to talent, and a systematic enemy to ingenuity.'

The curious misprint, here, is the name of Mr. Rowland Hill. Some other and perfectly different name must have been sent to the printer. Mr. Rowland Hill!!! Why, if Mr. Rowland Hill were not, in toughness, a man of a hundred thousand; if he had not had in the struggles of his career a stedfastness of purpose overriding all sensitiveness, and steadily staring grim despair out of countenance, the Circumlocution Office would have made a dead man of him long and long ago. Mr. Dickens, among his other darings, dares to state, that the Circumlocution Office most heartily hated Mr. Rowland Hill; that the Circumlocution Office most characteristically opposed him as long as opposition was in any way possible; that the Circumlocution Office would have been most devoutly glad if it could have harried Mr. Rowland Hill's soul out of his body, and consigned him and his troublesome penny project to the grave together.

Mr. Rowland Hill!!! Now, see the impossibility of Mr. Rowland Hill being the name which the Edinburgh Review sent to the printer. It may have relied on the forbearance of Mr. Dickens towards living gentlemen, for his being mute on a mighty job that was jobbed in that very Post-Office when Mr. Rowland Hill was *taboo* there, and it shall not rely upon his courtesy in vain:

140   ON THE NOVEL AND JOURNALISM

though there be breezes on the southern side of Mid-Strand, London, in which the scent of it is yet strong on quarter-days.[1] But, the Edinburgh Review never can have put up Mr. Rowland Hill for the putting down of Mr. Dickens's idle fiction of a Circumlocution Office. The 'license' would have been too great, the absurdity would have been too transparent, the Circumlocution Office dictation and partizanship would have been much too manifest.

'The Circumlocution Office adopted his scheme, and gave him the leading share in carrying it out.' The words are clearly not applicable to Mr. Rowland Hill. Does the Reviewer remember the history of Mr. Rowland Hill's scheme? The Novelist does, and will state it here, exactly; in spite of its being one of the eternal decrees that the Reviewer, in virtue of his license, shall know everything, and that the Novelist in virtue of *his* license, shall know nothing.

Mr. Rowland Hill published his pamphlet on the establishment of one uniform penny post-age, in the beginning of the year eighteen hundred and thirty-seven. Mr. Wallace, member for Greenock, who had long been opposed to the then existing Post-Office system, moved for a Committee on the subject. Its appointment was opposed by the Government—or, let us say, the Circumlocution Office—but was afterwards conceded. Before that Committee, the Circumlocution Office and Mr. Rowland Hill were perpetually in conflict on questions of fact; and it invariably turned out that Mr. Rowland Hill was always right in his facts, and that the Circumlocution Office was always wrong. Even on so plain a point as the average number of let-ters at that very time passing through the Post Office, Mr. Rowland Hill was right, and the Circumlocution Office was wrong.

Says the Edinburgh Review, in what it calls a 'general' way, 'The Circumlocution Office adopted his scheme.' Did it? Not just then, certainly; for, nothing whatever was done, arising out of the enquiries of that Committee. But, it happened that the Whig Government afterwards came to be beaten on the Jamaica question, by reason of the Radicals voting against them. Sir Robert Peel was commanded to form a Government, but failed, in consequence of the diffi-culties that arose (our readers will remember them) about the Ladies of the Bedchamber. The Ladies of the Bedchamber brought the Whigs in again, and then the Radicals (being always for the destruction of everything) made it one of the conditions of their rendering their support to the new Whig Government that the penny-postage system should be adopted. This was two years after the appointment of the Committee: that is to say, in eighteen hundred and thirty-nine. The Circumlocution Office had, to that time, done nothing towards the penny postage, but oppose, delay, contradict, and show itself uniformly wrong.

'They adopted his scheme, and gave him the leading share in carrying it out.' Of course they gave him the leading share in carrying it out, then, at the time when they adopted it, and took the credit and popularity of it? Not so. In eighteen hundred and thirty-nine, Mr. Rowland Hill was appointed—not to the Post Office, but to the Treasury. Was he appointed to the Treasury to carry out his own scheme? No. He was appointed 'to advise'. In other words, to instruct the ignorant Circumlocution Office how to do without him, if it by any means could. On the tenth of January, eighteen hundred and forty, the penny-postage system was adopted. Then, of course, the Circumlocution Office gave Mr. Rowland Hill 'the leading share in carrying it out'? Not exactly, but it gave him the leading share in carrying himself out: for, in eighteen hundred and forty-two, it summarily dismissed Mr. Rowland Hill altogether!

When the Circumlocution Office had come to that pass in its patriotic course, so much admired by the Edinburgh Review, of protecting and patronizing Mr. Rowland Hill, whom any child who is not a Novelist can perceive to have been its peculiar *protégé*; the public mind (always perverse) became much excited on the subject. Sir Thomas Wilde moved for another Committee.

---

[1] *OED* One of the four days fixed by custom as marking off the quarters of the year, on which tenancy of houses usually begins and ends, and the payment of rent and other quarterly charges falls due. From 1480. With 1840 DICKENS *Barn. Rudge* The twenty-fifth of March, one of those unpleasant epochs termed quarter-days.

CURIOUS MISPRINT IN THE *EDINBURGH REVIEW* 141

Circumlocution Office interposed. Nothing was done. The public subscribed and presented to Mr. Rowland Hill, Sixteen Thousand Pounds. Circumlocution Office remained true to itself and its functions. Did nothing; would do nothing. It was not until eighteen hundred and forty-six, four years afterwards, that Mr. Rowland Hill was appointed to a place in the Post Office. Was he appointed, even then, to the 'leading share in carrying out' his scheme? He was permitted to creep into the Post Office up the back stairs, through having a place created for him. This post of dignity and honor, this Circumlocution Office crown, was called 'Secretary to the Post-Master General'; there being already a Secretary to the Post Office, of whom the Circumlocution Office had declared, as its reason for dismissing Mr. Rowland Hill, that his functions and Mr. Rowland Hill's could not be made to harmonize.

They did not harmonize. They were in perpetual discord. Penny postage is but one reform of a number of Post Office reforms effected by Mr. Rowland Hill; and these, for eight years longer, were thwarted and opposed by the Circumlocution Office, tooth and nail. It was not until eighteen hundred and fifty-four, fourteen years after the appointment of Mr. Wallace's Committee, that Mr. Rowland Hill (having, as was openly stated at the time, threatened to resign and to give his reasons for doing so), was at last made sole Secretary at the Post Office, and the inharmonious secretary (of whom no more shall be said) was otherwise disposed of. It is only since that date of eighteen hundred and fifty-four, that such reforms as the amalgamation of the general and district posts, the division of London into ten towns, the earlier delivery of letters all over the country, the book and parcels post, the increase of letter-receiving houses everywhere, and the management of the Post Office with a greatly increased efficiency, have been brought about by Mr. Rowland Hill for the public benefit and the public convenience.

If the Edinburgh Review could seriously want to know 'how Mr. Dickens accounts for the career of Mr. Rowland Hill', Mr. Dickens would account for it by his being a Birmingham man of such imperturbable steadiness and strength of purpose, that the Circumlocution Office, by its utmost endeavours, very freely tried, could not weaken his determination, sharpen his razor, or break his heart. By his being a man in whose behalf the public gallantry was roused, and the public spirit awakened. By his having a project, in its nature so plainly and directly tending to the immediate benefit of every man, woman, and child in the State, that the Circumlocution Office could not blind them, though it could for a time cripple it. By his having thus, from the first to the last, made his way in spite of the Circumlocution Office, and dead against it as his natural enemy.

But, the name is evidently a curious misprint and an unfortunate mistake. The Novelist will await the Reviewer's correction of the press, and substitution of the right name.

Will the Edinburgh Review also take its next opportunity of manfully expressing its regret that in too distempered a zeal for the Circumlocution Office, it has been betrayed, as to that Tottenham Court Road assertion, into a hasty substitution of untruth for truth; the discredit of which, it might have saved itself, if it had been sufficiently cool and considerate to be simply just? It will, too possibly, have much to do by that time in championing its Circumlocution Office in new triumphs on the voyage out to India (God knows that the Novelist has his private as well as his public reasons for writing the foreboding with no triumphant heart!); but even party occupation, the reviewer's license, or the editorial plural, does not absolve a gentleman from a gentleman's duty, a gentleman's restraint, and a gentleman's generosity.

Mr. Dickens will willingly do his best to 'account for' any new case of Circumlocution Office protection that the Review may make a gauntlet of. He may be trusted to do so, he hopes, with a just respect for the Review, for himself, and for his calling; beyond the sound, healthy, legitimate uses and influences of which, he has no purpose to serve, and no ambition in life to gratify.

'Light Literature in France'
(*Saturday Review*, 5 September 1857)

JFS extends his 'Light Literature and the *Saturday Review*' (*Sat. Rev.*, 11 July 1857; p. 98), deploring that liberals in France, as in England, disparage their country. 'We do not by any means deny that French writers of fiction have often erred in this matter' (of representing the world as worse than it is), 'or that many of their books are very immoral indeed; but...' His judgments continue on the lines laid down in, for instance, 'Madame Bovary' (*Sat. Rev.*, 11 July 1857), and 'Balzac' (*Sat. Rev.*, 19 Dec. 1857).

Light Literature in France

A pamphlet called *Thirty Years of French Literature*, by M. Masson,[1] an assistant master of Harrow, which has been lately brought to our notice, appears to us remarkable enough to demand some attention. M. Masson is a Frenchman, who has, we believe, long been resident in this country, and writes its language with singular force and purity. Some time since, the editor of the *Revue des Deux Mondes*[2] offered a prize of 100*l.* for an Essay on the Decay of French Literature during the present century, and, without becoming a candidate for the prize, M. Masson has addressed to his adopted countrymen some remarks upon the recent literary history of their neighbours, which are curious, interesting, and singularly full of knowledge, but which seem to us to take a gloomier view of France and French society than the circumstances call for.

M. Masson's pamphlet deals successively with the poetry, the drama, and the romance of the last two generations; and after going through the land from Dan to Beersheba,[3] he pronounces it a sort of moral wilderness, in which nothing is to be found but a dreary atheistic materialism, haunted rather than varied by all sorts of unreal and sentimental efforts after something better and higher. We do not affect to possess so wide a knowledge of the subject as M. Masson shows; but we would submit to our readers some considerations upon the general subject which seem to us to be deserving of attention, although they are almost, if not altogether, ignored by most of those who express opinions in the present day about the condition of French society. We will confine ourselves to that part of M. Masson's Essay in which he stigmatizes, if not in express words at least by implication, the whole novel literature of France for the

---

[1] 1856. (Thirty years in thirty pages.) Gustave Masson, B.A. Univ. Gallic., Assistant Master at Harrow School, and Member of the Société de l'Histoire du Protestantisme Français.

[2] Founded 1829, bimonthly, with Balzac and George Sand among the contributors, by the 1860s the most widely read of the reviews.

[3] 2 Samuel 24:2, Go now through all the tribes of Israel, from Dan even to Beer-sheba, and number ye the people, that I may know the number of the people.

LIGHT LITERATURE IN FRANCE

last thirty years, as the outward and visible sign[4] of an unutterable corruption, spread through the whole fabric of French society. We cannot by any means agree in so sweeping a censure. It is true that many French writers deserve the severest reprobation that can be applied to them. We could name books, by distinguished writers, which the vilest shop in Holywell-street[5] could not expose for sale without coming under Lord Campbell's late Act.[6] But we do not think that the works of such writers as Sue, Charles de Bernard,[7] and Balzac, deserve to be described as 'slow dissolvents upon the generous feelings of the heart, which leave us unfit to cope with the realities of life.'[8] They are certainly not books for women or for children; but to men, and especially to men able to make those allowances and deductions which are necessary in drawing from novels inferences as to life, they may, we think, be neither unneeded nor unimpressive sermons. Most of them, as far as our experience goes, contain scenes which might be wished away, but many of them can, to some extent, and with some reservations, be depended upon as a man's observations upon life addressed to his equals. Before we condemn books for their immorality, we must remember that novels are only possible in a very peculiar state of society, and that if they aim at representing any portion of society as it exists, novelists must, from the nature of the case, confine their representations to a very small section of it. It is only when civilization has made much progress—when a class of persons sufficiently educated, and sufficiently at

[4] The Catechism in the Book of Common Prayer: An outward and visible sign of an inward and spiritual grace.

[5] JFS on letters to *The Times*, 'Groans of the Britons', p. 65. VERECUNDIA ('one who knows his place'): To THE EDITOR OF THE TIMES (15 Sept. 1857): Sir, I was much gratified by seeing an account in the police report of *The Times* of this morning of the suppression of at least one of the many shops which now exist in the metropolis for the sale of obscene works and pictures. How is it that so many more are left unmolested has long been a matter of wonder to me. ¶ I would direct your attention more especially to Holywell-street and Wych-street, in which are shops the windows of which display books and pictures of the most disgusting and obscene character, and which are alike loathsome to the eye and offensive to the morals of any person of well-regulated mind. The mischief, however, does not exist merely in the outward display alone—that is perhaps the least part of the danger; but, alas! that is nothing to the effect which such works are calculated to produce on the minds of those persons whose morbid desires induce them eagerly to peruse them, oftentimes to the destruction of their health, and, what is infinitely worse, to their souls' danger. ¶ Your powerful and influential paper is always ready to bring before the public. As soon as Mr. Perry read this report he wrote to the chaplain, to know whether his evidence was correctly reported, and on hearing that it was, he went down to investigate the subject. The inquest was concluded on May 3rd. Mr. Perry's inquiry began on May 16th, and ended on the 23rd (Ev. p. 492). These proceedings appear to have been known to, and were probably concerted with, the Home Office. (Rep. p. v) especially, when the scourge of cholera is ravaging our land, ought we not, as a Christian country, while so many means are taken to prevent all outward contamination, be also anxious to remove all matter contaminating and prejudicial to the soul? ¶ Cannot, then, as in the case of the shop in Castle-street, Leicester square, these dens of iniquity be suppressed? Surely, if the authorities have power to hold to bail in one case they have in another; and if they have the power, and do not exercise it (with the full knowledge that such places exist), they are surely highly reprehensible in permitting the existence of one of the greatest and most glaring nuisances—to call it by no harsher term—in the city of London.

[6] An Act for more effectually preventing the Sale of Obscene Books, Pictures, Prints, and other Articles. Royal Assent, 25 Aug. 1857; it made the sale of obscene material a statutory offence. Lord Campbell, the Chief Justice of the Queen's Bench, introduced the controversial bill, which was passed following the assurance that it was 'to apply exclusively to works written for the single purpose of corrupting the morals of youth and of a nature calculated to shock the common feelings of decency in any well-regulated mind.' JFS, 'The Mote and the Beam', p. 239 on obscenity, advertisements, and law reports in newspapers.

[7] Pierre-Marie-Charles de Bernard du Grail de la Villette (1804–1850), man of letters.

[8] Modified by JFS, Masson 27 on Balzac's novels: 'The effect they produce is that of a slow dissolvent, which acts gradually, but surely, upon the generous feelings...'

leisure to use books as toys, has arisen—and when, therefore, there is much luxury, and much idleness—that a novelist can be produced, or that novels could find readers. Such a society as we have described is sure to be in many ways immoral, and it is also sure to invest its immorality with a grace which, no doubt, makes it more dangerous than the coarser vices of simpler times. Is it, then, not to be represented at all? We think it should; and we also think that such representations are far from being calculated to injure those to whom they are addressed—the members, namely, of the society which they describe, or those who are hovering on its outskirts, or who have sufficient connexion with it to be able to understand and to sympathize with it. To our perceptions, such books as Balzac's *Scènes de la Vie d'un Célibataire*, or George Sand's *Horace*,[9] are amongst the keenest of all conceivable satires upon the vices of which their authors disapprove; and though the virtues which they praise are flighty and unsteady enough, it would be hard to deny that, so far as they go, they really are virtues.

A novel presupposes a certain degree of experience in its readers. Expunge a few pages of *Gerfaut*,[10] which may be called specifically immoral, and it is hardly possible to mention a book which, to a pure-minded man, who has seen something of life, would read a more terrible lesson of the danger of giving way to temptations which all men occasionally feel. The story turns, no doubt, upon the violation of the marriage tie, and it is true that M. de Bernard does not moralize upon the sinfulness of breaking the seventh Commandment, but we know of no story which more fearfully illustrates the danger and the misery of a marriage without affection, or which sets the wickedness and the shameful treachery of indulging an unlawful fancy, merely by way of amusement, in a more lurid light. It may be objected that the principal character is a man of great power, who may be called 'interesting', and that he is made the object, not of contempt, but of sympathy. Is it, however, the fact that men guilty of such vices are usually weak silly people, and would it be possible to impose upon men who have seen anything of the world by so shallow an expedient as that of representing them as such in novels?

M. Masson is rather severe upon the principle of *art pour l'art*[11]—of writing, that is, without any specific moral purpose. Surely, in so far as art is regulated by essential and eternal rules, it is its own justification. Art is but a version of life so contrived as to make a deep impression on the imagination. Unless, therefore, life is immoral, art can hardly be so. If, in point of fact, the wicked are not plagued like other men, neither tormented like other men, why should not the novelist say so? If the lessons of history are sometimes stern and hard to read, why should not those of fiction, which is its shadow, be so too? A novelist is no more disrespectful to morality in simply imitating the world as he finds it, than the analyst is disrespectful to geometry in representing the conic sections under algebraical forms. If, indeed, the novelist represents the world as worse than it is, that is a fault of art; and it is the more serious, because it may have bad moral consequences. We do not by any means deny that French writers of fiction have often erred in this matter, or that many of their books are very immoral indeed; but they do seem to us to have kept in view a fact which some of our most popular English novelists appear altogether to forget—the fact that a work of imagination ought to be considered, not as a child's play-thing, but as a great and serious undertaking, to be

---

[9] 1840.   [10] Charles de Bernard (1838).   [11] Masson 10–11.

LIGHT LITERATURE IN FRANCE

executed according to the rules of its own art, and not to be mutilated for the sake of pointing any moral which may strike the fancy of the writer.

We must finally protest against a way of speaking to which M. Masson gives some little countenance, and in which far too many of our own countrymen indulge. We cannot think, and do not believe, that France is utterly corrupt and degraded; and it annoys us to see how frequently Frenchmen of considerable talent and knowledge use language which implies that it is. We honour and love our own country beyond all others in the world, and we see much to dislike, and something to blame, in the French character; but surely it is worse than illiberal to deny that France is one of the very greatest nations that the world ever saw, or that its position in European politics and literature can only be considered as second even to our own by those who enter far more fervently into English forms of thought than any but Englishmen ever will. Where there is such vast power, so magnificent a history, such a wonderful accumulation of every gift that can adorn humanity, there must be great virtues. Mere military glory implies a great deal, but there is in France infinitely more than that. There must be a great deal of salt in a society of 35,000,000 souls which is not too corrupt to form a single, orderly, compact, and homogeneous body. We are all brought so near together in these days of railroads, that every member of the great European republic affects every other. England is certainly not very corrupt nor utterly effete, and if she is not, we may be sure that there must be a great deal of good in those with whom our intercourse is so constant and familiar. It would be to us the saddest thing in the world to be forced to think very ill of the social condition of such near neighbours and close allies; and we do not see that French light literature by any means obliges us to do so. Our views of morals may be widely different from theirs, and our practice may or may not be better, but we firmly believe that the principal difference between the novelists of the two countries is, that in France they address the most plain-spoken, and in England the most reserved, of modern nations.

'La Daniella'
(*Saturday Review*, 12 September 1857)

George Sand (1804–1876), woman of letters; pen-name of Aurore Dupin, baronne Dudevant.

La Daniella*

The novels of George Sand are seldom entertaining; and the last she has written, *La Daniella* is perhaps less entertaining than any of its predecessors. Whatever may be the merits of the writer, it is hard work reading through two thick volumes of a fiction where there is scarcely any plot—where the characters are sketched faintly, and hinted at rather than fully delineated—and where there is little to startle, amuse, or touch us. *La Daniella* has the great fault which marks all the recent productions of George Sand—it is very much too long. It is spun out with an audacious prolixity, as if the writer were amusing herself with seeing how much she could make the public read. Perhaps this prolixity may arise from a wish to meet the demands of the publisher for a two-volumed story; or, possibly, it springs from what is a very prominent characteristic of the writer's mind. George Sand is essentially reflective and self-contemplative— she writes because she feels, and as she feels. It is the world within, and not the world without, with which she occupies herself. Being, however, of an impulsive and passionate nature, certain subjects, such as the problems of social life and the range of artistic excitement, have taken a deep hold on her imagination. While these subjects were new to her, she worked them with a spontaneous life and freshness which enabled her in a great measure to dispense with action and incident in her fictions. Now that she has grown calmer, sadder—in one word, older—she gives us reflections as original and as suggestive as ever, but which, from the very fact that they are truer to life and nature, more soberly expressed, and more patiently elaborated, have less to stimulate and fascinate the reader. It is not that her powers have decayed, but their maturity itself makes her productions less effective. Secure of an attentive audience, she goes on page after page writing whatever comes uppermost, without regard either for those whom she addresses, or for the puppets of her romance. But, although *La Daniella*, in which she has indulged her genius to the uttermost, is tedious, spiritless, and flat, it bears abundant traces of a master-hand. It contains many passages which no one but George Sand could have written—passages full of subtlety, of a nobleness of aspiration, and of nice observation, and expressed with that wonderful grace, ease, and *abandon*, the command of which is the greatest of her gifts.

---

* *La Daniella*. Par George Sand. Paris: 1857.

LA DANIELLA

A reflective story-teller is never without specific purpose. In inferior hands this purpose degenerates into a moral or religious lesson, which the story is supposed to teach. But, with a great writer, it is nothing but the outpouring of the particular thoughts which happen to fill the author's mind at the time of composition. There is no distinction between the two, except in the degree of individuality and originality with which the writer approaches the subject. The theme of *La Daniella* is 'all for love'.[1] The book is an echo of the cry which we hear arising from the lips of so many of the leaders of thought in France, who are appalled at the growing taste for material happiness—at the ignorance, baseness, and poverty of soul which follow in the train of national avarice. M. de Montalembert[2] has recently made a spirited appeal to his countrymen against this, the greatest of moral curses that can beset a people, with the one exception of religious fanaticism—of the evil of which it falls short, because the weakly good recoil from avarice, but are attracted by bigotry. 'Even in romances', says George Sand, 'which would seem to be the proper home for an ideal more pure than that of the share list and the Bourse, I often see the expression of an impetuous desire for a treasure like that of the grottoes of *Monte Cristo*,[3] and am neither astonished nor scandalized at it. I see that in a society so uncertain and troubled as ours, while Europe trembles with fear and hope, between dreams of a fabulous prosperity and of a universal social cataclysm, men of vivid imagination rush into that terrible determination "to be rich or to die". It is one of the evils of our day, and we bring on ourselves an infinity of misery because we wish to build a big ship when we really need nothing more than a little boat.' It is the object of *La Daniella* to show that the man who builds the big ship sails through life distracted, anxious, and in danger, while the owner of the little boat has a tranquil, safe, and happy voyage.

In England, we never disconnect individual improvement from the scheme of constituted society. The virtue that is to be encouraged must be a virtue that will fit into the established order of public and religious life. The means to be adopted must be means which would practically answer in the case of men and women holding a certain position in English towns and counties. In France it is not so. The individual is not asked to take his proper place in the fabric of the State, to fall into the groove of patriarchal respectability, or to harmonize his thoughts with the influences of a recognized religion. The appeal is only to himself. He is asked to look into his own heart—to find out when and why he is best—to give free play to his generous emotions—to accept honestly the unalterable facts of human life. In *La Daniella*, a poor French artist, trained simply, and of a noble, quiet, thoughtful disposition, goes to Italy, and there is invited to visit the family of an English nobleman, to whom he renders assistance against a sudden attack of bandits. In the house of this nobleman, Valreg, the artist, meets a niece of the nobleman's wife, Miss Medora, and also Miss Medora's Italian lady's-maid, La Daniella. With the eccentric insolence of British wealth, Miss Medora makes violent love to the artist, who receives her advances with the utmost coldness.

---

[1] Dryden, *All for Love; or, The World Well Lost* (1678). 'In *La Daniella*, a poor French artist, trained simply...the life of a poor artist': JFS may have recalled Robert Southey, *All for Love; and The Pilgrim to Compostella. With some account of the writer, written by himself and an introductory essay on the lives and works of our uneducated poets* (1829).

[2] Charles-Forbes-René, comte de Montalembert (1810–1870), Catholic writer and politician.

[3] Alexandre Dumas (1802–1870). *Le Comte de Monte-Cristo* (serialized 1844–46).

He greatly prefers Daniella, who is consequently sent away by her jealous mistress. She meets Valreg again, when chance takes him near the village where her family resides. The end of it is, that she returns his passion, and, as she modestly expresses it, *se passant de prêtre*,[4] flies to his arms. He is touched by the generosity of her sacrifice and the nobleness of her character, falls seriously in love with her, and marries her. He refuses the offer of a competency[5] made him by his rich friends, and leads the life of a poor artist engaged in the decoration of a palace situated in the village where Daniella lives. Different circumstances arise to call out and strengthen the better qualities of the lovers. Valreg, as a husband and father, finds in his family the sphere which best admits of his becoming all that he aspires to be; and Daniella, heartily repenting a fit of furious jealousy to which she on one occasion gives way, learns to moderate the violence natural to an uneducated Italian. A companion of Valreg, an ambitious, needy, daring adventurer, tries to win the hand and wealth of Miss Medora; and it is in the contrast which this couple, with their folly, pettiness, and selfishness, present to the peaceful dignity of Valreg and his wife, that the moral of the story is to be found.

To English readers the moral is absurd. To tell a young Englishman, whom we wanted to improve, that the best thing he could do would be to make first a mistress, and then a wife, of an Italian lady's-maid, would be simply ridiculous. The whole thing is quite out of the range of English family life. We immediately begin to think how the young couple would be tabooed. No cousin would write to them. No maiden aunt would leave them a legacy. But if we get rid altogether of these very sensible considerations, leave England and English society entirely out of sight, and think merely of the course to be taken by an individual whose moral growth was not supported by external props, we find there is some meaning in *La Daniella*. Valreg and Daniella are thrown together—they are fond of each other, and their passion leads them on. Up to this point there is no lesson whatever. Very natural circumstances lead to very natural results. But immediately after this point is attained, the crucial test of Valreg's conduct begins. He is struck by the greatness of what Daniella has done for him—he finds in her the seeds of a noble character. Shall he give way to this emotion? Perhaps no question could be raised better fitted to try the worth of worldly notions, and to elicit the difference of opinion between the author and her adversaries. The more we consider it, the more shall we find that behaving well to a woman who is in our power goes down to the root of all that excellence which man, when looked on as isolated from society, can display.

The scene of the story is laid in the vicinity of Rome. There are many authors who can describe scenery more distinctly and effectively than George Sand; but there is no one who can surpass her in the power of giving an impression of the deep feeling with which the scenery described has possessed itself of the mind of the writer, or who more thoroughly carries the charm of personality, and of a subjective richness of meaning, into representations of the external world. She has a singular facility in marking out some features of what she wishes to paint, which stamp the scenery portrayed for ever in our recollection. The general description of the Campagna affords an excellent example of this:

---

[4] Bypassing a priest.
[5] *OED* A sufficiency, without superfluity, of the means of life, a competent estate or income. With 1749 FIELDING There is no happiness in this world without a competency.

There is a sort of failure in the effect produced by the plain of Rome. This arises from a want of proportion—the plain is too great for the mountains. It is a vast picture with a tiny frame. There is too much sky, and nothing is so formed as to arrest the attention. All is solemn, but tiring, like a sea in the level of calm. The very civilization of the country is so managed as to spoil it; for it just suffices to prevent the sensation of loneliness and the awe of real solitude.

This appears to us in the best style of subjective landscape-painting. And George Sand has two faculties which connect her with the more external view of nature, and give body to all she writes on the appearance of natural beauties. She has the eye of a colourist,[6] and she has the most lively interest in the various forms of animal life around her. Thus, in *La Daniella*, when she has to describe an old ruin where Valreg passes much of his time, she makes her sketch distinct and real, by noticing the animals which Valreg saw around him. She speaks of the little serpents, and of the way they crawled, of the kid[7] and the rabbits which he fed, of the abundance of scorpions, and of the curious rarity of butterflies. 'I know by sight', says Valreg, 'everything that grows and flies in the places where I have lived some time.' The author is speaking here herself, and it is her own tastes that she records. Nor is this less so in a passage where she describes the instinctive manner in which an artist gathers into his range of sight, and treasures up in the storehouse of his memory, every striking effect of form, of light and shade, of depth and harmony of colour, whatever may be the thoughts that otherwise occupy his mind, and however great may be the pressure which adverse external circumstances are exerting on him at the time. But although there are many fruits of this artistic sensibility scattered through the work, it is not these fruits that constitute the chief excellence of *La Daniella*. It is in the analysis of the less obvious relations of the sexes—of the treacherous delights of female friendship, and the rough differences of married lovers—that George Sand shows the full scope of her genius. *La Daniella* has much of this analysis wherewith to reward the patient reader. As a novel, it can never be popular; but it is not without importance as a sample of French literature, and it cannot fail to interest all who wish to watch the course through which so remarkable a mind as that of its author is carried in the progress of its development.

---

[6] *OED* A painter skilful in colouring. 1846 RUSKIN (of Gainsborough) The greatest colourist since Rubens. *figurative* Also said of descriptive writers. (WARTON, of Spenser.)

[7] *Le chevreau d'une chèvre* has more linguistic kinship than 'kid' has with 'goat'.

'Balzac'
(*Saturday Review*, 19 December 1857)

Balzac*

During the last thirty years,[1] novels have played a most characteristically important part in French literature. They have, indeed, acquired a sort of special character, which is as much associated with the words 'French novel' as various qualities of a very different kind are associated with such expressions as 'Scotch metaphysics'[2] or 'German theology'.[3] To this large and somewhat questionable class of productions, Balzac[4] was, we believe, the most prolific, as he was assuredly the most remarkable contributor. Between 1827 and 1848, he wrote, as Madame Surville tells us, 97 tales of various lengths, filling no less than 10,816 pages of the small one-franc volumes in which they have been lately republished at Paris, and which contain about as much matter as those of Mr. Murray's *Travellers' Library*.[5] We should on every account be glad to know something of the life of such a man; and though it is not yet satisfactorily written, we are occasionally favoured with instalments of the materials from which it will, we may hope, be ultimately produced. One of these, by M. Léon Gozlan,[6] called *Balzac en Pantoufles* we referred to about a year ago. We have now before us a production of somewhat the same size by the great novelist's surviving sister, Madame Surville. It is less amusing than M. Gozlan's book, but it throws, we think, more light on Balzac's character. He was the son of an army contractor at Tours—a person of a most original disposition—and of a lady who, though deeply attached to her son, showed her fondness by introducing a somewhat unusual degree of severity into all their relations. It is greatly to Balzac's honour that he seems through life to have felt that high degree of affection for his relations generally, and especially for his parents, which eminently

---

* *Balzac: sa Vie et ses Oeuvres, d'après sa Correspondance*. Par Madame L. Surville (née de Balzac). Paris: 1857.

[1] JFS on Gustave Masson's *Thirty Years of French Literature* (1856), p. 142. Masson 22–30 on novels, including Balzac's.

[2] See George Davie, *The Scotch Metaphysics* (2001), on the works of Thomas Reid, Dugald Stewart, Sir William Hamilton, Thomas Brown, and James Frederick Ferrier.

[3] Notably, David Strauss (1808–1874), whose work (1835–36) was translated by George Eliot as *The Life of Jesus, Critically Examined* (1846), and Ludwig Feuerbach (1804–1872), whose work (1841) was translated by her as *The Essence of Christianity* (1854). JFS on German, French, and English theology: 'Ecce Homo' (*Fraser's*, June–July 1866, not signed), a review of J. R. Seeley, *A Survey of the Life and work of Jesus Christ*. Seeley drew upon Strauss and upon Ernest Renan's *Vie de Jésus* (1863). JFS on English theology: 'An Orthodox Dean' (*Sat. Rev.*, 28 Feb. 1863). Both these essays are in *On Society, Religion, and Government*.

[4] Honoré de Balzac (1799–1850).

[5] Published by John Murray in the 1850s and 1860s.

[6] 1803–1866, novelist, author of *Balzac en Pantoufles* [in slippers] (1856; *Sat. Rev.* has '*on Pantoufles*').

BALZAC 151

belongs to the French national character. There was nothing very remarkable about his youth. He studied law from eighteen to twenty-one, at which age, greatly to his parents' disgust, he refused a very advantageous offer of a partnership with a *notaire*, and declared his wish to become a *littérateur* by profession. His father, with a very natural reluctance, allowed him two years to *faire ses preuves de talent*; and his mother, who thought that *un peu de misère* would perhaps cure him of his fancy, lodged him in a scantily-furnished garret, with an allowance on which he could just manage to live. Here he set to work of malice prepense[7] to become an author, and with infinite labour, composed a tragedy, called *Cromwell*,[8] which all his friends agreed in damning. He was accordingly recalled to his father's house, and lived there in an uncomfortable and anomalous position during the next six or seven years. During this time he wrote a number of tales which he never avowed, and to which, in obedience to his express wishes, his sister only alludes without naming them. At about the age of twenty-eight or twenty-nine, he turned from literature to speculation, and entered into several undertakings connected with printing, the capital being supplied by his parents. They appear, however, to have been not very successful, and he extricated himself from the business with the loss of all his money, a large debt—most of which was owing to his mother— and a considerable amount of experience in pecuniary matters. It is a most significant fact, that the first of his successful novels, *Les Chouans*,[9] was written under the pressure of these difficulties. In this we have an additional proof of the most important truth that can be impressed on authors—namely, that even a man of genius can write nothing worth reading which has any relation to human affairs, unless he is in some way or other really connected with the serious every-day business of life. If Balzac had accepted the offer made to him in early life, he would have seen a vast deal of the world whilst still young enough to appreciate and to describe it, and might have written his novels afterwards at his ease, without being constantly under the obligation—as for many years he was—of throwing off three or four novels a year, in order to place himself in a position either to take up his acceptances[10] or to get them renewed. In this, as in most of the affairs of his life, he showed the weakness which ran through the whole of his character. He was, as Madame Surville says in so many words, excessively vain, and he showed it by the extraordinary appetite for fame with which he was always devoured. *Etre célèbre et être aimé*, he wrote in very early life, were the only two things he cared for.

We do not pretend to have read the whole of his novels, but the specimens with which we are acquainted leave upon our minds no doubt that, in the school to which he belonged, Balzac was, in some respects, by far the greatest master that France has produced. The principal heads under which novels may be classified are comedies and romances. By comedies, we mean books which aim at painting life as it is, and by romances, those which depend for their interest upon the incidents which they describe, and in which the characters introduced are subordinate to the events and scenery. Mr. Thackeray's writings, for example, would all fall into the first class, whilst

---

[7] *OED Law* Wrongful intention generally (with *prepense*, malice aforethought).

[8] In verse (1819).

[9] A historical novel (1829) of which the title was revised more than once; the royalist insurgents against the French Revolution were led by Jean Chouan.

[10] *OED commercial usage* The act of formally accepting the liability to pay a bill of exchange when due.

152 ON THE NOVEL AND JOURNALISM

we should place Fenimore Cooper's[11] in the second. Here and there a man of extraordinary power combines both kinds of excellence, and of this rare combination Defoe and Scott are the most remarkable instances in our own country, and Balzac and Charles de Bernard in modern France. In the two great English writers whom we have named, the romantic element was the strongest. Robinson Crusoe is admirable as a character, but the name recalls the island rather than the man; and in *Waverley*, the march of events, and the strange society into which are introduced, throw into the shade in some degree the wonderful skill employed in drawing the Baron and Fergus McIvor. In the French writers, on the other hand, the comic element prevails, though the romantic element, especially in Balzac, is occasionally most powerfully developed, and there can hardly be a more interesting study of its kind than the effect produced by the union of the two. In Balzac's principal works, as our readers are doubtless aware, the stories and personages are all more or less connected; and his own theory about them was that they presented a vast and accurate picture of contemporary French life. Their merits are no doubt to be judged of by the degree in which they approach this ideal. It would of course be presumptuous for a foreigner to pronounce upon the accuracy of the picture; but the most ordinary observer may affirm some things respecting it with no fear of being mistaken. It has, we think, greater merits, in some respects, than almost any other prose fiction whatever. Looking merely at the extent and variety of the scenes and characters which it represents, we know of no series of works which can be compared to it. It contains portraits from every rank and from almost all the more important classes of French society, in Paris or the provinces. The power with which some of the characters are described is extraordinary, and the more so because their peculiarities are displayed without any of that minute dissection of motives which is so fashionable in this country, and yet without the melodramatic starts and fantastic tricks of expression which some of our most popular writers employ to cheat their readers into the impression that the animated puppets which crowd their canvas have real life and individuality. Nothing can be better worth attention in this way than the personages introduced into the *Scènes de la Vie Célibataire*.[12] The coarse cunning, reckless selfishness, and craft of Philippe Bridau; and the gay, careless honesty and somewhat improvident generosity and sensibility of his brother, the artist, are characters which even a foreigner can perceive to be exquisitely French and exquisitely true to nature; whilst the stolid stagnancy of the *bourgeois* society of Limoges, and the moody inactivity of the retired officers of the Grande Armée—bold, quick-tempered, and punctilious, but most characteristically incapable of extricating themselves from the vegetative life upon which the return of the Bourbons has thrown them back—fill up the outward and visible framework of French society with personages so curiously natural and appropriate that it is impossible not to believe in their truth.

The variety and life of Balzac's characters do not, we think, constitute their principal claim to attention. This is to be found in the impression which they produce—and which other facts abundantly confirm—of the extraordinary good faith with which they are drawn. M. Gozlan tells us, and Madame Surville confirms his statement, that Balzac conceived his various personages so vividly that they were to him exactly like

[11] (1789–1851).
[12] Subdivisions of the *Études de moeurs* that constitute *La Comédie Humaine*: Scènes de la vie privée...de province...parisienne...politique...militaire...de compagne...conjugale...célibataire.

real living men and women. He used to talk about them, and arrange the incidents of their careers, with precisely the same seriousness and fervour as he would have shown if he had been discussing the plans of real people. 'Savez-vous', said he one day to his sister, 'qui Felix de Vandenesse épouse? Une demoiselle de Grandville. C'est un excellent mariage qu'il fait là, les Grandville sont riches malgré ce que Mademoiselle de Belle-feuille a coûté à cette famille.' One of the characters in *Ursule Mirouet*,[13] a certain Captain de Jordy, excited the curiosity of Balzac's friends. M. de Jordy is represented as living at Nemours, weighed down by some secret grief, and Madame Surville was anxious to know the cause of it. 'I did not know M. de Jordy before he came to Nemours', was her brother's answer. Another proof of the strange vitality with which he endowed his characters was his practice of naming them, not out of his own head, but after any names over a shop which seemed to him to suit them *à priori*. '*Matifat! Cardot!* quels delicieux noms me disait-il. J'ai trouvé *Matifat* rue de la Perle au Marais. Je vois déjà mon Matifat! Il aura une face pâlotte de chat, un petit embonpoint, car Matifat n'aura rien de grandiose comme tu peux le croire.'[14] It is impossible not to see the same strange sort of sympathy between the name and the description which Sydney Smith,[15] with general applause and consent, affirmed to exist between a bishop of the Church of England and the name of Simon.

This good faith and profound sense of reality shows itself also in the way in which Balzac treats serious subjects. He believed so fully in all that he wrote, that he threw his characters into the business of life with as much vehemence and interest as he can possibly have employed in negotiating his bills. He counts up their resources in francs and centimes. He gives the most minute details of their speculations and of their views of art or politics, according to the positions in life which they fill. We have writers in our own country who turn novels into political pamphlets—generally to the great injury both of the story and of the politics, for they almost always fall into the mistake of railing *ab extra* at the management of affairs which they do not understand. Balzac was by no means open to this charge. He was anything but a mere destructive[16] in politics. He seems to have studied with considerable depth and acuteness, and with a genuine wish to understand their working, many of the institutions amongst which he found himself placed. How deep his knowledge of law, of administration, and of commerce, really went, an Englishman can only conjecture, but it is quite clear that he was at any rate free from that vulgar and presumptuous contempt for common opinions upon these subjects which so strongly characterizes a certain class of English novelists.

The key, as we believe, to this and to most of the other peculiarities of his style, is to be found in the fact that Balzac had a far higher conception of the objects and nature of his art than is usual in this country. He felt that novels were something more than

[13] Within Scènes de la vie de province (1841).

[14] '*Matifat! Cardot!* what delicious names, he said to me. I found *Matifat* on the Rue de la Perle au Marais [the Marais, a historic district in Paris]. Already I saw my Matifat! He'll have a cat's pale face and be on the plump side, for Matifat is to have nothing impressive about him, as you can well believe'.

[15] Sydney Smith (1771–1845; *ODNB*, author and wit). *Letter to Archdeacon Singleton*, an anecdote of the medieval prelate Simon of Gloucester was held to be an attack on M. H. Monk (Arthur Burns and Christopher Stray, 'The Greek-Play Bishop: Polemic, Prosopography, and Nineteenth-century Prelates', *Historical Journal* 54:3, 2011). Other such Simons: Simon of Sudbury, died 1381, bishop of London, then archbishop of Canterbury; Simon Sydenham, died 1438, bishop of Chichester.

[16] *OED* A person whose theory or practice tends to overthrow existing institutions or systems. (Chiefly dyslogistic). From 1832 *Examiner* The Radicals (or Destructives, as you are pleased to describe them).

154 ON THE NOVEL AND JOURNALISM

mere toys, to be kept down to the level of the most childish minds and the most babyish ignorance of life. He was well aware that they are works of art, to be constructed according to rules of their own, and to be valued for their inherent perfection, and not for any collateral purpose to which they might be made subservient; and this feeling naturally led him to deal far more fairly with the institutions under which he lived, and to study them in a much more generous and honest spirit than it is possible for any man to evince who devotes hundreds of pages to attacks on a misconceived and possibly non-existent abuse. He had an artist's aversion to the caricature and extravagance which are so conspicuous in many of our own novelists when they write upon the real business of life.

It must be admitted that the same temper of mind lies at the root of the most serious faults with which he is justly chargeable. Balzac has been repeatedly denounced as an immoral writer; and there can be no doubt that in some degree the charge is well founded, though, as we think, in a degree very much lower than that in which it is usually put forward. As we have already observed, he is especially remarkable for combining excellence in the comic and the romantic departments of fiction—using the word 'comic' as denoting all that relates to the observation of every-day human life, not only, or principally, in its ludicrous, but also in its gloomy and appalling aspects. So long as he is merely an observer and faithful depicter of what passes around him, we think that he is entitled to the full weight of the defence which, as his sister tells us, he made when charged with immorality. 'J'écris pour les hommes, non pour les jeunes filles.' A novel in England is in some respects like a sermon. It is addressed to an audience so very large and so very mixed, that a large proportion of the most important social and moral subjects must of necessity be tabooed. No London clergyman could preach to an ordinary congregation a sermon on the Seventh Commandment;[17] yet no one can doubt that if the proper hearers could be collected separately—and the materials would not be wanting—one of the most impressive and most important discourses which human lips could deliver might be founded on it. If Mr. Thackeray writes a novel, he is forced by the prevailing tone of writing, and especially by the fact that he will have many female readers, to leave untouched one large province of life; but in France the temper of the people is different, and we cannot blame a novelist for availing himself of the opportunity of showing how hideous vice is. But it is not merely as an observer that Balzac depicts vice. It furnishes most of the machinery to which the romantic parts of his novels owe their interest. In this way he constantly creates monsters, and needlessly dwells upon disgusting subjects for the sake of producing a dramatic effect, and sometimes, we fear, to gratify the pruriency of his readers. Nothing can excuse the author of such a story as *La Fille aux Yeux d'Or*.[18] It is altogether corrupt, abominable, and loathsome, nor can a single word be said in defence of it. It is not less true that the creation of such characters as Rastignac, De Marsay, and Delphine de Nucingen[19] was a very grave offence against morals. They are base, wicked, and hateful to a degree

---

[17] 'To Rest, the Cushion and soft Dean invite, / Who never mentions Hell to ears polite' (Pope, *Epistle IV, Of the Use of Riches*). For JFS it would be *solely* 'ears polite' that would be 'the proper hearers' of a 'discourse' on adultery.

[18] 1835.

[19] Eugène de Rastignac and Delphine de Nucingen appear in *Le Père Goriot* (1835); Count Henri de Marsay, in *La Duchesse de Langeais* (1834).

which no words can describe, whilst we also feel that they are not, and cannot have been, true to nature. Utter baseness and great intellectual power do not go together in real life, and should not be allied in novels. These characters are not gathered from general observation—they are at most the imitation of hideous exceptions. The same observation applies in some degree to the accumulation of horror upon horror which marks some of his most remarkable stories. Wickedness is not so dramatic as Balzac would have us believe; and needlessly to invest it with such a shape is in effect to give it a sort of sombre magnificence to which it is not entitled.

Whilst we admit that in the particulars which we have specified Balzac's writings are immoral, we maintain that these are by no means their commonest or most prominent features. Many of his books—and many of those which treat of vice—appear to us to be moral reading for those to whom they were addressed. The *Scènes de la Vie Célibataire*, *La Cousine Bette*, *Le Cousin Pons*,[20] are not very fit reading for boys or women (though we ought to remember that the adventures of *Clarissa Harlowe*[21] were prescribed to our grandmothers from the pulpit), but a man must be corrupt indeed before they could injure him. Many of the characters are no doubt as wicked as men and women can well be in this world, but we do not remember to have seen anywhere more impressive illustrations of the hideousness of vice.

We may conclude our observations on Balzac by pointing out one circumstance about him which has not been properly understood. We mean his relation to religion. In some parts of his books, expressions and speculations may be found apparently so subversive of all definite religious belief that Protestant readers might be inclined to look upon the great respect and apparent affection with which he always refers to Catholicism and to the priesthood as merely hypocritical. We cannot join in that opinion. He seems to us to illustrate very strongly a state of mind by no means uncommon amongst highly educated members of that church. He looks upon reason and faith as fundamentally distinct, and radically opposed to each other; so that a man may see his way, intellectually speaking, to opinions quite irreconcileable with any form of Christianity, and yet may have such a distrust of his own reason, and such a reliance upon the great external system before his eyes, that he may be a devout Catholic. Dr. Minoret, for example, in the novel of *Ursule Mirouet*, passes at once from materialistic atheism to Catholicism. It does not occur to him to argue the details. This principle is one of wide application, and very necessary to any right understanding of French literature.

---

[20] *La Cousine Bette* (1848), *Le Cousin Pons* (1847), the two parts of *Les Parents pauvres*.

[21] Samuel Richardson, *Clarissa; or, The History of a Young Lady. Comprehending the Most Important Concerns of Private Life. And Particularly Shewing, the Distresses that May Attend the Misconduct both of Parents and Children, in Relation to Marriage*. (By the editor of *Pamela*, 1747–48.)

'Mr. Dickens'
(*Saturday Review*, 8 May 1858)

Mr. Dickens*

The republication of Mr. Dickens's works in a collected form affords an opportunity for offering some observations on the position which the most celebrated novelist of the day occupies, and will in future occupy, in English literature. If popularity is to be taken as the test of merit, Mr. Dickens must be ranked next to Sir Walter Scott in the list of English novelists. For more than twenty-five years he has continued to publish an unintermitting series of fictions, most of which are probably more than twice as long as those to which the author of *Waverley* owed his fame, and might have owed his fortune if he had pursued it somewhat less eagerly. Besides his larger works, Mr. Dickens is the author of a great variety of smaller tales, and the conductor of one of the most successful of the periodical publications of the day.[1] In whatever he has undertaken he has obtained not only success, but an unbounded and enthusiastic popularity, which is manifested, whenever the opportunity offers, with all the warmth of personal affection. It is interesting to attempt to analyse the qualities which have produced such results. Nothing throws more light on the character of an age than the study of its amusements—especially its literary amusements; and Mr. Dickens has amused the public more successfully than any other living man.

Pickwick was first published, we believe, about the year 1832 or 1833,[2] when the Reform Bill had just been passed, and when what Mr. Carlyle has called—with the miraculous facility for inventing nicknames, which is not the least of his gifts—the Scavenger Age,[3] was in the first flush of its triumphant inauguration. We should be at a loss to mention any one who reflected the temper of the time in which he rose into eminence more strongly than Mr. Dickens. We feel no doubt that one principal cause of his popularity is the spirit of revolt against all established rules which pervades every one of his books, and which is displayed most strongly and freshly in his earlier productions. Just as Scott owed so much of his success to the skill with which he gave shape and colour to the great Conservative reaction against the French Revolution, Mr. Dickens is indebted to the exquisite adaptation of his own turn of mind to the peculiar state of

---

* *The Works of Charles Dickens*. Library Edition. London: Chapman and Hall, 1858.

[1] *Household Words*, every Saturday, March 1850 to May 1859. A dispute between the publishers, Bradbury & Evans, and Dickens, led to his replacing it with *All the Year Round* (from April 1859).

[2] *The Posthumous Papers of the Pickwick Club* (edited by 'Boz', 1837). First published in monthly parts, March 1836–Oct. 1837.

[3] Carlyle, *Latter Day Pamphlets,* 'The New Downing Street' (15 Apr. 1850): 'the long-expected *Scavenger Age*'.

MR. DICKENS

157

feeling which still prevails in some classes, and which twenty years ago prevailed far more widely, with respect to all the arrangements of society. So much cant had been in fashion about the wisdom of our ancestors, the glorious constitution, the wise balance of King, Lords, and Commons, and other such topics, which are embalmed in the *Noodle's Oration*,[4] that a large class of people were ready to hail with intense satisfaction the advent of a writer who naturally and without an effort bantered everything in the world, from elections and law courts down to Cockney sportsmen, the boots[5] at an inn, cooks and chambermaids. Mr. Dickens had the additional advantage of doing this not only with exquisite skill, and with a sustained flow of spirit and drollery almost unequalled by any other writer, but in a style which seemed expressly intended to bring into contempt all those canons of criticism which a large proportion of people were learning to look upon as mere pedantry and imposture. *Pickwick* is throughout a sort of half-conscious parody of that style of writing which demanded balanced sentences, double-barrelled epithets, and a proper conception of the office and authority of semi-colons. It is as if a saucy lad were to strut about the house in his father's court-dress, with the sleeves turned inside out and the coat-tails stuck under his arms. Whenever he can get an opportunity, Mr. Dickens rakes up the old-fashioned finery, twists it into every sort of grotesque shape, introduces it to all kinds of strange bedfellows, and con-trives, with an art which is all the more ingenious because it was probably quite undesigned, to convey the impression that every one who tries to write, to think, or to act by rule, is little more than a pompous jackass. It is impossible to describe the spirit of a writer of whose best books slang is the soul without speaking his own language. Mr. Dickens is the very Avatar[6] of chaff, and bigwigs[7] of every description are his game. The joviality, the animal spirits, and the freshness with which he acted this part in his earliest books are wonderful. We cannot mention any caricature so perfect and so ludi-crous as the description of Messrs. Dodson and Fogg, and that of the trial of *Bardell v. Pickwick*.[8] The mere skill of his workmanship would have unquestionably secured the success of such a writer; but the harmony between his own temper and that of his audi-ence must be appreciated before we can understand the way in which approbation grew into enthusiasm.

---

[4] In 'Fallacies of Anti-Reformers' (1824), Sydney Smith reviewed Jeremy Bentham's *Book of Fallacies*, concluding part III with 'a little oration, which we will denominate the "Noodle's Oration" '; included here, p. 161. JFS had opened his review of Edward Stillingfleet Cayley's *The European Revolutions of 1848* ('A Practical Man', *Sat. Rev.*, 29 Mar. 1856) with a shot at such: 'We greatly want a second Sydney Smith to write a new edition of the Noodle's Oration. Far be it from us to attempt more than a most distant imitation of that great original; but if such a work were executed, it would perhaps run somewhat as follows: "The political events of the last eight years show the immense difference between theory and practice. Englishmen are practical—foreigners are theoretical. It may not be true that Frenchmen live principally upon frogs, but they are nourished by abstractions. They use such abominable words as Liberty, Order, and Principle, which no Christian man can endure. They believe, that some things are false and other things true, and that some things are right and other things wrong—whereas, as Sir Archibald Alison has conclusively proved, that makes no difference at all. The one thing needful is what is practically right, and the one thing to be avoided is what is practically wrong..." '

[5] *OED* A name for the servant in hotels who cleans the boots. 1798, then DICKENS 'I'm the boots as b'longs to the house.'

[6] Of Dickens, again; p. 79.

[7] *OED* From the large wigs formerly worn by men of distinction or importance. A man of high official standing, or of note or importance (*humorous* or *contemptuous*). From 1731. 1855 *Household Words* All this solemn bigwiggery.

[8] *Pickwick Papers*, ch. xx, ch. xxxiv.

It would, however, be a great mistake to suppose that it was merely to banter that Mr. Dickens owed his marvellous success. Mere banter soon grows wearisome; and Mr. Dickens was led by nature as much as by art to mix up a very strong dose of sentiment with his caricature. From first to last, he has tried about as much to make his readers cry as to make them laugh; and there is a very large section of the British public—and especially of the younger, weaker, and more ignorant part of it—which considers these two functions as comprising the whole duty of novelists. It is impossible to deny, that certain classes of Englishmen and Englishwomen retain all the tendencies of Prince Arthur's young gentlemen in France, who were as sad as night for very wantonness.[9] They do not care for violent paroxysms of passion—they are disgusted by horrors. The outrageous rants, surgical operations, and *post mortem* examinations which afford such lively pleasure to Parisian readers, would be out of place here; but if anybody can get a pretty little girl to go to heaven prattling about her dolls, and her little brothers and sisters, and quoting texts of Scripture with appropriate gasps, dashes, and broken sentences, he may send half the women in London, with tears in their eyes, to Mr. Mudie's or Mr. Booth's.[10] This kind of taste has not only been flattered, but prodigiously developed, by Mr. Dickens. He is the intellectual parent of a whole class of fictions, of which the *Heir of Redclyffe* was perhaps the most successful. No man can offer to the public so large a stock of death-beds adapted for either sex and for any age from five-and-twenty downwards. There are idiot death-beds, where the patient cries ha, ha! and points wildly at vacancy—pauper death-beds, with unfeeling nurses to match—male and female children's death-beds, where the young ladies or gentlemen sit up in bed, pray to the angels, and see golden water on the walls. In short, there never was a man to whom the King of Terrors was so useful as a lay figure.

This union of banter and sentiment appears to us to form the essence of Mr. Dickens's view of life. In the main, it is a very lovely world, a very good and a very happy world, in which we live. We ought all to be particularly fond of each other and infinitely pleased with our position. The only drawback to this charming state of things is that a great number of absurd people have got up a silly set of conventional rules, which the rest of us are foolish enough to submit to. The proper course with them is good natured ridicule and caricature, which cannot fail to make them conscious of the absurdity of their position. Here and there, no doubt, is to be found a villain who has laid aside the dagger, the bowl, and the Spanish cloak, which by rights he ought to carry, for some one of the many costumes worn by Englishmen in the nineteenth century; and there are plenty of erring brothers and sisters who have lost all but their picturesqueness, which is in itself enough to constitute the highest claim to our sympathy. It would be no uninteresting task to trace the stream downwards from the fountain-head, and to show how this view pervades the long series of works to which we have referred, though the exigencies of fecundity and an enlarged acquaintance with the world have modified it very considerably, especially by way of acidulation.[11] We are all dear brothers and sisters in *Bleak House* and *Little Dorrit*, just as we were in *Pickwick* and *Nicholas Nickleby*; but we

[9] *King John*, IV i: 'Methinks nobody should be sad but I: / Yet I remember, when I was in France, / Young gentlemen would be as sad as night / Only for wantonness.'

[10] C. E. Mudie (1818–1890), of Mudie's Lending Library and Subscription Library; from 1852, premises on New Oxford Street. Booth's: fee-based circulating library based in Regent Street.

[11] *OED* 1849, of sap (literal).

MR. DICKENS   159

have reached a time of life in which family quarrels must be expected, and we have
learned that good-natured banter, when kept up for a quarter of a century, is apt, with
the kindest intentions in the world, to degenerate into serious and angry discussion. It
is all very well to cork a man's face[12] after a college supper-party, but if the process were
kept up for five-and-twenty years, whenever he took a nap, it might come to be worth
his while to require a special and serious justification for such conduct.

We cannot now attempt to trace the history of Mr. Dickens's publications, or of the
various stages through which his style and his opinions have passed, but we may briefly
indicate the literary position to which, in our opinion, he has attained. It does not
appear to us certain that his books will live, nor do we think that his place in literary
history will be by the side of such men as Defoe and Fielding, the founders of the
school to which he belongs. *Pickwick* stands as far below *Tom Jones* as it stands above
Dombey and Son or *Bleak House*. It is an exquisitely piquant caricature of the everyday
life of the middle and lower classes at the time to which it refers; but the general theory
of life on which it is based is not only false, but puerile. Caricature depends for its vitality almost entirely on the degree of wisdom which it veils, just as the ornaments of a
dress depend for their beauty on the materials which they adorn. The wit of *Henry IV*
or the *Merry Wives of Windsor* is like spangles on rich velvet—the wit of *Pickwick* is like
spangles on tinsel paper. Mr. Dickens's very highest notion of goodness does not go
beyond that sort of good-nature celebrated in the old song about the fine old English
gentleman who had an old estate, and kept up his old mansion at a bountiful old rate.[13]
He can only conceive of virtues and vices in their very simplest forms. The goodness
of his good men is always running over their beards, like Aaron's ointment[14]—the
wickedness of his villains is always flaming and blazing like a house on fire. The mixed
characters, the confusion, the incompleteness, which meet us at every step in real life,
never occur in his pages. You understand what he means on the first reading far better
than on any other. The only characters drawn from real observation belong to one or
two classes of life. All the oddities of London he has sketched with inimitable vigour;
but class characteristics and local peculiarities are of a very transient nature. Fifty years
hence, most of his wit will be harder to understand than the allusions in the *Dunciad*;[15]
and our grand-children will wonder what their ancestors could have meant by putting
Mr. Dickens at the head of the novelists of his day.

Though, however, we do not believe in the permanence of his reputation, it is
impossible to deny that Mr. Dickens has exercised an immense influence over contemporary literature, or that his books must always be an extremely curious study on that
account. Till our own days, almost every popular writer formed his style on the classical model. Even those who revolted most strongly against the canons of composition

[12] *OED* Blackened with burnt cork. Dickens, *Sketches by 'Boz'. Illustrative of Every-day Life, and Every-
day People*, 'Partially corked eyebrows'. JFS in his next paragraph here turns to Dickens and 'everyday life'.
[13] 'I'll sing you an old ballad / That was made by an old pate, / Of a fine old English Gentleman / Who
had an old estate, / He kept a brave old mansion / At a bountiful old rate / With a good old porter to relieve /
The old poor at his gate / Like a fine old English gentleman, / All of the olden time.'
[14] Psalm 133:2, It is like the precious ointment upon the head, that ran down upon the beard, even Aaron's
beard.
[15] Of *The Dunciad*, Swift had written to Pope on 16 July 1728: 'twenty miles from London nobody understands hints, initial letters, or town facts and passages; and in a few years not even those who live in London'
(*The Dunciad*, ed. James Sutherland, 3rd edn., 1963, xxxiii–xxxiv).

160 ON THE NOVEL AND JOURNALISM

current in the eighteenth century—Coleridge, Wordsworth, Southey, Charles Lamb, and their associates—had, almost without an exception, been taught to write. They maintained that the stiffness of the style then dominant arose from a misapprehension of the true principles of the art of literature; but that it was an art they never doubted. The first person of mark who wrote entirely by the light of nature, and without the guidance of any other principle than that of expressing his meaning in the most emphatic language that he could find, was Cobbett.[16] Though no two persons could resemble each other less in character, the position of Mr. Dickens with respect to fiction is precisely analogous to that of Cobbett with respect to political discussion. The object of the arguments of the one is to drive his opinion into the dullest understanding—the object of the narrative of the other is to paint a picture which will catch the eye of the most ignorant and least attentive observer. Mr. Dickens's writings are the apotheosis of what has been called newspaper English.[17] He makes points everywhere, gives unfamiliar names to the commonest objects, and lavishes a marvellous quantity of language on the most ordinary incidents. Mr. William Russell and Mr. Charles Dickens have respectively risen to the very top of two closely connected branches of the same occupation. The correspondence from the Crimea is constructed upon exactly the same model as *Pickwick* and *Martin Chuzzlewit*, and there can be no doubt that the triumphs which this style has attained in Mr. Dickens's hands have exercised, and will continue to exercise, very considerable influence on the mould into which people will cast their thoughts, and indirectly upon their thoughts themselves. We cannot affect to say that we look upon the growth of this habit with much satisfaction. It appears to us to foster a pert, flippant frame of mind, in which the fancy exerts an amount of influence which does not rightfully belong to it, and in which it is very hard for people to think soberly of others, and almost impossible for them not to think a great deal too much about themselves and the effect which they are producing. There is a sex in minds as well as in bodies, and Mr. Dickens's literary progeny seem to us to be for the most part of the feminine gender, and to betray it by most unceasing flirtations, and by a very tiresome irritability of nerve.

---

[16] William Cobbett (1763–1835; *ODNB*, political writer and farmer). 'Cobbett's Political Works' (*Sat. Rev.*, 7 July 1866; *Hor. Sab.* iii 230–49).

[17] 'Newspaper English' (*Sat. Review*, 9 Aug. 1856), p. 54.

Sydney Smith, 'The Noodle's Oration' From 'Fallacies of Anti-Reformers' (1824), Part III

What would our ancestors say to this, sir? How does this measure tally with our institutions? How does it agree with their experience? Are we to put the wisdom of yesterday in competition with the wisdom of centuries? (Hear, hear.) Is beardless youth to show no respect for the decisions of mature age? (Loud cries of hear, hear.) If this measure be right, would it have escaped the wisdom of those Saxon progenitors to whom we are indebted for so many of our best political institutions? Would the Dane have passed it over? Would the Norman have rejected it? Would such a notable discovery have been reserved for these modern and degenerate thins? Besides, sir, if the measure itself is good, I ask the honourable gentleman if this is the time for carrying it into execution—whether, in fact, a more unfortunate period could have been selected than that which he has chosen? If this were an ordinary measure, I should not oppose it with so much vehemence; but, sir, it calls in question the wisdom of an irrevocable law—of a law passed at the memorable period of the Revolution. What right have we, sir, to break down this firm column on which the great men of that age stamped a character of eternity? Are not all authorities against this measure—Pitt, Fox, Cicero, and the Attorney and Solicitor General? The proposition is new, sir; it is the first time it was ever heard in this house. I am not prepared, sir—this house is not prepared—to receive it. The measure implies a distrust of his Majesty's Government; their disapproval is sufficient to warrant opposition. Precaution only is requisite where danger is apprehended. Here the high character of the individuals in question is a sufficient guarantee against any ground of alarm. Give not, then, your sanction to this measure; for, whatever be its character, if you do give your sanction to it, the same man by whom this is proposed, will propose to you others to which it will be impossible to give your consent. I care very little, sir, for the ostensible measure; but what is there behind? What are the honourable gentleman's future schemes? If we pass this bill, what fresh concessions may he not require? What further degradation is he planning for our country? Talk of evil and inconvenience, sir! look to other countries—study other aggregations and societies of men, and then see whether the laws of this country demand a remedy or deserve a panegyric. Was the honourable gentleman (let me ask him) always of this way of thinking? Do I not remember when he was the advocate in this house of very opposite opinions? I not only quarrel with his present sentiments, sir, but I declare very frankly I do not like the party with which he acts. If his own motives were as pure as possible, they cannot but suffer contamination from those with whom he is politically associated. This measure may be a boon to the constitution, but I will accept no favour to the constitution from such hands. (Loud cries of hear, hear.) I profess myself, sir, an honest and upright member of the British Parliament, and I am not afraid to profess myself an enemy to all change and all innovation. I am satisfied with things as they are; and it will be my pride and pleasure to hand down this country to my children as I received it from those who preceded me. The honourable gentleman pretends to justify the severity with which he has attacked the noble lord who presides over the Court of Chancery. But I say such attacks are pregnant with mischief to government itself.

Oppose ministers, you oppose government; disgrace ministers, you disgrace government; bring ministers into contempt, you bring government into contempt; and anarchy and civil war are the consequences. Besides, sir, the measure is unnecessary. Nobody complains of disorder in that shape in which it is the aim of your measure to propose a remedy to it. The business is one of the greatest importance; there is need of the greatest caution and circumspection. Do not let us be precipitate, sir; it is impossible to foresee all consequences. Everything should be gradual; the example of a neighbouring nation should fill us with alarm! The honourable gentleman has taxed me with illiberality, sir. I deny the charge. I hate innovation, but I love improvement. I am an enemy to the corruption of government, but I defend its influence. I dread reform, but I dread it only when it is intemperate. I consider the liberty of the press as the great palladium of the constitution; but at the same time I hold the licentiousness of the press in the greatest abhorrence. Nobody is more conscious than I am of the splendid abilities of the honourable mover, but I tell him at once, his scheme is too good to be practicable. It savours of Utopia. It looks well in theory, but it won't do in practice. It will not do, I repeat, sir, in practice; and so the advocates of the measure will find, if, unfortunately, it should find its way through parliament. (Cheers.) The source of that corruption to which the honourable member alludes, is in the minds of the people; so rank and extensive is that corruption, that no political reform can have any effect in removing it. Instead of reforming others—instead of reforming the state, the constitution, and everything that is most excellent, let each man reform himself! let him look at home, he will find there enough to do, without looking abroad and aiming at what is out of his power. (Loud cheers.) And now, sir, as it is frequently the custom of this house to end with a quotation, and as the gentleman who preceded me in this debate has anticipated me in my favourite quotation of the 'Strong pull and the long pull',[1] I shall end with the memorable words of the assembled barons—*Nolumus leges Angliae mutari*.[2]

[1] Thomas Rowlandson (1757–1827; *ODNB*, artist). 'A Long Pull A Strong Pull and a Pull Altogether', anti-Napoleon political cartoon (1813).

[2] 'For all these reasons to all these demands our answer is, Nolumus Leges Angliae mutari' (we are unwilling to change the laws of England). The rejection, by King Charles I, of the Nineteen Propositions put to him by Parliament in June 1642; the Civil War began two months later.

'Gentlemen Authors'
(*Saturday Review*, 17 July 1858)

Gentlemen Authors

In the days when Pope lashed the victims of the Dunciad, there was struck out[1] a theory of the genteel pretensions of authors, which was very clear, and to those on the right side of the hedge very satisfactory. There was to be, on the one hand, a knot of polite well-bred men, possessed of true learning and genius, the companions of statesmen, the associates of fashionable wits, the oracles and models of an Augustan age. On the other hand, there was to be Grub-street[2] with its greasy historians and translators, its flea-bitten, bailiff-driven booksellers' hacks, its starving, low, virulent poets and dunces. But a hundred years have changed all that. The greatest literary man[3] of the last half of the eighteenth century came out of Grub-street and conquered the polite world by something that was better than gentility. Society, too, has fined off[4] into a series of imperceptible gradations, and in the world of authorship, as in the sphere of other callings, there is no saying where gentility begins or ends. Mr. Thackeray, in his last number of the *Virginians*,[5] has stigmatized some of his critics as 'Young Grub-street'. But Young Grub-street would not answer to the name, would hold up its head with imperturbable coolness, and be apt to call out 'Old Grub-street' in return. Society gains a great deal, if it also loses something, by this superficial equality; and although privately it is impossible not to make distinctions, convenience and courtesy equally bid us pronounce that all the authors of the present day are gentlemen.[6] Still there are certain literary occupations which at least make us wonder that a gentleman will venture to engage in them. There is, for instance, the province of contemporary biography, and of living on the bodily presence and the mental characteristics of an eminent man. And when the eminent man is himself a writer, then there are no limits to what may be said, or to the manner of saying it. The biographer can have his fling, and can gratify vulgar curiosity by the minuteness of his description, and himself by the ingenuity of

---

[1] *OED* To produce by a stroke of invention (a plan, scheme, fashion, etc.). (As against the other sense, To cancel or erase by or as by the stroke of a pen.)

[2] *OED* The name of a street near Moorfields in London . . . used allusively for the tribe of mean and needy authors, or literary hacks.

[3] Samuel Johnson ruefully characterized Grub-street as 'much inhabited by writers of small histories, dictionaries, and temporary poems'.

[4] *OED to fine away, down, off*: to become gradually fine, thin, or less coarse (*away*, from 1858; no citation with *off*).

[5] *The Virginians. A Tale of the Last Century* (1858–59). First pub;ished in 24 monthly parts, Nov. 1857–Oct. 1859; JFS, 'last number', meaning the latest. Reviewed by JFS (*Sat. Rev.*, 19 Nov. 1859).

[6] Pope: 'the Wits of either Charles's days, / The mob of Gentlemen who wrote with Ease' (*Imitations of Horace*, Ep. II i 106–7).

164   ON THE NOVEL AND JOURNALISM

his invidious praise. As an example—a rather singular example—we may take a portrait
of Mr. Thackeray, which has lately appeared in a paper called *Town-Talk*, and which,
as the whole literary world knows, has subsequently been acknowledged by Mr. Edmund
Yates.[7] It is not often that one gentleman author goes so plainly and directly into particulars about another, as Mr. Yates does in the following passage:

> Mr. Thackeray is forty-six years old, though from the silvery whiteness of his hair he
> appears somewhat older. He is very tall, standing upwards of six feet two inches, and as
> he walks erect his height makes him conspicuous in every assembly. His face is bloodless,
> and not particularly expressive, but remarkable for the fracture of the bridge of the nose,
> the result of an accident in youth. He wears a small grey whisker,[8] but otherwise is clean
> shaven. No one meeting him could fail to recognise in him a gentleman; his bearing is
> cold and uninviting, his style of conversation either openly cynical, or affectedly good-
> natured and benevolent; his *bonhomie* is forced, his wit biting, his pride easily touched—
> but his appearance is invariably that of the cool, *suave*, well-bred gentleman, who, whatever
> may be rankling within, suffers no surface display of his emotion.

To do this kind of biographical business is a strange pursuit for an author and a gentleman. If print were not the vehicle of expression, and a writer were not the subject, it
would be thought offensive to be so personal, and coarse to be so plainspoken. But
there is certainly the defence that contemporary biography sells well, and that, the
more personal and plainspoken it is, the better it sells. And even if Mr. Yates has, we
will not say endangered, but tested his reputation as a gentleman author by penning
and selling this hue-and-cry delineation of a fellow writer, it may perhaps be doubted
whether there is not a sort of justice in Mr. Thackeray being the victim; for Mr. Thackeray
is the great creator and support of the 'new profession'—that of what is euphemistic-
ally called lecturing, but what is really taking a man's personal appearance into the
market. When any one man has written works which have been read by thousands, and
has excited an interest in large classes of the population, there are sure to be a great
many persons that would like to see the man himself whose writings they know so well.
They like to see him, and to say they have seen him. Mr. Thackeray has thought, and
others have thought with him, that there was money to be made largely and easily out
of this curiosity. Why should he not show himself? There is a character in *Evelina*[9] who
goes to the play every evening, on the plea that he is willing to pay five shillings a night
in order that his friends may see he is alive. Mr. Thackeray effected the same object
much more cleverly, and made other persons pay him the five shillings, that they might
see he was alive. He took into the market his 'silvery hair', his 'bloodless and not particularly expressive face', his 'fractured nose', and his 'small grey whiskers'.[10] He sold a
good stare at them to thousands of curious and eager purchasers. Mr. Thackeray was a

---

[7] (1831–1894; *ODNB*, journalist and novelist). *Town Talk* (1858), in its first issue, praised Dickens, and in
its second, disparaged Thackeray in personal disrespects which led to Yates's expulsion from the Garrick
Club. As editor of *The World* he attacked JFS (22 Jan. 1879) in 'How I came to be a Judge'. *Life* 255: 'A notorious journalist asserted that the promise had been made on consideration of his writing in the papers on behalf
of the Indian Government. The statement is only worth notice as an ingenious inversion of the truth.'

[8] *OED sing.*: in earlier use, a moustache. (Including 1848 DICKENS.) JFS, in his next paragraph, quotes
it as 'whiskers'.

[9] Frances Burney (1752–1840; *ODNB*, novelist), *Evelina; or, a Young Lady's Entrance into the World*
(anon., 1778).

[10] Each of these, though within quotation marks, rewords the passage above.

GENTLEMEN AUTHORS

gentleman by birth and education, and he probably knew that this publicity[11] of private life—this coining money out of his personal appearance—was not a proceeding of a very high stamp. He was, we may suppose, aware that reserve and a hatred of vulgar notoriety are marks of a gentleman's character and bearing. But really the thing was so lucrative. There was nothing wrong in it; and why should he not put his pride in his pocket if he put a heavy purse there too? We do not pretend to quarrel with his decision; but there certainly is some reason why he should complain less than most men of being photographed by Mr. Yates. Mr. Thackeray makes money by showing himself at a lecture, and Mr. Yates makes money by describing what is shown. We do not pretend that the two things are exactly the same, but then Mr. Thackeray and Mr. Yates are not exactly in the same literary position; and if it was, as we hope, a descent for Mr. Yates to draw this biographical portrait, it was indisputably a descent for a man of honourable family and good education to make the tour of the platforms that bid highest for a peep at him.

It would, however, be very unfair if we did not acknowledge that it is extremely hard to sacrifice a large sum of money for a mere punctilio—that most men, and most critics, if tried, would prefer the money to so shadowy a thing as self-approbation—and that there are always a hundred good reasons why money should be made. Few men love themselves, or think more anxiously and wisely for themselves, than parents do for their children, while yet their hopes for their issue are high, and they have not been disheartened by bitter experience. Now, let us suppose that the darling of a family is a mischievous, olive-coloured, hump-backed little pickle. The parents promise themselves that they will keep and cherish this strange nursling for ever. But Barnum[12] comes that way, and settles that this is exactly the child for an 'Original Chinese Dwarf'. He proposes a moderate sum to the parents, and is repulsed with scorn. He is not to be beaten back, and bids higher and higher. At last the point is reached when the parents begin to hesitate. They picture all that they could do with the money, and are secretly a little flattered by the urgency of the speculator. Finally they are overcome by what they consider a sense of duty. It will be so obviously for the advantage of their little boy that he should be the Well-known Chinese Dwarf, and common prudence enjoins that they should look to the future, and provide a comfortable maintenance for the poor lad. And so the affair is arranged, and Jemmy goes away in a caravan.[13] If parents who act thus are guilty of a weakness, it is a weakness from which few would escape. It might indicate a more noble and generous feeling if they had preferred poverty and privacy for their darling; but after all they have acted prudently, and have done no harm. Just so, we must admit that all Mr. Thackeray would have gained by refusing to be Barnumized,[14] was something infinitesimal and inappreciable; and he would have lost a sum of money which the aspect of a bloodless face and a broken nose can rarely procure. To go to market with himself, and satisfy curiosity at a scale of prices regulated according to

[11] *OED* The quality of being public; the condition or fact of being open to public observation or knowledge. (1832 BENTHAM Publicity is the very soul of justice.) *specifically* Public notice; the action or fact of making someone or something publicly known; the business of promotion or advertising. 1842 DICKENS You will see that they are signed by the first writers in England, and that their object is. .*Publicity*.

[12] P. T. Barnum (1810–1891), 'a pushing American show-proprietor' (*OED*).

[13] *OED* A troop of people going in company.

[14] *OED* To exhibit with a lavish display of puffing advertisements. From 1851, with 1852 *Blackwood's* 'Barnumizing the prodigy through Europe'.

proximity, was not to do anything dishonourable. It was not anything ungentlemanly, like cheating at cards, or telling a lie. It was, at worst, an offence against taste; and all that could be said about it was that it tended to degrade literature and to foster the appetite for intrusion into other men's affairs, which is apt to be impertinently gratified at the special expense of authors. We can easily conceive that, although a man of Mr. Thackeray's sensibility would perceive that to do this was a departure from the strictest code of high feeling, yet calm philosophy would tell him that such a departure might be justified by a large pecuniary profit. We feel sure that, in some way or other, he thought it only due to himself or to others to let Barnum have his Chinese Dwarf; and it is certain that nine-tenths of any number of persons subjected to the same trial would have decided as he did, and that the few who might decide otherwise would have very little of palpable and visible advantage to show as a compensation for the money they rashly threw away.

We may even admit that it is a debateable point whether there is any derogation from his position in a gentleman going about in his literary caravan. It may be argued that he is still the same man, with the same feelings, opinions, and principles, and that he is only combating the essentially ungentlemanly notion that a man ceases to be a gentleman when he earns his bread honestly in an unusual way. Looking only to the individual, this is to a great extent true, and we must own that Mr. Thackeray is the same man alike when we have paid our five shillings for the privilege of looking at him, and when we have enjoyed it gratis. But if we turn our thoughts to the whole literary profession, we are inclined to think that the bad effect of a vendible publicity is discoverable. Mr. Thackeray might maintain that Mr. Yates was taking rather a liberty with him, if he had not himself provided his biographer with a sufficient excuse. That a man near the head of a calling should entitle his inferiors to take a liberty with him, is in itself an evil. At any rate, if we are not to say that it is derogatory to Mr. Thackeray to show himself, nor to Mr. Yates to photograph the show, we may venture to admire more unmixedly those who set themselves against this literary unreserve. It is not one of the least debts of gratitude that the country owes to the Laureate,[15] that he has always consistently maintained that a gentleman is not to be intruded upon, nor to intrude himself on others, because he has a gift for verse-making. If we recognise the common-sense which says that money is better than a punctilio, we may also sympathize with the nobler scorn which refuses to let fame degenerate into notoriety. No one who even knows Mr. Thackeray only by his books, and has not the honour of an acquaintance which the first gentleman in the kingdom might be pleased to possess, can doubt that he is a man of honour and high feeling. But he has made what, if judged on other than pecuniary grounds, appears to us a mistake. Against this mistake Mr. Tennyson has repeatedly protested, and we think that he has chosen the better part.[16]

---

[15] Tennyson, Poet Laureate since 1850. The protest: 'To –, After Reading a Life and Letters' (1849), and in poems still to come as well as in conversation (W. M. Rossetti, on Tennyson's 'fit of intense disgust after reading Medwin's book about Byron', 18 Dec. 1849).

[16] Traditional rewording of Luke 10:42: But one thing is needful: and Mary hath chosen that good part, which shall not be taken away from her. (In some translations, heightened to 'better' and even to 'best'.)

'Manon Lescaut' (excerpts)
(*Saturday Review*, 17 July 1858)

Antoine-François Prévost, abbé (1697–1763), *Histoire du Chevalier des Grieux et de Manon Lescaut* (1731), the final volume of *Mémoires et aventures d'un homme de qualité* (1728–1731).

Manon Lescaut (excerpts)*

To say that the writers of French fiction are always fluctuating between realism and sentimentalism[1] is only to say of them what is equally true of English novelists. But there is a thoroughness in French writing which there is not in English; and their realism seems more real, and their sentimentalism more sentimental than ours. They describe things and persons which we taboo, and justify themselves by saying that they do but paint what exists. On the other hand, they rise to heights of fancy and rhetoric, go back to first principles, and claim an intimacy with the Bon Dieu on which we should not venture. A hundred years ago, there was the Abbé Prévost to represent the realism, and Rousseau the sentimentalism, exactly as Balzac and George Sand represent them in our own time. The difference, however, which a century has made in the respective types is very considerable, and it is worth while to know what the realism of France was a century back, in order that we may compare it with its modern counterpart. We cannot say that the comparison is entirely in favour of the later generation. *Manon Lescaut*, the only one of the very numerous productions of the Abbé Prévost which has survived, has been the model of a conspicuous class of French novels, and more especially of the *Dame aux Camélias*.[2] But although M. Alexandre Dumas fils has copied closely the main features of his original, there is the widest possible interval between the execution of the two works. The Abbé Prévost, although he treats of courtesans and rogues, is always a gentleman. There is not the slightest approach to voluptuous materialism in *Manon Lescaut*; and we are sure that the author would have thought himself disgraced by the minute nastiness of his successor.

* * *

---

* *Histoire de Manon Lescaut et du Chevalier Des Grieux*. Par l'Abbé Prévost. Nouvelle Edition. Paris. London: Jeffs, 1858.

---

[1] 'Sentimentalism' (*Sat. Rev.*, 25 Dec. 1858), p. 188, and 'Sentimentalism' (*Cornhill*, July 1864), p. 223.

[2] *La Dame aux Camélias*, the novel (1848) by Alexandre Dumas the younger (1824–1895), became his play (1852) and then Verdi's opera, *La Traviata* (1853).

168 ON THE NOVEL AND JOURNALISM

Manon Lescaut is so great a favourite with the French public, that new editions are constantly being published, and they are almost all preceded by biographies of the author. There is much reason in this, for the life of the Abbé Prévost throws great light on the story which has made his name famous. From his life we gather the idea of a man of strong feeling, of tenderness, of an excited and passionate character, of little fixity of purpose, but still with a sincere desire not to suffer himself to be corrupted—controlling himself in his better moments, and disgusted by the coarser side of worldly pleasure, while fascinated by its more brilliant aspect. Above all, we apprehend him to have had something simple, genuine, and almost childish in his composition. *Manon* bears the traces of such a character. Its *naïveté*, its natural ease, its intensity of passion carry us through scenes, and familiarize us with persons, that would have been repulsive if treated by a man of vulgar sensuality. There is no morbidness, no apology for taking up such a subject, no wish to heighten or to disguise. The tale is told because to the author's mind it seems true, and because his readers will like to have it told. It begins at once, and rushes *in medias res* at the very opening. The first pages inform us how the Chevalier Des Grieux at seventeen met Manon at sixteen, how he saw her getting out of the coach at Amiens, and how instantly he fell in love with her. Thenceforward the story rolls on, and the history of the unhappy couple is pursued with that artless art which carries us forward, because only those things happen that seem inevitable. Manon is the most tender of mistresses until poverty threatens to knock at the door, and then she flies to a richer lover. But the Chevalier is too deeply attached to care about inconstancy, and waits patiently till his mistress returns to him. Friends and relations try to reclaim him, but in vain. He will do anything to stay near his Manon. He turns rogue, he cheats at cards, he lives by joining a combination[3] of sharpers;[4] and however often his mistress leaves him, he is overjoyed when she condescends to come back. He even joins with her in trying to plunder one of her rich admirers, and both are thrown into prison. At last she is condemned to be sent to America as a *fille perdue*; but he will not be shaken off, and accompanies her to New Orleans. Fresh intrigues threaten to break up their intercourse, when he carries her off with him into the wilderness, trodden only by the Indians, and there she dies in his arms. He is rescued by a friend, named Tiberge, who has never ceased to help him, although lamenting deeply the course of his long infatuation. The Chevalier returns to Europe, and then tells his story to a stranger, who had had an opportunity of showing him an accidental kindness; and so, without a word of reflection or sentiment, without any ending but what such a story would have in real life, ends a tale that is certainly one of the most remarkable creations of the French genius in the eighteenth century.

Some of the French critics have pronounced that the Abbé Prévost wrote *Manon Lescaut* by a happy accident. In his other tales the ease of narration becomes mere prolixity, and the passionate tenderness fades into a group of ordinary intrigues. And in *Manon Lescaut*, as in the productions of other novelists of that time—of Le Sage and Fielding—we scarcely feel the excellence of the work as we read it. The story is told so straight-forwardly, that we are neither invited nor permitted to analyse the pleasure it gives us. But when we look back we find that Manon and the Chevalier have been

---

[3] *OED* The banding together or union of persons for the prosecution of a common object: formerly used almost always in a bad sense = conspiracy, self-interested or illegal confederacy.

[4] *OED* A cheat, swindler, rogue; *esp.* a fraudulent gamester.

MANON LESCAUT 169

strangely interesting, and the lucky accident really consisted in the author either remembering or inventing the two characters. The former is the more probable, and it is impossible not to suspect that in Manon we have a reminiscence of the *engagement trop tendre* of the Abbé's youth. This woman, with her true attachment to and honest admiration of her lover, her unaffected determination not to be poor, her avowed hankering after the superfluities of life, her delight in tricking the rich fools she preys on, and her merriment when she gets her Chevalier to play this roguish game with her, is so life-like that she overcomes us with her reality, and claims something of the indulgence which we extend to a living person. The Chevalier again has a kind of gentlemanly melancholy about him which becomes a man of that quality, and makes us think twice before we damn him. He offends against every standard of judgment. His infatuated love is an insult to strict principle. He flies in the teeth of worldly wisdom by his invariable readiness to take a woman back who has deceived and left him. He violates common honesty in order that he may protract his guilty career. But so well is the unity of his character preserved, that all these offences seem natural. They are but steps in a career, which, looked at as a whole, excites pity and sympathy quite as much as disapprobation.

The Abbé, in a preface to his story, expresses a hope that *Manon Lescaut* may be found moral and edifying, because it shows the great misery into which illicit love brings those who entertain it. This sort of moral is not generally found, we believe, to be very efficacious. In the first place, the loss of future worldly prosperity has extremely slight weight with the class of persons that are capable of imitating the conduct of the Chevalier Des Grieux; and secondly, the misfortunes of the Chevalier are greater than come within the average experience of his imitators. The moral of the book, so far as it has any moral, lies at once in its reality and its reserve. If we assume that life as it is should be, within certain limits of decency, the theme of the novelist, there is much reason for saying that so very large and important a part of actual life as that occupied by illicit love cannot be overlooked. Who ought to write on this subject—and still more, who ought to read what is written—is a different matter. But taking it for granted that the theme ought to be handled for some readers, then the question of morality only arises as to the execution of the task, and it is possible that the execution may be moral; and it will be all the more likely to be so if it is free from moralizing. In this sense *Manon Lescaut* may be called a moral book. The object of such literature is to be real; and *Manon Lescaut* is eminently real. There is no idealizing vice, no confusing one kind of passion with another, no hesitation in painting the degradation of character that ensues. And if the book is realistic, the realism consists in the acceptance of consequences, and in the fidelity to a conception of character. There is none of that loathsome realism which has gone to such prodigious lengths in modern French novels, and which describes everything that the modesty of all, except the publicly immodest, would keep concealed. It argues the most singular depravation of taste that such things can be tolerated. It is quite true that prudery begets prurience, and that when the public discussion of illicit love is too rigidly excluded from literature, we have hankerings after it appearing in the most curious way. Mr. Albert Smith,[5] for instance, introduced in his

---

[5] Albert Richard Smith (1816–1860; *ODNB*, author, public lecturer, and mountaineer). In 1851 he ascended Mont Blanc; *The Story of Mont Blanc* (1852) became an entertainment that ran for 2,000

last 'Mont Blanc' a young lady, who expressed, with a sly look, a great wish to go to the 'naughty opera', and the applause and laughter of the audience amply justified him. But what could be more singular, if we reflect on it, than that an ordinary goodish girl should find food for mirth and playful allusion in the sin and sorrows of the *Traviata*? But all this is justification of treating the subject as it ought to be treated, and as it is treated in *Manon Lescaut*—with fidelity, with frankness, without sermonizing, but with largeness that looks to the whole of life, and an abhorrence of the brutality that unveils the *minutiae* of an intrigue. It is not the justification of treating it as it is treated by the younger Dumas and by Théophile Gautier.[6]

performances over six years; in 1854 Smith performed it before Queen Victoria and Prince Albert at Osborne House. (This note is more than usually indebted to Wikipedia.)

[6] The heroine of *La Traviata* is 'Marguerite Gautier'. She was played by Marie Duplessis, an obituary of whom was written by Théophile Gautier (1811–1872).

'The Spectator'
(*Saturday Review*, 14 August 1858)

Life 119, on what had become 'middle' articles: 'For such literature the British public had shown a considerable avidity ever since the days of Addison.'[1] In 'How to Write an Article' (*Sat. Rev.* 25 Oct. 1856), JFS had called a formidable witness: 'Mr. Macaulay describes, with his usual vigour and with more than his usual warmth, the wonderful versatility and beauty of Addison's contributions to the *Spectator*. "On the Monday", he says, "we have an allegory as lively and ingenious as Lucian's *Auction of Lives*; on the Tuesday, an Eastern apologue as richly coloured as the tales of Scheherazade; on the Wednesday, a character described with the skill of La Bruyère; on the Thursday, a scene from common life equal to the best chapters in the *Vicar of Wakefield*; on the Friday, some sly Horatian pleasantry on fashionable follies, on hoops, patches, or puppet-shows; and on the Saturday, a religious meditation, which will bear a comparison with the finest passages in Massillon." '[2]

The Spectator*

There are few more instructive branches of literary inquiry than the comparison of the different amusements of different generations. Light literature, in its manifold shapes, has become by far the most popular of modern recreations, and it is curious to trace the various forms which it has worn during different periods of its history. The vast differences between the reign of Queen Victoria and the reign of Queen Anne can hardly be displayed more concisely or more pointedly than by the contrast between the general character of the *Spectator* and modern fiction. The comparison, like other comparisons, will not go upon all-fours. There are parts of the *Spectator* to which the multifarious publications of our own day offer hardly any analogy. There are other parts of which it presents the pattern and germ with curious exactness, though the spirit is utterly different. Upon each of these divisions some observations occur which may not be without interest, as evidence of the changes which have come over a very important aspect of the national character.

The principal feature of the *Spectator*, to which nothing in our own day corresponds, is to be found in the moral essays with which it is so largely sprinkled. Why is it that whereas 150 years ago thousands of readers were delighted to buy and to read a speculation by Addison on Good-nature, or on the Immortality of the Soul, no one thinks of

---

* The Spectator. In *British Essayists*. 1823.

[1] Joseph Addison (1672–1719; *ODNB*, writer and politician). *The Spectator*, daily, 1711–12, by Addison and Sir Richard Steele (1672–1729; *ODNB*, writer and politician).

[2] Jean-Baptiste Massillon (1663–1742), preacher.

inserting such matter in any of our modern papers? We can hardly imagine how we should feel if we were to read some morning in the *Times* such a paragraph as this in an article on the vanity of ambition:

> There is scarce a thinking man in the world who is involved in the business of it, but lives under a secret impatience of the hurry and fatigue he suffers, and has formed a resolution to fix himself one time or other in such a state as is suitable to the end of his being.

Or what should we think if the *Examiner*[3] were to inform its readers that:

> When I look upon the tombs of the great, every emotion of envy dies in me; when I read the epitaphs of the beautiful, every inordinate desire dies out; when I meet with the grief of parents on a tombstone, my heart swells with compassion; when I see the tomb of the parents themselves, I consider the vanity of grieving for those whom we must quickly follow.

Is the disuse of such admonitions to be attributed to a dearth of Addisons, or to a tone of mind hostile to Addisonian reflections? There is probably much ground for each supposition. No one can read the moral dissertations in the *Spectator* without being sensible that they are conceived in a spirit which no man of genius could enter into now. We should be fully prepared to endorse, with but little qualification, Lord Macaulay's glowing praises of their beauty, and indeed, no one who is not accustomed to periodical writing can adequately appreciate the all but supernatural freshness and fertility of mind which they display; but it is impossible to read them without a feeling that if we could imagine an Eton boy's themes[4] written with ideal beauty, they would resemble them very nearly both in matter and in manner.

Opening the volumes at random, we find (No. 215) the greatest of English Essayists, under the heading of our old friend 'Ingenuas didicisse',[5] &c., discussing the advantages of education. Four paragraphs introduce the subject, setting forth how the soul is like a block of marble, the colours of which are brought out by the polisher. Then comes the example, in the case of two negro slaves, who murder their mistress because they cannot agree which is to marry her, and then commit suicide in despair. Three paragraphs conclude the dissertation, beginning respectively with the following characteristic observations:

> We see in this amazing instance of barbarity what strange disorders are bred in the minds of those men whose passions are not regulated by virtue and disciplined by reason...It is therefore an unspeakable blessing to be born in those parts of the world where wisdom and knowledge flourish...Discourses of morality and reflections upon human nature are the best means we can make use of to improve our minds and gain a true knowledge of ourselves.

In reading such sentences, the *Quæ cum ita sint*, the *Quod si*, and the *Genus humanum*[6] of our youth rise dimly before us; bringing with them the recollection that the *Spectator* was the most productive and the most easily worked of all the mines of what, with unconscious irony, we used to describe as 'sense'. It is a curious reflection how such

---

[3] Weekly paper (1808–86), founded by Leigh Hunt and John Hunt in 1808.

[4] *OED* An exercise written on a given subject, *esp.* a school essay; an exercise in translation.

[5] Ovid, *Pontics* book 2: *Ingenuas didicisse fideliter artes emollit mores, nec sinit esse feros.* (A faithful study of the liberal arts refines the manners and corrects their harshness.)

[6] The 'things being as they are', the 'what if', and the 'human race'.

THE SPECTATOR

173

compositions can ever have contributed so much as in fact they have contributed to the reputation of a man who is universally placed high in the list of English classics. The answer to the question is, we think, afforded in a great measure by the whole tone of the *Spectator*. It indicates the prevalence of a singular lull in the public mind—a state of feeling in which the great problems of life seem to have received a sort of good-humoured solution, and in which there is a general impression that all men of sense are agreed upon all matters of essential importance, so that nothing remains except to explain their sentiments to the mass of mankind as tastefully as possible. The simple gentle theology in which the Psalms, Cicero, Epictetus, and 'several heathen as well as Christian authors', are produced by turns as witnesses to the uncertainty of life, the immortality of the soul, and the emptiness of worldly distinctions—and the elegant, but singularly formal and even timid criticism in which it is shown how 'artfully' the author of *Chevy Chase*[7] introduces this and that sentiment, and how he wrote with the high moral object of preventing the feudal nobility from fighting, as Homer wished to show the Greeks the necessity of combination against Persia—are further illustrations of the same temper. The universal sentiment is that there are rules and measures on all subjects, human and divine, which are well understood and ascertained, and which it only remains to enforce by elegant remarks and appropriate classical quotations. It would be needless and almost impertinent in us to enlarge upon the extraordinary felicity and skill with which Addison and Steele betook themselves to this congenial task. We confine ourselves to pointing out that it would be simply impossible for men of their powers in the present day to write as they wrote, because the substratum of belief which enabled them to do so no longer exists. The most ignorant person would in these days steer clear of the marvellous blunder which we have quoted about Homer and *Chevy Chase*, for it is a matter of universal notoriety that there is a whole library of controversy about Homer, his relationship to the *Iliad* and the *Odyssey*, and the relations of the various parts of those works to each other; whilst, in regard to morals and theology, legions of controversialists, whose premisses and conclusions contradict each other in the wildest manner, lie in wait for any one who is rash enough to vent commonplaces upon the subjects on which they dispute.

The presence of this feeling of repose and security with regard to all the most important subjects of thought unquestionably gives a rather formal and shallow air to the more serious speculations of Steele and Addison; but it is at least equally plain, and equally worthy of our attention, that the same cause enabled them to understand, far better than is the case with their representatives in the present day, the true scope and province of that description of literature to which they devoted themselves. The prototypes of each of the main divisions of modern light literature are to be found in the *Spectator*. Sir Roger de Coverley and the other members of the Club are the legitimate progenitors of the most conspicuous of our modern novels, more especially of those which appear in parts; whilst the various sketches of manners—the Lovers'-club, the Liars'-club, the letters about Fulvia and Claudia, patches, snuff-boxes, and the like—contain the germ of that immense mass of comments upon all sorts of small social matters which fill our magazines, and overflow into the morning papers through

---

[7] *Life* 49, JFS as a child: 'He especially delighted . . . in "Chevy Chase" ', the medieval ballad.

174 ON THE NOVEL AND JOURNALISM

the activity of the gentlemen whose natural impulse it is, in all the vicissitudes of life, to console themselves by writing to the *Times*.[8]

It would of course be unfair to institute a comparison, in point of literary skill, between some of the greatest masters of the English language that ever lived and that very miscellaneous crowd of writers who instruct us at the present day; but it is well worth while to attend to the difference between the spirit which pervades the *Spectator* and that which shows itself under an almost infinite variety of forms amongst so many popular modern novelists. As the business of such writers is to appreciate and to paint delicate shades of feeling, they may be naturally presumed to be possessed of more than the average amount of sensibility, and therefore to participate in and to display more deeply than their neighbours the prevalent temper of the times. We shall accordingly find that no department of literature shows clearer traces of the depth and intensity of modern controversies upon all the most important subjects of inquiry than modern popular novels. The *Spectator*, as we have already remarked, assumes everywhere the existence of a sort of average state of feeling and opinion. Its object—as described in the dedication of the first volume to Lord Somers[9]—is 'to cultivate and polish human life by promoting virtue and knowledge'; and it may be read from end to end without the discovery of a single hint of the existence of anything more than very superficial controversies as to the objects indicated by that comprehensive formula. The great charm of the wit, the pathos, and the playfulness of the *Spectator*, and especially of Addison's contributions to it, is to be found in the narrowness of their range. They neither prove nor assert anything of much importance, nor are they meant to do so. The provinces of wit and business (perhaps because the writers in question were versed in both) are recognised as fundamentally distinct. The former is never allowed to encroach upon the latter; and, indeed, those who excel in it never show the slightest inclination to do so.

Nothing can afford a greater contrast to this than the present state of the same department of literature. The controversies of the last century have embraced every subject of importance to the welfare of mankind here or hereafter. There is perhaps hardly a single conception, theological, moral, metaphysical, scientific, or political, which they have not profoundly modified. The strong instinctive presumption which used to be felt by almost all men, however lively their fancies, and however quick their sensibilities might be, in favour of any well-established form of thought, has been almost entirely destroyed. Men of taste have all but universally fallen into the way of forming their views of the world around them not according to any fixed rules, but according to the prevailing temper of their own minds for the time being. The extent to which opinion has been superseded by sentiment is almost incredible, but the evidence upon the subject is to be found in every novel on every railway bookstall in the country. Modern novelists universally seem to assume, in a thousand indirect ways, that the principal question with regard to any man, any opinion, or any line of conduct, is not whether it

---

[8] 'Groans of the Britons' (*Sat. Rev.*, 22 Nov. 1856), p. 65.

[9] John Somers, Baron Somers (1651–1716; *ODNB*, lawyer and politician). 'My Lord, I should not act the part of an impartial Spectator, if I Dedicated the following Papers to one who is not of the most consummate and most acknowledged Merit. None but a person of a finished Character can be the proper Patron of a Work, which endeavours to Cultivate and Polish Human Life, by promoting Virtue and Knowledge, and by recommending whatsoever may be either Useful or Ornamental to Society.'

THE SPECTATOR 175

is right or wrong, true of false, wise or foolish, but whether it can be so represented as to enlist the reader's sympathies, or at any rate to make him understand and enter into the feelings of the party concerned. Sir Roger de Coverley is a mere amusement. His character embodies no particular view of life, and it proves nothing except the exquisite skill of Addison; but the case is totally different with Childe Harold, Ernest Maltravers,[10] or Nell in the *Old Curiosity Shop*. It would be unfair to say that Lord Byron meant to preach up pride and misanthropy—that Sir Edward Bulwer Lytton holds himself out as a serene philosopher, for whom life has no secrets and little interest—or that Mr. Dickens goes round to all the world to be kissed like a child at dessert. But it is not unfair to say that they respectively create characters who do act in this manner, and that they do so in a way which tends—not perhaps very logically, but still most effectively—to produce a certain sympathy with the temper so described. Addison's fictions are like fireworks throwing out different-coloured stars, which can be criticised according to their inherent qualities. Modern novels are like slips of coloured glass interposed between the eye and the face of nature, the effect of which is to give a colour to the common events of life whilst the attention is quite withdrawn from the colouring medium. Whig or Tory, Hanoverian or Jacobite, High Churchman or Low Churchman, could equally enjoy most parts of the *Spectator* without prejudice to their several creeds; but almost every modern novel is more or less a party manifesto, and indicates one of several views of life which would run through and colour opinion upon every subject whatever. If we were told that a man really enjoys and sympathizes with Mr. Thackeray, Mr. Kingsley, Mr. Dickens, or Mrs. Gaskell, we could give a very good guess as to his views upon any subject whatever.

We have often expressed our opinion upon the mischief which sermons in circulating libraries inflict upon society, but in connexion with our present subject it is curious to notice how completely the growth of the new school of fiction changes the whole character which fiction sustains. In former times, fiction, even in its highest form, was in the nature of a plaything. Sir Roger was a Tory, but Addison was a Whig. Falstaff was full of fun and humour, but Shakspeare sees through him. Henry V. casts him off, and we feel that it is as right that our old acquaintance should die in distress and neglect, as that Nym and Bardolph should come to the gallows. Dante loves Francesca, but Francesca is damned. All this is changed in our day. The universal postulate of novelists seems to be that sympathy cannot be wrong,[11] and that hard cases cannot be right. These writers appear to look upon the world as a vast stage, on which there is room for many actors and for many parts, and on which, if a man plays his part consistently and acts after his kind, no further demand is to be made of him. Or, to take another metaphor, they consider life as an equation which presents many roots. You cannot say that one root is more right than another. Any of them will satisfy the terms of the problem.

There is hardly any department of thought in which this temper may not be traced. It is expressly avowed and embodied in one of the most popular of modern scientific

---

[10] Ernest Maltravers, by the author of *Pelham, Eugene Aram, Rienzi*, etc. (1837).

[11] 'Hobbes's Minor Works' (*Sat. Rev.*, 13 Oct. 1866; *Hor. Sab.* ii 41–2): 'That men should have mixed motives, sympathies of which they are barely conscious themselves, and a very imperfect knowledge of the true character and tendencies of their own views, seems hardly to have suggested itself to Hobbes. Nothing, indeed, is more characteristic of the difference between our own and earlier ages, than their total want of that power of entering into the views and feelings of others, which in our days is so common as to threaten sometimes, and in some persons, greatly to weaken all moral distinctions whatever.'

176 ON THE NOVEL AND JOURNALISM

schools—a school, by the way, from which most novelists shrink with a pathetic and interesting distaste. A fatalistic science which recognises no object of thought except facts and modes of succession is the exact complement of a school of art which substitutes sentiment for opinion. There is the closest possible connexion—we might almost say that there is an absolute identity—between the theory which maintains that the rise, progress, growth, decline, and fall of nations proceed eternally according to a fixed unchangeable decree, and the picture which intimates (though it does not say, for its principle is to say nothing) that the proud and the humble, the licentious and the pure, the energetic and the lazy, act respectively after their kind, without being the objects of express praise or express blame, and in a manner which almost makes it impossible to look upon them as being moral agents at all. Closely connected, too, with this is the whole system of attack and defence by novels. Mr. Disraeli[12] wants to injure Mr. Croker, Mr. Dickens wants to vilify the Government, and they proceed to compose novels which give you a theory (more or less founded on facts) of the man or of the system, the only evidence of the truth of which is the ingenuity and the artistic consistency with which it is put together. It is not amiss to remind authors of this kind that amongst predecessors whom the most exorbitant vanity must recognise as superiors, the province of art was looked upon as being infinitely more narrow than they seem to consider it, whilst the execution of works of art was carried to a pitch of perfection quite inaccessible to writers whose works aim at fulfilling a function for which they are, and from the necessity of the case must continue to be, absolutely unfit.

---

[12] Benjamin Disraeli, earl of Beaconsfield (1804–1881; *ODNB*, prime minister and novelist). Both *Coningsby; or, The New Generation* (1844), and *Sybil; or, The Two Nations* (1845), expose the politician Rigby (based on John Wilson Croker, 1780–1857; *ODNB*, politician and writer). *Life* 222 and n.: 'In 1881, Lord Beaconsfield wrote to Lord Lytton: "It is a thousand pities that J. F. Stephen is a judge; he might have done anything and everything as leader of the future Conservative party." JFS told Lytton he was "very much touched and pleased by Lord B.'s kind words about me"; he felt however that "judging and bookwriting is my proper sphere" (9 Feb. 1881)'.

'Novels and Novelists' (excerpt)
(*Saturday Review*, 18 September 1858)

Novels and Novelists (excerpt)*

The question at issue is this—Are novels proper vehicles for direct political and social discussions, or is amusement their legitimate object? We cannot understand how any one who has ever seriously entered upon the discussion of political or social questions can entertain a doubt upon the subject. Such discussions universally turn upon questions of fact, and generally upon facts which are at once highly complicated and hotly debated. Let us look at any one of the numberless questions of this order which have lately engaged public attention. There is the question of prison discipline. It is pre-eminently a question of fact, and one, too, on which it is very difficult indeed to arrive at the truth. How does imprisonment affect those who are subjected to it? How do different systems vary in their effects? Does solitary or does separate confinement drive a man mad? Does the one or the other confirm him in vice? Does the one or the other lead him to reflection and repentance? What are the liabilities to abuse of each of these systems? How far do they place the prisoners at the mercy of a careless or harsh gaoler? What abuses have, in fact, existed, and how widely have they prevailed? Questions like these must be answered with the greatest care, fulness, and impartiality; and the answers must be weighed with the most deliberate scrutiny before any stable and comprehensive conclusion on the subject can be reached. How is the progress towards such a conclusion forwarded, in the most remote degree, by a man who comes forward with a picturesque but simply fictitious story, in which, with almost frantic violence, he proclaims that he takes one view of the subject, to the exclusion of all others—that separate confinement is a monstrous iniquity, that prisons are hells, gaolers devils, and judges beasts, asses, &c.? He may be right or he may be wrong; but his assertion is simply worthless as evidence of the truth of his theory: and it is excessively mischievous, because inconsiderate[1] people are, by their natural weakness, inclined to believe any one who makes strong assertions in an interesting manner. The fundamental vice of novels, considered as works of instruction, lies in the circumstance that the novelist makes his facts, and that, if he is charged with inaccuracy, he can always plead that he is writing a novel, and not a political treatise. He is always proving a truism for the sake of insinuating a *non sequitur*. No one doubts that such a prison as the gaol in *It is Never too late to Mend*, such a Government as the Circumlocution Office, such a Court as is

---

* *Novels and Novelists, from Elizabeth to Victoria.* By J. Cordy Jeaffreson. 2 vols. London: Hurst and Blackett, 1858.

[1] *OED* Of persons, etc.: not characterized by consideration; acting without deliberation; thoughtless, imprudent, indiscreet, careless.

depicted in *Bleak House*, such a state of society as is drawn in *Hawkstone*, such a system of slavery as is painted in *Uncle Tom's Cabin*, would be very bad things.[2] That is what these novels really prove; but what they insinuate is, that the system of English prisons, the English Government, the Court of Chancery, the state of the manufacturing districts in Yorkshire and Lancashire, and slavery in the Southern States of the Union, are, in point of fact, such as Mr. Reade, Mr. Dickens, Mr. Sewell, and Mrs. Stowe assert them to be. And the dexterity of the novelist is proved by the fact, that he inclines his readers to dispense with evidence the study of which would supersede his unsupported assertions. Such assertions are mere impertinences to which a man of real sobriety and fairness of mind would attach absolutely no importance whatever.

If a novel really were a useful instrument for political and social discussion, why should it not be extended to other matters, which turn equally upon questions of fact, though upon questions of a less extended and difficult kind. If Mr. Dickens has in his hand an instrument which enables him to teach us all about the procedure of the Court of Chancery, and to procure its reform, why should he not employ it in criminal as well as civil justice? Why not write a striking tale in a magazine or newspaper, to establish, before trial, the guilt or the innocence of Palmer[3] or Bernard?[4] It would of course be a monstrous absurdity and a gross wrong to an accused person to do anything of the kind. But why is it less unjust in principle to act in a similar way towards bodies of men, and to prejudge questions of great depth and intricacy, by excited, noisy, and constantly reiterated assertions? Of course we know quite well that philanthropic reforms are more important and more dignified pursuits than amusement, but it does not follow that either of them are improved by being mixed up together. To our minds, the consequence is that the one becomes false and the other dull, but there is unhappily no doubt at all that that large and petulant race which wishes to have the honours and the pleasures without the labour of thought, and to enjoy the feeling of being engaged in a dignified occupation, without preparing themselves for its prosecution by any preliminary education, welcomes the advent of earnest novels as a sort of royal road to the attainment of their wishes.

---

[2] 'Theodore Parker on Slavery' (*Sat. Rev.*, 14 Nov. 1863): 'Exactly in proportion to the degree in which such language is ill-suited to discussion it is well-suited for denunciation, and in certain states of public feeling no doubt denunciation is highly useful. When a crying evil is established by law, and goes on from generation to generation, people are fatally apt to come to look upon it as not being an evil at all; and no extravagance, either of language or of conduct, into which the Northern Americans may be at present betrayed, ought to blind us to the fact that for some sixty years the nation, as a whole, showed a degree of indifference to the existence among them of negro slavery, which every good and honest man must have regarded with disgust. There is no inconsistency between a dislike for Parker's way of expressing himself about absolute rights, and eternal laws, and other such matters, and a strong opinion that, after all, the feelings of which that language were the expression did him the highest honour. He saw—and proved by evidence which, though not perhaps very novel, is unanswerably cogent—that all the interests of the United States, moral and material, were fearfully injured by slavery; and he had the courage to express that opinion in marvelously forcible language, at a time when it required considerable courage to do so. He had also an undoubted claim to the great merit of having taught his countrymen a lesson which they and most other populations are apt to forget with fatal ease—namely, that there is such a thing as moral responsibility for the general character of institutions as well as for particular acts, and that those who contribute to the establishment or support of an institution selfish, degrading and pernicious to the souls and bodies of millions of men, incur a responsibility which is perhaps all the greater because it does not involve any positive act generally considered wrong and odious.' Also JFS, 'Olmsted's Texas' (*Sat. Rev.*, 21 Feb. 1857), p. 194.

[3] 'The Rugeley Poisoner'; see p. xv.

[4] Simon François Bernard, French radical implicated in Orsini's bomb, the attempted assassination of Napoleon III in January 1858.

'The *Revue des Deux Mondes* on English Romance' (excerpts) (*Saturday Review*, 2 October 1858)

The *Revue des Deux Mondes* on English Romance (excerpts)

Burns' prayer[1] that we might be enabled to see ourselves as others see us, has been answered by the great modern diffusion of periodical literature to a very surprising extent. We receive from day to day, from week to week, from month to month, and from quarter to quarter, endless information as to what different people think of us. To say nothing of novels—the principal aim of which may be described as that of giving brilliant exhibitions of almost every conceivable type of character, accompanied by the broadest hints as to the opinion which the writer entertains of them—writers of every calibre are constantly racking their ingenuity to discover points of national or individual character which they may take for the texts of direct special disquisition. An instance of this is afforded by an article in the last number of the *Revue des Deux Mondes*, in which a writer, who adopts the signature of Arthur Dudley,[2] gives us a dissertation on 'Anglo-Saxon Romance', suggested by a review of Mr. Charles Reade's novel, *It's Never too Late to Mend*, and Mr. Emerson's *English Traits*.[3] The general purport of the article is that the two books which we have mentioned may be accepted as faithful accounts of the English—or rather, to use the author's own phrase, of the Anglo-Saxons—and that Mr. Reade, in particular, had succeeded in seizing and in portraying very happily the leading points in our national character. The writer is of opinion that the basis of this character is rightly indicated in these works as being a combination of great romance with immense force of will, and that its most characteristic sphere of action in the present day is to be found in colonization, and whatever is analogous to it. Love, we are told, is the great mainspring of all English conduct. To marry the woman he loves is the great object which every young Englishman proposes to himself. It is this which drives young Englishmen all over the world, and inclines them to undertake every sort of difficult and dangerous enterprise, and gives the nation that intense energy of will which distinguishes it from every other race in the world. Towards the end of the article, the author qualifies the romance of this theory by bringing us down to very prosaic considerations. If emigration ceased to be available for 'les

---

[1] Robert Burns (1759–1796; *ODNB*, poet). 'To a Louse': 'O wad some Pow'r the giftie gie us / To see oursels as others see us! / It wad frae monie a blunder free us / An' foolish notion'.

[2] 'Adopts', not being (as would be the spirit of Romance) the son of Queen Elizabeth by her lover from childhood, Robert Dudley.

[3] 1856.

180   ON THE NOVEL AND JOURNALISM

cadets de famille',[4] we should have to give up the 'law of primogeniture'; and that would involve the sacrifice of love-matches, which would degrade the national character and destroy the force of the national will. It is curious to find that, after all, the rule in Shelley's case[5] and Fearne on Contingent Remainders are the true basis of our national greatness.

The whole theory, from beginning to end, is an odd instance of that ingenious, moderate, and cultivated extravagance which is so common in the present day, and which the popularity of such writers as Mr. Emerson and Mr. Reade—and they have much in common—has a strong tendency to produce. Every single member of the theory is a caricature of the most delusive nature. To begin at the beginning, why substitute the word 'Anglo-Saxon' for 'English'? It is a mere American vulgarism, and a very incorrect one. There neither is, nor ever was, such a race as the Anglo-Saxons. The Angles lived in one part of England, and the Saxons in another; they were mixed up with Celts, Danes, and Normans; and all these and some other tribes had been fused into a stock as completely national and individual as any race in the world, and radically distinct from any one of its component members, for full 500 years before there was a single English colony in North America. The Americans might as well call themselves Welsh, Scotchmen, or Yorkshiremen, as Anglo-Saxons; and as there is no more difference between an Englishman and an Anglo-Saxon, in the modern and vulgar sense of the word, than there is between a Frenchman and a native of France, we infinitely prefer the older, the simpler, and the more honourable title.

* * *

As for Mr. Reade's novels, if there is one thing about them clearer than another, it is that they are written entirely on French models. The violent situations, the glaring colours, the short sentences, the swagger and the bombast are all imitations of M. Dumas. It is hard to understand the simplicity which can accept *It's Never too late to Mend* as a series of pictures of English men and women as they are. We will venture to say that not a single character nor a single transaction in the whole book can be accepted as a fair representation of English life. The most favourable account which can be given of it is that it is a clever and well-constructed but violent melodrama, always trembling upon the verge of absurdity, and not unfrequently falling over it. It closely resembles the *Comte de Monte Cristo* or the *Trois Mousquetaires*,[6] and it would be just as absurd to draw general conclusions about the French character from the sayings and doings of Dantès, or Athos, Porthos, and Aramis, as to attach any importance to the proceedings of the many heroes of *It's Never too late to Mend*.

It is, however, upon this foundation that the criticisms of the writer in the *Revue des Deux Mondes* principally repose, though their relation to them is rather that of a sermon to a text than that of a verdict to evidence. For example, Mr. Reade makes George Fielding, the farmer, emigrate to Australia with Mr. Winchester the young squire, because

---

    [4] The children other than the oldest child.
    [5] A rule of law as to future interests in property, from Shelley's Case (1581), preserved with the support of Charles Fearne (1742–1794; *ODNB*, lawyer). *An Essay on the Learning of Contingent Remainders and Executory Devices* (1772). See p. 108.
    [6] 1844.

THE *REVUE DES DEUX MONDES* ON ENGLISH ROMANCE

both of them are in love, and want to make money enough to marry; and M. Dudley remarks that nothing can be more 'typical' than the way in which the young aristocrat and the farmer understand each other, or than the motive which acts upon each of them. We do not blame Mr. Reade for following the canons of his art. Of course, every one is in love in a novel, and all his actions flow from that fact. Of course, moreover, people make confidences to each other in such situations which they never make in real life. If they did not do so, how could the readers of the novel know what they were about? But it is surely the height of simplicity for a serious writer in a journal like the *Revue des Deux Mondes* to found upon such transparent literary artifices the strange conclusions to which we have referred. Can any reasonable person seriously maintain that the great bulk of the emigrants who have left this country for the colonies went there because they were in love? A large proportion of the early settlers went because they could not help it. Felony, and not love, was their ruling passion, and the Crown Courts had much more to do with their exodus than the law of primogeniture. Love is, indeed, referred to in the literature of the emigrants, but it is not in an exulting tone. The following was one of the most popular utterances of the early colonial muse:

> My curse rest on you, Justice Bailey,
> And gentlemen of the jury also,
> For transporting me from the arms of my Polly
> For twenty long years, as you know.[7]

Even when we come to what one of the Governors called with exquisite, and, let us hope, unconscious irony, 'the undetected part of the population', we shall find that they belonged, for the most part, to a class which has little to do with romance. The hundreds of thousands who left this country in 1847 and 1848 were mostly composed of starving Irishmen, who had loved not wisely, but too well[8]—as their enormous families and the potato famine[9] conclusively proved. The Emigration Office had plenty of work in those days, but it was not, either as related to England or to Ireland, of a very romantic character. Many thousands of poor men and women went to Canada, or to Australia, not in order to marry, but in order to live. The next great tide of emigration set in with the gold discoveries; and there, again, there could be no possibility of mistake as to the motive which took people abroad. It was the combined action of the thirst for excitement and the thirst for rapid and doubtful gain. There was, no doubt, a considerable sprinkling of *cadets de famille* amongst this class of emigrants, but it would be absurd to suppose that any large number of them went abroad in order to return and marry at home. In every instance it was a daring, and for educated men it was generally a rash action to go to the gold diggings, but it would in almost every case have been mere hair-brained[10] folly for such a man to go there if he meant to come back rich enough to be married. In almost every case such a step would have been equivalent to breaking off

---

[7] Later quoted in *Hist. Crim. Law*, i 172n: 'In my youth a ballad used to be sung which was said to be a genuine product of the hulks. It began "My curse rest on you, Justice Bayley..." ' The transportation of criminals was ending in the 1850s.

[8] Othello after he murders Desdemona: 'Then must you speake / Of one that lov'd not wisely, but too well' (V ii). JFS moves to 'romantic' and 'marry'.

[9] More than one and a half million immigrants from Ireland to America, 1845–55.

[10] *OED* hare-brained. The spelling hair-brained, suggesting another origin for the compound, is later, though occasional before 1600.

182   ON THE NOVEL AND JOURNALISM

an engagement, for it amounted simply to investing a man's whole property in buying a lottery-ticket at the antipodes, and going there to look after it. There is one kind of emigration which is confined to persons who may be called *cadets de famille*, and it is worth noticing that, in deciding upon it, the prospect of marriage has never in any instance any influence whatever. No one goes to India to marry. Till quite lately, the choice of the civil service as a profession had to be made at sixteen or seventeen, and the young civilian was on his way out before he was twenty.

No one, of course, either can deny, or would wish to deny, that the adoption of the principle that marriage ought to be based on mutual attachment, and not on money considerations, is a most important element in the English character, nor that it tends to enrich and fortify it; but instead of its being the basis of our national energy it is only one of its manifestations. No one would marry for money, instead of marrying for love, if he had confidence in his power of earning what money he wanted. It is the energy which causes the marriages, not the marriages which cause the energy; and both the one and the other would survive, with perfect indifference, the repeal of that wonderful 'law of primogeniture' which is in the singular position of being the palladium of all that we hold most dear, though it is not encumbered with the attribute of existence.

'Guy Livingstone' (excerpts)
(*Edinburgh Review*, October 1858)

George Alfred Lawrence (1827–1876). *Guy Livingstone* (anon., 1857; six editions by 1867). On this novel, 'muscular Christianity', 'the Muscular Novel', and Dickens, see Nicholas Shrimpton, *Dickens Quarterly* (June 2012).

Guy Livingstone (excerpts)*

'Guy Livingstone' is rather a favourable specimen of a class of books which are one of the most characteristic literary products of the present day. It is not a work of art, nor is it a novel with a moral, nor is it a satire, nor a sporting story, though it belongs in some degree to each of these subdivisions of the prolific genus of fiction. An anonymous writer thinks it well to invent a character whose works and ways, and general view of life, he puts before the world, with a sort of tacit request to be informed what the world thinks of such a personage. It is a little difficult to say what is the exact meaning and value of such a proceeding. To some extent, no doubt, the author must be taken to endorse his hero's views, for the mere fact of excogitating and publishing them to the world, gives them a currency which they would not otherwise enjoy; but we are left in the dark as to the real extent of this resemblance, and, as in photographic portraits, there is a scowl on the features which is essentially untrue. The author has always a perfect right to turn round on his reader with the assertion, that he had no intention of recommending his hero either for imitation, or even for sympathy. He may say, as Lord Byron[1] constantly did say—My 'Corsairs' and 'Giaours' do not embody my own views. I am a poet and a peer, amusing myself with literature, and caring nothing for the moral fitness of things. But in truth such pleas are merely evasive. All fictions, unless they are composed in an artistic spirit as rare as it is in many respects excellent, have a direct moral, and do, in fact, produce moral results on those who read them. To read an elaborate account of a person's life and conversation, specifying his feelings and

---

* *Guy Livingstone, or Thorough*. Second Edition. London: 1858.

---

[1] *The Corsair: A Tale* (1814); *The Giaour: A Fragment of a Turkish Tale* (1813). Byron to Thomas Moore (2 Jan. 1814): 'With regard to my story—& stories in general, I should have been glad to have rendered my personages more perfect & amiable if possible—inasmuch as I have been sometimes criticised & considered no less responsible for their deeds & qualities than if all had been personal. Be it so—if I *have* deviated into the gloomy vanity of "drawing from self" the pictures are probably like since they are unfavourable...I have no particular desire that any but my acquaintance should think the author better than the beings of his imagining' (*Byron's Letters and Journals*, ed. Leslie A.Marchand, iv, 1975, 13). To Annabella Milbanke (14 Oct. 1814): 'a long address in the M[ornin]g P[os]t to me—making me responsible for a sentiment in "the Giaour" though it is in the mouth of a fictitious character' (iv 208).

motives, is very like associating with him for a certain time; and it is hard to imagine any theory of authorship on which less responsibility attaches to the author of such a work, than that which belongs to a man who, being better acquainted than any one else with the character and conduct of another, introduces him to all his friends, and takes great trouble to make them intimate with him. If the person so introduced is a gambler, a blackleg,[2] and a bully, the introducer would be condemned for his conduct, even though he might himself be the most irreproachable of mankind. It is, perhaps, the fairest and the most convenient method of dealing with such cases, to leave the author entirely out of consideration, to accept, for the time being, the events and persons described as real, to discuss their character upon that supposition, and to leave the author to draw his own conclusions as to the degree in which he himself has been made the subject of praise or blame.

* * *

Apart from the radical defects of the character of the hero of the story, 'Guy Livingstone' contains one remarkable feature, which fits in very appropriately with the worship of strength and audacity pervading the greater part of the book. A strange undertone of melancholy runs through it. The author is always making little semi-pious reflections about his hero, which are evidently sincere, but which have a somewhat ludicrous air when they are compared with the drift of the story. It is tinged, like so many other productions in the present day, by a sort of gentle and half-repentant scepticism.

* * *

This habit is but one specimen amongst many of the inconveniences which necessarily attend novels written on the principle on which 'Guy Livingstone' is written. They, one and all, are meant to express a certain view of life in the loosest and most indefinite form. It is impossible to read such books, without seeing that the author is giving vent to a set of feelings and experiences which he has collected. All of them have a certain *blasé* air about them. They are a contrivance for enunciating idly, and without taking the trouble of definite arrangement, a set of impressions about the world which have grown up in the mind, and which do not exactly correspond with those which other people have put forward. Such views are, for the most part, crude and almost worthless, and when they are embodied in novels, they are invested with a false brilliancy, a false air of extent and profundity, and a degree of popularity totally disproportioned to their intrinsic value. For one person who has the will or the power to think, a thousand are ready to sympathise; and if a man possesses brilliancy enough to entertain, and imagination enough to interest, he may secure a vast amount of sympathy from vacant but susceptible people. It is an unmanly thing to have the sympathies moulded by such means as these, for, generally speaking, nothing can exceed the slightness and flimsiness of the doctrines thus preached, except the confidence of the preacher. They are a mere mouthful of froth. They say nothing, they prove nothing, they are nothing, but they addle a great many foolish brains, and prompt a vast deal of foolish conduct and unreasonable feeling.

[2] *OED* A turf swindler; also a swindler in other species of gambling.

'The Romance of Vice'
(*Saturday Review*, 13 November 1858)

The Romance of Vice

M. Emile Montégut[1] has published in the last number of the *Revue des Deux Mondes* a very sensible critique on *Fanny*,[2] and on the class of literature to which it belongs. What he fastens on especially is the sham poetry, and the real prosaic vulgarity, both of the vice which seeks in such books to be romantic, and of those who admire these books because they like to believe that they, too, could be at once romantic and vicious.[3] He asks his readers whether they have ever seen a gourmand of a type exclusively Parisian, who, having to spend eightpence on his dinner, will not satisfy his appetite on a good slice of roast beef, but has, at a bad *restaurant*, a dish of salmon, peas, and a *meringue*. He has an execrable dinner, but he procures himself the illusion of thinking he has had a good repast. Just so the personages in many French romances of the present day flatter themselves they have passions while they have only vices. And the success of the novel depends on its having this mixture of real vice and false sentiment. There is a considerable portion of society which likes to plate over its sensuality with a thin layer of tinsel passion. The hero of the romance and the hero of real life will like to fancy that, if they are as vicious, they are also as romantic as René.[4] Now the public which chiefly supports these books is a public entirely out of the line of romance. It is a public of ordinary thought, and occupied with very ordinary kinds of business. The supposition that the romance of René can be repeated in a society utterly unlike that in which it was written, is a pure chimera. All this is expressed with great happiness and force by M. Montégut, and we may find the point worth thinking of in England. It is true that our illusions of immorality are very different from the French type. We have got rid of cockney Don Juans.[5] But the influence of French literature on English society is very considerable; and so far as French novels do harm to persons who have any business at all to read them, they do so by throwing a tinsel plating over vice—by making the romance of vice seem a perfectly practicable arrangement, to be easily secured and enjoyed if the state of mind which gives the romance has been induced by an attentive study of the right models.

It is worth while, then, to think what the romance of vice demands—what are the qualities, mental, moral, and social, which are indispensable, if the desired halo is to be spread over the area of self-gratification. Chateaubriand is the author of the finest type

---

[1] (1825–1895), contributor to the *Revue* from 1847, becoming its chief literary critic in 1857.

[2] *Fanny* (1858, the year after *Madame Bovary*), by Ernest Feydeau (1821–1873).

[3] *OED* Of the nature of vice; contrary to moral principles.

[4] The type of the Romantic hero, from the fiction of François-René, vicomte de Chateaubriand (1768–1848), René's adventures being first published within *Le Génie du christianisme* (1802), and then separately (1805).

[5] Compacting the 'Cockney school' with which Leigh Hunt (1784–1859; *ODNB*, poet, journalist, and literary critic) was identified and John Keats (1795–1821; *ODNB*, poet) was mocked, with Byron, *Don Juan* (1819–24; *ODNB*, poet).

186   ON THE NOVEL AND JOURNALISM

of romantic vice that has been turned out; and M. Montégut terms him epigrammatically, but not untruly, *un gentilhomme breton catholique, athée et ennuyé*. At any rate, René exactly answers to this description. Now, the more we consider these epithets, the more we find ourselves removed from the field of vulgar immorality. A Catholic Atheist is a person so little akin to the ordinary thoughts of Englishmen, that many persons would be inclined to doubt the possibility of his existence. And yet no expression could better convey the belief in everything, combined with the belief in nothing, which shine through René. The Catholic Atheist has open to him some of the most exciting and thrilling sensations which can fall to the lot of man. He worships God, and yet curses Him; he feels the rapture of a wild adoration, and the despondency of a reproachful despair. There are human minds—probably not a few—through which such thoughts pass, not as eccentricities noted down for literary purposes, but as the things which, for the time, naturally and really occupy them. It is easy to understand that a person under such an influence finds a harmony in the mental contemplation of unusual crime; and, however literally absurd, there is a sort of psychological consistency in René wandering about the woods of America thinking of incest. But René is romantic, not because he thinks about vice, but because he has a certain range of thought and feeling.

If, again, we examine the real heroines of romantic vice, we see at once how different they are from the sham ones—how different, for instance, are Indiana[6] and Valentine[7] from Fanny. The difference lies in this, that in the characters of Indiana and Valentine there are elements which are unconnected with vice, and which are in themselves poetical. There is in Indiana an intensity of affection—a wild delight in the luxuriance of nature—a childlike concentration of all interest on a few objects. She is placed in a society where incidents are made to occur with tolerable probability, so as to illustrate and confirm certain views on the fundamental arrangements of social life accepted by the writer. The romantic element is the groundwork, and the vicious element is only the addition. It is not vice that is made romantic, but romance that is made vicious. It may be easy to imitate the vice, but the vice does not involve the romance—it has nothing to do with it. But it is very possible to bring to the vice the remembrance of the romance, and this is exactly what is done. It would be something if this were confessed to be a pure illusion, and if it were recognised that the romance accompanying vulgar vice under a peculiar system of training is a trick of the memory, and not a feeling really entertained, or a part of the character really existing. And we may observe that the confusion which hangs about the connexion of vice and romance is apt to distort literary and moral criticism, as well as to exercise a pernicious influence over action. When a writer of real power has thoughts that are uncommon, but genuine, and feelings that are spasmodic perhaps, and exaggerated, but the natural growth of a general state of mind, we may look at their expression as a study which is not at once to be set down as immoral because it leads us into the region of concomitant vices. But when, as in so many modern French novels, the vice is the main staple of the book, and the romance is merely thrown over it as an alluring garment, decking the rottenness and hideousness that lie beneath, we are not to extend to creations of a character substantially different the indulgence we accord to fictions where a species of misdirected nobleness is the mainspring of the drama.

Against the sham romance of vice there is no doubt that cynicism is a powerful, and, in a certain sense, the most appropriate antidote. It is, indeed, one of the two great antidotes

[6] From *Indiana* (1832), by Sand.   [7] From *Valentine* (1832), by Sand.

that literature has to offer. The creation and maintenance of a sound moral sense is not properly to be looked for in a purely secular literature. But to higher and better instruments of good, literature can add her own subsidiary aids. Cynicism is unpopular, because it is often employed to strip off the illusions from virtue; but it should be credited with the possibility of being used to strip off the illusions of vice. Cynicism does away with romance; and the romance which it does away with most swiftly and surely is the mock romance laid on to gild the vulgarity of wrong-doing. The nation and the age that in Chateaubriand produced the greatest painter of romantic vice, produced in Balzac the greatest of cynics. Under the painful touch of the withering genius of Balzac, the edifices of artificial romance crumble into nothing. He shows vice, as he shows the whole of human life, reduced to its skeleton shape. There is plenty of vice in Balzac, and he had that love of stirring up dirty puddles which seems inseparable from all but a very few French minds. But in his novels life is painted in so true a miniature—the component parts of a vicious society are so minutely analysed—the irony of fortune is so remorselessly followed out to all its consequences, that artificial romance seems not so much a failure or an imposition as an impossibility. Given a character in which desire is real but passion is absent, Balzac will show, as by a mathematical demonstration, that romance is out of the question. Cynicism may be defended on other grounds. It may be urged that virtue gains by being deprived of some of her illusions, or she would be apt to grow too sentimental. But it is only in relation to vice that the true significance and the true function of cynicism become apparent. To estimate the moral position of a writer like Balzac, we must not take him by himself. We must view him with reference to opposite writers, like George Sand or Chateaubriand, and we shall see what is the function which tales such as his are capable of discharging.

The other great literary antidote, as M. Montégut points out, is the expression of the ludicrous. A hearty laugh, if it can but be honestly raised, soon expels the poison from the mind. We are not speaking of ridicule aimed at a particular object, but of a general fund of humour, whether genial or stern—a sense of the comic, a quickness at catching the consequences of impossible data, a power of seeing the grotesque side of human waywardness and frailty. The dead-alive[8] seriousness of a bad French novel is blown into thin air by the light breath of even jovial high spirits, and much more by that of measured and discriminative laughter. 'Let us', M. Montégut says—'let us have some one to teach us what raillery is when we are overwhelmed with books like *Fanny*. If we cannot get the bold and deep laugh of Rabelais or Molière, let us be content with the ironical humour of Lesage.' Happily, in England, the race of laughers has never died away. Byronism[9] yielded rather to the fun than to the abuse it provoked. We may not otherwise have reason to be entirely satisfied with the kind of fun that shows itself so widely in the English literature of the day; but it certainly keeps us from some nonsense. If comic journalism and facetious novels have done even a little to keep us from an English counterpart of *Fanny*, let us pay them our debt of gratitude. As to the greater lights,[10] there can be no doubt that the succession of real humorists in our literature has acted as a bulwark against the invasion into English thought of the pestilent combination of mock poetry and sensualism.

---

[8] *OED* Dead while yet alive; alive but without animation; dull, inactive, spiritless. From 1591; 1840 Hood dead-alive, hypochondriacal old bachelor uncle. (JFS has 'deadly-lively' in 'Groans of the Britons', p. 68).

[9] *OED* from 1817, with 1857 *Fraser's Mag.* When Byronism was at its height, when... you could not be interesting unless you were miserable and vicious.

[10] Genesis 1:16, the greater light to rule the day, and the lesser light to rule the night.

'Sentimentalism' (excerpts)
(*Saturday Review*, 25 December 1858)

Sentimentalism (excerpts)

If we accept sentimentalism as the genuine expression of shallow feeling, we gain a means of estimating its value when it is exhibited in its highest as in its lowest forms. In the productions of modern authors, there is perhaps no better piece of sentimental writing than the description of the last days of little Paul, in *Dombey and Son*.[1] We feel at once that it does not rise above sentimentalism—the feeling that runs through it is shallow. The comparison of any really poetical description at all parallel to it—as, for example, that of Mignon, in *Wilhelm Meister*[2]– shows that we are kept throughout at a low level; and an examination of the passage in Mr. Dickens's work shows why we do not rise higher. Little Paul is represented as always haunted with the voices of the waves, and troubled by the presence of a flowing river which bears him on its current. These thoughts are, we believe, true to nature, and are such as would perplex the brain of an imaginative sickly child. They are, moreover, such as to afford available material to a real poet. But under Mr. Dickens's management they are brought completely within the range of sentimentalism, because they are repeated, dwelt on, and turned in every way, until we get the notion of a trick or cunning device in their being thus prominently worked, as we imagine, for producing an emotion of protracted pity. This harping on one or two thoughts, so as to awaken the attention to the trick by which it is done, belongs essentially to a sentimentalist. The feeling which is so explicit and so lengthy is sure to be shallow; but still it is feeling. The death of little Dombey has in it something really touching, and even poetical. The effect produced by the record of the fading away of the gentle child is one that leaves an impression on the memory. The passage might draw tears from eyes that are not accustomed to cry for nothing. It is sentimental, but its sentimentalism is of a decidedly high character.

So, too, in the greatest of all sentimental books, Sterne's *Sentimental Journey*,[3] there is genuine feeling; and this feeling displays itself most unmistakably in parts of the story where the bad side of sentimentalism is also brought out on a scale which has given the work so indifferent a reputation. The peculiarity of Sterne's book is that it exhibits a constant hovering on the edge of vice without actually approaching it, while this proximity to vice is always attained from the side of virtue. The Sentimental Traveller is the most gentle, benevolent, sweet-tempered of creatures. His affability

---

[1] ch. xvi, 'What the Waves were always saying'.

[2] *Wilhelm Meister's Apprenticeship* (1795–96), by Johann Wolfgang von Goethe (1749–1832).

[3] Laurence Sterne (1713–1768; *ODNB*), *A Sentimental Journey Through France and Italy. By Mr Yorick* (1768).

SENTIMENTALISM   189

and comprehensive charity lead him to take an interest in every one he meets, and he manages, as sentimentalists often do, to meet only those to whom he has an affinity—beggars, and old soldiers, and pretty women. For the latter class he has an endless courtesy, a patronising coquetry, and the fraction of a heart. The feeling that is so ready and so divided may well be called shallow; but there is a genuineness in it, and it is based on a perception of what is poetical and right, that distinguishes it on the whole from what it so often and so closely resembles—the prurience that seeks to heighten excitement by prolonging the preliminaries. Those who know the book will remember the scene where the *fille de chambre* visits the traveller in his hotel, and where, after some hesitation, described in Sterne's most *piquant* and objectionable manner, the traveller sends her away and locks the door.[4] This scene is enough to convince any one who reflects on it that Sterne had sounded the depths of sentimentalism. The feeling of the sentimentalist was shallow enough to lead him into the affair, but it was generous enough to get him out of it. He did not, like a man of high principle and deep feeling, abstain from expending sentiment on such an intimacy, nor, like a man of the world, did he proceed in a spirit of consistent prose. He did what both these classes of men would be apt to pronounce impossible—he stopped half-way.

If we are required to point the moral of sentimentalism, and, on Christmas-day, to rise or fall into a sermon, it is not difficult to do so. The evil of sentimentalism, more especially of sentimentalism in the higher walks of literature, is that it tempts readers to go further than the sentimentalist, and to take advantage of the shallowness of his feeling without being influenced by its genuineness. France used, not long ago, to send us shoals of sentimental novels calculated to produce this effect. Now, French romances are sunk far below sentimentalism; but the novels published a few years since by the more poetical romance writers had this great drawback—that on their shallow and prurient side they were easily appreciable, but their better side was too peculiar to the writer, or to some set of persons, to be intelligible to English readers. And of course, taken at its best, sentimentalism is a very imperfect thing. It is good that men should have shallow feelings rather than none; but shallow feelings are very dangerous guides, as Sterne has abundantly shown. No man who is sentimental, and who knows that he is sentimental, ought to rest satisfied. But to pass from sentimentalism to high feeling is a very difficult thing, and requires a serious effort, sure to be marked by numerous[5] failure; for it is a prominent tendency of sentimentalism to think things right, but not to think things wrong. The man of shallow feeling loves what is good, but he will not keep aloof from what is bad. The hatred of wrong is the great sign and triumph of deep

---

[4] Closing the chapter, 'The Conquest', after a prayer: 'As I finish'd my address, I raised the fair *fille de chambre* up by the hand, and led her out of the room—she stood by me till I lock'd the door and put the key in my pocket—*and then*—the victory being quite decisive—and not till then, I press'd my lips to her cheek, and, taking her by the hand again, led her safe to the gate of the hotel.' To be contrasted, as JFS knew but was not saying, with the close—if that is the (unpunctuated) word—of the final chapter, 'The Case of Delicacy': ¶ But the Fille de Chambre . . . had crept silently out of her closet, and it being totally dark, had stolen so close to our beds, that she had got herself into the narrow passage which separated them, and had advanc'd so far up as to be in a line betwixt her mistress and me: ¶ So that when I stretch'd out my hand, I caught hold of the Fille de Chambre's ¶ END OF VOL. II.

[5] With the singular (as here, 'numerous failure'), *OED* has numerous bliss, numerous business, and 1841 D'ISRAELI How long has existed that numerous voice which we designate as 'Public Opinion'?

feeling. How is this hatred to be excited and fostered in a breast that is a stranger to it? Perhaps it never can be brought beyond a certain point of growth, for the characters to which the hatred of wrong is natural will always be superior to those in which it is acquired. But the first great step towards the acquisition—the first stage of transition from sentimentalism to high feeling—is the conviction that bad things are bad. How that conviction is to be made permanent, strong, and fruitful, it must be left to every one to answer for himself; and Christmas-day is not, perhaps, a bad day for meditating on the subject.

'The History of British Journalism' (excerpt)
(*Saturday Review*, 29 January 1859)

The History of British Journalism (excerpts)*[1]

The combination of political and literary essay-writing with modern journalism is to some extent external and accidental. Periodical publication, though it is convenient both to authors and to their readers, is not essential to criticism, nor are leading articles necessarily inseparable from the news which forms their principal subject. Nevertheless it is of the utmost importance that the comments of journalists should be checked by the fullest information as to all public transactions, and especially by the accurate reports which do so much credit to English newspapers. The danger of a cheap press consists less in the circulation of erroneous opinions than in the deterioration of the machinery by which intelligence is collected from all parts of the world. If the daily papers of London should become unable to employ competent correspondents abroad and educated reporters at home, future historians of British journalism will have the melancholy task of recording its degeneracy and decline. The great super-structure of popular information rests on the narrow basis of three or four high-priced daily papers, which, for the most part, have little share in the vast circulation of the journals which they gratuitously supply with matter. There is reason to believe that only one of the original daily newspapers is largely profitable; and the decease of its few remaining rivals would leave no security for the maintenance of the present standard of journalism except the enterprise and patriotic spirit of the proprietors of the *Times*. Mr. Andrews suggestively remarks that among the cheap papers which have attained the largest circulation 'there does not occur the name of one leading paper'. It may be gratifying to find that the calmest of these journals are also the most popular, but the wide diffusion of harmless entertainment and superficial instruction will offer but a miserable substitute for the higher functions of the English press. 'The list of our public journals', says their enthusiastic chronicler, 'is a proud and noble list—the roll of an army of liberty', &c.—a police—a sentinel with watchfires which 'form a chain of communication with freedom wherever it exists'. 'For good or for evil the Press must go on now—no power on earth can arrest it.' Unfortunately, the power which is enthroned in Basinghall-street[1] will suffice to arrest any enterprise that does not pay; and in France an eloquent press has been effectually arrested by the simple application of superior force. The Assembly elected by universal suffrage made anonymous journalism

---

* *The History of British Journalism, from the Foundation of the Newspaper Press in England to the Repeal of the Stamp Act in 1855. With Sketches of Press Celebrities.* By Alexander Andrews, Author of 'The Eighteenth Century' (London: Bentley, 1858).

[1] Guildhall, the administrative centre of the City of London.

illegal—the President elected by universal suffrage annihilated the remaining liberties of the press. The demagogues who are at present attempting the overthrow of the English Constitution have repeatedly denounced the writers of newspapers with the fiercest intolerance. The influence of the press will perhaps be the most trustworthy safeguard of freedom as long as the principal journals maintain their present character; but an institution which stands alone in the world may not be exempt in England from the causes which have deprived it of freedom on the Continent and of dignity in America.

'The Minister's Wooing' (excerpts)
(*Saturday Review*, 22 October 1859)

Collected in *Essays*. Harriet Beecher Stowe's *The Minister's Wooing* was serialized in the *Atlantic Monthly*, Dec. 1858–Dec. 1859, then published first in England and then in the USA (1859). JFS: 'There never was an age in which there was so much novel writing, and so much theological speculation, as there is in our own' (on 'The Enigma', by 'An Old Chronicler', *Sat. Rev.*, 30 Aug. 1856; p. 59).

The Minister's Wooing (excerpts)

The special gift which appears to belong to particular writers of obtaining for their works what the French call a 'mad success'[1] is not a high one. The books which are read in every family and sold on every book-stall, which furnish popular platform speakers with half their arguments and all their illustrations, and which convert the author or authoress into the lion of the season, have seldom much substance; or, if they have, it is not to their substance, but to their popular defects that the rage for them is owing. The reason of this probably is, that the region of the mind to which such books address themselves is that which lies uppermost, and which has least permanence about it. In such cases, thousands of amiable and communicative people are ready to say, 'my own sentiments better expressed'; and as they like to get an excuse for talking about their sentiments, they find one in praising the book and the authors by whose means their wish has been humoured. It is not, however, by standing on the same level with the rest of mankind, and repeating their transient commonplaces in a piquant style that works of permanent importance are written. An author who looks beyond money and popularity must be, to some extent, in advance of his neighbours. Indeed, he is inexcusable if he is not, for it is his business to think, and theirs to act; so that, if his thoughts are not better worth having than theirs, he must be incapable of thinking to any purpose. A real work of art is not to be understood at a moment's notice. It will grow upon the world and educate the minds of the public at large to appreciate its beauty, and will thus have a sounder and more lasting popularity a few years after its production than it had at first.

For these reasons little sympathy was due to the extravagant admiration which *Uncle Tom's Cabin* excited here and in America; nor need any one be surprised at the fact that its popularity, like that of any other party pamphlet, has been as short-lived as it was

---

[1] Rather, what the French call a *succès fou*. *OED* A success marked by wild enthusiasm. First citation 1878. As against a *succès d'estime*, a critical rather than a popular or commercial success.

ON THE NOVEL AND JOURNALISM

extensive. The goodness and vice which ran down in unctuous streams from Uncle Tom, Eva, and Legree, were enough to make any one revolt against the book; and the same result was produced even more strongly by the egregious and scandalous injustice which always attends the *argumentum ad misericordiam*. The fact that Mrs. Stowe could describe the flogging to death of an old black in an affecting manner proved nothing whatever as to the general character and results of slavery. Mr. Olmsted's Travels[2] were as much superior to *Uncle Tom* in real importance, as evidence upon the subject of slavery, as they were inferior in accidental importance.

* * *

Mrs. Stowe occasionally appears to be struck with the reflection that she has chosen a strange subject for a novel, and she apologizes for it by saying that she could not have drawn a picture of New England as it was without giving theology its due prominence. The conclusion appears to be that she should have held her peace altogether. There really are some subjects which are too solemn for novelists, strange as such an opinion may appear. Of the many gross outrages on decency which have been perpetrated by French writers, none was so gross as the adaptation of the history of the Crucifixion[3] to the exigencies of the feuilleton.[4] But though there is, of course, an infinite difference in degree, and probably hardly less difference in execution, the principle of the *Minister's Wooing* is precisely the same. To some persons, Dr. Hopkins's[5] opinions may probably appear to be eternal truth; to others, they may appear—as a much less energetic version of them appeared to Wesley[6]—'blasphemy to make the ears of a Christian to tingle', and a justification for a call to the devils to rejoice, and to death and hell to triumph. Mrs. Stowe appears, to judge from her book, to incline to the former view. It is, indeed, true that, with that shuffling timidity which is the characteristic vice of novelists, she does not commit herself to anything, but talks about it and about it[7]—putting Dr. Hopkins and his views in all sorts of positions, looking at them under every possible aspect, contrasting them with the activity of one person, the apathy of another, and the commonplace vulgarity of a third, with that effectiveness which any one may obtain who

---

[2] Frederick Law Olmsted (1822–1903), whose dispatches to the *New York Daily Times* had been collected as *A Journey in the Seaboard Slave States* (1856), and *A Journey Through Texas* (1857). JFS: 'As an argument against slavery, his book seems to us worthy any number of *Uncle Tom's Cabins*; for he writes upon the subject without noise or passion, and contents himself with stating in a simple manner what he has observed, and what conclusions he has founded upon his observations' ('Olmsted's Texas', *Sat. Rev.*, 21 Feb. 1857).

[3] Evariste de Parny (1753–1814). *La Guerre des Dieux* (1799; banned, 1827), a blasphemous mock-epic which has a crucifixion scene In *Madame Bovary*, 'Old Bovary replied with a quotation' from it, calculated to offend the priest (Part 2, ch. iii).

[4] *OED* In French newspapers, a portion of one or more pages (at the bottom) marked off from the rest of the page by a rule, and appropriated to light literature, criticism, etc. 1845 *Athenaeum* The tendency of the newspaper feuilleton, in France, to absorb the entire literature of the day. JFS: 'Scenes of professional robbers talking argot are introduced which read just like bits of the *Mystères de Paris* or *Les Misérables*. In a word, the book is the natural product of an age of *feuilletons*.' (*Mémoires des Sanson: Sept Générations d'Exécuteurs*; *Sat. Rev.*, 7 Nov. 1863.) Seven generations: 'The office passed during the whole of this time [159 years] from father to son, and went out of the family at last chiefly because the present author had only daughters.'

[5] In the novel, the eighteemth century preacher, a disciple of Jonathan Edwards.

[6] John Wesley (1703–1791; *ODNB*, Church of England clergyman and a founder of Methodism).

[7] Pope, to the Goddess Dulness: 'For thee explain a thing till all men doubt it, / And write about it, Goddess, and about it' (*The Dunciad* iv 251–2).

does not shrink from peeping and botanizing upon their fathers' graves.[8] Whatever may have been the true value of the works of Jonathan Edwards[9] and Dr. Hopkins, a religious novelist owed them more respect than Mrs. Stowe has shown. The themes on which they wrote were far too awful for a novelist. The only question about them which can interest any rational creature is, whether they are true or false. The only circumstance respecting them on which a novel can throw any light is their relation to common life.

Now, every one admits that the average tone and temper of every-day existence is not our ultimate rule—that if theology is worth anything at all, it must form the rule and guide of our daily lives, instead of being guided by them; and, therefore, a novel which (as all novels must) takes daily life as its standing ground, and shows how it is related to theology, has no tendency whatever to show the truth or falsehood of the theological doctrines which it describes. In so far as Mrs. Stowe's book can be said to have any moral at all, it is that we ought to keep our minds in a sort of hazy devotional warmth, and hope for the best, and that any consistent or explicit theological belief upon the great topics which form the basis of theology is self-condemned. The semi-conscious approach to a cross between a sentiment and an opinion which appears to form the premiss of the book, is that no theological opinions are true which are either un-Calvinistical or very unpleasant; and that, as most Calvinistical doctrines are extremely unpleasant, and involve the damnation of a great many agreeable people, the mind ought to be kept floating in a sort of tincture of Calvinism which, if it ever were reduced to definite statements of any kind, might perhaps turn out not to be as bad as might be expected.

This is as near an approach to a moral as Mrs. Stowe's book will yield. It would be rash to offer it with confidence, or to contend that she is any way committed to the proposition (if it is one). Such as it is, however, it furnishes an admirable illustration of the truth of the assertion that novels on serious subjects are the curse of serious thought. The difficulty of serious reflection upon any subject, and especially on theological subjects, is incalculably increased by those who overlay the essential parts of the question with a mass of irrelevant matter, which can have no other effect than to prejudice the feelings in one direction or another. If there is ground to believe that agreeable people really will be damned, the probability or improbability of that opinion will not be affected in the remotest degree by setting before the world minute pictures of these agreeable people, and by asking pathetically whether it is really meant that such a fate can overtake men and women who laugh and joke, and eat their dinners, and make love, and enjoy themselves like all the rest of the world. Of course, no one doubts that, if it is true, it is a great pity. The one question which reasonable people can ask with any interest is whether it is true. Temporal punishments are often remarked upon in the same style. M. Hugo, for example, in the *Dernier Jour d'un Condamné*,[10] counted out the minutes of a man who was to be guillotined, and described in endless detail every separate sensation attending that condition. The inference suggested (of course, it was not drawn) was that society did not know what it meant by condemning a man to death;

---

[8] Wordsworth, 'A Poet's Epitaph': 'A fingering slave, / One that would peep and botanize / Upon his mother's grave'.

[9] (1703–1758), theologian, preacher in Massachusetts.

[10] Victor-Marie Hugo (1802–1885). *Le Dernier Jour d'un condamné à mort* (1829).

and that, if it did know, capital punishments would be abolished. The true inference was altogether the other way. People knew in general that it was very unpleasant to be guillotined, and they meant it to be so. The particular items which made up the total were quite immaterial, and M. Hugo's book was accordingly as much beside the mark at which he aimed as Mrs. Stowe's book is beside any mark whatever of a doctrinal kind.

It may be urged that the *Minister's Wooing* is merely a picture of a state of society, and that the authoress was not bound to do more than to paint it truly. But this is false in fact; for it is full of such vague hints at argument as have just been described.[11] And, besides this, the argument is bad in principle, for the book undoubtedly does produce an impression very unfavourable to Calvinism; and though that system is one which is open to observation it ought not to be attacked upon irrelevant grounds. Any one who describes things heartily and vividly takes up, for the time, the position described. By giving all the details of the eating and drinking, marrying and giving in marriage, which was going on in New England notwithstanding Dr. Hopkins and his Disinterested Benevolence—by throwing what she has to say into the form of a novel, and by winding up the story with a happy marriage—Mrs. Stowe virtually adopts the cheerful view of life, and rejects the awful one; and the only approach to a justification for this which the book contains is that the awful view is unpleasant. It is impossible not to resent this. Whatever may be asserted to the contrary, the fundamental beliefs upon which all human conduct proceeds do not depend upon inclination, but on conviction; and there is hardly any more urgent necessity for men or nations than that those fundamental convictions should rest upon grounds which, if they do not exclude doubt, at any rate show what is doubtful and what is not—what is light and what is darkness. Whether there is a God—whether we can argue respecting his character from any data except those which revelation supplies—whether there is any revelation at all, and if so, what are its limits, and what its interpretation—are the overwhelming questions on which hangs all human life. To these Dr. Hopkins and Jonathan Edwards gave one set of answers. Others would give very different ones, but it is by those only who can discuss these subjects upon those terms that either Calvinism or any other creed whatever can be properly criticised. To make any step towards the discovery of the truth upon these matters is the most important, as it is the most awful, enterprise which any man can propose to himself; and it is impossible not to feel a strong sense of indignation against those who nibble at such questions, gossip about them, and, as far as their influence extends, try to substitute for the adamantine foundations on which any genuine faith must rest the mere shifting sand and mud of personal sentiment and inclination.

* * *

The gospel of vagueness and sentiment has obtained a miserable currency in these times. We think that the sea will never come, the waves never beat, the floods never rage again, and we accordingly build our houses on the sand. This is a great evil; for even if it be true that society is so firmly organized that we have got to the end of those trials which search the heart and reins—if we have secured for ourselves and our heirs for

---

[11] 'Montaigne's answers to the two objections...appear to prove, when put together, that it is right to argue on religious matters, but wrong to require good arguments' ('Montaigne's Essays', *Sat. Rev.*, 3 Nov. 1866; *Hor. Sab.* iii 133).

ever that fair chance of being comfortable, provided we are industrious, which may be roughly taken as the meaning of the phrases 'civilization' and 'social progress'—it is still not the less important that our mental foundations should be firmly settled. We have still got to live, to marry, to educate children, to discharge some duty in life, and, after all, to die,[12] and go we know not where;[13] and there is something infinitely contemptible in doing all this in a blind, helpless, drifting way, with nothing to guide us but a strange hash of inclinations and traditions. If any spectacle can be sadder than this, it is that of clever, ingenious people who pass their lives in gossiping about the great principles in which their forefathers really did believe, and by believing in which they purchased for their children the inestimable privilege of being able, without conscious inconvenience, to do without any principles at all, and to pass their time in prattling over incongruities between their practice and the small remnant of their theories. The *Great Eastern*,[14] or some of her successors, will perhaps defy the roll of the Atlantic, and cross the seas without allowing their passengers to feel that they have left the firm land. The voyage from the cradle to the grave may come to be performed with similar felicity. Progress and science may, perhaps, enable untold millions to live and die without a care, without a pang, without an anxiety. They will have a pleasant passage, and plenty of brilliant conversation. They will wonder that men ever believed at all in clanging fights, and blazing towns, and sinking ships, and praying hands;[15] and, when they come to the end of their course, they will go their way, and the place thereof will know them no more.[16] But it seems unlikely that they will have such a knowledge of the great ocean on which they sail, with its storms and wrecks, its currents and icebergs, its huge waves and mighty winds, as those who battled with it for years together in the little craft, which, if they had few other merits, brought those who navigated them full into the presence of time and eternity, their Maker and themselves, and forced them to have some definite views of their relations to them and to each other.

[12] 'To educate children...and, after all, to die...their forefathers...their children': JFS's father had died the previous month, 14 Sept. 1859.

[13] *Measure for Measure*, III i: 'Ay, but to die, and go we know not where' (Claudio speaking as *un condamné à mort*).

[14] The iron steamship designed by Brunel, when launched the largest ship ever built. The maiden voyage took place in Sept. 1859, two months before JFS's evocation of her and of 'sinking ships'; he will have known that several men had been killed in an explosion as she then entered the English Channel.

[15] Tennyson, *The Lotos-Eaters* 161 (read, 'flaming towns'). Animating the whole of JFS's conclusion is Tennyson's passage on the Gods (from Lucretius): 'For they lie beside their nectar, and the bolts are hurled / Far below them in the valleys, and the clouds are lightly curled / Round their golden houses, girdled with the gleaming world: / Where they smile in secret, looking over wasted lands, / Blight and famine, plague and earthquake, roaring deeps and fiery sands, / Clanging fights, and flaming towns, and sinking ships, and praying hands. / But they smile...'

[16] Job 5:10, He shall return no more to his house, neither shall his place know him any more. (Given Tennyson within JFS's sentence, Job was perhaps further prompted by 'The Two Voices' 264: 'The place he knew forgetteth him.')

'A Tale of Two Cities'
(*Saturday Review*, 17 December 1859)

In 1856, JFS had written: 'There is a never failing interest in everything which throws light on the French Revolution—it seems as if we could never learn too much of the great event of modern times' ('Beaumarchais and His Times', *Sat. Rev.*, 23 Feb. 1856). For JFS, *A Tale of Two Cities* threw not light but darkness, and from it he could not learn much if anything. But his own interest in the French Revolution was never-failing, as is clear from what he was to write in 1863, 1864, and 1865. 1863: of 'the four centuries' prior to Gibbon in the eighteenth century: 'In order to understand the force of the appeal which Christianity made to men's feelings and understandings in those days, we must combine with the influences which it exercises at present something of that indignation against a whole world lying in wickedness, which gave so vehement an impulse and so strange a charm to the French Revolution' ('Gibbon', *Sat. Rev.*, 30 May 1863; *Hor. Sab.* ii 397). 'The French Revolution gave an extraordinary impulse to what may be called sympathetic literature. Ever since it fairly took hold, not merely of the understanding, but of the imagination of the world at large, a wonderful power of comprehending the questions which interested past times, and a strong propensity to pry into those which will interest our descendants, have been observable' ('Precursors', *Sat. Rev.*, 20 June 1863). 1864: 'The humour which M. Taine appears to consider as an incidental, occasional talent, is in reality one of his [Carlyle's] great qualifications for historical inquiry. The great merit of humour is that it usually means much more than it says. The mere turn of a phrase enables a man possessed of this gift to give a colour to a whole series of transactions, and thus to hint a meaning which it would many pages of explanation to assign specifically. This is the characteristic peculiarity of the History of the French Revolution which so much shocks and scandalises Mr. Taine. What he views as mere tricks and charades are a set of devices which enable the author to point out easily and transiently the slightly absurd character of the whole proceeding. The delicate flavour of contempt which pervades the whole book is that ingredient which delights almost all Englishmen, and which Frenchmen appear incapable of understanding, whether they themselves or others are its objects' ('A French View of Mr. Carlyle', *Sat. Rev.*, 4 June 1864). 1865, on Tocqueville: 'The chapters on the French Revolution have the great and almost unique merit, so far at least as our experience of histories of that event goes, of being written by a man who had had the patience to study with minute care the whole mechanism of the old Government and who had the fairness to do so with an impression on him that it had principles and a meaning, and was not a mere heap of corruption. A very large proportion of the writers who have handled this subject treat the old Constitution of France as if it had been a mere mass of rottenness, so fundamentally bad that it both invited and rendered necessary total and immediate destruction. There is nothing of this in De Tocqueville's view of the matter' ('De Tocqueville's Historical Fragments', *Sat. Rev.*, 22 July 1865).

A Tale of Two Cities*

There are few more touching books in their way than the last of the *Waverley Novels*. The readers of *Castle Dangerous* and *Count Robert of Paris*[1] can hardly fail to see in those dreary pages the reflection of a proud and honourable man redeeming what he looked upon as his honour at the expense of his genius. Sir Walter Scott's desperate efforts to pay his debts by extracting the very last ounce of metal from a mine which had long been substantially worked out, deserve the respect and enlist the sympathy which is the due of high spirit and unflinching courage. The novels, to be sure, are as bad as bad can be; but to pay debts is a higher duty than to write good novels, and as monuments of what can be done in that direction by a determined man, they are not without their interest and value. They have, moreover, the negative value of being only bad. They are not offensive or insulting. The usual strong men, the usual terrific combats, and the usual upholstery are brought upon the stage. They are no doubt greatly the worse for wear; but if they were good of their kind, there would be nothing to complain of. The soup is cold, the mutton raw, and the fowls tough; but there are soup, mutton, and fowls for dinner, not puppy pie and stewed cat.

In the *Tale of Two Cities*,[2] Mr. Dickens has reached the *Castle Dangerous* stage without Sir Walter Scott's excuse; and instead of wholesome food ill-dressed, he has put before his readers dishes of which the quality is not disguised by the cooking. About a year ago, he thought proper to break up an old and to establish a new periodical,[3] upon grounds which, if the statement—and, as far as we are aware, the uncontradicted statement—of Messrs. Bradbury and Evans is true, were most discreditable to his character for good feeling, and we might almost say for common decency, and in order to extend the circulation of the new periodical he published in it the story which now lies before us. It has the merit of being much shorter[4] than its predecessors, and the consequence is, that the satisfaction which both the author and his readers must feel at its conclusion was deferred for a considerably less period than usual. It is a most curious production, whether it is considered in a literary, in a moral, or in an historical point of view. If it had not borne Mr. Dickens's name, it would in all probability have hardly met with a single reader; and if it has any popularity at all, it must derive it from the circumstance that it stands in the same relation to his other books as a salad dressing stands in towards a complete salad. It is a bottle of the sauce in which *Pickwick* and *Nicholas Nickleby* were dressed, and to which they owed much of their popularity; and though it has stood open on the sideboard for a very long time, and has lost a good deal of its

---

* *A Tale of Two Cities*. By Charles Dickens. With Illustrations by H. K. Browne. London: Chapman and Hall. 1859.

[1] In *Tales of My Landlord*, 4th ser. (1832).
[2] *A Tale of Two Cities* (Nov. 1859; serialized in *All the Year Round*, Apr.–Nov. 1859, also as seven monthly parts, June–Dec. 1859).
[3] *Household Words* (weekly, 30 March 1850–28 May 1859), published by Bradbury & Evans; then *All the Year Round* (weekly, 30 Apr. 1859 till 1870 under Dickens's editorship), published by Chapman & Hall.
[4] In the Oxford Illustrated Dickens, 358 pages.

200   ON THE NOVEL AND JOURNALISM

original flavour, the philosophic inquirer who is willing to go through the penance of tasting it will be, to a certain extent, repaid. He will have an opportunity of studying in its elements a system of cookery which procured for its ingenious inventor unparalleled popularity, and enabled him to infect the literature of his country with a disease which manifests itself in such repulsive symptoms that it has gone far to invert the familiar doctrines of the Latin Grammar about ingenuous arts,[5] and to substitute for them the conviction that the principal results of a persistent devotion to literature are an incurable vulgarity of mind and of taste, and intolerable arrogance of temper.

As, notwithstanding the popularity of its author, it might be an error to assume that our readers are at all acquainted with the *Tale of Two Cities*, it may be desirable to mention shortly the points of the story. The Two Cities are London and Paris. A French physician, who has just been released after passing many years in the Bastille, is brought over to England, where he lives with his pretty daughter. Five years elapse, and the doctor and his daughter appear as witnesses on the trial for treason of a young Frenchman, who is suspected of being a French spy, and acquitted. A year or two more elapses, and the doctor's daughter marries the acquitted man, refusing two barristers, one of whom had defended him, whilst the other was devil[6] to the first. Then ten years elapse, and as the Revolution is in full bloom in Paris, all the characters go over there on various excuses. The Frenchman turns out to be a noble who had given up his estate because he was conscience-stricken at the misery of the population around him, and thought he had better live by his wits in London than have the responsibility of continuing to be a landowner in France. He gets into prison, and is in great danger of losing his head, but his father-in-law, on the strength of his Bastille reputation, gets him off. He is, however, arrested a second time, and turns out to be the son of the infamous Marquis who had put the father-in-law into the Bastille for being shocked at his having murdered a serf. On this discovery he is condemned to death, and his wife goes through the usual business—'If I might embrace him once', 'My husband—No! A moment', 'Dear darling of my soul',[7] and so forth. Next day, before the time fixed for his execution, the rejected barrister—the devil, not the counsel for the prisoner—gets into the prison, changes clothes with the husband, stupifies him with something in the nature of chloroform, gets him passed out of the prison by a confederate before he revives, and is guillotined in his place.

Such is the story, and it would perhaps be hard to imagine a clumsier or more disjointed framework for the display of the tawdry wares which form Mr. Dickens's stock-in-trade. The broken-backed way in which the story maunders along from 1775 to 1792 and back again to 1760 or thereabouts, is an excellent instance of the complete disregard of the rules of literary composition which have marked the whole of Mr. Dickens's career as an author. No portion of his popularity is due to intellectual excellence. The higher pleasures which novels are capable of giving are those which are derived from the development of a skilfully constructed plot, or the careful and moderate delineation

---

[5] *OED* Befitting a freeborn person. From 1611, ingenuous education; 1648 F. JUNIUS all kinde of ingenuous arts did flourish. Also ingenuously: With the education or culture befitting an honourable station. (With 1674 Those that are most ingenuously educated in Arts and Letters.)

[6] *OED* A junior legal counsel who does professional work for his leader, usually without fee. With 1849 LORD CAMPBELL *Lives Chief Justices* opinions—which were perhaps written by devils or deputies.

[7] Book the Third, ch. xi. (JFS is not punctilious as to Dickens's punctuation and sequence.)

A TALE OF TWO CITIES

201

of character; and neither of these are to be found in Mr. Dickens's works, nor has his influence over his contemporaries had the slightest tendency to promote the cultivation by others of the qualities which produce them. The two main sources of his popularity are his power of working upon the feelings by the coarsest stimulants, and his power of setting common occurrences in a grotesque and unexpected light. In his earlier works, the skill and vigour with which these operations were performed were so remarkable as to make it difficult to analyse the precise means by which the effect was produced on the mind of the reader. Now that familiarity has deprived his books of the gloss and freshness which they formerly possessed, the mechanism is laid bare; and the fact that the means by which the effect is produced are really mechanical has become painfully apparent. It would not, indeed, be matter of much difficulty to frame from such a book as the *Tale of Two Cities* regular recipes for grotesque and pathetic writing, by which any required quantity of the article might be produced with infallible certainty. The production of pathos is the simpler operation of the two. With a little practice and a good deal of determination, it would really be as easy to harrow up people's feelings as to poke the fire. The whole art is to take a melancholy subject, and rub the reader's nose in it, and this does not require any particular amount either of skill or knowledge. Every one knows, for example, that death is a solemn and affecting thing. If, therefore, it is wished to make a pathetic impression on the reader, the proper course is to introduce a death-bed scene, and to rivet attention to it by specifying all its details. Almost any subject will do, because the pathetic power of the scene lies in the fact of the death; and the artifice employed consists simply in enabling the notion of death to be reiterated at short intervals by introducing a variety of irrelevant trifles which suspend attention for the moment, and allow it after an interval to revert to death with the additional impulse derived from the momentary contrast. The process of doing this to almost any conceivable extent is so simple that it becomes, with practice, almost mechanical. To describe the light and shade of the room in which the body lies, the state of the bed-clothes, the conversation of the servants, the sound of the undertaker's footsteps, the noise of driving the coffin-screws, and any number of other minutiae, is in effect a device for working on the feelings by repeating at intervals, Death—death—death—death—death, just as feeling of another class might be worked upon by continually calling a man a liar or a thief. It is an old remark, that if dirt enough is thrown some of it will stick; and Mr. Dickens's career shows that the same is true of pathos.

To be grotesque is a rather more difficult trick than to be pathetic; but it is just as much a trick, capable of being learned and performed almost mechanically. One principal element of grotesqueness is unexpected incongruity; and inasmuch as most things are different from most other things, there is in nature a supply of this element of grotesqueness which is absolutely inexhaustible. Whenever Mr. Dickens writes a novel, he makes two or three comic characters just as he might cut a pig out of a piece of orange-peel. In the present story there are two comic characters, one of whom is amusing by reason of the facts that his name is Jerry Cruncher, that his hair sticks out like iron spikes, and that, having reproached his wife for 'flopping down on her knees' to pray, he goes on for seventeen years speaking of praying as 'flopping'. If, instead of saying that his hair was like iron spikes, Mr. Dickens had said that his ears were like mutton-chops, or his nose like a Bologna sausage, the effect would have been much the same. One of his former characters[8] was identified by a habit of staring at things and people with his teeth, and another[9] by a propensity to draw his moustache up under his nose, and his nose down over his moustache. As there are many members in one body, Mr. Dickens may possibly live long enough to have a character for each of them, so that he may have one character identified by his eyebrows, another by his nostrils, and another by his toe-nails. No popularity can disguise the fact that this is the very lowest of low styles of art. It is a step below Cato's full wig and lacquered chair which shook the pit and made the gallery stare,[10] and in point of artistic merit stands on precisely the same level with the deformities which inspire the pencils of the prolific artists who supply valentines to the million at a penny a-piece.

One special piece of grotesqueness introduced by Mr. Dickens into his present tale is very curious. A good deal of the story relates to France, and many of the characters are French. Mr. Dickens accordingly makes them talk a language which, for a few sentences, is amusing enough, but which becomes intolerably tiresome and affected when it is spread over scores of pages. He translates every French word by its exact English equivalent. For example, 'Voilà votre passeport' becomes 'Behold your passport'—'Je viens de voir', 'I come to see', &c. Apart from the bad taste of this, it shows a perfect ignorance of the nature and principles of language. The sort of person who would say in English, 'Behold', is not the sort of person who would say in French 'Voilà'; and to describe the most terrible events in this misbegotten jargon shows a great want of sensibility to the real requirements of art. If an acquaintance with Latin were made the excuse for a similar display, Mr. Dickens and his disciples would undoubtedly consider such conduct as inexcusable pedantry. To show off familiarity with a modern language is not very different from similar conduct with respect to an ancient one.

The moral tone of the *Tale of Two Cities* is not more wholesome than that of its predecessors, nor does it display any nearer approach to a solid knowledge of the subject-matter to which it refers. Mr. Dickens observes in his preface—'It has been one of my hopes to add something to the popular and picturesque means of understanding that terrible time, though no one can hope to add anything to the philosophy of Mr. Carlyle's wonderful book.'[11] The allusion to Mr. Carlyle confirms the presumption which the book itself raises, that Mr. Dickens happened to have read the History of the French Revolution,[12] and, being on the look-out for a subject, determined off-hand to write a novel about it. Whether he has any other knowledge of the subject than a single reading of Mr. Carlyle's work would supply does not appear, but certainly what he has written shows no more. It is exactly the sort of story which a man would write who had taken down Mr. Carlyle's theory without any sort of inquiry or examination, but with a comfortable conviction that 'nothing could be added to its philosophy'.[13] The people, says

---

[8] MR. JAMES CARKER, confidential clerk and manager in the firm of Dombey and Son.

[9] *Little Dorrit*, ch. i: 'When Monsieur Rigaud laughed, a change took place in his face, that was more remarkable than prepossessing. His moustache went up under his nose, and his nose came down over his moustache, in a very sinister and cruel manner.'

[10] Pope, *Imitations of Horace*, Ep. II i 336–7: ' "What shook the stage, and made the people stare?" / Cato's long Wig, flowr'd gown, and lacquer'd chair.'

[11] The preceding sentence of the Preface: 'Whenever any reference (however slight) is made here to the condition of the French people before or during the Revolution, it is truly made, on the faith of trustworthy witnesses.'

[12] 1837.   [13] Not an exact quotation, despite JFS's quotation marks.

A TALE OF TWO CITIES 203

Mr. Dickens, in effect, had been degraded by long and gross misgovernment, and acted like wild beasts in consequence. There is, no doubt, a great deal of truth in this view of the matter, but it is such very elementary truth that, unless a man had something new to say about it, it is hardly worth mentioning; and Mr. Dickens supports it by specific assertions which, if not absolutely false, are at any rate so selected as to convey an entirely false impression. It is a shameful thing for a popular writer to exaggerate the faults of the French aristocracy in a book which will naturally find its way to readers who know very little of the subject except what he chooses to tell them; but it is impossible not to feel that the melodramatic story which Mr. Dickens tells about the wicked Marquis who violates one of his serfs and murders another, is a grossly unfair representation of the state of society in France in the middle of the eighteenth century. That the French *noblesse* had much to answer for in a thousand ways, is a lamentable truth; but it is by no means true that they could rob, murder, and ravish with impunity. When Count Horn[14] thought proper to try the experiment under the Regency,[15] he was broken on the wheel, notwithstanding his nobility; and the sort of atrocities which Mr. Dickens depicts as characteristic of the eighteenth century were neither safe nor common in the fourteenth.

England as well as France comes in for Mr. Dickens's favours. He takes a sort of pleasure, which appears to us insolent and unbecoming in the extreme, in drawing the attention of his readers exclusively to the bad and weak points in the history and character of their immediate ancestors. The grandfathers of the present generation were, according to him, a sort of savages, or very little better. They were cruel, bigoted, unjust, ill-governed, oppressed, and neglected in every possible way. The childish delight with which Mr. Dickens acts Jack Horner, and says What a good boy am I, in comparison with my benighted ancestors, is thoroughly contemptible. England some ninety years back was not what it now is, but it was a very remarkable country. It was inhabited and passionately loved by some of the greatest men who were then living, and it possessed institutions which, with many imperfections, were by far the best which then existed in the world, and were, amongst other things, the sources from which our present liberties are derived. There certainly were a large number of abuses, but Mr. Dickens is not content with representing them fairly. He grossly exaggerates their evils. It is usually difficult to bring a novelist precisely to book, and Mr. Dickens is especially addicted to the cultivation of a judicious vagueness; but in his present work he affords an opportunity for instituting a comparison between the facts on which he relies, and the assertions which he makes on the strength of them. In the early part of his novel he introduces the trial of a man who is accused of being a French spy, and does his best to show how utterly corrupt and unfair everybody was who took part in the proceedings. The counsel for the Crown is made to praise the Government spy, who is the principal witness, as a man of exalted virtue, and is said to address himself with zeal to the task of driving the nails into the prisoner's coffin. In examining the witnesses he makes every sort of unfair suggestion which can prejudice the prisoner, and the judge shows great reluctance to allow any circumstance to come out which would be favourable to him, and

---

[14] Antoine Joseph Horn (1698–1720), Austrian officer, from the nobility (ordinarily entitled to be beheaded).

[15] Philip d'Orléans (nephew of Louis XIV), Prince Regent (1715–1723) because Louis XV was still a minor.

does all in his power to get him hung, though the evidence against him is weak in the extreme. It so happens that in the State Trials for the very year (1780) in which the scene of Mr. Dickens's story is laid, there is a full report of the trial of a French spy—one De la Motte—for the very crime which is imputed to Mr. Dickens's hero. One of the principal witnesses in this case was an accomplice of very bad character; and in fact it is difficult to doubt that the one trial is merely a fictitious 'rendering' of the other. The comparison between them is both curious and instructive. It would be perfectly impossible to imagine a fairer trial than De la Motte's, or stronger evidence than that on which he was convicted. The counsel for the Crown said not one word about the character of the approver,[16] and so far was the judge from pressing hard on the prisoner, that he excluded evidence offered against him which in almost any other country would have been all but conclusive against him. It is surely a very disgraceful thing to represent such a transaction as an attempt to commit a judicial murder.[17]

We must say one word in conclusion as to the illustrations. They are thoroughly worthy of the text. It is impossible to imagine faces and figures more utterly unreal, or more wretchedly conventional, than those by which Mr. Browne[18] represents Mr. Dickens's characters. The handsome faces are caricatures, and the ugly ones are like nothing human.

---

[16] *OED* One who proves or offers to prove (another) guilty; *hence*, an informer. Now restricted to: One who confesses a felony and gives evidence against his accomplices to secure their conviction. With 1855 MACAULAY The testimony of a crowd of approvers swearing for their necks.

[17] JFS's investigative history of an accusation of judicial murder: *The Story of Nuncomar and the Impeachment of Sir Elijah Impey* (1885; ed. Lisa Rodensky, 2013; *Selected Writings of James Fitzjames Stephen*, Oxford University Press).

[18] The last of Dickens's books to be illustrated by Hablot Knight Browne, 'Phiz' (1815–1882; *ODNB*, artist and illustrator). See J. R. Harvey, *Victorians Novels and Their Illustrators* (1970).

'Journalism' (excerpt)
(*Cornhill*, July 1862)

'The Sunday Papers' (*Sat. Rev.*, 19 April 1856): 'The *Dispatch* contains articles which are historically curious. They remind us of a time when journalism was quite a different thing, and journalists quite a different class of people, from what they are now', p. 46. On the word *journalism* itself, see the Introduction p. xix.

Journalism (excerpt)

Journalism will, no doubt, occupy the first or one of the first places in any future literary history of the present times, for it is the most characteristic of all their productions. A great humourist once even went so far as to assert that the true social and political history of the age in which we live never would, or could, be known till some competent person should write an account of the management and policy of the different newspapers which influence it so deeply, under some such title as *Satan's Invisible World Revealed*.[1] The admirable wit of the phrase, and the superficial resemblance of the sentiment to truth, excuse a good deal of injustice and of error in its substance.

The enormous reputation for both power and ability which our leading newspapers possess is due in a considerable degree to the impatience which every one feels of being governed in a prosaic way. No one likes to believe that the commonplace, unexciting scenes which he witnesses, or hears of, in the House of Commons really constitute the process of governing a great nation. People look for something more striking, and they find it in the notion of an invisible power called 'Public Opinion', produced as we suppose by a set of unknown persons of prodigious genius, whose names are mysteriously concealed by the editors of the leading London papers, by whom they are from time to time invoked for the purpose of directing the different branches of human affairs with which they happen to be specially familiar. Few people have a definite notion of what a

---

[1] Carlyle, *Sartor Resartus*, ch. 6: 'The Journalists are now the true Kings and Clergy: henceforth Historians unless, they are fools, must write not of Bourbon Dynasties, and Tudors, and Hapsburgs, but of Stamped Broad-sheet Dynasties and quite new successive Names, according as this or the other Able Editor, or Combination of Able Editors, gains the world's ear. Of the British Newspaper Press, perhaps the most important of all, and wonderful enough in its secret constitution and procedure, a valuable descriptive History already exists, in that language, under the title of *Satan's Invisible World Displayed*; which however by search in all the Weissnichtwo Libraries I have not yet succeeded in procuring'. George Sinclair (*d.*1696), Scottish mathematician, *Satan's invisible world discovered, of modern relations proving evidently against the saducees and atheists of this present age, that there are devils, spirits, witches, and apparitions, from authentick records, attestations of famous witnesses and undoubted verity* (1685).

newspaper really is, of the different classes of persons who write it, and of the real extent of its influence on the course of affairs.

Newspapers are composed of two principal parts—the original matter and the news. These two parts occupy different proportions in different papers. Daily papers are composed principally of news, and weekly papers of original matter. The original matter may be further subdivided into leading articles upon political subjects or incidents of the day, and reviews of books; and the news might also be divided into that which is provided for serious and businesslike purposes, and that which is provided for amusement. The words Intelligence and Gossip would describe not inappropriately the elements of which it is composed. Each of these departments of a newspaper is written by different people on different principles, and requires the employment of different kinds and degrees of ability; and in order to get an adequate notion of the complex whole called a Newspaper, it is necessary to know something of each of these different heads.

There is, however, one great leading principle which underlies all the rest, and which affects, and, indeed, may be almost said to determine, the character of every separate branch of journalism, though hardly any one who writes or thinks on the subject appears to keep it in sight. This is the fact, that a newspaper is beyond everything else a commercial undertaking. Whatever else it does or omits to do, it must either pay or stop. This is an alternative which it is impossible to evade. Here and there, possibly, a rich man, who can indulge his fancies without reference to his money profit, may amuse himself by setting up a paper simply for the expression of his own views; but this is not only a mere exception and anomaly, but it is an apparent exception which, in the strictest sense of the words, proves the rule. Even in such a case the paper cannot be sold, unless the public are disposed to buy it, though it may be printed; so that unless it complies with the conditions of commercial success it can exercise no sort of influence, and give no currency to the opinions which it expresses. This principle ultimately determines the character of all periodical literature whatever. A paper may guide, or bully, or flatter, or instruct, or amuse the public, or it may do all these things at different times and in different degrees, but unless it does for the public something which the public likes it does nothing at all. Whatever may be the tone and bearing of journalists, they are in reality the servants of the public, and the course which they take is, and always will be, ultimately determined by the public.

'Novelists' Common Forms'
(*Saturday Review*, 13 June 1863)

OED Legal and other phrases, *common form*. (*a*) a form of probate...; (*b*) a customary form of words used in the pleadings in actions at common law; (*c*) a form of words common to documents of the same species; hence *colloq.*, a formula, mode of behaviour, etc., of general application.

Novelists' Common Forms

When a conveyancer draws a deed, he begins by considering the special circumstances of the transaction, and after arranging and describing them to his satisfaction, he completes the draft by making his clerk fill up the blanks in a set of common forms applicable to all cases, and of which a store, duly labelled, is kept tied up in bundles to be used as occasion requires. This practice, with modifications, is adopted in most walks of life. The physician has his prescriptions, the clergyman has his commonplaces, and the speaker his perorations. It is, therefore, not only natural but inevitable that the novelist should have his peculiar methods of doing his work, and should repeat himself with variations. It is, however, undoubtedly true that a common-form novel excites feelings which are not excited by other common-form documents. If a man were to insure his life, for instance, he would not only not object to the policy on the ground that it was like all others, except in his name and in the amounts of the premium and of the sum assured, but he would feel suspicion and disquiet if it were not. Yet the same man will feel a certain sense of the ridiculous when, in reading a novel, he finds the secret which was betrayed by a turn of expression in the beginning of the first volume paraded as a tremendous disclosure towards the middle of the third; or when he is introduced to a gentleman with a stern countenance and flashing eyes, in circumstances precisely analogous to those under which he became acquainted only a week before with another gentleman with flashing eyes and a stern countenance. On the other hand, it is for the sake of the secret and the hero that he reads the story. Of all the dreary productions which the art of man can bring to light, none surely is more dreary than a strictly domestic tale with no story, no character, no anything except more or less skilful copies of every day life. A man who is afraid to be ridiculous, and cannot rise to being sublime, has no business to write novels. If the common forms in novels are at once ridiculous and indispensable, what is the true theory of them? The answer is, that the great bulk of the novels which are written are simply evils, and ought not to be written at all; and that even those which are worth writing contain an element of absurdity which ought to prevent both men and women from taking to that pursuit, unless they belong to a class so small that its living members might at any given moment be counted on the fingers.

208　　　　　　　　ON THE NOVEL AND JOURNALISM

The fact that the common forms in question are ridiculous is proved chiefly by universal consent; the reason why they are ridiculous is another matter. In one point of view, they are not ridiculous at all. A man who fully and consciously admits to his own mind, and who shows by his way of treating his readers that he does admit, that he is engaged in a purely commercial transaction, ceases to be ridiculous. No one laughs at a clown for making absurd faces. It is his trade to do so, and it is just as serious a matter with him to get the corners of his mouth up to his eyes as it is with a surgeon to perform an operation. So when a man has once set up a manufactory of novels, his Emmas and Julias are stock in trade, and the ridicule, if any there be, is transferred from him to his customers. No one laughs at a dressmaker for supplying ladies with crinoline, and by the same rule no one ought to blame a man like Mr. G. P. R. James for the 'two travellers' who 'might have been perceived'. Of such books the authors might say, in the words of the old song:[1]

> You may call them vulgar fairing,
> Wives and mothers most despairing
> Call them lives of men.

This, however, is a plea which the great mass of novelists would never put forward. They take a higher view of their performances, and consider them, not as articles of commerce made to order, but as works of art, produced, to some extent, because the author thinks that they ought to instruct and please mankind. To those who write stories in this temper, it is fair to use a different language. When a man selects a particular incident which has struck his fancy, and elaborates it into a three-volume novel, or even into a one-volume novelette,[2] it is fair to say to him, 'You would never have taken all this trouble if you did not think, not merely that this kind of thing is saleable, but that it has that degree of grace and prettiness about it which makes it desirable that it should be saleable'; and thus the fact that it is really ridiculous, and not graceful, is relevant. The proof that particular common forms are bad consists, therefore, in showing that, whereas they must be presumed to have been selected from the great mass of occurrences which the writer had to choose from, because they more or less vaguely indicate some doctrine, or excite and gratify some sentiment, the doctrine or sentiment so indicated or excited is false or injurious. A novel, not being a mere article of commerce, can never be considered as a mere matter of curiosity. It always either asserts or insinuates something or other, and the absurdity or otherwise of the common forms which novelists use depends upon the nature of the assertion or insinuation. A few particular instances will make this clear.

A common form has prevailed for a considerable time amongst novelists which was used with considerable effect by Mr. Dickens in *David Copperfield*, and which has been worked very hard since that time by many other writers. The hero is introduced hesitating between two mistresses, like an ass between two bundles of hay. He marries the inferior mistress of the two, all external beauty and accomplishment, and the other

---

[1] Caroline Oliphant, Lady Nairne (1766–1845; *ODNB*, songwriter), 'Caller Herrin": 'Oh, ye may ca' them vulgar farin', / Wives and mothers maist despairin', / Ca' them lives o' men.' JFS calls up a line of her poem 'The Land o' the Leal' (letter, 28 Sept. 1885; *Life* 348).

[2] *OED* A story of moderate length having the characteristics of a novel. Now frequently applied to a short romantic or sentimental novel of inferior quality. From 1814.

silently retreats into good works, and nourishes a hopeless passion for him. After a time, the first wife dies—in her confinement very often, which prevents the embarrassment of a family; and the hero, flying for consolation in a purely fraternal spirit to the lady with the hopeless passion, marries her after a more or less decent interval. The artistic advantages of this arrangement are obvious. You get an affecting deathbed, two courtships—one gay and the other grave—wounded affection, and probably a confidential female friendship chastened by mysterious reticences, all by the help of a process which enables the hero to have his cake and eat his cake. And what, it may be asked, is the harm? Why not tell people this pretty little tale if they like to hear it? What is the false assertion or improper insinuation which, as you must say, such a plot conveys? The answer is, that indirectly, and all the more effectively on that account, it gives a lesson of intense and even hateful selfishness. It is quite true that the writer does not in so many words praise his hero, or teach people to look forward to a second marriage as a sort of not unpleasant remedy for the possible misfortunes of the first, but that is the substance of it. By putting the man who goes through such an experience in an interesting attitude, and showing how he not only had the satisfaction of living with a pretty and attractive woman for a certain time, but how, when he had got tired of her, or had found out her weak side, she was happily removed, and a better supplied in her place, the writer whispers, in a subtle, indirect, ambiguous way, that a wife and a horse stand on the same sort of footing—that you may indulge your fancy by buying a showy mare, that very likely she will break down, and then you can get a more serviceable animal. The author is, and must be, a sort of deputy Providence for his characters; and when he shows his readers what a pleasant thing it is for the man whom he delights to honour to have two wives, one after the other, he is giving them a coarse and selfish lesson, however delicate may be the envelope in which it is enclosed.

A recent writer on America mentions another illustration of the same thing, far less offensive, but eminently characteristic. Mr. Dicey[3] informs us that all the popular novels in the United States have the same plot. A governess from the North goes into the house of a rich Southern planter, probably a widower. In due time the planter is converted from his belief in slavery, and elopes with the governess to the North, where, after more or less adventure, he lives happily ever after. Of course a good deal of this is purely local and artistic, but the sentiment running through it is obvious enough. Here you behold virtue rewarded, for what can be so virtuous as a Northern governess, or what such a reward to her as marriage with a converted Southerner? As, according to the old riddle, a salmon in the water is the thing most like a salmon out of the water, an unconverted Southerner must bear, especially for matrimonial purposes, a close resemblance to a converted one; and thus the moral of such stories would be, that the most blessed lot on earth is to be a victorious lecture-monger,[4] raised by the recognition of her virtues to the position of a rich lady. This can hardly be considered as a

---

[3] Edward Dicey (1832–1911; *ODNB*, author and journalist). *Six Months in the Federal States* (1863). *Life* 339, JFS's letter to Lord Lytton, 30 Aug. 1877, about essays on Egypt by Dicey: 'I think my cousin E. Dicey's articles in the XIXth Century are good, but I quite agree with you...'

[4] *OED* In formations dating from the middle of the sixteenth century onwards -*monger* nearly always implies one who carries on a contemptible or discreditable 'trade' or 'traffic'. (JFS on 'lecturing' by 'Gentlemen Authors', p. 164.)

210 ON THE NOVEL AND JOURNALISM

successful exposition of the sacred maxim that godliness[5] is great gain, and has the promise of this life as well as that which is to come.

The technical common forms of novelists constitute a separate and a curious subject. They are adopted probably because they are found to answer. Why they should answer is a curious question, but there is little hope of solving it. Why should brown trousers be commoner than grey, or *vice versâ*? These forms may, however, be regarded by the outside and untechnical world with an excusable curiosity. Is it, for instance, really true that when men make offers of marriage they always say, 'Take my hand, it is the hand of a gentleman'? Mr. Trollope, if any one, ought to know, and many passages from his works might be quoted in support of the proposition. In one of his recent works there are some five or six offers of marriage, and each of them contains this clause, or something like it. Such forms as these are perfectly harmless. It is, indeed, a pity that technical names should not be invented for them, so that their peculiarities might be announced in the advertisements. It would not be a hard matter to produce formulas by which any number of such books as *Guy Livingstone*,[6] for instance, might be written by any one who could hit off the particular trick of style. Take a giant with knotted muscles, and some women for him to love or flirt with—alternate between inchoate[7] adultery and inchoate seduction, flavoured with scowls, reticence, and the affectation of being unaffected—and you have only got to change the names and vary the Greek quotations in order to make as many novels as the public will buy. It must be a strange sensation for the author to bring on the stage his fourth or fifth giant with knotted muscles, and to tell the reader for the tenth time, in a sort of confidential aside, that he does not hold him up as a model of virtue, with his hard face and evil smile. Such a giant must in time become a sort of Frankenstein.[8] 'Master', he might say, 'I have held a man out at arm's length and choked him. I have swung out my mighty fist from my left hip and felled to the ground a man bigger than myself. I have crumpled up a silver cup between my fingers in the agony of death, and what on earth am I to do now?' If his master would or could have the kindness to tell him to go to his own place and stay there, it would be a satisfaction to his readers and himself.

---

[5] 1 Timothy 6:6–7, But godliness with contentment is great gain. For we brought nothing into this world, and it is certain we can carry nothing out.

[6] See p. 183.

[7] *OED* Just begun, incipient; in an initial or early stage. With 1765 BLACKSTONE *Comm*. If a boy under fourteen, or a girl under twelve years of age, marries, this marriage is only inchoate and imperfect. Also 1821 SYDNEY SMITH Many inchoate acts are innocent, the consummation of which is a capital offence.

[8] *OED* The name of the title-character of Mrs. Shelley's romance *Frankenstein* (1818), who constructed a human monster and endowed it with life. Commonly misused allusively as a typical name for a monster who is a terror to his originator and ends by destroying him. From 1838 GLADSTONE They [mules] really seem like Frankensteins of the animal creation. (The first instance complete with the 'destroying him', 1889.)

'Mr. Thackeray' (excerpts)
(*Fraser's*, April 1864)

Not signed, following *Fraser's* usual practice. For JFS and Thackeray, see 'Barry Lyndon', p. 71.

Mr. Thackeray (excerpts)

Mr. Thackeray's melancholy and unexpected death[1] makes it natural to take some notice of the general character of his writings.

There has been much controversy on the moral effects of novels; and it is only of late years that the public at large, and especially the religious public, appear to have given way to irresistible force, and to have admitted by their conduct, and also by their teaching, that novel-reading is not wicked, and that it is even possible that a novel may be a good and useful book. The denunciations against novels which may be read in old-fashioned sermons are still as good as when they were first written, yet no one reads them. Baxter[2] says, 'Another dangerous time-wasting sin is the reading of vain books, play-books, romances, and feigned histories. I speak not here how pernicious this vice is, by corrupting the fancy and affections, and putting you out of relish to necessary things; but bethink you, before you spend another hour in any such books, whether you can comfortably give an account of it unto God?' Elsewhere he says, 'Another point of sensuality to be denied is the reading or hearing of false and tempting books, and those that only tend to please an idle fancy, and not to edify. Such as are romances and other feigned histories of that nature, with books of tales and jests, and foolish compliments, with which the world so much aboundeth that there's few but may have admittance to this library of the devil.' He goes on to show how these works 'ensnare us in a world of guilt', 'dangerously bewitch and corrupt the minds of young and empty people, and rob men of much precious time.' And he concludes with these emphatic exhortations, which afford a strange contrast to the tone of modern reviews, even if they are of the stricter sort: 'Therefore I may well conclude that play-books, and history fables, and romances, and such like, are the very poison of youth, the prevention of grace, the fuel of wantonness and lust, and the food and work of empty, vicious, graceless persons; and it's great pity they be not banished out of the commonwealth.' 'All these considered, I beseech you, throw away these pestilent vanities, and take them not into your

---

[1] On 24 Dec. 1863.

[2] *A Treatise of Self-Denial* (1675), by Richard Baxter (1615–1691; *ODNB*, ejected minister and religious writer). His admonition: 'In necessary things, unity; in doubtful things, liberty; in all things, charity.' *Life* 80: 'A very different writer [from F. D. Maurice] of whom he read a good deal at college was Baxter, introduced to him, I guess, by one of his father's essays.'

212   ON THE NOVEL AND JOURNALISM

hands, nor suffer them in the hands of your children, or in your houses, but burn them as you would do a conjuring book, and as they did, Acts xix. 19,[3] that so they may do no mischief to others.'[4]

These vigorous denunciations embody, in plain words, a sentiment which, in our own days, is altogether worn out, in so far as novels were its object. It was, however, exceedingly powerful in its day; and long after it had ceased to be openly or generally avowed, it continued to exercise a very perceptible influence, not only over the opinion which the public entertained of novels and their writers, but over the opinion which novelists entertained of themselves and their works. With some striking exceptions, a certain Bohemian air hung about our principal writers of fiction for a length of time. A humorist is almost always a person of more than average sensibility, and these qualities are almost certain to put their possessor more or less in opposition to the established state of things. Both Fielding and Smollett[5] are memorable instances of this; and though memorable names—such, especially, as that of Walter Scott—might be mentioned on the other side, it will be generally found, as was the case with Scott himself, that their attachment to what exists is owing, to a great extent, to the fact that they have been able to throw an air of romance over it. If he had not managed to idealize Scotland, and to see his bare-breeched Highlanders in a romantic point of view, Scott, hard-headed and sensible as he was, would hardly have managed to write the Waverley novels, however much he wanted to buy land. The moral novelists—such as Richardson, Miss Edgeworth, and Miss Austen[6]—who are to fiction what Arminians[7] are to theology, belong to a different class. The whole colouring of their works is derived from a mental atmosphere altogether unlike that of the rebellious sentimentalists who seem to consider that wit, irony, and pathos are the instruments by which a just estimate may be formed of human affairs. For the last thirty or five-and-thirty years the writers who in the last century would have been prominent members of the literary opposition, have obtained an entirely new position, and have exercised a considerable influence on the whole course of thought. Novel writing has become not only a business, but by far the most lucrative branch of literary industry. A really good novel, by a well-known writer, is worth its weight, not in gold, but almost in five-pound notes. Thousands of pounds have of late years been paid for the right to publish a single edition of a story in numbers. After being published in numbers they are thrown into cheap editions, and find wings of one sort or another with which they fly over the whole face of the country. Their influence is enormous. They are the favourite national indoors amusement. All men and all women read them, and many women read nothing else. Modern popular novels have far more influence over the morals of the public, and over their views of life, than the stage and the pulpit put together. Novels and newspapers have a sort of analogy to Church and State. The one represents to innumerable readers the active and business-like, the other the contemplative view of things. There are thousands upon thousands of young people, and a considerable number of people no longer young, whose principal experience of argument and discussion is derived from leading articles, and whose notions of the character and prospects of the world in which they live,

---

[3] Acts 19:19, Many of them also which used curious arts brought their books together, and burned them before all men.

[4] Read, 'any others'.   [5] Correcting Fraser's, 'Smollet'.   [6] Correcting Fraser's, 'Austin'.

[7] Or Remonstrants, followers of the Dutch Reformed theologian Jacobus Arminius (1560–1609).

MR. THACKERAY 213

of the nature of its institutions, and, in a word, of the general colour of life, are taken principally from novels. Whether we like it or not, such is the state of things to which, by a great variety of causes, we have been brought; and it ought to be recognized, if we are to try to estimate the nature of the influence which particular writers have exercised.

Mr. Thackeray was thrown, at the age at which people choose their professions, into the full current of light literature, and became one of the most prominent directors of that great outburst of the pathetic and impulsive view of things which has just been referred to. Its first beginnings were contemporary with what almost every one of a sufficiently ardent turn of mind to take a prominent part in fiction, regarded as the advent of a political millennium. The Reform Bill, and other measures of the same sort, had discredited all existing institutions, and the general temper of the times led men to look with favour on all new schemes, and to listen willingly to every one who was inclined to denounce or to banter the standing usages of society. The old Bohemianism of the ragged authors of the eighteenth century was transformed into political, literary, and social radicalism.

* * *

His scrupulous modesty and adherence to fact produced at least two effects on Mr. Thackeray's novels worth noticing. It accounts for much of the air of pathos which they wear. In one of the volumes of miscellanies there is a frontispiece representing a dwarfed figure with a large head. He is removing a laughing mask attached to a cap and bells, and underneath appear the author's own features, wearing a strange look of half bewildered sadness—the face of a man who has hardly shaken off an unpleasant dream. Again and again, in various parts of his books, the impression under which this little figure was drawn is conveyed to the reader by casual allusions, by turns of expression, by a thousand subtle intimations to the effect that the actor was rather tired of his part, and never heartily liked it. When a sensitive man is under a constant temptation to write about himself and his own feelings, he inevitably acquires a certain degree of mannerism, and it is impossible to be quite sure whether his feelings are entirely genuine. A person who, from a feeling that he ought to be dissatisfied with his occupation in life, is constantly telling himself that he is dissatisfied with it, probably hardly knows himself whether he really is so or not. There is no reason to suppose that Mr. Thackeray would have liked any other pursuit better than the one which he adopted, or that he was better fitted for any other; but, considering the arrogance which is the besetting sin of popular writers, it is much to his credit that he should have felt the weak side of his calling, and should have regretted to see his hand[8] subdued to what it worked in as no doubt it often was. A writer by profession must by the necessity of the case write a good deal that would not sell if it had not his trade mark on it; and he must almost always

[8] Shakespeare, Sonnet 111: 'That did not better for my life provide, / Than publick meanes which publick manners breeds. / Thence comes it that my name receives a brand, / And almost thence my nature is subdu'd / To what it workes in, like the Dyers hand'. (JFS has 'public' half a dozen times in these few pages.) Dickens's Preface to *Bleak House* quotes from these lines (p. 78); as Dickens had done, JFS renews this of Shakespeare's, and again in 'Luxury' (*Cornhill*, Sept. 1860): 'Such descriptions ["of virtuous mechanics who refresh themselves after a hard day's work by reading metaphysics"] are either totally false, or applicable only to the rarest exceptions. An all but universal experience conclusively proves that the mind is subdued to what it works in.'

feel that if his income was otherwise secured, and if he had energy enough to write at all under such circumstances, he would be able to write much better books than he is ever likely to make in the way of business.

It is a considerable thing, and shows a true perception of a man's real value, for so popular a writer as Mr. Thackeray was, to be able to bear this in mind. The flattery poured upon popular novelists, living or dead, in the present day, is a disgrace to what is technically called literature. Hardly any other class of men, except here and there popular preachers, get publicly cried over by their colleagues. When eminent men in other lines of life die, people do not put articles into newspapers or magazines, leaving out the Mr., putting in at length all the Christian names, and blubbering about them and theirs as if the fact that a man wrote novels made him and his affairs, and all the feelings of his friends and family, public property. To those who care for the maintenance of that wise reserve which is to all sturdy virtues what enamel is to teeth, such demonstrations are extremely unwelcome. If a man cannot control his feelings, let him go home, and cry his eyes out if he pleases; but he ought not to come before the public till he has washed his face and brushed his hair.

Besides producing this general impatience of the work in which he was engaged, Mr. Thackeray's genuine modesty and adherence to his own limits produced a noticeable specific effect on his writings. It contributed largely to the want of plot which is to be seen in all his books. This, no doubt, was partly due to the practice of publishing novels in parts—a practice far more advantageous to the novelist than to the novel; but the moral ground for it is to be found in the inherent honesty and simplicity of the man. A young gentleman in search of a profession once asked a venerable relative high in the Church what he thought of his becoming a doctor. 'No', was the reply, 'I see a providential obstacle. You have not humbug enough about you.' The same obstacle prevented Mr. Thackeray from excelling in what is often considered the most attractive and even the most intellectual part of novel-writing—the devising of plots. He had very little turn for this. If by any accident he brings in an unexpected incident or strange turn of events, you feel that he is tacitly despising his own trick. For instance, at the end of *Philip*,[9] where the old coach upsets and is broken, whereby the will lost for many years is discovered, and the necessary fortune is sent in the right direction, there is a sort of intentional, or at least conscious clumsiness about the whole proceeding, which shows that the writer must have laughed at it himself. His caricature plots—the plots of the prize novels,[10] for instance, or of *Rebecca and Rowena*[11]—are much more ingenious than the plots of his principal works. The latter are without an exception what Baxter called feigned histories. They are fictitious biographies extending over a considerable space of time, and depending for their interest, not on any particular combination of circumstances, but on a succession of events, long enough to bring out naturally, and without perceptible effort, the leading characteristics of the personages of the story. No doubt this way of writing is apt to be dull. It cannot be denied that by

---

[9] *The Adventures of Philip on His Way Through the World. Shewing who Robbed him, who Helped him, and who Passed him by* (1862).

[10] 'Comic Journalism' (*Sat. Rev.*, 1 Mar. 1856): 'Some of Mr. Thackeray's *Miscellanies*, his prize novels for example, are admirable.' 'Mrs. Caudle's Curtain Lectures' (*Sat. Rev.*, 1 Nov. 1856): '*Punch's Prize Novels* were works of art' (Thackeray's parodies of Sir Edward Bulwer-Lytton, Disraeli, and others).

[11] *Rebecca and Rowena. A Romance upon Romance* (by Mr. M. A. Titmarsh, 1849; first version, *Fraser's*, 1846, as 'Proposals for a continuation of "Ivanhoe"').

MR. THACKERAY   215

the time that Pendennis leaves his chambers in the Temple, we, the readers, are as tired of them as he must have been; and long before Philip reaches the end of a career which has no particular termination after all, we get to feel that we know as much about him as we much care to know. On the other hand, a writer in whose works the ludicrous element, whether in its simple or in its pathetic shape, has so very large a share, could hardly, without a certain contempt for himself, make his plots good, in the sense in which the plots of A. Dumas, for instance, are good. A reflective man, whose eyes are open to the grotesque side of human affairs, and especially to his own relation to them, can hardly fail to be struck with the absurdity of his own position, when he sits down to construct an elaborate series of adventures, coincidences, hairbreadth escapes, mistaken identities, and the like, which he is afterwards to describe with a sprightliness which will pass for real interest and emotion. To compose a plot calculated for descriptions of the deeper, sterner, and more tragic emotions, is a task on which serious labour might well be bestowed; but a man must rather overrate the value of a laugh if he is willing to take so much trouble to devise the telling of it; and a mind essentially humorous and pathetic will find occasions for the display of those gifts rather in the common routine of life than in forced unnatural situations. It is one of the great merits and beauties of Mr. Thackeray's style that his pathos is introduced in the most perfectly natural way, and never forced into artificial prominence. Death-bed scenes—which some writers would dwell upon as if they could not be content without actually rubbing the onions into their readers' eyes—are by him almost always left in the background, and rather indicated than described. He does not make us stand by the bedside of poor old Sedley, or give a minute description of the way in which Amelia received the news of George's death.[12]

* * *

Considered as a picture, *Pendennis* is admirably good; but considered as a sermon, it is open to serious objection. Pendennis ends by putting his head under his wife's apron-string, and taking it for granted that it is his bounden duty and privilege to submit himself in important matters to the direction of one so pure and holy. A youth of irresolute scepticism culminating in a marriage founded on what may be called the religion of a mother's grave, is, after all, a very poor thing. It is very well to describe it; but it should be described somewhat contemptuously. Indeed, Mr. Thackeray in his later novels, *The Newcomes* and *Philip*, does not flatter Pendennis. He shows that his wife always had the upper hand of him, and that, as is usually the case where the is the better horse, the grey mare had her weaknesses.[13] There is a fine dash both of prudery and priggishness in Laura's matronly years, at the time of life when she is always hugging a child to her bosom and talking to it and at her husband; and the careful observer may detect a certain openness to flirtation, always in the most strictly correct and Madonna-like way, in the saintly eagerness with which she bestows sisterly or filial caresses on her husband's attractive friends, Colonel Newcome and Philip.

* * *

[12] Joseph Sedley, Amelia Sedley, and George Osborne, in *Vanity Fair*.
[13] *OED* Proverb (the wife rules the husband).

The defect of all Mr. Thackeray's later novels, all the good-humored ones, is the want of backbone in the male characters. Esmond and George Warrington (of *The Virginians*)[14] have little more in them after all than Pendennis. Esmond, in particular, as he himself frequently observes, is a perfect fool about women. As soon as he cares about a woman he lets her do what she likes with him. It is to please a woman that he intends to be a clergyman, becomes a soldier, and commits high treason; and George Warrington has a similar weakness in a less degree. This is always admitted, by the parties concerned, to be a fault and a weakness; but it is easy to see that they and the author are barely sincere in blaming it. They seem to think it both an amiable and a venial weakness. In reality, a man thoroughly given over to such a state of mind would be perfectly contemptible. There is something horrible in the levity of a person who will hold every scheme and object of life at a woman's disposition; and it is nothing less than a great crime to be willing to take the responsibility of contributing to civil war and revolution, for no other purpose than that of pleasing a woman who, after all, cared for nothing but the notoriety of the matter. It is, however, consolatory to find that even in novels women are represented as not liking this sort of admirer. Beatrix serves Esmond perfectly right in jilting him for ten years. If he was so weak as to submit to such treatment from her it was entirely his own fault. It is the unpleasant feature, or, at least, one unpleasant feature, in almost all Mr. Thackeray's writings, that he generally puts love in the light of an amiable weakness, which turns out happily, if at all, by chance rather than by design. It would be sad to be obliged to believe that one of the most important affairs in life is always, or, at least, generally, and in the natural course of things, managed in this blind way, at the bidding of a mere violent passion, springing up, one hardly knows how, and acting, when it has sprung up, with unaccountable and uncontrollable violence. This notion of the matter, however, is much like other parts of Mr. Thackeray's view of life. It is all impulse and passion, sometimes fervent, more often languid, but seldom guided by reflection.

---

[14] The sequel to *Henry Esmond*, with the references to 'Esmond' here being to the earlier novel.

'Senior's Essays on Fiction' (excerpt)
(*Saturday Review*, 23 April 1864)

Nassau Senior (1790–1864; *ODNB*, political economist). *Life* 44, on the household of Sir James Stephen: 'A next-door neighbour for many years was Nassau Senior, the political economist, and one main author of the Poor Law of 1834. Senior, a very shrewd man of the world, was indifferent to my father's religious speculations. Yet he and his family were among our closest friends'. JFS, 'Autobiog.': 'A Benthamite of the Benthamites, a Utilitarian of the Utilitarians, wild about political econmy on which he was a distingushed writer, and one of those dogmatic liberals who in my experience are amongst the most intolerant of mankind' (*Life* 44 n.). JFS was soon to review 'Senior's Historical and Philosophical Essays' (*Sat. Rev.*, 22 Apr. 1865): 'Their general characteristics are those of their author's profession. Before all things Mr. Senior was a lawyer. His mind was intensely legal, and that in the good sense of the word. That is to say, he understood the nature and value of evidence, he knew an argument when he saw one, he always wrote with a distinct meaning in his mind, and there is no nonsense or sophistry to be found in his compositions. On the other hand, he had not much imagination; and this defect sometimes led him, not only to leave out of account matters which he ought to have considered and which really bore upon the question in hand, but also to put up with a word, instead of finding out what the word meant.' Senior's essay on France, America, and Britain gave JFS the opportunity to consider verdicts on whole nations: 'The article itself is a long and very able denunciation of the behaviour of each of the three nations in question in all, or nearly all, their external relations for the last thirty or forty years. It is full of information as to passages in modern history which every one knows by name, though few know them accurately, and is almost as unsparing an attack on the wickedness of mankind in their collective capacity as is to be found in modern literature. At the same time, it cannot be called unjust. It is like the summing up of a hanging judge in a very bad case of murder. Both America and France, France in particular, are found guilty upon every count and after any number of previous convictions. England, though most severely reprimanded, is still recommended to mercy, on the ground of one or two redeeming features of character.'

Senior's Essays on Fiction (excerpts)*

Mr. Senior's volume is a good illustration of the old remark, that men whose occupations are dry and severe have a special liking for reading and criticizing novels. Nearly the first of his writings which attracted any attention were his reviews of the Waverley Novels, written whilst he was still a practising conveyancer. The reason of this is not to be sought entirely in the pleasure of contrast. The fact is due, to a great extent, to the scope which the criticism of novels affords to several of the harder qualities of mind.

---

* *Essays on Fiction*. By Nassau W. Senior. London: Longman & Co., 1864.

ON THE NOVEL AND JOURNALISM

A novel is a collection of imaginary facts, on which the critic has to make his remarks without the trouble of investigating the truth of the statements before him, or searching into collateral or illustrative topics. He looks the book over and considers what it suggests, what are the propositions which may be extracted from it, and what is their value. It is, in short, an excellent text for as lively a sermon on subjects of general interest as a man happens to have it in him to preach. Hence the criticism of novels often comes to show at least as much of the opinions and feelings of the critic himself as of the novels which are the subjects of his remarks. This is specially the case with Mr. Senior. His articles on the Waverley Novels show a keen relish for their beauties, but the principal interest of them lies, not so much in the descriptions of Sir Walter Scott which they contain, as in the reflections which they suggest to the critic himself. They are vigorous, spirited essays, full of shrewd remarks, connected together by the fact that they were all suggested by different parts of the Waverley Novels. For instance, the description of the siege of Torquilstone Castle in *Ivanhoe* leads Mr. Senior to ask how Scott managed to make it so vivid. This suggests a careful inquiry into the way in which descriptions may be made lively, and the special means employed by Scott for that purpose. The method in the present instance is then shown to consist in putting an account of part of the scene to be described into the mouth of a supposed eye-witness, who is supposed to be repeating her own first impressions on the subject to an experienced person who, though prevented from looking on himself, knows from experience enough about the matter to bring out the interesting points by judicious questions. Thousands upon thousands of readers have been charmed with the vigour and beauty of the description, but few indeed would either appreciate the difficulties to be overcome, or the mental resources displayed by Scott in dealing with them, unless they were pointed out by some one who was accustomed, not only to enjoy, but to heighten his enjoyment by analysing its constituent elements.

'Detectives in Fiction and in Real Life'
(*Saturday Review*, 11 June 1864)

'There is little scope for ingenuity in the detection of crimes.' Come 1887 and *A Study in Scarlet*, Sherlock Holmes would seek admissions.

Detectives in Fiction and in Real Life

Of all forms of sensation novel-writing,[1] none is so common as what may be called the romance of the detective. Indeed, one very popular author seems to think that the only striking incident that ever varies the monotony of every-day life is the discovery of a mysterious murder by a consummate detective. Whether the contrast between the stern prose of the officer and the awfulness of the offence, or whether a Pre-Raffaellite[2] delight in the representation of familiar objects, is the true source of the popularity of this kind of plot, it would be rash to decide; but of the fact itself there is no doubt. That an *atra cura*,[3] or rather a *caerulea* or dark-blue *cura*, sits behind every criminal, and hunts him down in a second-class railway carriage with the sagacity of a Red Indian, the scent of a bloodhound, and an unlimited command of all the resources of modern science, appears to be a cherished belief with a certain class of novelists. One eminent member of the craft goes so far as to talk of the science—perhaps the word used was the philosophy—of detection, as if it were a subject on which public lectures were read at Scotland Yard by a well-paid professor. It may perhaps be a little ungracious to object to what may be described as a well-tried, serviceable, common form which has sold a considerable number of popular novels, and which, in the natural course of things, may be expected to sell several more; but, to any one who has any practical acquaintance with the proceedings of detectives and with the transactions which they try to detect, this detective-worship appears one of the silliest superstitions that ever were concocted by ingenious writers. The stories by which the popular notion about them was created and is maintained are all framed upon the same model and all involve the same fallacy,

---

[1] *OED* sensation. An excited or violent feeling. Also, in generalized use, the production of violent emotion as an aim in works of literature or art. 1863 *Q. Rev.* A sensation novel, as a matter of course, abounds in incident. 1864 *Edin. Rev.* Two or three years ago nobody would have known what was meant by a Sensation Novel. (JFS: 'He is a convert to all the modern anti-capital-punishment theories, and has evidently caught the style of French sensation novelists.' *Memoires des Sanson: Sept Générations d'Exécuteurs; Sat. Rev.*, 7 Nov. 1863.)

[2] *OED* Pre-Raphaelite: Also -Raffael-. 1851 The attempts of a few young men who style themselves the Pre-Raffael-ite school.

[3] Horace, Odes iii 1.40: post equitem sedet atra Cura (behind the horseman sits black Care). JFS moves to light blue or dark-blue, in uniform. *OED* cites 1860 *Dict. Slang* Blue, a policeman.

and the facts of every-day experience show how complete a fallacy it is. Perhaps the earliest story of the kind was that in which Edgar Poe[4] described the discovery, by a man of great detective genius, of a horrible murder in a lonely house at Paris. This eminent person ascertained, by a series of profound reflections, that the supposed crime must have been committed, not by a man, but by a baboon,[5] and by advertising for the person who had lately lost a baboon he brought to light the real agent in the tragedy. Perhaps an earlier illustration may be found in the old Eastern fable about the man who, by observing the grass, the flies and bees, the footmarks and the twigs, along a track over the desert, was enabled to inform those whom it concerned that they had lost a camel of such and such a height and colour, laden with honey on one side and spice on the other, lame of such a foot, and forming part of such a caravan.

All these stories are open to the same criticism. Those that hide can find. The person who invented the riddle and knows the explanation is of course able to pretend to discover it by almost any steps, or by what really amount to no steps at all, and thus he can easily convey the impression of the exercise of any amount of sagacity on the part of the person who is supposed to make the discovery. In real life, and especially in the real life of policemen, such discoveries are hardly ever made; and if any one takes the trouble of comparing the actual experience of courts of law with the fictions of novelists as to the extraordinary genius displayed by the detective police, they will find that hardly anything that can be fairly described as remarkable or even peculiar ability is ever shown by the police in finding out a crime. There are a certain number of almost mechanical precautions which they get to know, and which they take, as a matter of course, when a crime is committed. For instance, if plate is stolen, they will give notice at once to all the pawnbrokers in London, or any other town in which the offence has taken place, and this, of course, will sometimes lead to detection. So they will trace bank-notes through a number of hands by the simple process of going to the Bank of England, and showing a note which has been paid over the counter to the banker who paid it in, the customer from whom the banker received it, and so on. They are also acquainted with the head-quarters of thieves and burglars, and get to know some few of their ways and characteristic tricks; but when a crime is committed out of the common routine, and by a person who does not belong to the class of criminals, it is wonderful how helpless they are. They make brilliant discoveries in novels, but in real life next to nothing is due to their sagacity. Point out an obviously guilty person who has absconded, and they will often hunt him down with both skill and perseverance, but they are almost powerless in discovering who the guilty person is. Any one who took the trouble to do so might soon make out a fearfully long list of undiscovered crimes. As to the common offences against property, it is enough to say that a whole army of marauders live in comfort, and even in occasional splendour, by committing them. There are in England thousands of professional thieves, robbers, burglars, and coiners, to say nothing of people who make a living by extortion. Even in regard of murders, there is every reason to believe that a majority are undiscovered, to say nothing of those which are unsuspected;

---

[4] Edgar Allan Poe (1809–1849), 'The Murders in the Rue Morgue' (1841), with the Parisian detective, C. Auguste Dupin.

[5] Rather, Ourang-Outang (so in Poe), hominoid as a baboon is not. *Life* 238, on JFS's lack of interest in evolution or in Darwin: ' "What difference can it make", he asks, "whether millions of years ago our ancestors were semi-rational baboons?" '(from *Sat. Rev.*, 22 May 1858).

DETECTIVES IN FICTION AND IN REAL LIFE

and of persons actually brought to trial somewhere about 25 per cent are acquitted. It is hard to doubt that the majority at least of these persons owe their escape to defects in the evidence against them. It can scarcely be that so large a number of really innocent persons are wrongfully suspected. There is one department in which detectives have the fullest opportunity and the strongest encouragement for the display of their supposed sagacity. When a man is unlucky enough to get into the Divorce Court he will almost always employ detectives, and it is marvellous to see how little good he gets by it if the persons whom he employs go one step beyond the commonest possible exertions, not so much of ingenuity as of industry. It requires a very humble effort of skill to show that A. B. and C. D. stopped at such an hotel; but as soon as the energetic detective goes beyond this humble line and betakes himself to boring holes through doors and other such devices, he usually impresses the Court and jury with the belief that he is simply a bungler.

These remarks are intended to discredit, not the police, but the novelists. The simple truth is that, under a system of law and rules of evidence like our own, there is very little scope for the sort of cunning with which novelists delight to credit the normal detective of a sensation novel. It is possible that the sort of gifts which they describe may have been possessed, or have been supposed to be possessed, by the old French police; but then it must be remembered that French public feeling will tolerate many things which would be altogether intolerable to Englishmen, that French tribunals are satisfied with evidence on which no English jury would act, and that French police officers are never cross-examined. If the feats of the old French police had been submitted to the tests of truth imposed by the laws of this country, it would probably have appeared that they had, in reality, far less to boast of than they supposed, and that many of their supposed triumphs were, in fact, nothing but mares'-nests. Nothing is less trustworthy than that which claims to be behind-the-scenes information. It is one of the commonest experiences of all persons who are practically acquainted with the administration of justice to be told that there is 'no moral[6] doubt' whatever of the guilt of such or such a man. When the reason is asked for, the answer is generally altogether unsatisfactory, and as often as not it amounts at most to a guess on the part of the police or the prosecuting attorney, of the truth of which they have persuaded themselves without any reasonable grounds, and merely on account of the disposition which men have to stick to the hypothesis by which they have once accounted for a thing in their own minds.

The explanation of the whole matter is to be found in considering the nature of crimes and of the evidence by which they are shown to have been committed. A crime is almost always an act of a somewhat violent and more or less dramatic character, unless, indeed, it be a secret fraud. It is always committed for some reason or other, and

---

[6] *OED* Used to designate that kind of probable evidence that rests on a knowledge of the general tendencies of human nature, or of the character of particular individuals or classes of men; often in looser use, applied to all evidence which is merely probable and not demonstrative. *moral certainty* : a practical certainty resulting from moral evidence; a degree of probability so great as to admit of no reasonable doubt. *The Times* (26 Nov. 1864): 'The sole power of these men consists in a moral certainty that their victims will not prosecute. Let that certainty be removed, and all their power is gone'; p. 240, with JFS, 'The Mote and the Beam' (*Sat. Rev.*, 3 Dec. 1864). JFS, *The Indian Evidence Act* (1872) 36: 'what is commonly called moral certainty, and this means simply such a degree of probability as a prudent man would act upon under the circumstances in which he happens to be placed in reference to the matter of which he is said to be morally certain.' (JFS often chooses 'reasonable'; 'whether he feels a doubt about it which he will call reasonable . . . whether they have a reasonable doubt', *Gen. View 1863* 238–9.)

is generally followed by some marked change in the conduct of the person who has committed it. In almost every case the motive and preparation for the offence, its execution, and the subsequent behaviour of the criminal are matters which, if they can be ascertained, mark off in a sufficiently decisive and distinctive way some one person, or some small class of persons, from the rest of the community. Nobody but the thief or the receiver pawns the stolen goods. Nobody but a clerk or a servant who has the opportunity of doing so embezzles money, and if he does, he is obliged to alter his accounts so as to avoid discovery. If a man passes bad money it is pretty certain that he will try to get as much change for his bad shilling as he can. Nor does any one deliberately commit murder unless he has some object to gain by the death of his victim, and proposes to make some sort of change in his own arrangements on account of it. Thus in every case, or almost every case, of crime, there are pretty broad tracks, leading to and from the actual offence itself, and showing the way in which it was committed. No doubt there are exceptions, and it is upon these exceptions that sensation novelists fasten. A crime sometimes occurs of which it is extremely difficult to trace the history, but to such cases our English rules of evidence, generally speaking, extend impunity. Where there is no power to keep suspected persons in prison, and constantly worry them by interrogatories; where every form of hearsay is rigidly excluded from consideration; where nothing is allowed to be given in evidence which is not immediately connected with the very point at issue, there is little room left for the sort of ingenuity ascribed to detectives. There either is or there is not evidence of the crime. If there is evidence, there is, generally speaking, little skill required for its detection; if there is not, all the skill in the world will not supply its absence without deliberate perjury and forgery. Any one may convince himself of this who will take the trouble to study the evidence given in any important criminal case. Palmer's trial,[7] for example, was justly celebrated as an instance in which every relevant fact was brought out and marshalled with unequalled skill and industry; yet there was not a single curious or ingenious piece of testimony given in the whole trial, if indeed we except the scientific evidence, which stood on a basis of its own. The only ingenuity shown in the whole matter was shown by the gentleman who first suspected that a crime had been committed. When he had once put forward that notion, the task of finding out where Palmer had bought the poison, what he had done about his friend's bets, and the like, was all plain sailing enough. Indeed, skilfully as the case was got up, and lavish as was the expenditure upon it, no one ever found out what became of the greater part of the money which Cook received for his bets, and which Palmer no doubt stole; yet this is just the sort of thing which the imaginary detective ought to have discovered with hardly an effort. Many hundred pounds' worth of bank-notes are paid to a man on a race-course. His friend murders and robs him; where are the notes? They never were traced. In a novel, there would have been sure to be some mysterious yet simple and ingenious dodge by which they would have been discovered; but this is just the difference between the detective of fiction and the detective of real life. The whole matter may be summed up very shortly. There is little scope for ingenuity in the detection of crimes, because, if there is evidence, it is almost always easy to produce it; and if there is none, it is altogether impossible to get it. The sphere of ingenuity is in making guesses, and the whole object of English courts of law and rules of evidence is to exclude guesswork.

[7] See p. 104. Jan-Melissa Schramm addresses the evidence in the Palmer trial, *Testimony and Advocacy* 123–7.

'Sentimentalism' (excerpts)
(*Cornhill Magazine*, July 1864)

Not signed, following the *Cornhill*'s practice. JFS furthers his 'Sentimentalism' (*Sat. Rev.*, 25 Dec. 1858), p. 188.

Sentimentalism (excerpts)

Sentiment is no more than feeling, and sentimental is the adjective of that substantive. So far, therefore, as etymology goes, sentimental ought to be synonymous with feeling (the adjective). In fact, the sense of the word is considerably narrower. It is a dyslogistic[1] word, implying that the person or thing qualified, is distinguished by a misapplication of the tender emotions. A sentimental person is a person, in some unfavourable way, remarkable for the part which the tender feeling plays in his or her character. A person would not be called sentimental merely for having peculiarly strong feelings; nor even for having feelings easily excited and warmly expressed, unless the person who used the epithet meant to convey a shade of disapprobation by it. In short, to be sentimental means to display or indulge tender emotions in an improper manner; and thus the question what we mean by sentimentalism becomes an inquiry into the occasions on which, and the manner and degree in which, tender feeling ought to be expressed and encouraged.

* * *

Any one who watches with care the common use of language, will be surprised to see how accurately popular feeling and the common use of language apply this principle. Analyze any popular writer, any well-known scene, which would generally be called sentimental, and ask why it is so stigmatized, and the answer will always be, because it appears, from the turn of the sentences, or the extent to which the author dwells upon a painful subject, that he had ceased to think naturally and simply about the fact, real or supposed, which originally drew out the feeling, and had begun to think about himself, and how cleverly he could describe the sources of tender emotion, and how pleasant it was to stimulate their action.

This will explain how sentiment may be, and often is, theatrical and affected without being insincere. When Mrs. Siddons[2] frightened herself into hysterics by her own acting,

---

[1] *OED* Expressing or connoting disapprobation or dispraise; having a bad connotation, opprobious. (The opposite of *eulogistic*.) Very much Bentham's word, from 1802 on.

[2] Sarah Siddons, née Kemble (1755–1831; *ODNB*, actress), born to the great family of actors.

there can be no doubt that she really was in a state of genuine emotion. One of the great charms of Mr. Carlyle's *History of the French Revolution* is the clear perception which he has of the fact, that the fierce, violent nonsense of many of the famous scenes in the revolution was sincere as well as nonsensical. The swearing, the swaggering, the protesting was genuine in its way, though the actors in the strange melodrama seem to have had continually before their minds' eyes the reflection that they were wonderfully fine fellows for figuring in such a performance. The volunteers who went to fight on the frontiers had a natural love for the bombast with which they were fed, and licked it up as a dog does a pat of butter; but they really did mean the greater part of what they said, and their reason for going beyond what they meant was, that they liked the sentiment which their position created so much, that they could not resist the temptation of increasing their enjoyment by exaggerated language.

Perhaps the strongest illustrations (if some living authors are excepted) supplied by literature of delight in the mere sensation of tenderness, and of systematic indulgence in it, are to be found in the works of Sterne and Rousseau. In every page of *Tristram Shandy* and the *Sentimental Journey*, Sterne revels either in tenderness or in picturesqueness, and whichever he happens to be indulging in for the moment, his motive appears to be the same. The emotion itself, apart from its suitableness to the matter in hand, is delightful to him. He likes to make himself and some of his readers cry about Corporal Trim or Le Fevre's death-bed, just as a man might like to eat something particularly nice. Rousseau's sentiment is, perhaps, less specific, and more genuine; but he does so thoroughly enjoy the process of describing himself and his own feelings, he is so passionately eager after sympathy, that he, like Sterne, feels for the sake of feeling. He sits down deliberately to be tender, and, when he has done it, he rubs his hands, and says, 'Ha, ha, I am warm; I have seen the fire.'

There is no difficulty in explaining the fact that the taste for indulging in this particular kind of enjoyment is usually considered somewhat contemptible. The reason is, that people feel, and feel rightly, that there is something mean in valuing that which is in itself so serious, and so closely connected with the highest objects of life, for the mere specific pleasure by which it is accompanied. The occasions which excite tender feelings are, generally speaking, those in which a high-minded and generous person would be inclined to forget himself and his own sensations, in the effort by which those sensations are produced, and instead of trying to heighten his feelings by such devices as elaborate language and luscious descriptions, would not care about them at all, and would express them only so far as might be rendered necessary for the sake of others. For instance, the description of a death-bed is solemn and affecting, so long as it is confined to the statement of matters which the writer reasonably supposes to be interesting to those whom he addresses. Every expression which is put in either because he enjoys the interest of dwelling upon the matter, or in order to heighten the emotion of himself or his reader, is justly chargeable with being sentimental. In real life, the distinction may instantly be detected. It is impossible to mistake what is now-a-days called sensation writing when you see it. Whether it takes the shape of minute detail, or ghastly calmness, or conscious unconsciousness, the trail of the serpent[3] is over it all.

---

[3] *The Trail of the Serpent; or, Three Times Dead* (1861 reissue of *Three Times Dead; or, The Secret of the Hearth*, 1854), by Mary Elizabeth Braddon, married name Maxwell (1835–1915; *ODNB*, novelist).

SENTIMENTALISM

225

The general maxim that, in real life, people ought not, as a rule, to permit themselves to dwell on the specific pleasure which attends tender emotions, but ought, when such emotions are excited, to think principally of the object which excites them, explains many of the most characteristic features of our national manner. It shows, for instance, why it is that we are usually so careful to repress all public demonstrations of feeling, indeed all demonstrations of feeling, except those which are witnessed only by persons who fully share in them. The justification of such expressions of feeling is that they are necessary for the purpose of enlisting the sympathies of the person to whom they are made. If they were made publicly, they would of necessity be submitted to people who did not sympathize with or care for them. This would make no difference if the mere pleasure of the feeling itself were the object; and the fact that it does make all the difference shows that the pleasure attending the sense of the emotion is one which our habits of thought and feeling incline us to keep in the background. It is only on the rare occasions in which they are fairly overpowered by their feelings, that people, at least in this country, display emotion publicly. In other parts of the world, where the same restraint is not practised, the satisfaction taken in the actual sensation and expression of tenderness is more prominent, and is more commonly recognized as a legitimate source of pleasure.

The case of literature, and especially of fiction, is different and peculiar. The object of a poem or novel is to give pleasure, and to give, amongst others, that sort of pleasure which is derived from the excitement of the tender emotion. Hence the pleasure of tender feeling must be contemplated directly and expressly by poets and novelists; and this, no doubt, constitutes a real exception to the general rule, that the pleasure of tenderness ought to be enjoyed incidentally. The exception, however, is subject to the proviso that tenderness ought not to be put into a literary work in larger quantities than would be wholesome in that portion of real life which the literary work influences. Thus, a short song produces a slight effect on the mind while it is being sung, and serves as an artificial means for exciting tender feeling at pleasure. There is no harm in making it as tender as may be. It is like a pill, which a man can take when he wants it. A three-volume novel takes a good deal more time to read, and operates on a larger surface. It is read for its general effect, and describes a variety of things. The quantity of tenderness which ought to be put into it will vary according to the total effect which it is likely to produce, but there generally ought to be some.

* * *

Perhaps the worst result which the absence of the tender feelings produces on the character is that sort of hypocrisy which lays claim to them. When closely considered, this illustrates the observations already made. It is a great mistake to suppose that a hypocrite's feelings are not in a sense genuine. They are rather artificial than fictitious. A man who professes to have fine feelings, probably has, in general, a certain real taste for the pleasure of sentiment, considered as a pleasure. While Becky Sharp was actually pleading before her eyes in an interesting way, old Miss Crawley really did for the moment feel kindly towards her. The hypocritical sentimentalist is emphatically a sentimentalist in the bad sense of the word. Having little real tenderness, he gets up an artificial tenderness, because it is intrinsically pleasant.

226   ON THE NOVEL AND JOURNALISM

Joseph Surface[4] illustrates this, though his sentimentality was rather what we should now call sententiousness; but, for the time, he probably believed more or less in his own platitudes. Rousseau and Sterne illustrate, in its highest degree, the effects of treating tenderness as a luxury; and their well-known histories show what a purely selfish luxury such an indulgence may be. In our own days, such characters (never very common) are probably somewhat rarer than they formerly were. There never was so critical an age as the one in which we live, nor one which directed its criticism so unsparingly against that particular form of hypocrisy, which takes its rise in the abuse of tenderness. Our hypocrisy upon such matters runs in the opposite direction.

Though the pressure of the fear of ridicule and the general habits of society is so strong that it is by no means common, in these days, to have in people's manners well-marked evidence of the abuse of the tender feelings, there is much reason to fear that those feelings are, in fact, indulged in excess, and do exercise considerably more influence over the conduct of mankind than is desirable. The proofs of this abound in every direction. In almost every subject, in literature, in politics, in religion, in the tone taken by the public questions of all sorts, there is abundant evidence that great and increasing weight is attributed to the sentimental view of things. People appear to act, upon almost every occasion, on the principle that a pleasant feeling is rather an end to be desired for its own sake, than an index pointing to the attainment of a desirable object lying beyond. A thousand proofs of this might be given, but our limits confine us to a few. One signal one is to be found in the influence which novels exercise, not in their proper and natural sphere as amusements and works of art, but as irregular and informal arguments. A novel is, from the nature of the case, an appeal to feelings, and to feelings for their own sake. A novelist never lays down a proposition properly limited and supported. He confines himself to drawing pictures, which act powerfully, but always more or less indistinctly and indirectly, upon the feelings. Novels can hardly ever be thrown into the form of propositions capable of being distinctly attacked or defended. In so far as they are arguments at all—and they certainly operate as such very powerfully—they are arguments by way of association. They associate a strong feeling of disgust, or sympathy, or pity, with a particular class of facts; and they suggest to idle readers, or to any reader in an idle mood, conclusions which they do not really prove. Capital punishments, to take a single illustration, have often been attacked by novelists. The mode of attack generally is to describe the process of putting a criminal to death, in such a manner as to terrify, or even, perhaps, to sicken the reader. Hence, when he hears of capital punishments, he remembers the description which he has read, and shudders himself into the conclusion that things so terrible ought to be done away with. The question, whether the association supplies an argument against or in favour of the punishment is one which, from the nature of the case, a novelist cannot discuss. It is out of his province to appeal to the reason; he acts upon the will—but by the force of association more powerfully than the most elaborate arguments could act upon it. This explains what is the sting of the imputation of being a sentimental writer. It is a way of charging people with being either weak, or dishonest, or both. It implies

---

[4] Richard Brinsley Sheridan (1751–1816; *ODNB*, playwright and politician). *The School for Scandal* (produced 1777).

SENTIMENTALISM

that a man tries to gain his ends not by legitimate means, but by appeals to the passions, by trying to dissuade people from doing what is disagreeable merely because it is disagreeable, and not because it has a general tendency to produce a balance of pain over pleasure, or, in other words, because it is wrong. That a particular rule produces pain is no argument at all against it; for every rule does and must do so. The only relevant assertion is, that it produces pain on the balance; and, for this purpose, it must not only be debited with the pain, but credited with the pleasure, which it produces. A sentimental book is like a cooked account. Its object generally is to make things pleasant, and, as such, it shows that the person who states it, is either weak, ignorant, or fraudulent.

'Mr. Matthew Arnold and his Countrymen'
(*Saturday Review*, 3 December 1864)

JFS had been guardedly grateful to Arnold in 1859: 'It is the infirmity of all who take a clear and strong view of a particular subject to find a great difficulty in admitting into their minds the belief that any other view of it should appear equally natural to other people...we are grateful to him for putting before us, with equal ingenuity and perspicuity, a side of the question which is certainly not familiar in this country' ('Mr. Matthew Arnold on the Italian Question', *Sat. Rev.*, 13 Aug. 1859, on the dispute between church and state in Italy). Arnold's lecture, 'The Function of Criticism at the Present Time', was delivered by him in Oxford as Professor of Poetry (29 Oct. 1864, 'The Functions...'), and published in the *National Review* (Nov. 1864). JFS contested it in 'Mr. Matthew Arnold and his Countrymen' (*Sat. Rev.*, 3 Dec. 1864). Arnold responded both within the Preface to his *Essays in Criticism* (1865), and by adding remonstrative footnotes to his lecture. (Excerpts below, p. 235.) *Essays in Criticism* was itself promptly reviewed by JFS, as 'Mr. Matthew Arnold Amongst the Philistines' (*Sat. Rev.*, 25 Feb. 1865; below, p. 245). JFS's titular '···his Countrymen' had moved Arnold in 1864 to contemplate writing 'My Countrymen', which duly appeared in the *Cornhill* (Feb. 1866), with further jousting by JFS, 'Mr. Arnold on the Middle Classes' (*Sat. Rev.*, 10 Feb. 1866; p. 247), and 'Mr. Matthew Arnold on Culture' (*Sat. Rev.*, 20 July 1867; p. 251).

Mr. Matthew Arnold and his Countrymen

Mr. Matthew Arnold has contributed to the first number of the new series of the *National Review* a paper on the functions of criticism at the present time, which is an excellent specimen of that peculiar turn, both of style and thought, with which of late years he has so often amused and rather surprised his readers. Few readers of the better class of periodical literature need to be told that Mr. Arnold is a very clever man, possessed in an unusual degree of some very uncommon gifts. He is always brilliant, good-natured, entertaining, and even instructive. There is generally a certain degree of truth in what he says, and, whatever its nature may be, there can never be any doubt about its good faith. Mr. Arnold's utterances may not be the result of any profound meditation, but they at least represent genuine likes and dislikes. He does really work himself, at any rate for the time being, into an esoteric enthusiasm for the particular point which he enforces. It is also to be noticed that his points are always of the same kind. His self-imposed mission is to give good advice to the English people as to their manifold faults, especially as to their one great fault of being altogether inferior, in an intellectual and artistic point of view, to the French. He is so warm upon this subject that he has taught himself to write a dialect as like French as pure English can be. Indeed, it is a painful duty to admit that his turn for French is so strong that the undefiled

MR. MATTHEW ARNOLD AND HIS COUNTRYMEN

well[1] is sometimes very near defilement. Take such a sentence, for instance, as the following: 'But Burke is so great because, almost alone in England, he brings thought to bear upon politics, he saturates politics with thought; it is his accident that his ideas were at the service of an epoch of concentration, not of an epoch of expansion.' We can almost hear the head-voice,[2] with its sharp nasal ring, and see the eloquent hands gracefully turned outwards, as if to point first to the epoch of concentration and then to the epoch of expansion, with which a French lecturer would hand us this neat little sentence. The exquisite French-English in which Mr. Thackeray so much delighted is only a very little more of a caricature.

Mr. Arnold's present object is to make English criticism ashamed of itself and conscious of its own contemptible character. Like all that he writes, his article is very pretty reading, but from first to last it appears to us to be fundamentally wrong, and, in particular, it totally fails to apprehend that against which it is directed. The truth is that, like his French models, Mr. Arnold has quick sympathies and a great gift of making telling remarks; but, also like them, he has hardly any power of argument. At least, if he has, he rarely shows it. His general object in the paper before us is to defend some observations which he had made elsewhere on the functions of criticism; but the greater part of it is composed of illustrations of the poverty and vulgarity of the modern English mind, with an attempt to explain the cause and the remedy. The cause of our unfortunate condition is, he says, our constant anxiety about immediate practical results. The remedy is that criticism, and thought in general, ought to be disinterested. 'And how is it to be disinterested? By keeping aloof from practice; by resolutely following the law of its own nature, which is to be a free play of the mind on all subjects which it touches; by steadily refusing to lend itself to any of those ulterior political practical considerations about ideas which plenty of people will be sure to attach to them, which perhaps ought to be attached to them, which, in this country at any rate, are certain to be attached to them quite sufficiently, but which criticism has really nothing to do with. Its business is simply to know the best that is known and thought in the world, and, by in its turn making this known, to supply a current of new and fresh ideas.'

In illustration of his meaning, he tells us that the French live by ideas. Speaking of the French Revolution, he says, 'That a whole nation should have been penetrated with an enthusiasm for pure reason' (can Mr. Cobden[3] have been looking at the *National Review*?), 'and with an ardent zeal for making its prescriptions triumph, is a very remarkable thing... The French Revolution derives from the force, truth, and universality of the ideas which it took for its law, and from the passion with which it could inspire a multitude for those ideas, an unique and still living power.' It failed in practice by attempting to give an immediate practical application to those 'fine ideas of the reason'; but we English, who are great in practice, never ascend to ideas at all. A member of Parliament blasphemously said to Mr. Arnold, 'That a thing is an anomaly I consider to be no objection to it whatever.' We think ourselves a wonderful people—*teste*[4] Mr. Adderley, who made a speech to that effect to the Warwickshire farmers, and

---

[1] Spenser, *The Faerie Queene*, IV ii xxxii: 'Dan *Chaucer*, well of English vndefyled'.

[2] *OED* One of the higher registers of the voice in singing or speaking; applied both to the second register (that immediately above the *chest-voice*), and to the third register or falsetto. From 1849 DICKENS.

[3] Richard Cobden (1804–1865; *ODNB*, manufacturer and politician).

[4] *OED* on the authority or evidence of.

230 ON THE NOVEL AND JOURNALISM

Mr. Roebuck, who said so to the Sheffield cutlers; but criticism ought to see how short we fall of anything like ideal beauty. Mr. Roebuck spoke of the 'unrivalled happiness' of England. Mr. Adderley spoke of 'the Anglo-Saxon race...the best breed in the whole world.' Mr. Arnold, representing the higher criticism,[5] read in a newspaper that a woman named Wragg was in custody at Nottingham for child murder. Of this the higher criticism says: 'Wragg! If we are to talk of ideal perfection, has any one reflected what a touch of grossness in our race, what an original shortcoming in the most[6] delicate spiritual perceptions, is shown by the natural growth amongst us of such hideous names—Higginbottom, Stiggins, Bugg...and the final touch, *Wragg is in custody?* The sex lost in the confusion of our unrivalled happiness.' Criticism ought to show that Wragg should have been called (say) Fairfax; and that, instead of saying 'Wragg is in custody', the brutal journalist should have said, 'And so, on that cold November night, the door of Nottingham gaol was shut behind our sinful sister.' To the general public this way of putting it may not seem to make much difference, but Mr. Arnold thinks otherwise: 'Mr. Roebuck will have a poor opinion of an adversary who replies to his defiant songs of triumph only by murmuring under his breath, "Wragg is in custody", but in no other way will these songs of triumph be gradually induced to moderate themselves.' We do not envy the higher criticism if it has to go about 'murmuring *Wragg is in custody*', till all after-dinner speeches rise to the level of ideal beauty.

More serious functions, however, do present themselves for criticism in the other illustrations given by Mr. Arnold. He tells us, for instance, that 'the British Constitution, seen from the speculative side, sometimes looks a colossal machine for the manufacture of Philistines.' Then criticism, looking at the Divorce Court,[7] 'in which the gross, unregenerate British Philistine has indeed stamped an image of himself'...'may be permitted to find the marriage theory of Catholicism refreshing and elevating.' Some parts of the marriage theory of Catholicism, as expressed in Suarez' *De Matrimonio*,[8] would, by the way, form an appropriate appendix to the *Times'* report of the Codrington case.[9] Dr. Colenso[10] is a mere Philistine of rather a contemptible kind, though M. Renan[11] (with whom Mr. Arnold by no means agrees) is quite the reverse: 'Bishop Colenso's book reposes on a total misconception of the essential elements of the religious problem as that problem is now presented for solution. To criticism, therefore...it is, however well meant, of no importance whatever. M. Renan's book attempts a new synthesis of the elements furnished to us by the four Gospels', and such a synthesis 'is the very essence of the religious problem as now presented.' The higher criticism, of course, knows what the religious problem is, and how it is presented, and therefore it treats M. Renan with respect, and Bishop Colenso with the most curious kind of contempt—the contempt of a benevolent elder sister for the little girl who

---

[5] *OED* criticism, *specifically* higher criticism. From 1836. 1881 ROBERTSON SMITH A series of questions affecting the composition, the editing, and the collection of the sacred books. This class of questions forms the special subject of the branch of critical science which is usually distinguished from the verbal criticism of the text by the name of Higher or Historical Criticism.

[6] 'the more', Arnold.

[7] The Matrimonial Causes Act (1857) abolished ecclesiastical jurisdiction in matrimonial matters, and made possible, by court order, secular divorce.

[8] Francisco Suárez (1548–1617), *De Justitia et Jure* and *De Matrimonio* (Paris: 1861).

[9] Pursued in 'The Mote and the Beam' (*Sat. Rev.*, 3 Dec. 1864), p. 239.

[10] John William Colenso (1814–1883; *ODNB*, bishop of Natal).

[11] Ernest Renan (1823–1892), *The Life of Jesus* (1863; English tr., 1864).

MR. MATTHEW ARNOLD AND HIS COUNTRYMEN

thinks that the world is a sham because she has discovered that her doll is stuffed with straw.

Mr. Arnold's theory, diffused over more than twenty pages, may be shortly expressed thus, for the most part in his own words:

'The prescriptions of reason are absolute, unchanging, of universal validity.'

It is the function of the higher criticism to discover and state these prescriptions of reason, leaving to others the inferior task of adapting them to practice.

English criticism is deficient in caring only for immediate practical results, putting on one side the prescriptions of reason.

Unless by some means this is remedied, the nation's spirit 'must in the long run die of inanition'.

Let us now consider what this theory is worth. Mr. Arnold overlooks two considerations which dispose of his whole argument about the present state of English criticism. These are, first, that there is in England a school of philosophy which thoroughly understands, and on theoretical grounds deliberately rejects, the philosophical theory which Mr. Arnold accuses the English nation of neglecting, and that the practical efforts of the English people, especially their practical efforts in the way of literary criticism, are for the most part strictly in accordance with the principles of that philosophy. Secondly, that whereas, according to his own system, practice and theory form different spheres—practice to be regulated by a view to immediate results, theory by a view to pure reason (whatever that may be)—and whereas practical objections only ought to be applied by him to practical inquiries, and objections drawn from pure reason to theoretical inquiries, yet again and again he objects to specific practical measures on theoretical grounds.

First, there is in England a school of philosophy which perfectly understands, and on theoretical grounds deliberately rejects, the philosophical theory which Mr. Arnold accuses the English of neglecting. Mr. Arnold's whole essay assumes the truth of the transcendental theory of philosophy. Englishmen are merely practical, they have no philosophy in them at all, because they set on one side 'prescriptions of reason, absolute, unchanging, and of universal validity.' This is just like saying a man has no religion because he is not a Roman Catholic. Mr. Arnold surely cannot be ignorant of the fact that, from the days of Hobbes and Locke to those of Mr. Mill and Mr. Bain,[12] the most influential of English thinkers have utterly denied the truth of transcendentalism, and have constantly affirmed that all knowledge is based upon experience and sensation. This may be true, or it may be false, but it is just as much entitled to be called philosophy as anything else. Now the commonest acquaintance with this view of things will show that in principle, though of course not in detail, it justifies the common run of English criticism—that is, of the remarks which English people make on passing events for practical or literary purposes. Take, for instance, Mr. Arnold's member of Parliament who did not object to anomalies. What Mr. Arnold viewed as his blasphemy really amounts to this: Political institutions exist for the purpose of producing a maximum of happiness, in the wide sense of the word. Experience alone can show what institutions, in a given case, will produce that result. Experience is either in the inductive or in the deductive stage. It is in the inductive stage until its results have

---

[12] Alexander Bain (1818–1903; *ODNB*, psychologist).

fallen into the shape of general principles, like those of mathematics, which can be applied at once to particular cases. When they have, it is in the deductive stage. Our political experience has not yet reached the deductive stage. It is still inductive. But, in considering institutions inductively, it can be no objection to them that they are anomalies—*i.e.* that they vary from some principle asserted to be true, for induction considers them only as facts, and does not, and by its very nature cannot, recognise the truth of the principles which they are said to contradict. Before Mr. Arnold lectures the English nation on their want of logic, he ought to understand that a man may deny his major[13] without denying the force of syllogisms in general. The member of Parliament meant, 'Your general principles being false, it is no objection to any institution that, judged by them, it is anomalous.' No man out of a madhouse ever says, Admitting the truth of your premises and the form of your syllogism, I deny the truth of the conclusion.

In fact, no nation in the world is so logical as the English nation. Once get it well convinced of the truth of a general principle—which is, as it ought to be, considering how hard it is to state general principles correctly, a very hard task—and it will do anything. For instance, the English nation believes in political economy, and the consequence is that it is the only nation in the world which has established free trade. The new Poor Law and the Bank Charter Act were based upon the principles of the same science. Bentham persuaded the English nation that the greatest happiness of the greatest number was the true rule for legislation, and every part of the law has been reformed by degrees by the application, more or less skilful and complete, of that abstract principle. Newton persuaded the English nation that the force of gravity varies inversely as the square of the distance, and this doctrine, with its consequences, was accepted and worked out to its practical results by the English nation before any other people fully took it in. Mr. Mill has persuaded the English nation that men ought to argue, not from universals to particulars, but from particulars to particulars, and the practical influence of this highly abstract principle is seen in that state of criticism to which Mr. Arnold objects. Our modern Indian policy has been governed by the abstract principle that the natives ought to be civilized on the English pattern. When abstract principles like these are embraced by and do influence the English people most deeply, is it just, or even decent, to talk about 'British Philistines' because we English do not choose to recognise as eternal truths a set of platitudes which may be proved to be false? And is it better than sophistry to try to bolster up the credit of these platitudes, in the face of their notorious failure, by saying that they are true in the sphere of absolute reason, and that, in order to purge our grossness, we ought to go and live in that sphere, murmuring under our breaths 'Wragg is in custody'? Our English notion is, that the only test by which you can judge of the truth of a general principle is its application to facts. If it will not open the lock, it may be a very pretty key, but it is certainly not the true one. It is from facts only that principles can be got, and it is by facts only that their truth, when they are got at, can be tested. Mr. Arnold is like a man who says to a painter or a sculptor, 'What a gross Philistine you are to pass your time in chipping at that hideous stone, dabbling with that nasty clay, or fiddling about with oil-paints and canvas! Why do you

---

[13] *OED* major. Logic. major term: the term which enters into the predicate of the conclusion of a syllogism. major premiss, major proposition: that premiss of a syllogism that contains the major term.

MR. MATTHEW ARNOLD AND HIS COUNTRYMEN

not at once rise to the sphere of pure reason, and produce, as I do in my dreams, statues and pictures of eternal and absolute beauty?'

Mr. Arnold, like other transcendentalists, is very shy of giving us an eternal truth to look at. He does, however, try his hand at one, and a better illustration of that great maxim, 'I never heard of an eternal truth without thinking of an infernal lie', has seldom been seen: 'The prescriptions of reason are absolute, unchanging, of universal validity. *To count by tens is the simplest way of counting.* That is a proposition of which every one from here to the antipodes feels the force; at least, I should say so if we did not live in a country where it is not impossible that any morning we may find a letter in the *Times* declaring that a decimal coinage is an absurdity.' This is a marvellous passage. The Decimal Coinage Commissioners declared against the scheme. One of them was Lord Overstone.[14] Imagine Mr. Matthew Arnold asserting that Lord Overstone is incapable of abstract thought on his own subjects! Apart from this, Mr. Arnold is not only wrong, but so clearly wrong that there is probably little hope of convincing him of it. What he calls a self-evident proposition is, in the first place, not abstract; in the second place, it is not true; and in the third place, if it were both abstract and true, it would not prove the consequence connected with it. First, it is not abstract. The abstract proposition is that, if any system of notation whatever be given, there will be some convenience in making the base of that system the unit of tables of weights, measures, and coinage. This is, no doubt, true. But some other abstract propositions are also true, one of which is that to be a multiple of many factors is a convenience to which regard should be had in choosing a base of notation. Now, the number ten has but two factors, two and five, both of which are prime numbers, and ten is therefore a very inconvenient base for a system of any kind. Twelve, on the other hand, is highly convenient, being divisible by four factors, of which two only are primes. Hence there is a balance of advantages. To count by tens has the advantage of taking as your unit the base of an established system of notation. To count by twelves has the advantage of taking as your unit a number in itself far more convenient for that purpose. The advantage of counting by twelve is principally felt in small calculations done in the head. The advantage of counting by ten is principally felt in large calculations done on paper, and is not felt till you get past twenty. Hence a system of pounds reckoned on the decimal basis, and shillings and pence reckoned on the duodecimal basis, combines two sets of advantages. On the other hand, the decimal system is notoriously inconvenient for small transactions.

To sum up—our transcendentalist supposes himself to be stating an abstract proposition when he is stating a concrete one. Instead of saying 'to count by tens', he should say, 'to take as your unit an established base of notation.' He supposes himself to be stating a true proposition when he is stating a false one. It is not true that to count by tens is the simplest way of counting, or that it is the most convenient, unless you add the very material clauses—'ten being given as the base of notation', and 'except for numbers under twenty'. Lastly, he supposes himself to be stating a complete proposition when he is stating one which is incomplete; for it does not follow that, because a particular way of counting is the simplest, any special system of coinage ought to be adopted. To count by ones, to have a separate name for each number, would no doubt

---

[14] Samuel Jones Loyd, Baron Overstone (1796–1883; *ODNB*, banker).

be simpler than to count by tens, but no one advocates such a system. Let it be observed that each of these objections is theoretical. Mr. Arnold may call his countrymen gross Philistines as much as ever he pleases, but they will always be able to reply—We object to what you call your theories, not because they are theories, but because they are not true theories, but arbitrary generalities, which we can show to be rash, false, or at best incomplete.

The second objection to Mr. Arnold's theory is that, according to his own view, theory and practice form different spheres—practice to be regulated by a view to immediate results, theory by pure reason. Yet he constantly objects to practical measures on theoretical grounds. Thus, he says that the Divorce Court is a hideous institution, and that it is refreshing to turn from it to the Catholic marriage theory. What relation, on his principles, is there between the two things? By his own rule, he cannot inquire into, and has no right to notice, the hideousness of the Divorce Court. That is a practical question, a matter of business to be decided on common earthly grounds. The Catholic marriage theory, we suppose, is a matter of pure reason. Let each have its sphere, but unless and until pure reason can work out its marriage theory in a sufficiently definite shape to solve every practical question connected with the marriage law, those who hold it have no other right to call the Divorce Court hideous than the authors of the Divorce Act have to call them visionary. If theorists are not sure enough of the truth of their theories to take the responsibility of putting them in practice, they have no right to depreciate the rule of thumb. When Don Quixote refused to try his sword on the second edition of his helmet,[15] he surely renounced the right to sneer at less romantic wares. When Mr. Arnold has got a theory which will fully explain all the duties of the legislator on the matter of marriage, he will have a right to abuse the Divorce Court.

Much the same may be said of Mr. Arnold's criticism on Dr. Colenso. His book, he says, is 'of no importance whatever' to criticism. It 'reposes on a fundamental misconception of the essential elements of the religious problem.' M. Renan's book, on the other hand, deals with the very essence of the religious problem. 'For saying this' (in *Macmillan's Magazine*), says Mr. Arnold, 'I was greatly blamed, because I was told that I was a liberal attacking a liberal; yet surely I had a right to say that a man in pursuit of truth had taken a false method.' Certainly some of Mr. Arnold's readers thought, and still think, that, considering how desperately hard the lower criticism was on Dr. Colenso, the higher criticism might have chosen some other victim, or some other time for scourging that particular victim. It was not, however, for this alone that Mr. Arnold was blamed, but for something very different. It was for the way in which he argued that it was a crime against literary criticism and the higher culture to attempt to inform the ignorant. He was blamed for saying much which was summed up in these words, 'Knowledge and truth, in the full sense of the words, are not attainable by the great mass of the human race at all.' In reference to the matter in hand, this meant, 'Ordinary English people have no business to have any opinion on the question whether or not the whole of the Pentateuch is true. The higher minds have, but the great bulk of the nation ought to leave such matters to M. Renan and a few others, and it is bad taste, a low vulgar thing, to address them on the question.' This was very different from

---

[15] The First Part, ch. xxi. Of the high Adventure and rich prize of Mambrino's Helmet. (A barber's brass basin.)

MR. MATTHEW ARNOLD AND HIS COUNTRYMEN

saying that Dr. Colenso's method was false. It said that his object was bad. Granting the goodness of the object and the truth of the assertions, it was simply absurd to deny their relevancy. Indeed, Mr. Arnold did not deny it. His point was, that the book ought not to have been written. This is altogether inconsistent with his present view, which is, that practice and theory ought to be divorced. Theory ought to sit on a hill retired,[16] and argue high about a new synthesis of the four Gospels, and care nothing for practice. Let it, then, care nothing for practice, but do not let it attack practical men for making practical remarks. Dr. Colenso wrote *ad populum*. Mr. Arnold denied his right to do so, but it is very hard now to change the charge, and to blame him for having addressed the higher culture of Europe in a popular way. Dr. Colenso's book may or may not repose on a false conception of the religious problem, though it is a strong thing to assert that a critical inquiry into the Old Testament must, under all circumstances, be simply worthless; but Mr. Arnold's criticism certainly reposes on a false conception of Dr. Colenso's book. Indeed, his two criticisms 'repose' on conflicting conceptions, and, as in the case of other attempts to sit on two stools at once, the result is grotesque.

The way in which Mr. Arnold treats Dr. Colenso is an excellent illustration of the fundamental weakness which affects all that he writes. With all his ability, he sometimes gives himself the airs of the distinguished courtier who shone so bright and smelt so sweet when he had occasion to talk with Hotspur about the prisoners.[17] He is always using a moral smelling-bottle, like those beloved countrymen, who, at foreign *tables d'hôte*, delight to hold forth on the vulgarity of 'those English'. Dr. Colenso condescended to do a sum about the '800 and odd pigeons'.[18] Mr. Arnold is almost ready to faint, till he is consoled by the thought of M. Renan and his sublime synthesis. He reads or looks at the Codrington case (which certainly had a strong scent about it), and, murmuring under his breath, 'Gross unregenerate British Philistines', flies in despair to the Catholic marriage theory, which purifies the country of Rabelais, Diderot, Faublas, Montépin,[19] and M. Dumas *fils*.

MATTHEW ARNOLD
FROM THE PREFACE TO *ESSAYS IN CRITICISM* (1865)

Several of the Essays which are here collected and reprinted have had the good or the bad fortune to be much criticised at the time of their first publication. I am not now going to

---

[16] *Paradise Lost*, ii 557–61: 'Others apart sat on a Hill retir'd, / In thoughts more elevate, and reason'd high / Of Providence, Foreknowledge, Will, and Fate, / Fixt Fate, free will, foreknowledge absolute, / And found no end, in wandring mazes lost.' To JFS, what went for Arnold goes also for the very different phenomenon that is Carlyle. 'His career and present position embody more fully than those of any other man the especial advantages and disadvantages of the literary temperament—the turn of mind which leads its possessors to sit on a hill retired and make remark upon men and things instead of taking part in the common affairs of life' ('Mr. Carlyle', *Sat. Rev.*,19 June 1858; *Essays* 243).

[17] *Henry IV*, Part I, I iii.

[18] Arnold, questioning Colenso's literalistic calculation 'as to the account in Leviticus of the provision made for the priests: "If the priests have to eat 264 pigeons a day, how many must each priest eat?"' ('The Bishop and the Philosopher', *Macmillan's Mag.*, Jan. 1863). Leviticus 12:6–7, She shall bring a lamb of the first year for a burnt offering, and a young pigeon, or a turtledove, for a sin offering.

[19] François Rabelais (1494–prior-to-1553), his scabrous stories of Gargantua and Pantagruel. Denis Diderot (1713–1784), philosophical sceptic. *Les Amours du chevalier de Faublas* (1787), a scandalous novel by Jean-Baptiste Louvet de Couvray (1760–1797). Xavier Henri Aymon Perrin, Count of Montépin (1823–1902), whose novels were judged obscene.

ON THE NOVEL AND JOURNALISM

inflict upon the reader a reply to those criticisms; for one or two explanations which are desirable, I shall elsewhere, perhaps, be able some day to find an opportunity; but, indeed, it is not in my nature—some of my critics would rather say, not in my power—to dispute on behalf of any opinion, even my own, very obstinately. To try and approach Truth on one side after another, not to strive or cry, not to persist in pressing forward on any one side, with violence and self-will,—it is only thus, it seems to me, that mortals may hope to gain any vision of the mysterious Goddess, whom we shall never see except in outline, but only thus even in outline. He who will do nothing but fight impetuously towards her on his own, one, favourite, particular line, is inevitably destined to run his head into the folds of the black robe in which she is wrapped.

I am very sensible that this way of thinking leaves me under great disadvantages in addressing a public composed from a people 'the most logical', says the *Saturday Review*, 'in the whole world.' But the truth is, I have never been able to hit it off happily with the logicians, and it would be mere affectation in me to give myself the airs of doing so.

* * *

FROM 'THE FUNCTION OF CRITICISM AT THE PRESENT TIME'
Essays in Criticism (1865) with Arnold's footnote additions

But the prescriptions of reason are absolute, unchanging, of universal avidity; *to count by tens is the simplest way of counting.**

* A writer in the *Saturday Review*, who has offered me some counsels about style for which I am truly grateful, suggests that this should stand as follows: *To take as your unit an established base of notation, ten being given as the base of notation, is, except for numbers under twenty, the simplest way of counting.* I tried it so, but I assure him, without jealousy, that the more I looked at his improved way of putting the thing, the less I liked it. It seems to me that the maxim, in this shape, would never make the tour of a world, where most of us are plain easy-spoken people. He forgets that he is a reasoner, a member of a school, a disciple of the great Bentham, and that he naturally talks in the scientific way of his school, with exact accuracy, philosophic propriety; I am a mere solitary wanderer in search of the light, and I talk an artless, unstudied, every-day, familiar language. But, after all, this is the language of the mass of the world.

The mass of Frenchmen who felt the force of that prescription of the reason which my reviewer, in his purified language, states thus: *to count by tens has the advantage of taking as your unit the base of an established system of notation,* certainly rendered this, for themselves, in some such loose language as mine. My point is that they felt the force of a prescription of the reason so strongly that they legislated in accordance with it. They may have been wrong in so doing; they may have foolishly omitted to take other prescriptions of reason into account;— the non-English world does not seem to think so, but let that pass; what I say is, that by legislating as they did they showed a keen susceptibility to purely rational, intellectual considerations. On the other hand, does my reviewer say that we keep our monetary system unchanged because our nation has grasped the intellectual proposition which he puts, in his masterly way, thus: *to count by twelves has the advantage of taking as your unit a number in itself far more convenient than ten for that purpose?* Surely not; but because our system is there, and we are too practical a people to trouble ourselves about its intellectual aspect.

To take a second case. The French Revolutionists abolished the sale of offices, because they thought (my reviewer will kindly allow me to put the thing in my imperfect, popular language) the sale of offices a gross anomaly. We still sell commissions in the army. I have no doubt my reviewer, with his scientific powers, can easily invent some beautiful formula to make us appear

MR. MATTHEW ARNOLD AND HIS COUNTRYMEN

to be doing this on the purest philosophical principles; the principles of Hobbes, Locke, Bentham, Mr. Mill, Mr. Bain, and himself, their worthy disciple. But surely the plain unscientific account of the matter is, that we have the anomalous practice (he will allow it is, in itself, an anomalous practice?) established, and that (in the words of senatorial wisdom[20] already quoted) 'for a thing to be an anomaly we consider to be no objection to it whatever.'

* * *

How serious a matter it is to try and resist, I had ample opportunity of experiencing when I ventured some time ago to criticise the celebrated first volume of Bishop Colenso.*

* So sincere is my dislike to all personal attack and controversy, that I abstain from reprinting, at this distance of time from the occasion which called them forth, the essays in which I criticised the Bishop of Natal's book;[21] I feel bound, however, after all that has passed, to make here a final declaration of my sincere impenitence for having published them. The Bishop of Natal's subsequent volumes are in great measure free from the crying fault of his first; he has at length succeeded in more clearly separating, in his own thoughts, the idea of science from the idea of religion; his mind appears to be opening as he goes along, and he may perhaps end by becoming a useful biblical critic, though never, I think, of the first order.

Still, in taking leave of him at the moment when he is publishing, for popular use, a cheap edition of his work, I cannot forbear repeating yet once more, for his benefit and that of his readers, this sentence from my original remarks upon him: *There is truth of science and truth of religion; truth of science does not become truth of religion till it is made religious.* And I will add: Let us have all the science there is from the men of science; from the men of religion, let us have religion.

* * *

When one looks, for instance, at the English Divorce Court—an institution which perhaps has its practical conveniences, but which in the ideal sphere is so hideous.*

* A critic, already quoted, says that I have no right, on my own principles, to 'object to practical measures on theoretical grounds', and that only 'when a man has got a theory which will fully explain all the duties of the legislator on the matter of marriage, will he have a right to abuse the Divorce Court.' In short, he wants me to produce a plan for a new and improved Divorce Court, before I call the present one hideous. But God forbid that I should thus enter into competition with the Lord Chancellor! It is just this invasion of the practical sphere which is really against my principles; the taking a practical measure into the world of ideas, and seeing how it looks there, is, on the other hand, just what I am recommending. It is because we have not been conversant enough with ideas that our practice now falls so short; it is only by becoming more conversant with them that we shall make it better. Our present Divorce Court is not the result of any legislator's meditations on the subject of marriage; rich people had an anomalous privilege of getting divorced; privileges are odious, and we said everybody should have the same chance. There was no meditation about marriage here; that was just the mischief.

If my practical critic will but himself accompany me, for a little while, into the despised world of ideas; if, renouncing any attempt to patch hastily up, with a noble disdain for transcendentalists, our present Divorce law, he will but allow his mind to dwell a little,

---

[20] Psalm 105:22, To bind his princes at his pleasure, and teach his senators wisdom.
[21] 'The Bishop and the Philosopher' (*Macmillan's Mag.*, Jan. 1863), affiliated to Arnold's essay on Spinoza.

first on the Catholic idea of marriage, which exhibits marriage as indissoluble, and then upon that Protestant idea of marriage, which exhibits it as a union terminable by mutual consent—if he will meditate well on these, and afterwards on the thought of what married life, according to its idea, really is, of what family life really is, of what social life really is, and national life, and public morals,—he will find, after a while, I do assure him, the whole state of his spirit quite changed; the Divorce Court will then seem to him, if he looks at it, strangely hideous; and he will at the same time discover in himself, as the fruit of his inward discipline, lights and resources for making it better, of which now he does not dream.

'The Mote and the Beam'
(*Saturday Review*, 3 December 1864)

'One day last week the *Times* contained an excellent article on a couple of scoundrels who were convicted at the Old Bailey...'

* * *

AN EDITORIAL IN *The Times* (26 Nov. 1864)

Few convictions and sentences deserve to be received with more satisfaction than those of the two quacks, HENERY (or WRAY) and ANDERSON, which we reported from the Central Criminal Court yesterday. These men are examples of a class of miscreants who extort enormous sums by practising the most infamous tortures upon the worst and weakest parts of human nature. Their system is as simple as it is infamous. A person imagines himself to be suffering from some illness, about which, from motives of false delicacy, he is unwilling to consult a regular practitioner. He sees one of the advertisements of these quacks, which, to the disgrace of our Press, are scattered broadcast over the country, and is induced to apply to him. From that moment he ceases to be a free being, and if he cannot summon up the courage and determination displayed by the prosecutor in this case, he is a slave under the lash of the quack he has applied to until he compounds with his tyrant for some monstrous ransom. The quack knows that his victim has resorted to him from combined motives of fear and shame, in order to avoid anything approaching to exposure. He knows, therefore, that he may demand almost anything, without, as a rule, being in any danger of resistance. First of all the victim is supplied at enormous charges with some stuff or other which is not even intended to benefit him; he soon finds he is being gulled, but when he endeavours to withdraw from the trap, he is threatened with exposure unless he continues to submit to the demands made upon him. In this case the unfortunate prosecutor had paid 86*l*. in half a year before he attempted to break loose, and six months after he had ceased to receive advice or medicine he was attacked by a further demand for 150*l*. Upon his refusal to submit to this extortion two letters were written to him threatening to publish the matter. Fortunately, he had the prudence and courage to put the letters into the hands of his solicitor, and to prosecute the writers. It is very rarely indeed, however, that persons can make up their minds to face the annoyance and disgust which such a resistance entails, and these tactics are all but always successful. It is notorious to medical men that hundreds—nay, thousands of pounds are being constantly extorted in this way. Persons in a good position will pay almost anything to avoid the exposure they are threatened with. In this instance, however, the prosecutor resisted successfully; a conviction was obtained on the charge of conspiracy, and the prisoners were sentenced each to two years' imprisonment with hard labour.

We rejoice that two of these scoundrels have at last met with some punishment, and we hope it will encourage other victims to their practices to resist and prosecute. To do so is to perform a public service, for one such conviction weakens the chains of every other

240   ON THE NOVEL AND JOURNALISM

slave to this tyranny. The sole power of these men consists in a moral certainty that their victims will not prosecute. Let that certainty be removed, and all their power is gone. We regret, indeed, heartily, with Baron BRAMWELL, that it was not possible to award a heavier punishment. As he said, it is impossible to conceive a more abominable offence. It is a sort of moral garotting by the foulest possible instrument. It is not merely, said the Judge, one robbery that is committed, but a succession of robberies. The bodily pain, moreover, that is inflicted by physical violence is nothing to the moral suffering of living in a constant sense of fear and shame. Add to this the abominable nature of the means employed, and it is not too much to say that the ruffian who is sentenced to penal servitude for a garotte robbery is a worthy member of society compared with the wretches who carry on this infamous trade.

We do not discharge the unpleasant duty of making these remarks from any notion of affecting the criminals themselves, for they must be dead to all human feelings before they can engage in such a trade. But to give publicity to their proceedings may be the means of saving many victims from their toils; and there are one or two means in the power of the public by which their system of extortion may be greatly checked. First of all, we appeal to the Press to consider whether it is not disgraceful to promote the ends of these wretches by publishing their advertisements. It is impossible to plead that these advertisements are inserted in ignorance of their meaning, for no man of common sense can be blind to what is meant by their suggestions. Every one, in fact, knows the sort of advertisement we allude to, and we are sorry to add that every one is daily liable to be insulted with it. In the best-conducted and most costly papers, as well as in the least respectable, may be seen these vile baits. Let it be considered that these advertisements are the very instruments by which this infamous business is carried on. It is solely through the allurements held out in them that persons are induced to avoid a regular practitioner in the vain hope of a speedy and secret treatment. And, worse than this, such advertisements in innumerable cases are the means of creating the very evils of which they advertise the remedies; and the extortion practised is, probably, of even less importance than the moral evil thus produced. If, therefore, our contemporaries would resolutely exclude from their columns any advertisements of this nature, they would strike at the very root of this infamous trade, and prevent an incalculable amount of moral corruption. We are satisfied that they have only to consider the matter to decide on this course at once.

But there are other ways of advertising, which are equally, if not more, pernicious. There are institutions in the metropolis which, under different names, are filled with the most disgusting representations. These places are advertised in every thoroughfare of London by the gratuitous distribution of papers. It is hard to believe that powers do not already exist to put down such exhibitions. The police have large powers under Lord CAMPBELL's Act, and it might be considered whether the term 'pictures, drawings, or other *representations*' would not include the models exhibited in these places. But, at all events, if no existing Act is ample enough to meet the case, there never was more urgent need of some extension of the law. It is idle to prohibit indecent pictures and prints, as was done by Lord CAMPBELL's Act, if representations infinitely more offensive to public morality are to be passed over. We are satisfied that we shall be supported by the whole medical profession in saying that no useful end whatever is answered by the institutions we are denouncing. In fact, the medical journals have for years endeavoured to put them down. We earnestly trust either that the police will find that they have the power to interfere, or that the Government will obtain the necessary powers at the earliest possible opportunity. It is sufficiently unpleasant to have to notice such a subject at all, and we hope it may prove sufficient to have once drawn attention to it. Probably none but medical men are fully aware of the magnitude of the evil, but we believe it is serious enough to demand the most prompt and vigorous measures.

* * *

The victim of the blackmail was a captain who had been badly wounded in the head when serving in the Crimea, and his consultation 'about a disease from which I was suffering' derived from the conviction that masturbation drives you mad; in the blackmailers' terms, 'spermatorrhœa, brought on by self-pollution', 'by base habits'. (*OED* 1858 spermatorrhœa, seminal flux. 1879 doubtless exists as a disease although rare.)

JFS: 'The daily press in general, and the *Times* in particular, would do well to remove the beam from their own eye whilst extracting the mote from the advertising columns of their neighbours.' Matthew 7:3–5, And why beholdest thou the mote that is in thy brother's eye, but considerest not the beam that is in thine own eye? Or how wilt thou say to thy brother, Let me pull out the mote out of thine eye; and, behold, a beam is in thine own eye? Thou hypocrite, first cast out the beam out of thine own eye; and then shalt thou see clearly to cast out the mote out of thy brother's eye.

The Mote and the Beam

One day last week the *Times* contained an excellent article on a couple of scoundrels who were convicted at the Old Bailey of extorting money from a young man whom they had deluded into consulting them about a malady, real or imaginary. These rascals received the severest punishment which the law could give—namely, two years' imprisonment and hard labour. The *Times* remarked, with perfect truth, that this was far too light a sentence, that they were as much worse than garotters as a systematic receiver of stolen goods is worse than a common thief, and that the means which they used were, to those used by garotters, what prolonged torture is to transient violence. In all this we heartily agree, and amongst the fruits which the next session of Parliament is to bring forth it may be earnestly hoped that one will be an Act, in a single section, assimilating the case of those who extort by exposing their patient's diseases to that of those who extort by accusing of infamous crimes; and if, in addition to the penal servitude which can be, and already is, awarded in the last-mentioned cases, flogging were superadded to both, the public at large would be well pleased, and the infamous wretches who carry on such practices would be addressed by the only argument which they are certain to be able to understand.

The *Times*, however, did not stop here. It very properly said that to publish the filthy advertisements which enable these wretches to carry on their robberies was in some degree to partake of their guilt; and it added, that those loathsome mock-scientific exhibitions which are to be seen in some of our leading thoroughfares were nuisances of the same kind, which ought to be abated in the same way by the strong hand of the law. This is perfectly sound doctrine. We would even go a step further. Why not make it penal either to publish, or distribute in the streets, or post on the walls these filthy things? It would be no difficult matter to draw an Act which would effectually put down the scoundrels who live upon the agonies, bodily and mental, of a number of poor lads, who, having yielded to the temptations of youth, exaggerate the consequences and character of their fault, and, instead of going to a respectable surgeon—who would both cure them, and respect their confidence, as a mere matter of course—put themselves in the power of gangs of ruffians who are capable of ruining them utterly in body and soul. We have been far too mealy-mouthed in this matter. There can be no real reason why common decency should not be protected, and why the streets should not be purged, once for all, from foul advertisements and still fouler exhibitions.

Upon all this we are happy to agree with our contemporary, and probably no decent person would be inclined to dissent. The evil is one of those which no human creature would stand up to defend if any one would denounce it. We cannot, however, stop here. There is a point on which we should hardly agree so readily. The daily press in general, and the *Times* in particular, would do well to remove the beam from their own eye whilst extracting the mote from the advertising columns of their neighbours. It is quite true that the most innocent lad or the purest woman may read the *Times* advertisements from end to end without meeting anything to offend the eye or stain the imagination. From the announcements of births, deaths, and marriages, down to the end of the 'want places', all is perfectly proper; but can the same be said of the news? What about the report of Codrington *v.* Codrington?[1] Which is worst—to put, for the sake of a few shillings, into the corner of a paper, an advertisement which, however filthy, cannot be called attractive even to the most degraded, and which would hardly be read by any one to whom it could do any moral harm; or to promote the sale of the most popular and influential paper in the world by filling five or six columns a day for three or four days together with a story more attractive, more immoral, more coarsely expressed, more closely studded with every filthy detail which could excite and gratify the prurient curiosity of young people hovering on the verge of innocence, than the most voluptuous imagination of the most impure of French novelists?

We are accustomed to boast, and not unjustly, of the morality of English fiction. It is perfectly true that, on the whole, though they are open to objections on other grounds, English novels are pretty clean. Our sensation romances turn, for the most part, on murder; and if they do happen to derive their interest from breaches of the seventh instead of the sixth commandment, they generally avoid details. This may seem cold praise, but it certainly does put even our worst writers on a somewhat higher level than the worst writers amongst our neighbours. But what is to be said of our newspapers? Are there any other journals in Europe, or even in America, which would degrade themselves in so loathsome a manner? It is said that the most notorious member of the New York press owed its early success to the adroitness with which its enterprising editor mingled dirty stories, gleaned from various sources, with authentic commercial news; but the American press of the present day gives far less prominence than our own to the wretched garbage which has to be brought forward in courts of law. The *Times* seems to revel in it. It reports dirty trials with a detail and apparent relish which makes

---

[1] Admiral Henry Codrington (1808–1877) divorced his wife Helen in 1864, she being accused of adultery with a Colonel Anderson, and also of a lesbian affair with the publisher and women's rights activist Emily Faithfull. In retort, it was alleged that Codrington had himself 'neglected the society' of his wife for that of a Mrs. Watson, and that one night he had 'come in a night dress from his own room into the respondent's room and got into the bed where the respondent and Miss Faithfull were then sleeping together, and had attempted to have connexion with Miss Faithfull', but was prevented from 'effecting his purpose' by Miss Faithfull's resistance (*The Times*, 19 Nov. 1864).

THE MOTE AND THE BEAM 243

one wonder where it gets its reporters.[2] No doubt they possess for the most part a certain kind of talent. The *Times'* reports of law proceedings are, as a rule, very well done, and it is no secret that the conductors of that journal have so laudable an anxiety on this subject that, both on the circuits and in London, they usually employ barristers for the work. What must a man of education, a member of a liberal profession, a gentleman probably by birth and position, be made of who condescends to such degradation as that of reporting in the Divorce Court in the style approved of by the *Times?* Of course a barrister is often engaged in dirty cases. There is more or less dirt in a surprising proportion of trials, both civil and criminal. In such cases he only does his duty by taking a full note on the back of his brief of the evidence which is given; but does it follow that he ought to use means to give, say, a hundred thousand readers an opportunity of reading such matter? What would be thought of a judge who should needlessly publish at full length his notebooks, or a selection from them? Yet, if he were to do so, he would do nothing half so bad as the *Times* did in the case in question, and habitually does in similar cases.

We wish it to be observed that our censure is founded exclusively on the way in which the class of trials in question is reported. It is, of course, neither to be expected nor wished that a newspaper should exclude from its columns every reference to wickedness, or even every reference to sexual immorality. There must be many things in newspapers which are not exactly fit for the reading of boys or women. No doubt the Divorce Court must be open, and some notice must be taken of its proceedings, but the question is, how much? Is it necessary to put every casual reader as nearly as possible in the position of a juror, at the expense of polluting many thousands of minds with a vast mass of that very class of details which has given an infamous notoriety to a considerable number of French novels? If, in Mrs. Codrington's case, the object of the *Times* had been the legitimate one of informing the public in a general way of the working of the new Court and the new Act, the whole of the material facts might have been compressed into a single column of dry statement, which would have attracted no one whatever. For instance, what useful purpose was served by giving at full length all Mrs. Watson's evidence as to Mrs. Codrington's conversations,[3] or by giving *verbatim*, in question and answer, the evidence of Miss Faithfull, or by printing at full length that most filthy letter signed 'Lilian'? All these facts, and many others on which we have no wish to dwell, could serve no other purpose than that of stimulating and gratifying prurience. They were of absolutely no public importance whatever. They were, no doubt, more or less relevant to the particular questions which the jury had to decide, and were properly submitted to their consideration; but they illustrated no general principle, and threw light on no subject on which it is well for the public at large to be warned or instructed. If their publication is to be justified on the ground that they give to mankind at large information as to a side of human nature which usually remains concealed, precisely the same may be said of the nastiest parts of Rousseau's *Confessions*, or the foulest productions of the author of *Madame Bovary* or *Fanny*.[4] It would be quite as justifiable, and much less pernicious, to publish detailed accounts of the

---

[2] Dickens, *Our Mutual Friend* (Book the First, ch. xvi): 'And I do love a newspaper. You mightn't think it, but Sloppy is a beautiful reader of a newspaper. He do the Police in different voices.'). SLOPPY, a foundling, adopted by Betty Higden.

[3] *OED* 3, Sexual intercourse or intimacy.   [4] See 'The Romance of Vice', p. 185.

diseases of the patients in the foul ward of a London hospital, as to seduce boys and girls all over England into familiarity with the impure secrets of such a household as that of the Codringtons. Probably half the boys at the public schools, all the students at the Universities, and a large proportion of young ladies in gentlemen's families, owe to the filthy cases published in the *Times* an acquaintance equally precocious, needless, and vivid with all the details of adultery. They know what sort of acquaintances may lead to it, what sort of letters people write about it, when, where, by what devices, under what opportunities it is committed, how it may be concealed, how it may be found out, how it has to be proved in courts of law. In fact, they get from the Divorce Court a natural history of the offence. The reports of this tribunal might be headed 'Adultery-teaching by example'. All this they find in a journal which, in its own way, is moral in a high degree, and which, when it has occasion to refer to the filthy reports which it publishes, always regrets that the call of public duty is imperative.

This last excuse might perhaps be believed if the call of public duty was ever obeyed in dull cases, but it is not. Nasty cases are tried by scores at the assizes, and are generally described by the reporters as 'unfit for publication'. Nay, when the offenders in the Divorce Court are obscure, uninteresting people, their wretched doings are described in a manner suitable to their obscurity. It is only when gentlemen and ladies of sufficient position to excite curiosity as to their misdeeds misconduct themselves, that public duty inexorably demands the pollution of many thousands of minds. The flimsiness of this plea of public duty is well illustrated by the fact that, when the question of establishing the Divorce Court was under consideration, the *Times* used constantly to argue in favour of it on the ground that a single case would be tried once for all and disposed of, and that thus public duty would not force them to tell the same nasty story three times over. It would seem, from the length at which they now report single trials, that public duty is a hard mistress. If she must not publish the same dirty story three separate times, she insists upon having three times as much dirt as there used to be in each separate story.

Every one knows his own business best, but we would respectfully submit to our contemporary that decency would be the best policy. We can understand the importance of popularity with the debauched classes, but the *Times* ought to recollect that it has a large respectable circulation, and it ought to know that, if an alteration is not made in its system of reporting, it will come to stink in the nostrils of every master of a household which contains members likely to be polluted by such stories as the one which has occasioned these remarks.

'Mr. Matthew Arnold amongst the Philistines' (excerpts) (*Saturday Review*, 25 February 1865)

Mr. Matthew Arnold amongst the Philistines* (excerpts)

Two or three months ago we made some observations on an article of Mr. Matthew Arnold's, in the *National Review*, on the functions of criticism. Mr. Arnold has republished that and some other essays in an excellent little volume, which contains, amongst other things, a preface replying in the most goodhumoured manner imaginable to his various critics, and several notes levelled at our article. We have, on former occasions, remarked upon most of the essays thus republished, and we do not mean to return to them. They have very good points. Some of them are exceedingly interesting, and all of them display a remarkable power of appreciation. Thus the essays on Heine, on Marcus Aurelius, on the Pagan and the Mediaeval Moral Sentiment, and two others on Maurice and Eugénie de Guérin, are all full of interest, and will introduce the great bulk of Mr. Arnold's readers to topics with which they are not likely to have been familiar previously, and to a mode of treatment which he is certainly right in considering as uncommon in English periodical writing. We heartily wish them success. They form a most agreeable volume, written in excellent taste by a refined and highly cultivated man. There are, however, other matters in the book on which we should wish to say a word or two in a tone, if possible, as goodhumoured as that of Mr. Arnold himself. His retorts upon our criticisms are in perfect good temper, and some of them are very happy. His Preface is a curiosity, coming as it does from a man who has suffered many things from many reviewers, and is determined to be no better, but rather to become worse, and to go on not only repeating, but even exaggerating, the sins for which it was their painful duty to take him to task. Like the early Christians exposed to wild beasts in the arena, Mr. Arnold has been baited by reviewers. For instance, he is attacked by Mr. Wright, the translator of Homer, and by one 'Presbyter Anglicanus', whom he accuses of writing, not merely in the *Examiner*, but in 'half a dozen of the daily newspapers' as well. The *Guardian* has acted toward him the part of a 'kind monitor', and has charged him with making jokes. He stands in awe of the 'magnificent roaring of the young lions of the *Daily Telegraph*', though whether they have actually assailed him or not does not appear; and the *Saturday Review* has treated him most unkindly. His attitude in the midst of this storm of censure is almost as peaceful as that of Daniel in the

---

* *Essays in Criticism*. By Matthew Arnold. London and Cambridge: Macmillan & Co.

den of lions, seated, as the showman[1] observed, on his three-legged stool and reading the *Times* newspaper. He returns blessings for curses, gently reproves the *Examiner*, gravely exonerates the *Guardian* from the faintest suspicion of levity, suggests for the Editor of the *Saturday Review* the honour of a statue in a temple dedicated to Philistinism, and asks Mr. Wright—who, it appears, lives at Mapperley—for information about Wragg, the young woman whose arrest Mr. Arnold so feelingly deplored in his remarkable contribution to the *National Review*. We will not object to the statue which he proposes for us, and let him have all the honours of the small war which we have carried on; nay, we will even tell him something about Wragg. She is still in custody in Nottingham Gaol, and will be tried at the assizes to be held there sometime between the 9th and 13th of next month. The only objection to Mr. Arnold's Preface is that it is too goodnatured. There is no pleasure in hitting a man who will not hit you back again; who says meekly that it is not his nature to 'dispute on behalf of any opinion . . . very obstinately'; who cares little for argument, and 'has a profound respect for intuitions'; who thinks that truth is something to be seen, and not to be proved; and who, strong in that conviction, sees exclusively by his own inner light, and, like the humming-bird when pressed in the chase (to quote the showman a second time), retires into his interior by creeping down his own throat, whence, illuminated by the inner light, he smiles benignantly on his baffled pursuers.

Admitting that it is not easy to argue with any one who takes such an ethereal view of things, and has such a pleasant way of slipping through every difficulty, we must notice one or two of his replies, inasmuch as they illustrate the texture of his mind and the principles which pervade every word that he writes.

* * *

As matters stand, we cannot but suspect the real truth to be that Mr. Arnold, like every other decent person, has been much disgusted by the reports of the Divorce Court trials; that he knows little or nothing about jurisprudence, or about the way in which law-makers ought to deal with marriage or with the other great interests of life; and that he feels pleasure in using vague and big phrases about 'the Catholic idea' and 'the Protestant idea', 'married life according to its idea', &c. &c., without attaching any particular meaning to those words.

It is no reproach to any one to be a man of taste and not a man of thought, but he ought not to deny to the whole English nation the power of thinking, merely because their thoughts do not happen to be expressed in a way which suits his taste. He ought also to try to understand that people may be influenced by difficult as well as by easy theories, and that in this complicated world the difficult theories are very often the true ones.

---

[1] At a Folkestone fair, Mr Showman displays 'Daniel in the lion's den, sitting on a three-legged stool, reading off the New Testament' (*The Smuggler*, by James Marsh, serialized in *The Visitor and Lady's Parlor Magazine*, NY, Aug. 1840). Seamus Perry, identifying this, adds *New Monthly Magazine* (month 1833, p. 196), which also presents, at a fair, "a faithful representation of Daniel, sitting on a three-legged stool, in the Lion's Den." ' (In a list within inverted commas, Perry notes, suggesting less a source than that JFS was thinking of whatever its author was thinking of.)

'Mr. Arnold on the Middle Classes' (excerpts)
(*Saturday Review*, 10 February 1866)

Mr. Arnold on the Middle Classes (excerpts)

The last number of the *Cornhill Magazine* contains one of those odd articles which Mr. Matthew Arnold so much delights in writing. It is called 'My Countrymen', and is written apparently in order to teach that degraded part of creation, the British middle classes, what the intelligent foreigners think about them. The article begins by referring to some advice which we had the honour of tendering to Mr. Arnold about a year ago, on the impropriety of describing the whole English nation as a parcel of miserable Philistines, destitute of all the higher mental gifts, and especially of a certain quasi-divine power of understanding and believing in ideas which it appears belongs exclusively to the French. Mr. Arnold was struck, he tells us, by this article. It made him 'make a serious return on himself', and he resolved never to call his countrymen Philistines again till he had thought more about it. In the course of his meditations, he found that other people besides the *Saturday Review* were opposed to him. In the face of Mr. Bazley, the member for Manchester, the *Noncomformist*, the *Daily News*, and the *Daily Telegraph*, by all of which authorities he was contradicted, he found it impossible to persist in his old accusations. He decided that he would never call his countrymen Philistines any more, and he recorded his resolution in a beautiful and appropriate Scriptural quotation. 'He that is unjust let him be unjust still, and he that is filthy let him be filthy still, and he that is righteous let him be righteous still, and he that is holy let him be holy still.'[1] We should be sorry to suggest that Mr. Arnold has broken his good resolutions by describing the unfortunate Philistines as unjust and filthy, but it appears to us that he thinks there are few just men, and not many clean beasts, on this side of the British Channel. His way of conveying his impression as to the 'filthiness' of the unclean animals who ought to rush violently down the cliffs at Dover and Brighton is by repeating the views taken by (possibly ideal)[2] foreigners of our national character, and communicated to him during a foreign tour of some months which he lately made upon public business. He shows us what a terrible opinion our foreign friends have formed of us, and he tells us by implication that we may or may not be Philistines, but that foreigners consider us as such, and that, in his own opinion, they have much the best of the argument. It is worth while to state the arguments of his foreign friends, and to say just a few words on them. It may be true that we care too little what foreigners think about us, and, whatever else may be said of Mr. Arnold, no one will deny that few people can

---

[1] Revelation 22:11.

[2] *OED* Existing only in idea; confined to thought or imagination; imaginary: opp. to real or actual. Hence sometimes, Not real or practical; based on an idea or fancy; fancied, visionary.

248   ON THE NOVEL AND JOURNALISM

be better qualified to repeat in a pleasant half-foreign style the commonplaces about England and things English which happen to be current for the moment amongst literary foreigners.

* * *

Many questions suggest themselves to the mind on reading Mr. Arnold's vehement invectives against the middle classes. Who are the middle classes, and why does Mr. Arnold hate them so bitterly? Are inspectors of schools members of the middle class, or the ordinary run of professional men? Or is 'middle class' only an elaborate name for small shopkeepers?[3] Mr. Arnold vouchsafes one little gleam of information on such points, though even in that he runs into a curious confusion. He thought to himself, 'As to our middle class, foreigners have no notion how much this class with us contains, how many shades and gradations in it there are, and how little what is said of one part of it will apply to another.' As this would have afforded a conclusive answer to the whole tirade of the 'foreign friends', Mr. Arnold of course did not say it, for if he had his paper would simply have shown how very little foreigners know about England. By referring to it, however, Mr. Arnold shows that he has adopted a form of composition which obliges him to give conclusive answers to what he wishes to represent as unanswerable arguments against himself, and to pretend that the answers are inconclusive. To affect to be beaten by a man of straw, who not only will not knock you down but cannot even stand on his own legs, is to repeat the misfortune of the little boy who made his right hand play at chess with his left, and, intending to give the right hand the victory, ended the game by a stalemate. Having thought, in his own mind, of the conclusive answer to the foreign friend, Mr. Arnold of course could only feebly hint at a very small part of it:

> Something of this sort I could not help urging aloud. 'You do not know', I said, 'that there is broken off, as one may say, from the top of our middle class a large fragment which receive the best education the country can give, the same education as our aristocracy, which is perfectly intelligent, and which enjoys life perfectly. These men do the main part of our intellectual work, write all our best newspapers, and cleverer people, I assure you, are nowhere to be found.'

Some of these gentlemen, we rather think, are inspectors of schools, and Mr. Arnold is better qualified to describe their merits than to point out how ludicrously unlike the truth the description of the life of the rest of the middle classes is. To say that the intelligent foreigner's description of the English middle class does not fit that small section of it of which the writer knows the habits and feelings, is like desiring a person who abuses a picture-gallery, on the supposition that it contains only one picture, to take notice that there is one other picture to which his charges do not apply. The true answer is that the collection contains several thousand pictures, and that his remarks have but the very slightest possible bearing on any one of them.

* * *

---

[3] Adam Smith: 'To found a great empire for the sole purpose of raising up a people of customers, may at first sight appear a project fit only for a nation of shopkeepers. It is, however, a project altogether unfit for a nation of shopkeepers; but extremely fit for a nation whose government is influenced by shopkeepers' (*The Wealth of Nations*, 1776, Book IV). (Attributed to Samuel Adams, likewise 1776, and to Napoleon, as '...boutiquiers'.)

MR. ARNOLD ON THE MIDDLE CLASSES 249

It is hardly worth while to write seriously upon such a subject, and yet the greatness of the nation to which we belong is a topic on which the coldest of cold Englishmen can hardly write merely in the tone of banter, however trifling may be the occasion which leads him to treat of it. Amongst thirty millions of men and women there will of course be found a vast mass of dull, commonplace, stupid people, whose lives must look to bystanders, whether countrymen or not, drearier than they really are. If such persons are free, and accustomed as such to speak their minds on all sorts of subjects with perfect openness, they will no doubt talk a vast deal of nonsense, and lay themselves open to any quantity of criticism. There are, moreover, real faults in the English character, and some of them are in a rough way caricatured by Mr. Arnold's foreign friends; but if any one seriously doubts whether England is a great nation and is doing a great work in the world, let him look, not at the position which our country may hold for the time being in the opinion of foreign diplomatists, or at the phrases which happen to be fashionable in French or German society about our middle class (of which they know considerably less than they know about the feelings of polar bears and walruses), but at a few broad facts.

England is the only great European country which enjoys political freedom to its full extent, and has succeeded in reducing it to a practical shape. The prospects of political freedom all over Europe depend largely on its success and permanence in England.

England is the only great country in which the religious controversies of the day, controversies deeper and more important than those which caused the Reformation, have taken a practical form, and are likely to lead to definite practical results. What in France and Germany is confined to a small class of learned men is coming to be preached on the housetops in England to a people slow to be convinced, but apt to be much in earnest in acting on their convictions.

England governs with absolute power 150,000,000 of people in India. The English Government there is labouring honestly and vigorously to use its power for the good of those millions, and to lead them on to changes, political, moral, and religious, hardly exemplified before in the history of any part of the world.

England exercises a qualified and ill-defined supremacy over Canada, South Africa, Australia, New Zealand, and various other places of less importance. These regions will be the homes of many millions of English people in another century, and their fortunes may be influenced most deeply, for good or evil, by English legislation and English thought.

Look well at these four facts, think what they mean, try for a moment to take their measure, and then ask whether it is worth while to give even a passing thought to the opinion which the Prussians may form of our attitude in the Danish question. Think, too, for a moment of the intense and varied energy with which millions of men are working out different bits of one or more of these vast problems. Remember that every ship loaded by the despised shopkeeper, every order taken by the vulgarest traveller, every article written in a penny paper, every vote given by a 10*l.* householder,[4] goes to make up the vast whole which constitutes the action of England on the world; and if you still sneer at the general result, and still fail to see the lines of greatness and majesty through the dust and sweat and noise and turmoil which obscure what they

---

[4] The Reform Act of 1832 gave the vote to all householders who paid annual rental of £10 or more.

develop, you despise human life itself. There are those who think otherwise, and who would prefer to grind in such a mill, ever so roughly, ever so coarsely, ever so meanly, all the days of their life, to the most aesthetic form of dawdling that could be invented by a joint committee from all the *cafés* and theatres between the Mediterranean and the Baltic.

'Mr. Matthew Arnold on Culture'
(*Saturday Review*, 20 July 1867)

Mr. Matthew Arnold on Culture

It was hardly to be expected that Mr. Matthew Arnold would descend from his professorial chair without a parting fling at the Philistines. He has selected 'Culture' as the subject of his concluding lecture, which is republished in the *Cornhill Magazine* for July, and has already elicited very various strictures from different quarters. One of his critics is prepared to admit all that he has urged on the importance of culture, in the extended sense here given to the term as including the highest ideal and harmony of 'beauty, sweetness, and light'—with the reserve, however, that to make it consciously the main object of pursuit is to sacrifice all about it that is best worth attaining, which in a certain sense is true. Another thinks it sufficient to meet his commendation of Oxford for, theoretically at least, recognising his ideal, with irrelevant sneers at the bigotry of Oxford Toryism, as though it were any disproof of the general scope and tendency of University education in producing a certain cultivated habit of mind to say that Convocation has bullied Professor Jowett and ejected Gladstone. The real question at issue between Mr. Arnold and his opponents, of whom he here takes Mr. Bright[1] and Mr. Frederick Harrison[2] as the typical representatives, lies deeper, and is certainly not an unimportant one. It comes, as we understand it, pretty much to this—whether action, and chiefly political or commercial action, is the great end of life, so that all which does not directly promote it, and still more whatever even temporarily retards it, is trivial, if not positively injurious; or whether, strictly religious considerations apart, humanity has not some higher interests than are represented by tariffs or Reform Bills, and to which the latter stand at best in the relation of means to ends. Indeed, it might be considered a phase of the old controversy about the true nature of happiness. Much that Aristotle says of the harmonious play and balance of faculties which comes into his definition of happiness is not unlike Mr. Arnold's definition of culture. On the other hand, Mr. Bright thinks culture synonymous with 'a smattering of the two dead languages', while Mr. Harrison can see no use in it except for a critic of new books; nay, in a political point of view it is worse than useless, it is a positive nuisance, with its turn for small fault-finding, and disinclination for rough-and-ready methods of settling things. 'The man of culture is in politics one of the poorest creatures alive.'

Mr. Arnold appeals in defence of his own view to the analogy of religion. The Bible says that 'the kingdom of God is within us',[3] and in like manner culture consists in an

---

[1] John Bright (1811–1889; *ODNB*, politician).

[2] Frederic Harrison (1831–1923; *ODNB*, positivist and author).

[3] Luke 17:20–1, The kingdom of God cometh not with observation: Neither shall they say, Lo here! or, lo there! for, behold, the kingdom of God is within you.

ON THE NOVEL AND JOURNALISM

internal condition of the powers of the human soul, and not in any of the external adjuncts which may indirectly contribute towards such a state, but cannot produce it, and still less become a substitute for it. He might have quoted, with equal fitness, another text. 'Is not the life more than meat, and the body than raiment?'[4] The advance of mere material and mechanical civilization may indeed multiply the opportunities and remove the hindrances of increasing knowledge, but still it must ever remain true that 'the railway and the steamship' are neither the measure nor the subject-matter of 'the thoughts that shake mankind'.[5] If religion regards wealth as only valuable according to the use men make of it, so also, in relation to the equilibrium and perfection of all the spiritual energies of humanity, wherein true culture consists, wealth is only a means to an end. Bodily health and muscular vigour is no more the essence of culture than of Christianity. Neither, again, is the liberty for every one to say and do what he likes, which is the Paradisaic Utopia of Mr. Bright and the *Daily Telegraph*, much better than a fools' Paradise, unless we have got people to like what is true and good, or, in other words, to dwell in a congenial atmosphere of sweetness and light. Mr. Arnold contrasts culture with religion, as embracing a wider range of aspiration, and insisting on a more complete standard of internal perfection. The one is content with teaching us to subdue our 'animality', while the other will not allow us to rest till all the higher faculties have attained their full development, and are attuned to a faultless harmony. The Puritans deserved high praise, he thinks, for their stern consistency in working out their religious ideal, but they were terrible Philistines for all that. They had nothing of sweetness, and not too much of light. True, but then their religious ideal was a narrow and one-sided one. And a good deal which Mr. Arnold brings under the head of culture seems to belong quite as much to the perfect expression of the religious character. There is surely some truth in the old-fashioned idea of the Christian gentleman, which implies that the Christian and the chivalrous type have a good deal in common. Or, to take a modern example—which Mr. Arnold certainly will not object to, as it is a favourite one of his own—the elements of religion and of culture are so indissolubly blended in the lofty moral 'distinction' of Eugénie de Guérin,[6] that it is difficult to say where one ends and the other begins, or to draw the line where they shade off into each other. That is a very different type of excellence no doubt from the Puritan's, but it is at least as far removed from the perfection of mere intellectual culture with the animal nature unsubdued, which the lecturer also holds to be quite inadequate. And his constant adoption, as though instinctively, of Scriptural language to clothe his own estimate of the meaning and value of culture points to a similar conclusion as to the intimate connexion, not exactly in Mrs. Proudie's[7] sense, between 'civilization and Christianity'. Mr. Arnold's great abhorrence is for vulgarity. He quotes with emphatic, we had almost said with unctuous disgust, the motto of the *Nonconformist* newspaper, 'The dissidence of Dissent and the Protestantism of the Protestant religion', and contrasts it with St. Peter's words, 'Finally, be of one mind, united in feeling';[8] but his extract proves at least that the Nonconformist maxim sins no less against the laws of religion than of

---

[4] Matthew 6:25.

[5] Tennyson, *Locksley Hall* 164–6 (1842) 'Summer isles of Eden lying in dark-purple spheres of sea. // There methinks would be enjoyment more than in this march of mind, / In the steamship, in the railway, in the thoughts that shake mankind.'

[6] (1805–1848), woman of letters.   [7] Wife to the Bishop in Trollope's *Barchester Towers* (1857).

[8] 1 Peter 3:8, Finally, be ye all of one mind, having compassion one of another.

MR. MATTHEW ARNOLD ON CULTURE   253

culture. He dislikes it because it is vulgar, not because, as he insists, it is unscriptural, just as some years ago he severely censured Bishop Colenso for his criticisms on the Pentateuch, not because they were false—for he seemed disposed to admit that they might be true—but because there was a vulgarity in obtruding questions on public notice which disturbed the popular belief. Mr. Arnold's sympathies would evidently gravitate towards what George Eliot somewhere calls 'a great, roomy, universal Church',[9] but he has a nervous horror of all kinds of 'religious organizations' for active purposes, and, we suspect, would look on any systematic efforts, say for the conversion of the heathen, or the promotion of Ragged Schools[10] or boys' Homes, or the reclaiming of prostitutes, as scarcely less 'fussy' and vulgar than 'the hideous and grotesque illusions of middle-class Protestantism' whereof the *Nonconformist* is the theological exponent. In rebuking the impatience which those who are eager to be up and doing feel at that 'turn for small fault-finding'—in other words, for minute and delicate criticism—which is incidental to a highly-cultivated mind, he seems to forget that all action would be paralysed if we waited to decide on our method of procedure till every criticism had been discussed and answered.

It is very characteristic of Mr. Arnold that he selects Abelard[11]—whom Mr. Harrison would probably regard as no better than a clever sophist—as the great apostle of mediaeval culture. So far there is nothing to object to. But we doubt if he would be ready to do equal justice to the merits of Abelard's great opponent. There is too little of dignified repose about St. Bernard[12] to suit Mr. Arnold's ideal; he made too much 'fuss' about orthodoxy, and the Crusades and the current morality of the age, and several other practical matters beneath the attention of a philosopher. Yet St. Bernard was certainly a greater man than Abelard, and we are by no means sure that he had not more of 'sweetness and light' about him. Butler points out that the passive contemplation of suffering, without any effort to relieve it, tends to deaden our sympathies rather than to quicken them, and all experience goes with him. It is true in the same way that the quiescent pursuit of self-culture, even in its highest forms, unaccompanied by an active interest in the social or moral problems that surround us, is more likely to enervate and demoralize our mental energies than to brace them. It is only fair indeed to say that Mr. Arnold accepts as a necessary evil what he cannot bring himself to admire or to approve. He would very likely admit that St. Bernard's work was requisite for the due development of European society, but he would regret that St. Bernard was sacrificed to it. Money-getting and busy industrialism, vulgar as they are, are beneficial for the future; but the main body of Philistines, whose function is to be hewers of wood and drawers of water for the chosen people of culture in the coming ages, are sacrificed. The misplaced zeal of some of our youthful gymnasts may provide a sounder physical type for the next generation; but the present generation of boys meanwhile is sacrificed. Puritanism and Nonconformity were required for the moral and religious education of the country; but Puritans and Nonconformists were sacrificed by wholesale.

---

[9] *Romola* (1862–63), ch. xxi: 'Altogether this world, with its partitioned empire and its roomy universal Church, seemed to be a handsome establishment for the few who were lucky or wise enough to reap the advantages of human folly.'

[10] *OED* a free school for children of the poorest class. 1843 *Times* Advt. [headed] 'Ragged Schools'. 1847 COCKBURN in favour of what are now called 'ragged schools'.

[11] Peter Abelard (1079–1142), French philosopher.

[12] Bernard of Clairvaux (1090–1153), canonized 1174.

The battle of freedom of speech must be fought out, but 'the young lions of the *Daily Telegraph*', whose roaring is neither cultivated nor melodious, 'in the meanwhile are sacrificed'. There is a great deal of truth of course in all this, but it strikes us that a theory which has to leave so broad a margin for exceptions can hardly be a complete *rationale* of the facts of the case. Mr. Arnold has a strong grasp of one aspect of the truth, and it is a very important one, but he falls into a very common kind of mistake when he puts it forward as the whole truth.

Still, after making all deductions, the view dwelt upon in this lecture is incomparably higher and truer than its opposite. We prefer the liberalism of the apostles of culture to the liberalism of Bright and Beales,[13] which is not altogether so unlike the old Puritan fanaticism, only that it has more of the political and less of the religious element about it. It was a pious wish of George III. that the time might come when every one of his subjects would be able to read his Bible; but still the example of Scotland has proved that some very ugly exhibitions of religious feeling may co-exist with a minute familiarity with the written word, if they do not sometimes spring out of it. And even in a country which realized the fondest dreams of our Reformers, where every man had his vote, to say nothing of voting by ballot, there might be many things considerably the reverse of perfection. If to deserve success is better than to win it,[14] to know how to make the noblest use of influence is better than to possess it. What a man is matters more than what he does; but then, again, what he is depends fully as much on what he does as on what he knows. Culture alone will not give sweetness, nor even 'flexibility', though it is an immense, and ordinarily an indispensable, assistance in acquiring those qualities. Moreover, bodily culture, of which Mr. Arnold speaks so slightingly, formed an integral part of that Greek ideal of perfection to which he rightly attributes so high a spiritual significance. The Greek palaestra[15] corresponded to the modern cricket-field. But there is no present danger of physical education, or mechanical and commercial industry, being at a discount. Culture is far more liable to be depreciated than to be overvalued. That without what he happily calls the 'glow of life and thought', which is the result of culture in the largest sense of the word, material comfort and political freedom can as little give worth and perfection to our moral being as food and clothing can give vigour to our animal organism without the glow of health, is the lesson which Mr. Arnold designs to teach. And we may be grateful to the teacher without altogether agreeing with him. It is just the lesson which, in an age and country like our own, men have the least inclination, and the greatest need, to learn.

---

[13] Edmond Beales (1803–1881; *ODNB*, radical), president of the Reform League which issued in the Reform Act of 1867.

[14] Addison, *Cato* I ii: "'Tis not in mortals to command success, / But we'll do more, Sempronius; we'll deserve it.'

[15] School for wrestling, for example.

INDEX

Abelard, Peter 25
Act of Toleration (1688) 26
Addison, Joseph 16, 171–5
Aeschylus xxi
Alford, Henry 40
Alison, Sir Archibald 61, 86
Aristotle 11
Arnold, Matthew 228–38, 245–54
Arnold, Thomas xxix
Austen, Jane 59–60, 88, 212
  Emma 8
Austin, Lieutenant William 116–22, 125–7

Bain, Alexander 231, 237
Balaklava, battle of 31
Balzac, Honoré de 99, 143–4, 150–5, 167, 187
Barnes, Albert 87
Barnum, P. T. 165–6
Barrow, George 114
Baxter, Richard 211
Beales, Edmond 254
Bede 65
Beecher Stowe, Harriet
  The Minister's Wooing 193–7
  Uncle Tom's Cabin 3, 178, 193–4
Bentham, Jeremy 217, 236–7
  The Book of Fallacies 106, 157
Bernard, Simon François 178
Bernard of Clairvaux 253
Birmingham Gaol 116–17, 133–5
Boston, Thomas 40
Boswell, James xvii
Bousfield, William 48
Bradley, Edward, *Verdant Green* 89
Bright, John 251–2, 254
British Museum 42
Brontë, Branwell 131
Brontë, Charlotte
  Jane Eyre xxii, 8, 59, 130
  Life of Charlotte Brontë (E. C. Gaskell) 105,
    107, 130–3
  Shirley 131
  Villette 131
Brontë, Emily, *Wuthering Heights* 9
Browne, Hablot Knight ('Phiz') 204
Browne, Sir Thomas 14
Buckle, Henry Thomas xxv–xxvi
Burke, Edmund 102
  *Philosophical Enquiry into the Origin of Our Ideas
    of the Sublime and Beautiful* xv
Burney, Frances, *Evelina* 164
Burns, Robert 179
Byron, George Gordon, Lord Byron 175,
    183, 187

Calcraft, William 34
Campbell, Sir Colin 31
Campbell, John, first Baron Campbell 96
capital punishment 34, 51–3, 195–6
caricature xxx–xxxii, 157–9
Carlyle, Thomas xxii, 66, 156
  History of the French Revolution xix, 3, 198,
    202, 224
  Sartor Resartus 2, 205
Cayley, Edward Stillingfleet 157
Chateaubriand, François-René 185–7
Chesterfield, Philip Stanhope, fourth earl of
  Chesterfield 2–3
Church Missionary Society 38
Clarendon, Edward Hyde, first earl of
  Clarendon xxii
Clark, William George 1
Cobbett, William 160
Cobden, Richard 229
Cockburn, Sir Alexander 127
Codrington v. Codrington 230, 235, 242–4
Coke, Sir Edward 102
Colenso, John William 230, 235, 253
Coleridge, John Duke 121
Coleridge, Samuel Taylor 160
Cook, James 102
Court of Chancery 78–9, 82, 84, 109, 161, 178
crime and punishment 47
  Birmingham Gaol 116–17, 133–5
  executions 34, 51–3, 195–6
  homicide xxxiv
  imprisonment for debt 78–9, 83–4
  letter to the *Times* 67–8
  trial scenes 20, 239–44
Crimean War 1, 27–34, 86–7, 160
Cumming, John 48, 87
Cunningham, Emily xxx, 77
Cupples, George, *The Green Hand* 61–2

Daily Telegraph 252, 254
Dante Alighieri 175
Davie, Donald xxxvi
De Bernard du Grail de la Villette,
  Pierre-Marie-Charles 143–4, 152
De Guérin, Eugénie 252
De Montalembert, Charles-Forbes-René, comte de
  Montalembert 147
De Parny, Evariste 194
De Toqueville, Alexis 198
death penalty 34, 51–3, 195–6
decimal coinage 233, 236
Defoe, Daniel 17, 159
  A Journal of the Plague Year 68
  Robinson Crusoe 19, 21–6, 57, 107, 152

256 INDEX

detective novels 219–22
Dicey, Edward 209
Dicey, Thomas Edward 115
Dickens, Charles xvi, xix, xxx, xxxiii, 23, 43, 51,
    63, 65, 98, 103–5, 138–41, 176
  Bleak House xxxii, 14, 22, 78–9, 81, 84, 158–9,
    178, 213
  caricature xxx–xxxii, 157–9
  David Copperfield 14, 16, 24, 79, 208–9
  Dombey and Son 14, 159, 188
  Hard Times xxx
  Little Dorrit 79, 82, 91–7, 107–15, 123, 128–9,
    133–9, 158
  Martin Chuzzlewit 160
  Nicholas Nickleby 14, 158, 199
  The Old Curiosity Shop 14, 16, 175
  Oliver Twist 14, 79
  Our Mutual Friend 243
  Pickwick Papers 77–9, 84, 156–60, 199
  sentimentality 13–15, 77, 80, 158, 188
  A Tale of Two Cities 198–204
Diderot, Denis 235
The Dispatch 44–8
Disraeli, Benjamin, earl of Beaconsfield 176
Divorce Court 221, 230, 234, 237–8, 242–6
Dove, William 54–5
Dryden, John 61
Dumas (the younger), Alexandre 147, 180,
  215, 235
  La Dame aux Camélias 167

Eccles (Eagle), Solomon 68
Edgeworth, Maria 17, 59, 212
  Castle Rackrent 72
  Murad the Unlucky 3
  To-morrow 3, 18
Edinburgh Review 133–41
Edwards, Jonathan 195–6
Egerton, Francis, first earl of Ellesmere 88
Elias, John 40
Eliot, George 150, 253
Empson, William xx, xxvi
'English character' 229, 231, 247–50
evidence xx, xxiii, xxix, xxx, 221–2
The Examiner 172
executions 34, 51–3, 195–6

Fenimore Cooper, James 62, 152
Feuerbach, Ludwig 150
Feydeau, Ernest, *Fanny* 185–7, 243
Fielding, Henry 17, 26, 103, 159, 212
  Jonathan Wild 71
Flaubert, Gustave, *Madame Bovary* 99–103,
  194, 243
Frederick the Great, of Prussia 72, 75
French literature
  Balzac 99, 143, 150–5, 167, 187
  De Bernard du Grail de la Villette,
    Pierre-Marie-Charles 143–4, 152
  Dumas, Alexandre (the younger), 147, 167, 180,
    215, 235

Flaubert, *Madame Bovary* 99–103, 194, 243
Hugo, Victor 51, 195–6
Light Literature in France 142–5
Montaigne xix, xxxii–xxxiii, 99, 196
Prévost, *Manon Lescaut* 167–70
Rousseau, Jean-Jacques 167, 224, 226, 243
Sand, George 19, 144, 146–9, 167, 186–7
Sue 51, 69, 143
French Revolution 156, 224, 229, 236
  Carlyle's *History* xix, 3, 198, 202, 224
  A Tale of Two Cities xix, 3, 198–204
Fullom, Stephen Watson 87

Galton, Francis 1
Gaskell, Elizabeth Cleghorn 88
  Life of Charlotte Brontë 105, 107, 130–4
  Mary Barton 20–1, 59
  Ruth 21, 59
  Sylvia's Lovers 21
Gautier, Théophile 170
Gibbon, Edward xxii–xxiii
Gladstone, William Ewart 251
Godfrey of Bouillon 54
Godwin, William, *Caleb Williams* 8–10
Goethe, Johann Wolfgang von, *Wilhelm
  Meister* 188
Goodford, Charles Old 7
Gozlan, Léon 150
Grant, James 88
Greg, William Rathbone 114
Guizot, François 86

Hale, Sir Matthew 102
Haliburton, Thomas Chandler 88
Hallam, Henry 114
Hamilton, William 114
Harrison, Frederic 251, 253
Hassall, Arthur Hill 108
Hastings, Warren xxiv
Hawker, Robert Stephen 87
Helps, A. 86
Herodotus 102
Hill, Sir Rowland 104–5, 114, 139–41
Hobbes, Thomas 175, 231, 237
Hogarth, William 94
Homer 173
Hood, Thomas 87
Hopkins, Samuel 194–6
Horn, Antoine Joseph 203
Housman, A. E. xxviii
Hughes, Robert Edgar 1
Hugo, Victor 51
  Le dernier jour d'un condamné 195–6
Hunt, Leigh 185

Impey, Sir Elijah xxiii–xxiv

James, G. P. R. 88
James, Henry xix, xxiii
Jerrold, Douglas 46, 63–4
Johnson, Samuel xvii–xviii, xxi, 61, 163

INDEX

journalism xvi, xviii–xxi, 205–6
  Grub-Street 163
  'History of British Journalism' 191–2
  law reports 239, 241–4
  letters to *The Times* 65, 174
  'newspaper English' 54–8
  religious journalism 35–42
  The Spectator 171–6
  Sunday papers 43–8
Jowett, Benjamin 39, 251

Keats, John 185
Kewsy, Serjeant 8
King, Peter John Locke 68
King's College, London 42
Kingsley, Charles, *The Voyages and Adventures of Sir Amyas Leigh, Knight* 16
Kirwan, William 66
Kossuth, Lajos 46

Lamb, Charles 160
Lardner, Dionysius 87
Lawrence, George Alfred, *Guy Livingstone* 183–4, 210
Layard, Austin 86
The Leader 50–2
legal fictions xxxiii–xxxv
Lesage, Alain-René, *Gil Blas* 17, 19
Lever, Charles 88
Levine, David xxxi
libel law 117
Lloyd's Weekly Newspaper 44–6
Locke, John 231, 237
Lockhart, John Gibson 11, 21–2
Longfellow, Henry Wadsworth 87
Lord's Day Observance Society 43
Louis-Philippe, King of France 129
Louvet de Couvray, Jean-Baptiste 235
Lytton, Sir Edward Bulwer, first Baron Lytton xxiv, 88, 109, 175
  Eugene Aram 16
  My Novel 19

Macaulay, Thomas Babington, Baron Macaulay xxiii–xxiv, 41, 85, 171–2
Mackay, General Hugh 41
Mansfield, William, earl of Mansfield 108
Marochetti, Carlo xxxii
Marryat, Captain Frederick 61–2, 88
Marsh, Catherine M. 87
Massillon, Jean-Baptiste 171
Masson, Gustave 129, 142, 144–5, 150
Maurice, Frederick Denison 40
Merivale, Charles 114
Militia Bill (1852) 66
Mill, John Stuart 36, 231–2, 237
Milton, John, *Paradise Lost* 101, 235
Montaigne, Michel de xix, xxxii–xxxiii, 99, 196
Montégut, Émile 185–7
Montépin, Xavier Aymon Perrin, Count of Montépin 235

Moore, Thomas 87
Morning Herald 44
Muntz, Philip Henry 68
Myers, Annette 66

Napoleon III 66, 178
Newman, Francis 41
News of the World 44–5
Newton, Isaac 232
Newton, John 38, 40
Nightingale, Florence 41
The Nonconformist 252–3
Northcote, Sir Stafford 111
Norton, Caroline, *Lost and Saved* 65, 99
novels and novelists xvi, xix–xx, xxiv–xxv, xxxiii, 1–26, 104–34, 177–8, 183–4, 207–10, 219–22, and passim

Olmsted, Frederick Law 194
Orwell, George xv
Overstone, Samuel Jones Loyd, Baron Overstone 233
Oxford Union 42

Paley, William 11
Palmer, William xv–xvi, 37, 50–3, 89, 178, 222
Parker, Theodore 178
Paul, Sir John 37
'Philistines' 247, 251–3
Phillips, Charles 104
Phillips, John 114
Poe, Edgar Allan 220
Ponsonby, Arthur, Baron Ponsonby of Shulbrede 27
Pope, Alexander *Essay on Man* 41
  The Dunciad 159, 163
Prévost, Antoine-François, *Manon Lescaut* 167–70
Prisoners' Counsel Act (1836) 104
Punch 46, 57, 63–4

Rabelais, François 235
Railroad Bookselling 85–90
railways 115–16
Reade, Charles, *It is Never Too Late to Mend* 105–9, 116–29, 133–8, 177–81
The Record 38–42
Redpath, John 115
Reform Acts, Reform Bills 149, 156, 213, 251, 254
religious journalism 35–42
Renan, Ernest 150, 230, 234–5
Revue des Deux Mondes 142, 179–82, 185
Richardson, Samuel 212
  Clarissa Harlow 155
  The History of Sir Charles Grandison 107
Rodensky, Lisa xvi, xxiii–xxiv, xxx, 7
Rousseau, Jean-Jacques 167, 224, 226, 243
Rowlandson, Thomas 162
Ruskin, John xxx–xxxi, 14, 134
Russell, William Howard xix, 27–34, 160
Russell, Sir William Oldnall 47

INDEX

Sand, George 19, 144
  La Daniella 146–9, 167, 186–7
Sandwith, Humphry 86
Saturday Review 98
Schramm, Jan-Melissa 104, 222
Scott, Lydia Robinson, Lady Scott 105
Scott, Thomas 38
Scott, Sir Walter, *Waverley Novels* 4–6, 22, 88, 109,
    152, 156, 199, 212, 218
  The Black Dwarf 16
  The Bride of Lammermoor 16
  The Heart of Midlothian 107
  Ivanhoe 218
  Rob Roy 16
Scott, William, Baron Stowell 12
Senior, Nassau 217–18
sentimentality, sentimentalism 13–15, 77, 158, 167,
    188–90, 223–7
Sewell, William, *Hawkstone* 18, 178
Shakespeare, William
  King Lear 57
  Measure for Measure xxvii–xxviii, 197
  Othello 7, 101, 181
  Sonnets 213
Shaw, Sir Charles 66
Shelley, Mary, *Frankenstein* 210
Sheridan, Richard Brinsley 226
Siddons, Sarah 223–4
Simeon, Charles 38
Sinclair, Catherine 88
Smith, Adam 248
Smith, Albert Richard 169
Smith, Sydney 153, 157, 161–2
Smith, William 86
Smollett, Tobias 17, 212
  Peregrine Pickle 95
Somers, John, Baron Somers 174
Southey, Robert 160
Soyer, Alexis 88
Spearman, Alexander 114
The Spectator 171–6
Steele, Sir Richard 171, 173
Stendhal, Marie-Henri Beyle xxv
Stephen, J. K., son of JFS 49
Stephen, Sir James, father of JFS xxxii, 65,
    114, 217
Stephen, Leslie, brother of JFS xv, xvii–xviii, xxx,
    49, 65, 71, 105
Stephen, Oscar Leslie 115
Stephens, Henry 86
Sterne, Lawrence 226
  Sentimental Journey 188–9, 224
  Tristram Shandy 68, 224
Strauss, David 150
Suarez, Francisco 230
Sue, Eugène 51, 69, 143
suicide 91–2
Sunday papers 43–8

Surville, Laure (née Balzac) 150–1, 153
Swift, Jonathan 15, 82

The Tablet 37
Taine, Hippolyte 198
Taylor, Alfred Swaine 102
Taylor, Henry 86, 114
Taylor, Jeremy xvii
Taylor, John Pitt 48
Tennyson, Alfred, first Baron Tennyson 40,
    87, 166
  Locksley Hall 252
  The Lotos-Eaters 197
Thackeray, William Makepeace xxiv, 6, 64, 88, 97,
    100, 138, 151, 154, 164–6, 211–16, 229
  The Adventures of Philip 214, 215
  Barry Lyndon 71–6
  The History of Pendennis 3, 6–8, 19–20, 71, 75
  The Newcomes 9, 75, 215
  Vanity Fair 3, 16, 19, 71, 75, 215, 225
  The Virginians 163, 216
Thackeray Ritchie, Anne 71
Thesiger, Frederic, first Baron Chelmsford 127
Thomas, William Moy 3
Thompson, William (Bendigo) 129
The Times
  law reports 239–44
  letters to 65, 174
Titmarsh, M. A., *Rebecca and Rowena* 214
Tocqueville, Alexis de 99
Trevelyan, Sir Charles 111, 114
Trollope, Anthony 252
Trollope, Mrs Francis 88
Trollope, T. Adolphus xxv
Tupper, Martin 87
Turnley, Joseph 88

Venn, Henry (1725–1797) 38
Venn, Henry (1796–1873) 38
Venn, Jane Catherine 38
Vicars, Captain Hedley 40, 87

W. H. Smith & Son 85, 89
Walmsley, Sir Joshua 42
Watson, Rev. H. W. xvii
Waugh, Evelyn, *Scoop* xix
Weekly Times 44–6
Wesley, John 194
Wheeler, J. Talboys xv
Wilberforce, William 38
Wilson, Rev. William Carus 105
Wiseman, Nicholas, Cardinal Wiseman 38–9
Woods, Nicholas Augustus 27–34
Wordsworth, William 160

Yates, Edmund 164–6
Yonge, Charlotte M. *The Heir of Redclyffe* 3,
    59, 86